TRUE STORIES

*Tales From the Generation
of a New World Culture*

Garrick Beck

iUniverse

Handwritten inscription:

Suzanne Wolbers

Art Over Authority!!
It's People who can make the community of character that can rescue our species & our world!!

— Garrick Beck

TRUE STORIES

Tales From the Generation of a New World Culture

Copyright © 2017 Garrick Beck.

All rights reserved. No part of this book may be used or reproduced by any means, graphic, electronic, or mechanical, including photocopying, recording, taping or by any information storage retrieval system without the written permission of the author except in the case of brief quotations embodied in critical articles and reviews.

iUniverse books may be ordered through booksellers or by contacting:

iUniverse
1663 Liberty Drive
Bloomington, IN 47403
www.iuniverse.com
1-800-Authors (1-800-288-4677)

Because of the dynamic nature of the Internet, any web addresses or links contained in this book may have changed since publication and may no longer be valid. The views expressed in this work are solely those of the author and do not necessarily reflect the views of the publisher, and the publisher hereby disclaims any responsibility for them.

Any people depicted in stock imagery provided by Thinkstock are models, and such images are being used for illustrative purposes only.
Certain stock imagery © Thinkstock.

ISBN: 978-1-5320-2601-0 (sc)
ISBN: 978-1-5320-2600-3 (hc)
ISBN: 978-1-5320-2602-7 (e)

Library of Congress Control Number: 2017909482

Print information available on the last page.

iUniverse rev. date: 08/01/2017

Dedication

To my parents, Julian Beck and Judith Malina, who founded The Living Theatre and set in motion so much more.

To my children, Eden, Robin, and Tameron, who are already carrying forward the ideals described in this book.

And to the Children of Earth, who all deserve to inherit a peaceful and beautiful world.

Also by Garrick Beck

- *The Rainbow Oracle,* Editorial Collective, Visionworks press, Eugene, Oregon, 1972

- *Plant & Grow! Teacher's Guidebook for an Outdoor Children's Gardening Program* with Paula Hewitt, Trust for Public Land, New York, 1993

Table of Contents

Acknowledgments vi

Introduction vii

PART 1: Meetings with Amazing People (1954–1959) . . . 1
   1. Dorothy's Story 2
   2. Nina's Story 8
   3. Naphtali's Story 13
   4. Spenser's Story 17
   5. Opening Night 20

PART 2: Acting & Action (1964–1967) 31
   6. The Siege of the Brig 32
   7. Exile in Italy 40
   8. Highschoolers Against the War 46
   9. In the Treasure Box 57
   10. Jimmy and Jimi's Stories 63

PART 3: Higher Learning (1967–1969) 69
   11. On the Quays of Paris 70
   12. War, War, What's it For? 75
   13. Sanctuary 87
   14. Something New 97
   15. The Ivory Tower Crumbles 108
   16. In the Labyrinth 113
   17. Looking for Answers in a Mad, Mad World 118

PART 4: Live Alive (1969–1970) **127**

18. Clues & Keys 128
19. To the End of the World. 135
20. Familiar Musing 146
21. Renaissance Faire. 154
22. The Turning Point 159

PART 5: Toad Hall & Beyond (1970) **167**

23. Kaushal Puts his Finger on It 168
24. Toad Hall and Beyond 173
25. Festival Summer 182
26. Emerald Lakes 195
27. V Is for Vortex 203
28. Calm in the Storm 213

PART 6: Into the Woods (1970–1971) **219**

29. How The Whole Thing Works 220
30. Frank and Lois's Story 233
31. Equinox 240
32. Christmas 1971 253

PART 7: On the Trail with the Rainbow Rock
              (1971–1972) **261**

33. The Hopi, the Hippies, the Missing Tablet
    and the Beautiful Blue Corn (Part 1) 262
34. Kitty & Elizabeth & Another Nina 270
35. Visionworks Press 282

PART 8: World Family Gathering Comes True (1972).. **289**

36. At the Gates 290
37. Gathering for the First Time. 307
38. Is it the End or Beginning of the Rainbow Trail? 319

PART 9: Back to the Woods (1973–1982) **323**

39. A Hint to the Things that Remain Hidden 324
40. Forest Magnificence 338
41. Life on the Farm 348
42. Q7 358
43. The Hopi, the Hippies, the Missing Tablet and the Beautiful Blue Corn (Part 2) 364
44. Solar Epiphany 370
45. Journey to Mexico 379
46. Short Takes 291
47. Saskatchewan A.I.M. 409

PART 10: In the Canyons of the City (1983–1987) . . . **421**

48. Gardenopolis 422
49. The Return of the Theatre 440
50. Percival's Story 447

Epilogue 456

Photo Credits 460
Index 464
About the Author 469

Acknowledgments

Most of all I would like to acknowledge and thank all the many people who participated in the stories told here who are *not* mentioned because of my lack of memory amid the turbulence of the times. These people deserve to be included in this book and so I must lump you all together in this heartfelt appreciation. Without the many participants, friends, family, supporters, activists, contributors and accomplices these stories never could have come to be. So many people carried the banners, walked the trails, sowed the seeds and baked the bread, who are not named in this accounting, and yet on the strength of their efforts these stories were actually able to occur. To all of you I give my deepest appreciation.

Further, I must give my thanks to each of the people who read these chapters and corrected names, places, dates, and who caught typos, suggested *mots justes*, asked for better descriptions, unscrambled jumbled parts and in general helped me create a better book. Tera Rutecki, Sid Small, Ellen Light, Bana Devi, Carol Kushner, Kenn Kushner, Fred Nemo, Mimi Leland, Peggie Morrison, and especially Karen McPherson.

Particularly I would like to thank Raquel Shapira for designing the book and especially the cover; Ian G. Ensign for masterful copyediting; Jackie Betz, Jay Kurley, Mary Nissen, Paula Watson, Julie Kirkpatrick, Christine Datz and Andy Stone for guidance in the development of the Children's Gardening Program; Tom Walker for his Living Theatre archival memories and references; Terri Faires and Joanee Freedom for their recollections of the Buffalo Party; Michael Crater for double-proofing; and my wife, Jenny Felmley for her careful advice and endless encouragement.

Introduction

I was born in New York, on Manhattan, the Island Continent in mid-May of 1949. My parents, Julian Beck and Judith Malina, were the founders of The Living Theatre, an innovative, radical, Off-Broadway theatre company. Some of the early stories in this book recall experiences I had as a young actor with the troupe and adventures with amazing characters whose paths the theatre crossed.

"True Stories" traces a passage from the Beatnik 1950s through the anti-war protests in the mid-1960s and then into the late 1960s' blossoming counter-culture scene in Portland, Oregon whose Goose Hollow enclave was the next major 'flower power' neighborhood up the coast from San Francisco's legendary Haight-Ashbury. From there the trail heads out to the Oregon hills where the communal lifestyle was in full frolic.

These tales include an account of the Vortex 1 Biodegradable Festival of Life held outside Portland, which is probably the largest, least-reported-about rock n' roll festival of that entire era. Following that I recount the generally-unknown tale of the beginnings of the Rainbow Gatherings – collective, spiritual, peacefully anarchic village-like gatherings in public forestlands that have continued and sprouted around the world to the present day.

Sections of this book will bring you to Native American protests in Canada, adventures in North Africa, arts libre in Mexico, as well as Paris, London, Berlin, and Rome. Some of these stories contain mysteries that may yet get to be figured out.

Episodes often point to someone who exemplifies ideals or inspired others. Sometimes these are well-known people and there are glimpses of Allen Ginsberg, Jack Kerouac, Ken Kesey and Timothy Leary among others; but just as often the characters exposed are largely unknowns: people who in a particular moment I observed standing up and acting in a way that stood for all of us, for the betterment of our earth or our human predicament.

Finally the tales return to their roots, back to New York City where the community garden movement and the creation of a children's gardening program turns vacant lots into neighborhood havens.

The stories I tell here map an arc of activity that is continuing to evolve and spread across the earth. But this is not the sole story, nor group of stories that define the emergence of our New World Culture.

Many other events covered parallel ground. There are many other movements that coincide in purpose with the movements described or birthed in these tales.

The roots of protest grow from many gardens. That's one of the remarkable things about this New World Culture: it doesn't have a chief, an office, an official history, nor any such thing as a central origin, except of course in a spiritual sense, so it belongs to everyone who gives it a place in their actions.

The Civil Rights Movement, the Feminist Movement, the Gay Rights Movement, the Occupy Movement and many, many others are all part of worldwide phenomena whose unity has hardly been noted, and yet, here it is across the globe, showing itself in current movements for environmental and human rights causes.

The old system of competitive currencies, national boundaries, bloodcurdling religions and ruthless corporations is broken and no one is going to be able to fix it. It certainly won't fix itself. The bankers aren't going to wake up tomorrow and begin to feed the needy; the corporations aren't going to hold their next board meetings and decide to enrich and uplift the lives and fortunes of their workers, nor to see to the protection of our environment; the religious fanatics are nothing but dangerous and destructive, and the governments – even the best of them, the boondoggled 'democracies,' – aren't going to give up their ties to the campaign contributors that keep them in power, nor to the lobbyists who bribe them shamelessly, nor to their own outmoded fearful ideologies.

No, the solution has to come from somewhere else. And it is already in motion. The fact that this New World Culture is still basically flying under the radar is to our advantage: we haven't been seen as a worldwide threat to the power elite. Nope, just a bunch of fragmented people's movements. But that is not the case. Without a centralized power system, without a single organization as such, the human species – through a thousand and one community movements, liberation movements, free expression movements, equal justice movements, environmental and ecological movements – is moving toward a world in which the values of our whole human community are being elevated. And this is going to continue to expand and save our butts, literally save our very lives, from the blind, ignorant, greedy, aggressive powers of the nation state corporate system.

The corporate state system and its allies the banksters tell us that peace isn't profitable enough. They tell us that the only way to pay for everything is through war economy. We are so busy using military aid to prop up dictatorships to 'help' our economy that we are unable to prop up our own economy enough to steer ourselves out of poverty and into abundance and prosperity. So we lose ourselves as an example of a successful commonwealth and it's no wonder that people struggling to come out from under the burdens of repressive regimes don't hold the corporate state as an ideal model. Then the dictatorships we have propped up get overtaken by people's movements, which arm themselves with the weaponry our country had provided to their oppressors. No wonder the world is such a mess.

That old world order cannot feed itself, nurture itself, care for its young, care for its old, care for the bountiful earth, its rivers and streams, its water sources, its fields, its forests, its oceans. It can't care for those, nor for the people who inhabit its land and its cities. It can't do it because it doesn't have the strength of will nor the insight about what it takes to do it. It is too blinded by greed and pursued by fear of itself to take the necessary steps to solve the problems.

So the people independently are going to do it. All across our globe, without regard for political parties, without old-style intolerant absolutist religions, without loans from the greedy bankers, without all those outmoded systems – people are coming to an understanding that like a great patchwork quilt of many colors and many stripes and many pieces – we are forming alliances for kind and supportive causes that will literally save us from ourselves.

We believe in the vision of a peaceful earth, that this is not a fantasy. We believe in the ideal of environmental harmony, that this is not a fantasy. We believe in the dream of equal justice and equal rights, that these are not fantasies. We believe in the hope of a kind and beautiful future for humanity, that this is not a fantasy.

We are, each of us in our own very small ways, taking actions that altogether are like the many drops that make a wave and the many waves that make a tide and these tides are going to change the course of history. We are here. This culture is here. It is evolving and growing every day and just slowly right now, right now becoming aware of itself. Nothing can stop it. We are actually the force of human evolution at work – and at play, because like the young-at-heart dreamers we are, we do things with joy and joyousness, and beauty and art and fun.

Even in the face of all the terrible things going on around us, we are not giving in, we are not giving up, we are not giving out. We are pursuing our goals of peace and environmental harmony with intense efforts, and yet with humor and with all the available arts we are keeping ourselves cool in the midst of this evolutionary struggle.

The saga of humans seeking freedom extends through the ages right up into our very own time, and the voices of those who have courageously advanced civilization will speak through our lips if we just stand up for the Rights of the Downtrodden, and for the Living Spirit of the Earth.

The question remains: How much more destruction is going to go on before we pull it together and evolve out of the old, outmoded ways?

We need to learn to see beyond the separations of national boundaries, absolutist religions, and ethnic or class divisions. We need to see the money system as a transitional process in between a world economy based on scarcity and competition, and a world economy based on abundance and cooperation. We need a different, new way of doing things, of providing for ourselves. The old system seems to be based on competition, and the belief that humans evolved to our position on earth because we out-competed other species. I think we evolved because we learned to co-operate with each other, to live and work together in teams and tribes and families. We need to re-learn from these ancient experiences to bring what's needed today into the future. We need to educate ourselves – and all the young people everywhere, to see ourselves as one human family.

I hope these stories leave some clues and some answers about how that can be done.

Simply put, this collection of tales is about the emergence of a New World Culture, a culture of tolerance for people's differences, a culture of respect for the earth and its bounty and its beauty. Without planning it as such, a New World Culture has grown out of the freewheeling ideas of the Beats, the Hipsters, the progressive artists, the peaceful anarchists, the communal idealists, the ecological activists and so on. This culture has roots across the world. It is thriving. It crosses all political lines and religious divisions. It is a genuine world movement and it stands as counterpoint to the New World Order with all of its outmoded nation-states.

Let the tales begin.

PART ONE

Meetings with Amazing People
(1954–1959)

In which the foundation blocks of the New World Culture are revealed to have already been set in place by the generation of artists, poets, playwrights, musicians, anti-war political activists, feminists, and spiritual visionaries who blossomed in the Bohemian and Beatnik eras.

1. Dorothy's Story

The breezes of the Cold War between The Imperial Soviet and The American Empire blew chills into the rosy-cheeked smiles of the 1950s.

Just when we Americans thought we had figured out how to live the good life because we had some elementary security and well-being, and televised entertainment in the living room of every home every evening, here come these honchos from the power elite telling us we're going to have to build bomb shelters. Every building in New York has to have one or designate a cellar or basement room as the bomb shelter. Signs are going to be posted in public buildings to direct people.

Not only that but the whole city—New York, the Empire City—is going to practice taking shelter together. You didn't have to be an Einstein to figure out that hiding in the downstairs hallway of the school, or the boiler room of the apartment building, or some designated office basement is not much protection from the heat of one of those hydrogen atom explosives. Still at the sound of the sirens it's going to be "Everyone off the streets!" and, in theory at least, everyone down into the basements in all five boroughs of New York City. Anyone found outside will be arrested. No, I am not kidding. This was the Cold War.

At the same time in a little house on Chrystie Street, just off the Bowery in Lower Manhattan, dwelt a small band of Catholics devoted to service to the poor. They took vows of poverty, and lived among the people who they served, helped with health problems, clothed, fed and sheltered at their 'House of Hospitality.'

They published a newspaper called *The Catholic Worker* and that's what they were called themselves, Catholic Workers. They also had a farm in the countryside where they could retreat or rehabilitate. The group was founded in the 1930s by a woman who had converted from Protestantism and helped to begin this independent sect.

Twenty-five years later, here she is, Dorothy Day, telling people that these bomb tests and shelter drills are an abomination, an offense to the eyes of God.

She and the Catholic Worker people are planning a public protest. A young anarchist (and poet), Jackson Mac Low, had been helping serve at the Catholic Worker's kitchen. Jackson was a performer in my parents' Off-Broadway theatre company, The Living Theatre. He had been cast in Racine's *Phedre* and called in to say he would have to miss a rehearsal for the demonstration. And he invited my mother, Judith Malina, and others from the Theatre to join him.

So Jackson and Judith from The Living Theatre joined the small band of Catholic Workers publicly outside City Hall when the sirens started howling. The whole cityscape emptied of people. It got very quiet.

Then the police came. They ordered everyone to leave City Hall Park and take shelter. And when no one left, they arrested all of the demonstrators.

Over the next several years these annual demonstrations—on the day of the yearly shelter drill—grew in size. At the first only a dozen people, then the second year just a few over two dozen, then hundreds, then a thousand. By the early 1960s many thousands. Everyone couldn't be arrested. There was a great deal of communication at these yearly demos, where people isolated in the long sleepy Fifties began to meet and discover each other. The protests got too big to be contained; people all over the city weren't taking shelter, and the Shelter Drills came to an end.

It was from this burgeoning scene that many of the more famous 1960s peace action and civil rights groups sprouted and grew.

But the second of these many shelter-drill demonstrations was the one that affected me most. The entire group was arrested, and sentenced to thirty days in the city's prisons. Judith spent her time in the Women's House of Detention, a towering brown building at the north end of Greenwich Village, and my father, Julian Beck, did his in the Bronx repository affectionately—dreadfully—nicknamed 'the Tombs.'

Let me tell you, I woke up with a perfect understanding that my own government can be seriously wrong.

I knew that my parents were both kind, caring people who were always teaching me, showing me right from wrong, encouraging me to do good; and that they had done nothing bad—except speak up for what they thought was right and good for everyone. And the government, 'my government,' was putting them in jail.

I have been skeptical ever since of government authority. Of bomb testing. Of the usefulness of jails. Or of getting justice in the courts.

Julian wrote me regularly from jail, long pencil-printed letters.

Judith's thirty days in the custody of the state were spent in a cell with Dorothy Day.

I was mercifully sent to summer camp before sentencing time. The whole thing was difficult enough even from a distance.

During Dorothy's stay in the Women's House of Detention she told the other 'girls'—that's what the prisoners there were all called—Dorothy told them she'd come back to visit them come Christmas Eve.

And indeed she did. She—and the Catholic Workers—organized a group of Christmas carolers to sing on the blustery eve of Christmas to the six tall sides of the women's prison: the group moving from adjacent to the Jefferson Courthouse on Sixth Avenue to the traffic island in between Sixth and Greenwich, then onto the busy sidewalk of Greenwich Avenue itself, next up along Patchin Place and one last stop by the alleyway where an odd bend in the architecture faced the bricks of the back of the Courthouse.

Figure 1. Christmas Eve, 1957. Author, center, between Judith Malina, Julian Beck. Dorothy Day at far right. (Photographer unknown: Courtesy the Estate of Judith Malina, 1957)

They had mimeographed texts of the carols but most of the people there knew the songs already. Of course Julian and Judith were there, and some of their friends from The Living Theatre. And myself. This was where I was exposed really for the first time to Christianity. I had to ask about what the lines in the songs meant or what the stories in the songs were about. And I saw, plain as day, plain as the crisp cold air of Christmas night that these sweet people were singing to let the inmates know something very deep and simple and beautiful. And a few of the prisoners hollered back requests, some asked for pop tunes and the choir obliged as best it could.

And the next year the little choir grew a bit larger and came back again. Some of the same prisoners were still inside; some were in again on new charges. Most, statistics showed, were in for prostitution or heroin.

For years I spent Christmas Eves caroling there. I learned all the verses to "Good King Wenceslas." The 'girls' came to expect us, they lit and waved matches, they hollered "We love you!" from inside the glass brick windows. Some of the prisoners who'd been released joined us. They were out, had jobs, families, but they came down here, hoping to find us, to sing.

It must have been about the fifth or sixth year we were doing this, while we were along the Greenwich Avenue side, facing the main entrance of the prison when one of the doors swung open and a portly woman, a woman with many keys came out. She was in uniform and she slowly went to the corner and crossed the street approaching us.

When she stopped and stood next to us she had our attention. She spoke carefully, even kindly. "I know you mean well, but you have no idea how upset you make the girls. They cry and cry after you're gone. You remind them of all the things they can't have out here, all their loved ones that they miss.

"Inside, we give them a nice Christmas program. Those who want to sing the songs can sing them. They get an extra nice meal and then to bed. Then you come and all that peaceful quiet turns into crying and sobbing all night long.

"I know," she continues, "I've been here years and I've seen the difference these times you've been coming. If you care about these girls, let them get their rest."

There was a moment as quiet as the twinkle of a star.

Then Dorothy was speaking, in fact agreeing that we all cared about these girls very much and that that's why we were all here, "In fact the very best Christmas present we could give these girls is some time with their families."

She leaned just slightly closer toward the Warden. "You know, you could let those girls go home for Christmas. That would stop their crying. That's what Jesus Christ would do if He had those keys."

In the space between moments I saw Dorothy the Saint extending like an elder Mary the true meaning of the Blessed Heart, and the Warden uniformed in Satan's army, herself chained by Beelzebub's keys.

For a moment she smiles a tiny smile at Dorothy, then her face regains her sternness and she looks down and shakes her head "No." Slowly she backs up, quickly shaking her head. She's frightened. She saw more than she had wanted to see. She re-crosses the street and, still shaking her head in broad series of "No's," she relocks herself into the prison building.

It was clear to me from that moment, that the inner truth of religion wasn't bounded by the various sects we call Christianity, Buddhism, Judaism, Islam, Hinduism, Anyother-ism. No, the truths that spiritual insight gives are boundless and belong to anyone who gives them voice.

For months afterward I hummed the Christmas carol tunes. I got in trouble for humming them in the hallway at Hebrew school. I still hum them, "Good King Wenceslas looked out da da da da daa daaaa...."

For years I went back every Christmas Eve. Even long after my parents had migrated to Europe. Then, one year they tore that rat hole of a prison down. No doubt they built another one somewhere else, but as I write these words a beautiful community garden full of trees, flowers, benches—open to the public—rests on that spot.

Dorothy's life has been chronicled by a number of religious and socialist writers and if the Catholic Church has enough good sense, they'll recognize her as a Saint. I sure did, and she still stands in that moment, tall as the centuries, shimmering in the robe of bravery, gently, firmly speaking words that illuminate the way.

2. Nina's Story

The earliest productions of The Living Theatre took place in our big shag-carpeted living room on West End Avenue in the seasons just after my birth. There, people gathered for '...an evening of plays,' as the watercolored announcements put it, consisting of four short poetic fanciful pieces by poet Gertrude Stein, playwright Bertolt Brecht, poet Garcia Lorca, and philosopher Paul Goodman. The setting was very informal and it brought together circles of artists, dancers, painters, sculptors, and poets, who might be interested to attend such exotic entertainments.

The effects were beyond the facility of even a large, well-lit, well-carpeted living room. So in the following seasons my father, Julian Beck, tall, bald-headed, sharp-featured, elegantly spoken and my mother, Judith Malina, small, dark-haired, finely-featured, and unquenchably creative, took a lease on the Cherry Lane Theatre downtown in Greenwich Village. There they brought together a theatre company for a two-year run in what was becoming known as the Off-Broadway movement. They ran "An Evening of Bohemian Theatre" with plays by Picasso, Alfred Jarry, more Gertrude Stein, and poets Eliot, Ashbery and Rexroth.

Then they rented a small loft in a wood-frame building on upper Broadway where for another two years they produced a string of wild, small but jewel-like productions: Auden's *The Age of Anxiety*, Strindberg's *The Spook Sonata;* Cocteau's *Orpheus;* Fredrick's *The Idiot King;* and Pirandello's *Tonight We Improvise;* Racine's *Phedre;* and Goodman's *The Young Disciple*. That's where they began to evolve the involve-the-audience and improvisational theatre we later became infamous for. These were days of experimentation and I played the roles of the various small children these esteemed authors had written into their works: I was murdered by a wicked king, seduced by an elder sister, and played children's games in the on-stage gardens of poetic imagination.

Into this mix of actors, actresses, poets and painters, into this whirlwind of people forever auditioning, rehearsing, and performing came a completely unique creative spirit, Nina, who was, it seemed, set down among us to grace us for a time.

Allow me to introduce one of the un-told heroes, actually a 'shero,' of modern times.

Originally her name was Shirley Gleaner. Her parents were egg farmers from New Jersey. She appeared (as did so many future members of the theatre's company) as a volunteer to help with the thousand whatevers of theatrical production: costumes, sets, lights, props and programs. Of course, she wanted also to act, to be on the stage in the hot lights of performance.

Although the exact details of her personal epiphany are beyond me, I do know that she was suffused by a vision in which she was told that what the world needed Right Now was a dose of Love and Beauty—and that she was to be in this moment the incarnation of Venus, Aphrodite, the Love Goddess.

Figure 2. Nina Gitana. (Ruth Kuzub: Courtesy the Living Theatre Archives, 1960)

She grew her hair long and flowing, with ribbons.

She marched right out of the beatnik somber black clothing

and into—unheard of at the time—paisley and flower prints. She painted on orange and purple eye shadow. She put glitter in her hair. She began talking in verse and rhyme. She laughed gleefully at the foolishnesses of the modern industrial 1950s. She dressed in ethnic mirror-covered garments and danced across the streets trailing multi-colored scarves. And, she took a new name, Nina, from the spectacular Bizet opera, *Carmen*.

She got busted dancing naked in the Washington Square Park fountain. And then she moved in with the theatre's producers—our apartment! She lived on the couch in the room my father used for his painting studio.

From the mosaic of those memories let me just open the refrigerator in search of a snack...and find the usual sparse selection of beatnik edibles. Nina approached and removed a full jar of jam. Opening it she began to spoon it into her mouth.

"Nina, you can't just eat jam," say I.

"Oh, and why not? It's delicious. Don't you like jam?"

"Sure, but, you need bread or peanut butter to go with it."

"Nonsense!" She replies. "Try some. Let's eat it together." Her eyebrows raised, and her eyes twinkled a mischievous twinkle.

She smiled a broad smile and handed me a spoon. While we ate, Nina mapped out her reasoning. "Everyone's always denying themselves pleasures, and for no good reason. Just like this jam, there's food enough to go 'round to feed all the hungry people, but no one will take it out of the fridge. Why? They're too afraid there won't be enough for tomorrow, and so we let people starve today."

"Yumm," I said.

"Why, think of a world with everyone well-fed. We could have music filling the streets, people dancing, laughing all the time, helping each other. Do you think that would be so bad?"

"No, not so bad."

"Well why isn't it? Because everyone's too busy planning and working for tomorrow's riches to enjoy today's. Ahhh," she sighed slowly, dreamily, "to enjoy the riches of this moment, now that's what living is for! We have to dance and sing, no one else can do it for us!"

She took me by both hands and lightly swirled us both in a circlet across the kitchen linoleum.

"Oh yes," she laughed, "life and its pleasures are all yours, but you, you must open the door, reach for the jam, and don't forget to ask if anyone else would like some too!"

She smiled her twinkly-eyed smile, stopped spinning and picked up the jam. We dug in together with our spoons until we had reached the bottom of the jar.

Nina was *always* like that. She played wooden flutes in the morning sunlight. She went downtown and returned with strange packages in colored cellophane, which when opened had the most exquisite smells—incense! The Hindu cones, the joss sticks, the green Japanese spirals. Aromas filled the house.

One day she announced a banquet: many of Julian and Judith's friends were invited. In preparation Nina unrolled big India print bedspreads as a tablecloth diagonally across the floor. She decorated the house with flowers. And spread out bowls of fruit, dates, black plums, cheeses, carafes of cider, juices; sweet smells and music did fill the air.

Everyone who showed up thought she was a bit mad, as she danced among us serving and pouring, in her parrot-colored skirt. Yes, even the Beatniks thought she was a wee bit too way out. And she was. But she was onto something. Something about where joy comes from and where happiness sits, always ripe and always tasty, and these grownups, they were just missing it. No, the Beatnik writers, artists, and poets dressed in their black turtlenecks and tees, their black jeans and dark glasses didn't just up and adopt her style nor her philosophy, even though her banquet was a delightful success.

But every one of those sunglassed, black-clad beatniks took a piece of Nina, an image of Nina and put it, wrote it, planted it in their poems, their novels, their songs and their plays. I tell you now, after these many years, that undoubtedly Nina was the first, the very true and original first Hippie. It wasn't until a decade plus later that I began to see her fashion, her sense of beauty erupt in the youth culture of America. And erupt it did, in all the many colors and flagrant free forms that Nina could have dreamed of. She showed it to all the Beats. The California left coasters as well as the New Yorkers all cruised through the Off-Broadway Theatre's scene in the course of those years. She let her free flag fly, she sang in the streets of cold-war America, in the gray-suited times of conformity, she let 'em have it, and maybe she was dismissed by the people who saw her as a strangewoman, but somehow, somehow, the images she left behind on the retinas, or in the imaginations of her peers were translated into characters in their art, their books, their poems; and then, on beyond Beatnik, they emerged fresh and delightful in the amazing decade that followed.

I know I've heard it said that Cuban revolutionist Che Guevara said that it was Jesus who was the first Hippie. But in our times, in our century, Nina was the very first one.

Later, she moved to a very quiet ashram where in dignity and decorum she practiced her meditations, did her yoga, ate her natural foods, cultivated her garden and fruit trees, and lived happily and beautifully to a ripe old age.

3. Naphtali's Story

Down the hill on West End Avenue, three blocks from our apartment stood New York's Public School 75 where I went for kindergarten and then six years of grammar school.

Multi-everything as New York really is, the kids I met and played with were Puerto Rican, Black, Italian, Irish, Jewish, White, Arabic, Greek, South African and other first world, second world, third world backgrounds. Year after year we played handball or box ball on the sidewalks, stickball in the streets, tag on the rooftops, and soccer and touch football on the park hill's slope. No supervision, no grownups. Just us kids, all different types and stripes, some different languages, certainly different Gods, having a good time together, keeping score, playing fair most of the time, working out our differences for hundreds of afternoons. Sure sometimes there were fusses, even fights, but it was the function of the rest of the group to pull the squabblers apart.

No doubt about it, these early experiences left me certain that kindness and meanness are found among all kinds of people, that you can't tell just by looking just what kind—or unkind—of a person a person is. No, you have to meet 'em, greet 'em in goodwill and find out bit by bit from there.

Out of respect for my mother's family's religious beliefs, I was sent on weekend mornings to the Hebrew school at Temple Ansche Chesed just a few blocks in the other direction up the avenue. There we were taught the Bible stories and Hebrew songs and customs, and about the recently founded State of Israel, but mostly we played with clay, drew with crayons and played. The intent was to teach us our culture and heritage but not to disturb the blending-in process that most Jewish families in New York were trying to accomplish at that time within the American culture. It wasn't much different from regular public school.

Facing West End Avenue and attached to the Hebrew school, was the big Anche Chesed Synagogue, where a lot of the neighborhood congregated on Saturdays and holidays. We went only on the major holidays, mostly to keep the peace with Judith's mother, Rose, for whom this all still had importance. The adults whispered back and forth in the pews, chatting about who's whatting with whom, and who got promoted, and where so-and-so vacationed; and when we kids could get away, it was off to the lobby to wait –or even better—outside onto the curb for a game of touch football with the parking signs as goalposts. Ahhh, the playful fulfillment of childhood religion.

Then one holiday, my parents said we were going to a different synagogue, and I could go, if I was going to pay attention and be well behaved. It was Succoth, the holiday where we build a house (a room, really) made of fruit and harvested corn, melons, grapes, and vegetables in which to give harvest season thanks.

But, in the sleep-late style of late-night theatre people we were good and late for the morning service and when we arrived at this tiny shoebox of a synagogue, there was no one there. The place was plain, very plain. There were no vaulted ceilings, no elaborate geometric patterned painting (which was so much the style for synagogues in New York at the time), no plush cushioned pews, and no chandeliers. Just a plain long room with a wooden ark for the scrolls at one end, and a little wooden platform for the reader or speaker.

We walked in slowly, quietly. We were more than half past late.

We went forward toward the front of the room and there were voices through a doorway at the back. Julian poked his head through that doorway and in a moment, out strode a man the likes of which I had never seen before. He wore a long cream colored robe. He was a big man, huge, and with a long, full, bushy gray-white beard. He was rocking a bit, side to side, as he walked loudly saying, "Ju-dit, Ju-dit," which was the way he said my mother's name. "Ju-dit, Ju-dit," as he came closer.

Then he caught sight of me. His eyes quickly glanced at my mother and back at me and in one swoop his big arms picked me up and he pressed me close to his body and his big thick scratchy beard. Then he kissed me, and again and again. It was the first time I'd ever been kissed by a man other than my father or grandfather. He was rocking with me now in his arms slowly and affectionately from side to side. I could feel his big heart beating in his chest and I looked up at his big kind smiling face, and there, there his eyes were just slightly teary.

I had never met anything like this before. He looked like somebody right out of the Bible picture books. There was suddenly more to this religion stuff than I had seen so far. This guy had something else going on that was far different from what I was being shown up at the big synagogue on 100th Street.

The seasons proceeded with further occasional visits to this Carlebach Shul, usually on Saturday mornings during the Hebrew holidays, where this rabbi, Naphtali Carlebach, held forth. His immigrant congregation was devout but not austere. Amidst the order of the service people whispered, women and men both leaving the separated sides of the prayer hall to chatter away in the building's lobby, or outside where the view down 79th Street opened across the park to the beautiful, broad flowing Hudson River along whose currents this city had risen.

Inside the shul, the congregants prayed by davening, that is chanting in unison and in silence the repetitive prayers and swaying back and forth in synch with the Holy Names recited during the formal prayers, and through the almost-ageless ritual of reading the Torah scrolls aloud bit by bit, week after week through the year, each year reading the whole of the first five books of The Bible.

But then came the time for the old rabbi's lecture, his weekly sermon to the congregation. Sometimes the Rabbi talked on world events, or the problems of the community, the problem of faith, all the usually pulpitory topics; but almost always he would illustrate his remarks with a story, from the ancient texts, a Mishnah, passed along from the rabbis of hundreds of years ago, or sometimes a tale from just beyond the century and the sea; from the old country from which our previous generations had migrated. Sometimes he spoke in German with Hebrew phrases, but frequently he held forth in English and it held my attention.

One particular sermon told about a child who had retreated from the world by refusing to come out from under the kitchen table, removing all his clothes, and claiming to be a chicken who would eat only crumbs off the floor. No amount of reason or force makes any difference, the child retreats under the table and squawks and chirps amid begging to be thrown some crumbs.

Finally the rabbi of the town is called in to help find a cure. And what does he do? He climbs under the table with the child. Removes his clothes as well and goes after the crumbs, too. This initiates an interchange between the child and the Rabbi, which results eventually in the child coming out re-encouraged to face the world.

And how the rabbi brought to life the conversations between the boy and the rabbi, mimicking first one then the other, has never left me, nor has the lesson of the story.

At the finish of the tale there was a strong long silence from the congregation, an awkwardly long pause, and then he began explaining, all very fast, so that I didn't follow all of it. Years later I came to know that this story was an elaboration—his twist—on a tale Rabbi Nachman of Breslav made famous two hundred years before.

Often I make of it that we are like the child under the table, fearful of our world. But then there are times, when I see the story is really about the Rabbi, our grown self, who needs to solve the problem—even in the face of insane situations—and where we draw the insight and the strength for that.

4. Spencer's Story

In the back of a car a man makes quarters appear and disappear. His hands are empty. Now they flash the silver.

A collection of blue bottles lines his shelf top.

He published his stories in typewriter font on long brown paper pages.

He appeared like a traveling magician—whatever that may be—at our door.

Not much taller than I. A tweed sport coat. Round expressive face already explaining that I should let my parents know he was here, and he added, along with his name, "The Storyteller." In moments I was back letting him know they'd be to the door in a minute. I asked, "Storyteller?" "Yes," he said plainly, "I tell stories. Just like some people build houses or drive taxicabs, I tell stories."

"Are you here to tell my parents a story?"

"Well, maybe, we'll see." And then down the hall came Julian and Judith welcoming him in.

'Boy' was his name. Not Spencer 'till much later. Everyone called him Boy. Maybe because of his youthful demeanor.

He taught me how to palm a quarter, seeming to make it appear and disappear in my hands. He explained distraction as the fundamental element of surprise in all art.

And a storyteller he was. In a constant chuckle of ironic imaginings he conducted conversations, and performed his work at café readings, and dozens of other illuminated literati gatherings.

In the years ahead I traipsed across the Village to the venues of his recitals. Small crowded galleries, the side room of a tavern, an apartment where everyone sat on the carpeted floor. Ginsberg was charmed. John Cage listened intently. Dancers, painters,

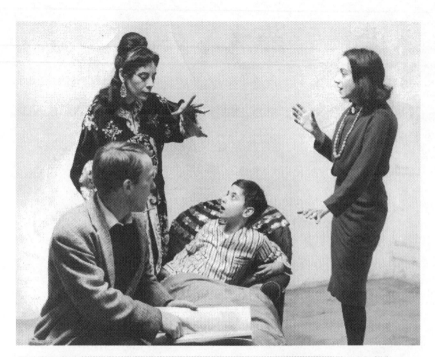
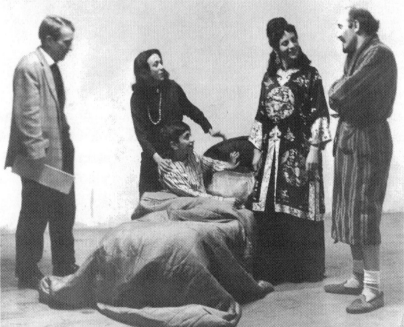

Figures 3 & 4. In rehearsal for Spenser Holst's play, *The Devil's Mother.* From the left: Spencer Holst; my mother, Judith Malina; the author; Nina Gitana and Jerome Raphael. (Ruth Kuzub: Courtesy the Living Theatre Archives, 1960)

actors, writers, poets clustered 'round this Yoda-like figure who dispensed his art like a street-corner oracle.

He never told 'folk tales,' only original work. And he never really 'told' them aloud. Rather he read them verbatim each time. Twenty or so years later I asked him about this. Why when he surely had the pieces memorized he could just as easily—and surely just as expressively—have told them without the aid of the text in front of him?

"First because every word, each word wants to be exactly right," and he went on for another moment or two about the rhythm, the cadence, the 'sound' of it, but then he interrupted himself to say, "It's really because these stories are made for someone to read out loud to somebody else."

In a time when increasingly the language of our legends, our myths, our tales was being taken over by advertiser-driven media, here's Spencer ambling along like Diogenes with his lantern, or Herodotus with his scrolls of storypapers, telling tales that reflect our strengths, our weaknesses, our hopes, our superstitions, our desires and our selves.

We become his frogs, his dancers, his wildebeests, his garbage collectors, his typewriter repairmen, his zookeepers, his goblins, and then it's time to go, back into the streets and on with our lives.

Spencer lived in a converted artist's loft and collected blue bottle glass. He wore grandfatherly sweater vests, or tweed coats to mask the wild imaginings that went on inside his brain.

I saw that he practiced his art, refining his twists of the tongue, the way a refinery purifies hot precious metals. Indeed each word counts. And I saw that even the most abstract works of art have a story to them. Where do they pick up the eyes of the viewer? Where do they take us, lead us, transport us? Where do they set us back down in our own 'real' world?

In one of his tales a goblin music teacher turns his various students into goblins themselves. Spencer turned me into a storyteller.

5. Opening Night

From the cell window Judith and Dorothy shared during their month in the women's prison there was a view up Manhattan's Sixth Avenue that included a vacant old Hecht's department store on 14th Street, adorned with a big red-on-white 'For Rent' sign.

Judith envisioned this as a theatre.

So it was that Julian and Judith scraped together the money to lease the top three floors of the old department store and invited the arts community at large of the Bohemian and Beat generations to work on creating a theatre inside the vacant hulk of a building.

There were three similar floors, each partitioned by huge panels covered in antiquated wallpaper, dusty now and hanging in some places in long swirling torn strips like giant apple peelings or the dusty curlicues of an illustrator whose project had been abandoned—and abandoned it was and had now fallen, or risen, into our hands.

We tore down the partitions; we swept up the years of dust and dinge, and then came architects, builders, painters, and electricians. Some Hungarian freedom socialists did all the plumbing. Each of the three floors was divided roughly in half, the long way, and Julian and Judith set about making use of the space so that not just a theatre but a community of artists would have space to flower.

Up at the top floor were the prop-making, set building, and tech areas along with the costume room. The far half of the top floor with its own entrance on 14th Street was leased to Merce Cunningham and his dance troupe. They used that space for the next five years for their rehearsal studio.

The middle floor held the Living Theatre office, and a string of nine dressing rooms all adjoined by a 'green room,' that is, a place where actors could meet and greet visitors, or visitors could wait for their actor friends to emerge either in costume before the show, during intermission or street-dressed after the show.

The far half of this second floor was split into just three large rooms. One, a gallery for art exhibitions, another a practice room for lessons: voice lessons, movement lessons, and of course, acting classes.

And the third, the third deserves a book of tales all to itself because this third room, the one at the back, became a peace action office, an organizational place for an array of independent activist groups.

It was out of this office that I first saw anti-Vietnam War protests. Freedom Bus rides into the deep South during the rise of the Civil Rights movement were organized from this room. From there mailings for sit-ins at the Atomic Energy Commission were folded, stamped and sent. From there day trips were scheduled to the sunny south shore of Connecticut, to the Groton Submarine base, where Julian and Judith (Judith! She doesn't know how to swim!) went out in a rowboat into the bay in front of an armed nuclear war sub to protest its launching.

It was in the midst of this—over the next four years—that I picked up the fine art of organizing communications in the service of a cause. I learned about getting the fliers from the printer, about how to fold fliers in thirds so they fit into envelopes, about endlessly stuffing envelopes, about address labels, rolls of stamps, maps for strategies during demonstrations, telephone trees, poster printing, putting up posters, press releases and I learned also: that people will pull together long and hard if the work at hand is something they believe is good and important and true. And here 'true' means that there is some truth that needs to be told, or for whatever reason—the truth isn't being told and for the good of the many the truth needs to come out.

There was a General Strike for Peace, that HQ'd in that room that had grown out of the Shelter Drill protests and in turn was overtaken by the force of the anti-war movement that eventually focused on Vietnam. One group's plan called for a daily walk that would slowly but surely cover each and every street in New York City, passing out peace literature and talking with people they encountered. I went on a couple of those outings. Paul Prensky, a solidly-built tawny-bearded physics teacher, and John Harriman, a lanky goateed labor organizer from the Midwest, were the map bearers, and off we went into the five boroughs of the vast city. We carried literature about all the peace and pacifist causes from around the world; African peoples protesting colonial rule, fallout from above-ground nuclear tests—these were real issues in that time. Then came stories of a secret war, a war America was fighting that it didn't want its people to know about. And we began making leaflets about Vietnam.

All this and more spun from the ghost of the department store. We built the walls to make the rooms. I learned to use mortar and to level and to point bricks.

Downstairs the plan called for a great big lobby with kiosks for vending small press poetry magazines and espresso coffees and Turkish delight.

Huge walls were scraped bare to the brick and the columns that really held up the middle of the whole building were alternately covered with crinkled aluminum foil or eye-popping super-vivid bright orange paint.

A sculptor made a wild snaking copper pipe drinking fountain and I watched the master enamellist Paul Hultburg fit the tiles that covered the doors that led into the theatre itself. Creamy white orange enamel swirls facing the lobby on the doors' outside and facing within the theatre, gloss black and pearl...so the grand opening wasn't just another play in another facility, it was the opening of a theatre built, cemented together and painted by a circle of artists and supporters and friends.

The first opening night in this new Living Theatre was set for January 13, 1959 and the play going up was to be William

Carlos Williams' *Many Loves*, a three-act piece where in each act the same actors played out different romantic relationships. There was, in what would only later be seen as typical Living Theatre style, a prologue and epilogue that drew the audience into their own relation with the cast, so as the audience entered the theatre from the lobby the crew was still busy setting up, lights were still being set, furniture hurriedly arranged on stage, the stage manager was saying it's ok, just let everyone in, and the house manager was encouraging people to find their seats even among the still ongoing stage preparations. I sat on the front of the stage with actor/comedian Murray Paskin and I ran his lines with him. That means: held his script and read him his cues while he ran his lines, practicing. We paid almost no attention to the audience filling up the seats.

Then the stage manager announced that we were ready at last, and we all left the stage, the curtain was closed, the house lights went down, and the play began.

Many times, people would later say, "Oh yes, the performance I saw, the company wasn't completely ready when they let us in, so we got to see the final preparations for the show." Some, who would see the play more than once, got it. "Oh, the beginning, the part with everyone bustling about, that was in the script!"

Same with the epilogue where the director came out and announced that two of the 'actors' in the play had actually decided to marry, had proposed and accepted that very evening and there they were, ushered onto the stage, arm in arm at the end of the curtain call, to a rousing round of applause from the rest of the cast and the stage crew—and of course from the real audience as well.

But my role, my part came at the end of the third act. I played a child, nine years old, sick home from school, upstairs asleep, while Mom downstairs—onstage—sweeps and irons clothes in the kitchen, waiting for the doctor.

When he arrives—because I'm asleep upstairs—they fall to

talking...about all the usual stuff of life. They know each other since going to the town's high school years ago and they talk about all what's happened to them since then, their friends, people they know, their lives, hopes, problems...all the stuff people talk about in the beginnings of courtship. Ultimately they start to seduce each other and wind up, at last on the kitchen table in a passionate embrace. Suddenly I enter, excitedly, in pajamas, with stuffed animal,

"Daddy, Da-"

and realize it's not Daddy come home to check on his sick child.

I had, in the words of the director, "To stun everyone in the whole audience in that one moment." They had to gasp, startled, or squirm in their seats. And in that one long moment while the embrace slowly separated, I played it so seriously, mouth slightly open, startled myself, experiencing the new found realities of life. There was a full house, and at the end of the show, lots of applause. For the actors that isn't the end, really just the beginning, as they say...'The Opening.'

After all the people and noise backstage, after taking off the makeup and changing from the costumes, it was uptown to the opening night party to wait for the reviews.

This practice has changed since then, with multiple 'opening nights.' First some 'previews' that are really openings, then an 'opening' for friends, supporters, patrons and patronesses, then a 'press opening,' then a commercial 'opening,' then maybe another 'press opening,' trying to get the writers and reviewers in who couldn't be at the first or other openings. It's a rather drawn out process nowadays, but then, in 1959, there was a single preview with special friends invited as a 'practice audience,' and then, simply The Opening with press writers packed among friends, supporters and ticket buyers. The New York dailies would come out an hour or two after midnight and the reviews would be there in black and white making or breaking the plays.

Uptown at the party rampant, I'm dressed in my fringed flannel cowboy shirt. Most of the beatniks are overdressed, many sporting ties, white shirts, jackets, looking dressed up for the opening. Parents of young actresses mix with the poets of New York. Liquor is abundant at a serve yourself bar. Smoking grass is pretty much confined to the very backmost room, where FM radio plays Jazz, and lights are low, shaded deep red brown, violet tones.

Upfront in the big room someone hands all the women long-stemmed roses. Conversations flash and dash. Painters parry parlays past philosophy professors. 'Literary Lions' pose for the photographer in the library. The Beatniks are at play themselves. Beatniks? What did I know? To me these are the people from the audience, friends of actors, relatives come to celebrate and hope for good reviews. Poet Gregory Corso explains Life and Death to an older mystified couple. Jack Kerouac pays attention to me, lets me ride on horsey back around the carpeted floor. His friends look on, disapproving of us both.

5. Opening Night

Figures 5 (previous page) & 6. Jack Kerouac, Allen Ginsberg, Gregory Corso, Eileen Fulton (far left bottom) at the opening night party at our apartment following the debut of W. C. Williams' *Many Loves*, New York City, January 13, 1959. (Don Loomis: Collection of the author, 1959)

Figure 7. Judith Malina looks on while Eileen Fulton reads the NY Times' review of *Many Loves*. (Don Loomis: Collection of the author, 1959)

Someone runs upstairs with the Times' review passing out copies of the newspaper. Judith clutches one, reading. Eileen Fulton—she has since acted for forty years on the TV soap, *As The World Turns*,—Eileen peers over Judith's shoulder and they read together. Someone cheers.

Figures 8 & 9. Poet Allen Ginsberg (with Gregory Corso and Jack Kerouac) shows me how to blow over the champagne bottle's top to make a rhythm sound while I pop paper bags as percussion. (Don Loomis: Collection of the author, 1959)

The dean of the New York performing arts writers, Brooks Atkinson, a critic known for his own elegant writing as well as his accuracy on the public pulse, applauded W. C. Williams' play and the engaging way it touched the audience.

Rapidly the party moved toward the kitchen where a refrigerator loaded with cold champagne was being unloaded bottle by bottle, glasses raised, toasts made.

Later, alongside a tableful of empty and mostly empty champagne bottles, Allen, the poet, Ginsberg shows me how to blow over their tops and make a rhythm sound. Boo - buh - Ba - boo - Buh - Buh - boo boo boo. I show him how to blow up paper bags with your breath and - Bwammm - pop them loud on the palm of my hand. Boo - buh - Ba - boo - Bwammm! - Buh - boo boo boo.

At the end Jack Kerouac lying down by the door, cigarette still in his hand, waited for his friends to finish goodbye-ing and head off into the cold clear night.

It was a wonderful opening. Everyone had a wonderful time.

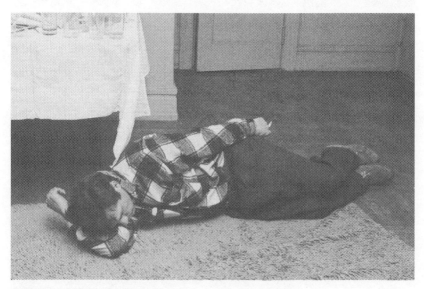

Figure 10. Kerouac lying down by the door, cigarette still in his hand, waited for his friends. (Don Loomis: Collection of the author, 1959)

Figure 11. Julian Beck and Judith Malina incredibly happy after the opening of their new theatre. (Charles Rotmil: Courtesy the Estate of Judith Malina. 1961)

PART TWO

Acting & Action

(1964–1967)

In which the forces of repression take notice of the emerging powers of the youthful arts and political movements, and in which these newfound energies come to express themselves in nature, in music, in the seeds of community, and in many other actions.

6. The Siege of "The Brig"

Four and a half years later, in 1963, I was returning from school as usual, bookbag in hand, to the 14th Street theatre where *unlike* usual, crowds have filled the street and police cars line the curb. *What is going on?!* Actors and actresses lean and wave from the windows. Stage ropes and pulleys haul baskets of groceries up to their waiting hands, which guide them into the windows. Police bullhorns are ordering crowds to disperse. Protestors are walking in lines on the sidewalk apparently in support of the people inside the building!

I approach the front door of the theatre. An officer stops me. "Theatre's closed. You can't go in there."

"I'm supposed to go in," I tell him.

"No one can go in. The theatre's been shut."

"Oh. Uh-huh, well, I have to do my homework and my parents are in there. And that's where I go after school."

He shakes his head and directs me to talk to the commanding officer. The Man-in-charge is sitting in his patrol car looking very unhappy. "Watzup?" he asks.

I repeat my story and he repeats his foot cop's story. So I go round to the front of his car and start unloading my schoolbooks and open my ring-binder notebook on the hood of the car.

He gets out and comes round too. "Whattaryou doing?" he asks head cocked sideways.

I tell him, "I'm doing my homework. That's what I'm supposed to be doing. If I don't do it I'll get in trouble. Big trouble. I can't do it on somebody else's car."

People from the protest lines in the street are coming over. Some of them recognize me. "You know this kid?" the cop-in-charge asks them.

"Yeah, his parents are inside the theatre," they tell him.

"It's OK," I tell him, "I can do my homework right here." The math book is opening; pencil and paper are spreading out on the hood of the commander's car. "I'm only here until eight this evening. Then I go back home uptown. You'll be here till then?"

The officers talk and decide to let me in the building. Up the stairs I go, entering the besieged Living Theatre from the sea of rush hour 14th Street.

What's happened is this: for years the theatre company had been trying to get its not-for-profit tax status, and although they'd filed and re-filed the reports, and lived up to the proper conditions the status had been repeatedly put off. The theatre had been in court with the tax authorities over this. The proper status was being denied because of the theatre's political and socially outspoken productions. In the end, years later, The Living Theatre's case was won, and the court ordered the government to pay them one dollar—exactly one dollar—in damages.

The on-going Living Theatre production was Ken Brown's *The Brig*, an astonishing play that detailed a single day in the life of a US serviceman serving time in a US Marine Corps jail. This, coming on the edge of Soviet protest writer Solzhenitsyn's enormously popular novel, *A Day in the Life of Ivan Denisovich*, painted a reverse picture of the Cold War ideology, where our military prisons might as well be run by the bad guys.

Also recently, the Living Theatre was—as ever—planning another desperate fundraiser to keep the theatre alive, out of the jaws of closure. Keep those marquee lights burnin' on 14th Street! The theatre's press releases for the fundraiser claim that it will shut its doors if such-and-much isn't raised by such a date. Well, this was the excuse the IRS used to come over and seize the building: that the business was about to shut down and therefore the IRS had to seize the property because of the theatre ticket taxes that they were in court over!

So the IRS guys show up and announce that if the money for the taxes isn't immediately forthcoming, they will seize the

Figure 12. On the Set of Kenneth H. Brown's play, *The Brig*. (Photographer unknown: Courtesy the Living Theatre Archives, 1963)

property. And they do. What does that mean 'seize the property'? You can't just pick up a building and put it in a wheelbarrow and roll it away. No, the IRS guys have to put tags on everything and put seals—big stick-on labels—across all the doors, but first they have to order everyone out of the building.

A lot of the acting company and stage technicians, were inside working at the theatre. A lot of them had been part of the freedom rides into the Deep South over the past two years, and participants in the non-violent protests and the sit-ins. And they just sat in, right there in front of the guys from the IRS.

Well, the IRS went and got the New York City Police, who politely, and wisely I believe, told them that since the building had already been seized, it was now Federal—not city—property and the city cops' jurisdiction ended right there at the front door.

They'd need Federal Marshals to haul these people out of there, and because they were going limp refusing to walk out on their own, they'd need a lot of marshals, and besides it was Friday evening now and it would take at least until Monday for the Fed cops to pull the operation together.

So the people inside the theatre were leaning out the windows sending down pulleys and hooks and rope and receiving baskets of food and supplies to hold out through the days ahead. The IRSies had finished stickering doors and tagging objects and, like guys on the clock, had gone home for the day.

Most of the people inside the theatre were up on the middle floor, that's where the best opening windows were, in the main office and gallery room. Already some of the theatre members who weren't inside the building when it was 'seized' had snuck into the theatre from over the adjacent unseen roof. More were on their way.

I strode up the stairwell—with its amalgam of pressed gold leaf and brilliant Crayola crayon as décor on the walls (a collaborative effort by my father, Julian, and the extraordinary artist Ray Johnson)—and passed the entrance to the big lobby, rounded the corner by the backstage door, upped the next flight of stairs and emerged in the big green room by the dressing rooms. Sunlight was streaming in from the broad, opened Sixth Avenue windows.

Figures 13 & 14. My parents, Julian Beck and Judith Malina, in the office at the 14th Street Theatre. (Photographers unknown: Courtesy the Estate of Judith Malina, 1964)

Julian, Judith, and most of the cast were in the big office. Activity equal to theatre in its most full-tilt preparation for production swirled about me. Phones rang, in came baskets of fruit, tools were being brought to the roof to rig ropes. I was a surprise.

"Garry, How did you get inside?" several voices asked, startled to see me. My parents looked up, big smiles at seeing me, and I tell them my tale.

Jenny Hecht, one of the company actresses and daughter of the famed screenwriter Ben Hecht, always animated with her golden frizzy-hair bouncing, puts her arm over my shoulder, and with a theatric sweep of her hand before us, announces in her high-pitched voice, "Welcome to the siege of The Brig!"

There was, as there often is in standoff situations, an exuberance at first, simply *because* the status is a standoff, and not a loss already. I experienced this same upbeat quality many times again: In 1967 at the occupied student center at MIT during the student's 'protection' of an AWOL Vietnam soldier; at the Buffalo Party Convention in 1971 in Washington state where 20,000 Acid Rock Buffalo Political Party Conventioneers were shut down—besieged—by the Washington State Police; later that same year at the protesters' seizure of the Canadian Indian Center outside Winnipeg; and in 1972 at the first Rainbow Gathering high up in the Rocky Mountains by Strawberry Lake, Colorado.

But here on the corner of 14th Street in this busiest of cities, this was for me the very first of these hole-ups, peaceful outlaws on the inside and out-of-whack government on the outside.

Press was being notified, crowds of supporters were demonstrating in a long circular line of marchers along the sidewalks, set painters were poster painting signs which were lowered out the windows to the marchers: Help Save the Living Theatre.... Shut The IRS Not The ARTS...No Taxes For The War....

I went and sat among the green room chairs, books sprawled open doing my French, my math, my history. Nighttime settled. People ate. The demonstration on the street below quieted down a bit and inside the cast and crew began preparing to sleep in for the night.

Toward the late of the evening it was usual for me to head uptown, and bed down at home. Julian spoke with me in the big neon-lit theatre office. On his desk before him were a couple of small piles of papers, a few postcards and some letters. "Here, put these in your book bag. Just slip them into the book pages." I looked at the papers: some poems by poets, a letter from Tennessee Williams, a postcard from ee cummings. Judith looked on from over my shoulder. I leafed through the pieces they had gathered.

"These are treasures," said Julian. A few treasures they wanted to preserve from falling into the hands of the IRS. Not money or valuable tools, or business records. No, these were little ink marks on paper, little typewriter letters on bond and onionskin, just that. But they were writ by the Hand of Art, that same hand that through the ages has sculpted, played the lute, painted and poeted and performed; the Hand which has through beauty and truth shown humanity to humanity. I put the pages delicately into my math book, ma gramaire francaise, my history notes. "They won't know what they're looking at even if they do check my bag," sez I.

Getting out was easy. A policeman was stationed at the door. I opened it from inside and simply told him I was going uptown because I was going to stay at my Grandmother's. And I was out on the street.

It always feels in these situations that the boundary between the two parts, where people are being kept in or kept out, is a very strong spiritual place. Maybe because when we transit—go across—from one to the other the difference is so clear, the difference between one way of the world and another way of the world is so strong, with only an imaginary line enforced by armed might between the two. So the differences are made clear to our eyes, differences which are usually hidden in the everyday stuff of our getting about, so that we don't usually see how close we are to the inside of the prison walls, and also how close we are to real freedom.

By the following morning there was a plan in motion. That evening the theatre would perform *The Brig* within the besieged building and those lucky enough, or daring enough or whatever enough to get themselves inside would get to be the audience. Now the siege itself had its own drama. The plot within the plot. Of course, not all the actors were in the building...yet. Still, the play *was 'The Brig'* and all the actors had drilled in precision training for months as practice for the mindset of the play. During any 'at rest' moment during the play or rehearsals they had been required to stand at attention and to read the US Marine Corps field manual. Yes, this acting crew had some preparation for scaling walls, entering through basement ducts and wiggling in marine style crawl over the rooftops.

Soon the city police mounted extra forces, along the adjacent roof, at the back and sides of the building. The longstanding friendship with our neighbor the Pet Store owner led to a number of 'audience members' entering his premises and gaining access up through his back ceiling and into the stairwell to the top floor dance studio.

The IRS had Con Edison shut the power to the building to try to prevent the show, but the theatre techies rigged up another power line and by the time the lights came back on, our 'audience' had more than doubled.

The play was played, but eventually the Federal Marshals came in great numbers, I think about fifty of them.

When the company saw them arriving, they went downstairs from the offices and dressing rooms and went onto the set of *The Brig*. This stage set was surrounded by a prison yard fence, which in turn surrounded a prison compound, which contained among its facilities an inner lockup, a solitary cell. Each of these levels was constructed of real metal fencing and real locks and real bars.

So the actors went down to the theatre and locked themselves inside the yard, then they locked themselves inside the compound and finally they locked themselves inside the solitary cell.

When the marshals burst in first they went upstairs to the offices where all the activity had been visible from the street, but no one was there.

Finally of course, they found everyone, (where else?) in the theatre! They had to break into the locked fence area, then break the locks into the prison compound, and finally into the cell within, in order to remove these people, carry them out from the prison of the theatre, down the stairs, into the waiting police wagons below, and then drive them through the city streets to other buildings where they were brought first inside one locked gate, then another, and finally inside real prison cells in our real world.

Figure 15. Padlocked for Non-Payment of Back Taxes, the Living Theatre Defies the Law... (New York World Telegram & Sun: 1963)

7. Exile in Italy

By early summer the theatre company had departed for Europe where—at that time—they could work paying far less in US taxes, and be secure from political harassment while the lawyers began a long paper argument over whether The Living Theatre had been unfairly singled out for prosecution by the U.S. government.

This was the start of what was to become a very long tour. It caravanned itself across several continents, and dozens of countries, cultures, and languages. It kept the theatre on the move for more than twenty years. After a while it seemed less like a tour and more like an exile. Pilgrims playing to the footlights in a dozen different languages, in a thousand different theatres, in the capitals of Europe and the souk markets of North Africa, in the fifth largest town in Finland and ultimately into the streets, the hospitals, the asylums, the favelas, the inner cities.... This tour was a long way from the 'theatre crowd' of New York's Broadway or London's West End. It was a very long way as well from the artsy stages of Off-Broadway and Greenwich Village.

When I first caught up with the travelers, after living out the school season in the home of my energetic grandmother, Mabel Beck, who had volunteered to watch over me, while (in her words) my parents ran away from home—when I first caught up with the tour, the company was inhabiting a marvelous wood-floored Italian villa in Velletri just an hour's drive from Rome. The wooden flooring stands out, since long ago the forests of Italy were all cut down and stone flooring became the rule, so this wood-floored villa had a genuine elegance to it.

My arrival there sticks in my mind like a boat from the Middle Ages going over the falls at the edge of the Renaissance. Beyond the entranceway of the villa, into the great hall, purple and golden

Figure 16. Velletri, Italy, June 1965. Living Theatre members including Steve Ben Israel (with guitar), Jimmy Tiroff, Petra Vogt, Judith Malina. (Photographer unknown: Courtesy the Estate of Judith Malina, 1965)

lights flashing, exotic electric musical notes swooning from guitars, people in the huge living room dancing slowly, wearing soft wide velvet clothes, patterned in the most bright colors. It was June of 1965.

In the big kitchen a few of the actors were preparing an evening meal for everyone, speaking in Dutch, Italian, German, French, English, communicating with each other in an easy hodgepodge of words and gestures. Clearly not all of these people were in the theatre company that had left New York just a few months ago.

The expansive villa with its large rooms and many chambers was an ideal place for The Living Theatre to hole up and rehearse. But more than just that, it was an ideal place for the friends of the theatre, other artists, performers, musicians, and political sympathizers to come and not simply visit for a day, but to bed down and become part of the process The Living Theatre was itself becoming: a community process, a collective process, a clan, a tribe of artists, an arts culture alive and budding.

The music wafted up the great wood staircase and through the rooms above.

There was a property nearby which belonged to a convent. The nuns' field was blazing with bright red poppies. Soon the season was ripe for the nuns to work the field, and they did—harvesting the poppy ooze, moving up and down the slope, hunching over in their habits.

In the ancient manner of tithing they left the edges of the field alone and when the nuns had concluded their harvest for the season, quickly the townsfolk made their way to the edges of the field to harvest what they could, and the theatre folk went too. It was the common thing to do, and though it wasn't a talked-about issue in the town, it was the way people got a little 'O' for their own use.

We let the razor-gotten scrapings dry out in small metal candy drop tins. After a few days there was enough to smoke some of the stuff, at night, around the yellow light of the kitchen inhaling the sweet aromatic vapors.

On a regular schedule the company was preparing and rehearsing in the villa's large open rooms. The new plays were *Frankenstein*, an adaptation of Mary Shelley's epic brought to modern life on a monstrously huge stage set which became the monster's head itself and a three-story tall monster, grown from the police state of modern times, threatening the audience...and the other new play was *Mysteries*, actually titled *Mysteries and Smaller Pieces*, in which the company enacted rituals and visions seeking to draw the audience into an inner space, a space of enigma and wonder.

Further along the tour the company acquired VW mini-buses or vans as they're now called, to travel the European landscape; but before the vans, we went by train. So we departed the sweet hillside town, driving to Rome's rail station and embarking by train for the next shows. At each new town we lugged luggage to our pensione, a sort of small hotel where everyone stays.

Then we are off to rehearse. In one city some friends of the producer want to make a recording of the audio from one of the scenes from one of the plays. They have arranged for us to meet at a studio where a small sound recording system is set up.

This particular scene had been brought to the company as a 'theatre exercise' which had been learned in India. First we all stood in a ring, shoulders close to each other's shoulders, then extended our arms over each other's shoulders forming a tight circle of people, held close by each other.

Bill Shari, a scientist turned actor, explained what to do next, "Just listen to the silence, then listen to the breath of the person on each side of you, feel their breathing, hear the sound it makes, listen to the rhythm of their breathing, and bring the sound of it into yourself, feel it and breath out the sound you hear."

It sounded like mighty strange instructions to me. Bill went on, "Don't hum, don't sing, don't try to make a pretty sound or an unpretty sound, just breathe and listen and breathe again, when you hear and feel the sound inside of you, let your breath bring it out."

We got very quiet. For a long time all I could hear was people breathing, then slowly, very slowly, I heard a deep slow sound from around me, as though the deep hidden gears of a slow moving gigantic machine were turning, creaking along. The sound rose through the throats surrounding me and I felt the sound from the left and right drawn into me and my own breath. It was easy then just to let the sound out on the next breath, and I felt that slowww deep sound pass through me and out into the room joining the others. Another breath and I was letting it happen as naturally as though I had done this or heard this before. There was a rumbling harmony I seemed to be part of, that I was helping to make, but that came from somewhere before or beyond or within, or around me, like the turning of some giant gear or the axis of the

Earth. The sound I was drawing from my nearest companions, and that they were drawing from theirs, seemed to come and go round the circle, and through all of our lungs and out, upwards and surrounding us like a reverbrating *chord*, propelling us toward deeper, fuller breaths and a resounding higher bell-like chime, like a hundred bells at once, like the hum inside the hive, like the sound of all the leaves of fall crackling, like the waves on all the shores crashing at once—more sounds than I could name, in one clear unity of pitch and tone and harmonic beauty.

Slowly again the sound came down, quieted, became softer, just a shade, a shadow of what it was, then softly like a whisper of lovers coming to sleep in each others arms, quiet came round us again.

Figure 17. The Chord from The Living Theatre's Mysteries and Smaller Pieces. (Photographer unknown: Courtesy the Living Theatre Archives, 1965)

"Did you turn the recording tape on?" asked a voice.

When I returned to the United States I heard about this thing, this 'chanting' again. I heard it called an Omm, but the theatre always called it a Chord. And when I heard about it in the US it was always with some kind of guru up at the front of a class leading the chants one breath-sound at a time or a group of people sitting cross-legged, apart from each other like in classroom school rows, doing three long chanted Omm breaths or something like that, never as intense as the arms-over-shoulders holy-donut of voices in celestial harmonies.

The theatre used this Chord in the new play, '*Mysteries*,' in a scene following a Jackson Mac Low poem called *Street Songs*. Julian would sit center stage, lit by a single small spotlight and intone the lines to Jackson's poem, lines which reflected the populist social causes of that era, and after some time actors and actresses sitting among the audience would join in, echoing those lines. Slowly we would come join Julian on the stage, first walking in a circle together, then joining hands, arms, forming the circle, coming to the stillness and finally joining together in the Chord. It was always one of the most memorable moments in the theatre. Sometimes whole parts of the audience would rise to the occasion, coming onstage too, putting their arms over the shoulders of those in front of them and lending their voices to the swell of the sound.

8. Highschoolers Against the War

Word was finally leaking out about the war. Even at this late date in history, as I sit writing this chapter in the first years of the 21st century, the public media and today's historians still gloss over the outrageousness of the US government's attempt to hide *entirely* its Vietnam involvement from the American people.

There was a long painful period where the 'official position' was that there wasn't any war; that we were only advisors to the South Vietnamese; that we, the Americans, weren't involved in any shooting, any warfare. No, only slowly after much public denial did the truth come out. A few brave reporters from outside the mainstream press, much pooh-poohed by officialdom as being commie sympathizers, wrote and photographed. And then the boys started coming home, wounded, shredded, maimed, blinded, too many to be accounted for by incidents and accidents. Like a wave turning, the extent of our military involvement came to light.

And that led to a long and ugly debate, still unresolved really in this country about the rightness or wrongness of our intentions and involvement.

From a pacifist or peace activist point of view of course, all war is wrong: a barbaric, crude, inferior method of solving differences. But most of America wasn't—and still isn't—peace activist or pacifist, and so the hinge pin of the nationwide debate turned on the rightness or wrongness of supporting the South Vietnamese in the battle with the North Vietnamese.

Unfortunately, this is not some out-of-date historical argument. It is a crucial question that dogs us today and will follow us into tomorrow because we are again and again going to be faced with very similar questions.

Do we, as a democracy, support dictatorial nations in their

conflicts with nations of opposing economic, or religious or political views?

The majority of the nation for a time said "Yes" to this, arguing that the Communist menace was so dangerous to our way of life that it was a cause of national security to support any nation in their battles with the commies, even if those nations were totalitarian or dictator run.

Sadly in this, there was a lot of fluff in the air about South Vietnam's 'democratic elections'—a hoax; and a lot of earnest talk about all those resources the communists would acquire if they won—rubber, tin, oil, minerals.

I disagreed, believing that there is no reason to support dictators anywhere, regardless of whether they were capitalist economic bastions, fascist economic bastions or whateverist economic bastions. By doing so, we degrade and debauch all the ideals of democracy that we supposedly stand for.

The full history of that war is a subject for long historical analyses, dating back through the European colonialization of Southeast Asia, and I will spare you my version of that chronicle. Still, there was at first only a small number of Americans who were willing even to believe that there was a war going on at all. And then only a small number of Americans who believed that particular war was anything but a righteous crusade against godless Communism. And then slowly, a growing number of Americans who learned about what was happening and thoughtfully drew their own conclusions.

The result was a growing revulsion at what we, what _we_ were doing, and finally an outcry from the heart of this country the like of which had never been heard before. And the tide turned, even the tide of war, which is so often shored up by the strongest of powers, even the tide of war turned, and the troops came home.

But this didn't happen by the wave of a magic wand, nor even by some vote or election. It happened because a few were able to *demonstrate* something to the many.

The first thing that had to be demonstrated was that it was

OK to demonstrate at all. Today this may seem like an obvious truth, but then, just a few decades ago, there was a lot of opposition to your cousin or your friend or you even demonstrating at all. You were demeaned, ridiculed, shouted at, spat upon, pushed, shoved, physically attacked right here in America just for participating in a legal mild-mannered demonstration.

But the demonstrations went on. And one of the early things to become apparent was just how many people—when given a way to voice their views—would come out and do so.

Just back from Italy in the fall of 1965 I began going by subway, after school, into the downtown maze of lower Manhattan's skyscrapers to work at the 5 Beekman Street headquarters of an amalgam of peace group offices where I folded flyers, addressed envelopes, collated mailings, and just generally helped as an office gofer and do-fer.

It was easy. I had all my peace office experience from working in the General Strike for Peace offices that had graced the far end of the second floor of the 14th Street Living Theatre.

The next phase of this involvement for me had to do with the distribution of the fliers. As each new revelation of our 'commitment' in Vietnam came to light and the debate of 'negotiations' vs. 'bomb 'em into the next world' escalated, new (usually one page) hand-out and mail-out fliers were written and produced by the folks at War Resisters League, Workshop in Nonviolence, and later at the various coalition groups like the Fifth Avenue Peace Parade Committee.

Some people would go and hand these out at college campuses, or union meetings, or wherever, whenever they could. So, on my way back uptown I'd get off the subway at 59th Street and walk the two blocks back to 57th, picking a street corner not far from Carnegie Hall, where I'd stand and hand out 200 or 500 of these broadsides to the passersby until my pile was gone and it was then time to continue uptown to face the regular order of homework assignments.

It was an unbelievable learning experience, this business of handing out fliers. First came the art of timing in the approach to handing something to a stranger. Next was the one line you had time to utter while peeling the flier from the pack and poising it toward the oncoming human being, "Would you take one of these, Sir?" "Would you take one of these, Ma'am?" Always asking the question, offering the item. Never pushy, thrusting. No problem if someone didn't want one. The next person was coming along the busy street less than a moment away.

I watched the seasons turn by the daylight's measure as the evenings provided their daylight and sunset and darkness and as fall turned to winter and to spring again. I stood my ground in the face of ten thousand comments. From thoughtful readers who stood a moment to glance, read and reflect, to bombastic retorts about who conned me into giving out this dreck and how pitiful it was that the communist faggots against our country had somehow duped this poor boy into giving out their literature.

But there were many who stopped to talk for a moment or two, and for them I would forgo the handing out of the fliers and focused on the human interaction at hand. Some spoke seriously about why they supported our troops and to these I responded earnestly, countering each argument as best as I could, honing my skills in communication, learning to get to the point—to suss out what point each arguer held close to heart, and why. To the serious questioners, I gave information, using and expanding my own inventory of facts and history to persuade and when I could, to convince. To those who had their own agenda of ideas I listened. There is nothing as boring as someone who won't listen back, and I learned from these speakers the roster of arguments sold to the American public as the combined party line about why we were 'over there' and what we-the-public believed we were doing. Without knowing and understanding the opposition's arguments it is impossible to plan or to act effectively against them.

Never in my life did I pack so many encounters into such a dense experience. Never before had I felt so close to the real pulse of a people. I was closer than the pollsters, closer than the politicians, closer than the press to what was going on in the heads of huge numbers of people about this far off war. And I knew—in a way that the media surely didn't report—how uncertain so much of our public was, how ready at least to consider ideas counter to the mainstream ideas. And especially how the continued revelations of deception by America's leaders were causing alarm bells to ring in the minds of a great part of the public.

Meanwhile back at Peace Action Central some of the office folk were concerned about "What is this kid doing taking a ream of fliers out of the office just about every day?" I had told them where I 'worked' handing them out, but since I was alone doing this, and the Peace Movement was (not without justification) concerned about sabotage and misfunction, two guys from 5 Beekman showed up early one evening at my outpost, just looking at me going at it, meeting, greeting and passing along the important documents of our time.

"No kidding, you're really doing it."

"Of course I'm really doing it. This is a great corner. Lots of activity. Here, have a handful and help out."

So for that one evening at least there were three of us putting the news and info into the public's grasp.

But many evenings others stopped and asked to help pass them out. And I learned the basic principle of recruiting from our own ranks to get the jobs done. Above that, people volunteered to help downtown at the office, people became inspired to join local groups in their own home areas, and I learned also one of the primary truths about making changes in our world: *It is the one-to-one human contact that has effect.* All the tools, the fliers, or even TV ads for that matter, may be helpful props or good for reference, or good for enforcing a belief someone already has, but it is far and away human-to-human communication that affects people most, that makes us think and consider our ideas, and the ideas of others. The human contact is more powerful than any media, than any government announcement, than any textbook. The primary means of evolving human ideas is person-to-person communication. The other media may be useful in maintaining a status quo, or for boosting an emotional level of support or opposition, but for change—real change—there is absolutely nothing like person-to-person communication.

This little grass roots approach to communication about the war was of course only one of many, many personal efforts by people all over the country who felt as I did. But we all felt it together, and we could feel the wave and ourselves part of the swell of the wave. And even though the dirty little war was still going on, and the horror of the war was leaking rapidly into the conversations in the dining rooms, and the televisions of the living rooms—we were getting a heady feeling from making progress in the war of ideas against the ruling powers of the corporate state.

Back at good old #5 Beekman I met up with a couple of other high school volunteers. The bonding was quick and we compared notes, the Bronx, Queensboro, Manhattan. We folded fliers and stuffed envelopes for any number of peace action groups and we became a peace group of our own.

The New York chapter of the Student Peace Union met twice a month around an old marred-up dark-wood table in a whitewashed room high in the towers of lower Manhattan; five or six of us, maybe eight at a big meeting. The large old office windows reflected sunlight off the next building's bricks through the fall and spring, and in the winter the long fluorescents lit the high ceilings with a glare that bore down on the table as we flopped our student briefcases down beside us and pulled up chairs to plan something in the real world to make a difference.

At first we just talked about our schools' policies toward speaking up, about what different demonstrations we'd each been to, and a lot of hotly spoken ideas about the war. Peace seemed to mean the end to 'the war' more than some kind of way to be, or feel or live. There was a lot of anger around that table. And why not? Everyone knew people a few years older than ourselves, or maybe just a year, who were over there fighting, or who had already come back to tell it like it really is, or who had come back already dead.

And, of course, there was the draft.

That meant everyone had to go—or find a way out. You could get a four year deferment for college, or get out by being certifiably gay or certifiably crazy; or if you were a woman you were out automatically; or there were a host of medical reasons and a host of loony stories of how to make your heart beat so fast they won't take you, or join the National Guard, so you wouldn't have to go over to Nam, but maybe if there were riots at home in the anti-war streets or the ghettoes of underprivileged America—you could get arrested and jailed right here at home. Or you could get a job working in a munitions factory, then you wouldn't have to go to the war. There were lots of ways to beat the draft, but as more and more of America's young didn't want to go, the Army got tougher about letting people get away.

The medical exemptions got full scrutiny. Conscientious Objector status—long a refuge of peace people—who usually served their army time as disaster relief people, medics, or humanitarian support workers, were shipped right over to be medics on the battlefields.

Men over the age of eighteen had to carry their draft card with them at all times. That was a card with your military status on it. Each status had code letters and numbers for student, medical exemption, too crazy, etc. and 1-A meant a prime target for the draft. Lots of young people were frightened, some just tried evading the draft; not responding to the mailed notices, not appearing for the army's physical exam which they scheduled for you. Sometimes the law came for people at their addresses who hadn't appeared for service. Some of these people went to jail. Some folks beat a trail north to Canada....

The time was right for an anti-draft movement. And we,

highschoolers who hadn't turned eighteen yet, hadn't yet had to register for the draft, had the good idea of a Highschoolers Against the Draft demonstration.

We knew what to do. We'd been the nuts and bolts volunteers for a dozen different demos for a dozen of the different fragmented peace groups of that time and we put our heads together to plan a demonstration ourselves. Really it was Linda's idea. She was a sharp thinking student from an immense public high school in Brooklyn. She spoke it up and the rest of us went along.... It just seemed like a bright move, a way to mobilize young people—whom we were already in touch with—and a way to reach people we weren't yet in touch with who shared our sympathies and most important, a way to reach the larger high school population—to encourage thinking about the issue—and not with just the general question of: Is the war wrong or right?—but with the very specific (and frightening) aim of asking the gut-searing questions "What're you gonna do if you're drafted?" and "Should there be a draft at all?"

We chose a date that would jibe with the city's high school schedule, so as not to land on finals week, a date in the spring of 1967. We wrote and printed flyers. We raised money for a sound truck. We spoke with Dave McReynolds and Ralph Di Gia, the iconic workhorses and spokespeople of War Resisters League, about helping us get a street closure permit for the demonstration. We chose a street right outside a church that was anti-the-war for religious reasons. The church could offer support, bathrooms, telephones. We tried to figure out who would be good speakers that we could actually get to come to the rally and who could folksing between the speeches.

We plotted together about the theme of the demonstration being against the draft, which was not seen as such an extreme position as a blanket opposition against the Vietnam War—nor as extreme as pacifism against all wars. Why not just let those who believe in this war go fight it but leave me, and those of us who don't believe this war is worth fighting or dying for—let us alone?

This was a clearheaded view for a highschooler to take and it was easier getting support for this than for more comprehensive anti-war positions.

Still we wanted the demonstration to demonstrate why this war in particular was loathsome. Who were the powers in South Vietnam we were supporting? What was their system of government? What kind of villains, torturers, plutocrats were we becoming in league with? And what were our motives? Political or economic? What chemicals, defoliants, Jellied Gasoline, were we igniting over valleys, villages, waterways? What lies were we being told at home? What lies were the boys in the field being told?

We started to fundraise; first, just from ourselves and best friends and cohorts. Then a flyer with a phone contact was put out. It had an address (at 5 Beekman, naturally) and bold letters announcing the demonstration. We began to pass these out at school and I began to hand these out at my usual station on West 57th Street, aiming in particular for those not yet of draftable age. It was an exuberant feeling to be part of a movement whose cause I felt was so right, and where now, instead of working as a junior level volunteer, I was able to be part of making something happen among my own generation.

Our meetings grew as other highschoolers joined the project. Then one afternoon we had a visit from several students from SDS; this was a nationwide college peace group: Students for a Democratic Society. They had formed chapters on most major American college campuses. They were responsible for hundreds of campus demonstrations against the war, against university complicity in war projects research and manufacture, against on-campus recruiting, against war technology research; they were responsible for bringing thousands of people to support other peace groups' demonstrations in dozens of cities. They spearheaded the movement action that became called 'Burning Your Draft Card' and that's just what it was: students burned their draft cards in public. This was an arrestible offence and it just outraged the mainstream public. It was considered very radical. But students and more students did it; TV cameras rolled on images of heaps of flaming cards and crowds of students flagrantly tossing their cards into the fire. This was heady stuff for peaceful, 'affluent' America to digest.

I had been to demonstrations in D.C., or marches on Fifth Avenue in New York, which had featured SDS speakers. With keen remembrance I can still see and hear black-bearded Carl Oglesby, an SDS speaker at a huge coalition peace march & rally in Washington, mapping out historical parallels and differences between this war and the American Revolution. Sometimes a good speaker can share panoramic perspectives and overviews that show the full terrain of a broad subject; sometimes they can inspire actions and sometimes they can give us the gift of clear explanations of what we already wordlessly know to be true. Oglesby from SDS did exactly that.

And now SDSers were coming to take an interest in our own doings. I couldn't have felt more proud. Again around the well-marred old wood table more than a dozen of us from the Student Peace Union listened to the three SDS'ers. They offered us use of their office, a phone where they could answer and take messages, guidance for running the demonstration, help with finding speakers and musicians, plus they offered to help with any problems or mediate any disagreements we might have among us, and so on. When they left the meeting I felt a glow of camaraderie, because it seemed the larger movement was putting its arm over our shoulder.

But not everyone in our group thought so. In our own session afterwards Linda, her reddish brown hair swirling as she shook her head, said "No way. These organizers want to take over our whole thing. They'll end up doing it all for us, and then telling us how and what to do!"

Others agreed. And I listened. There was a sense of independence here that each of us valued. And there were clues about the upcoming clashes yet-to-come within and among the peace groups, clashes on account of peace movement bureaucrats fighting for power and control, clashes which would later damage the movement enormously.

Still we worked with the SDS office people. They were very supportive even if we didn't take them up on all they offered.

The day came and in the sunlit afternoon on West 4th Street a little over four thousand highschoolers showed up. I remember being in the crowd just floored that so many students from all over the city would come out to demonstrate. I remember some of the older speakers looking out over the crowd of young heads and faces and saying to each other, "Lookit that, there may be hope after all." Two young women sang a song they'd written about the flowers you wouldn't have to lay on our graves because these young men weren't going to die for the war.

The New York press ran with the story, "Students Speak Out Against the Draft...."

I learned two great things from this. One was that independent-minded people can get together and do things that make a difference, make a stir in the social fabric and succeed even if they are young and without funding, commercial ties or celebrity sponsors. It's the *ideas* that drive the process forward. The other lesson was that The City granted us the ability to close the street for the duration of the event and to use a sound truck, even though virtually all City officialdom including the Police Department, the Traffic Department and their officers were war supporters. Yet, they supported our right to disagree and to hold open demonstration against the war and against what were their views. The key lesson here is that real democracy supports the right of dissent. And it was nice to see The City supporting our rights.

9. In the Treasure Box

In most of my youthful summers I had been sent out of the city—it seemed like a journey to another world—north to the wooded lands of Massachusetts where I became for eight weeks first a camper and then later a junior—and then senior-counselor at a summer camp named Wamsutta. An old apple orchard as well as a lake graced the property, which had long ago been home to Revolutionists during the Colony's War for Independence.

New England educators Samuel and Leah Sleeper founded it after the Second World War. They built and ran the camp along with their three able sons, Marty, Arthur and Bob. Their marvelous jack-of-all-trades handyman, Winthrop, wiry and muscular, practically lived in his workshop and seemed (in that stoic can-do Yankee way) to be able to build or repair anything.

There were eight campers to a cabin, a dozen or more cabins all told, and with only minimal changes my cabin of friends grew up many summers together, learning tennis and archery, playing baseball and basketball. It was an idyllic time.

These summer adventures were paid for, in my case, by my grandparents who thought it was a suitable gift to both myself and my parents, freeing them up to work on the theatre's next production without the hanging on for attention of an out-of-school child; and giving me a vacation with sports to be played, in a place with peer group companionship and solid American values.

Little did they know where this would lead.

Of all the various activities—while I liked tennis and softball, and the drama program was small and wonderful—I loved hiking along the trails, camping in the woods, and canoeing on the lake best of all. Maybe it was the stories around the sparkling campfire, or the wandering along the paths with names like 'The Blueberry Trail,' or the packing of packs and hiking out into the woods—going that extra mile, literally, from the country setting of the summer camp into the leaf-strewn, forest-canopied, New England rocky, brush-covered forest.

Little did *I* know where this would lead to.

As our cabin full of friends became young teens, we became the camp's waiters and junior counselors and worked with the senior counselors at one or another of the activities. I opted for Woodlore, which is what they called their hiking, camping and canoeing program, and became the assistant to the Woodlore counselor. By the time I 'graduated' into his shoes—ahem, into his hiking boots—I had lots of ideas about the program I wanted to run.

Looking ahead from there, little did I know that this was the beginning of a lifelong involvement with nature education. In-the-field <u>and</u> in-the-forest <u>and</u> on-the-farm <u>and</u> in-the-city ventures and adventures bringing people—especially young people—into hands-on and feet-first contact with the natural elements and the precious never-to-be-forgotten connections that fuse in our experience when we learn about our place in the eternal ecosystem that is our real home, how we are a part of it, and even how it extends into us. As a counselor, an instructor, and an educator, this whole lifelong process got started there in that Woodlore program.

I began with the seven knots: Square, Two Half Hitches, Clove Hitch, Bowline, Sheetbend, Sheepshank and the grand knot for setting up camps in the woods: The Tautline Hitch.

As soon as a whole cabin mastered those (so the more skilled were encouraged to aid the less dexterous), it was on to pitching tents. Those were summers before pop-domes or fiberglass poles. We used two-part surplus 'shelter halves' kind of like large pup tents that had to have the two identical pieces attached to each other to make a whole tent. First I carefully showed them how to set one up. Then they paired up and each pair had to put the halves together and pitch the tent. And then—this was the best part—they'd choose whoever they thought was most adept at it and that camper would stand to one side while I'd fold up the tent, neatly stacking it with all its poles, ropes and stakes. Next I'd blindfold the other seven campers. Only they, the blindfolded, were allowed to touch the tent while the eighth, the one camper standing aside—the only one able to see—had to give directions, as the rest of them struggled to get it set up right. Me with stopwatch in hand, one camper frantically calling out confusing instructions, and the other seven pushing and pulling at the canvas, getting tangled in the lines, fumbling the stakes and as often as not knocking the whole thing back over. It made for a good lesson.

Next they were up to fire building and wood gathering. I taught getting your starter wood and your firewood in order in a 'wood continuum,' a progression of sizes from the smallest tinder used for starting, to twigs, sticks, branches and finally logs. "See how the smaller stuff has more surface in contact with the air than the bigger logs? No? Watch: we'll split a big piece open; you can see more surface touching the air now, can't you? OK, we'll split those pieces again, and open more wood to contact with the air. Imagine if we did that again and again until the whole log was tiny tiny pieces. There'd be lots more surface of wood touched by air. Fire needs air to 'breathe,' to combust, to burn, and to get it started you need lots of air for the amount of wood. That's called the surface-to-air 'ratio.' Can you say, Ray-she-oh? Good. That's *math* and you *will* get taught about it later on in school, but for now, understand that you need the very smallest pieces of wood you can find—because these have the largest 'surface-to-air ratio'—to get your fire started, and slowly, methodically add larger and larger and larger pieces up from there. Got it?" (The small campfire I've been building is now flaming away at our feet.) "Kids, this is what our ancestors in the caves knew. Today we talk about it as science. But it *is* knowledge....And now...it's yours."

At the end of the lesson: teams were each provided only one match, and would race to boil a #10 can full of water, into which we put a little soap, so when it boiled, it really boiled over and everyone could see.

After that came knife and axe safety, and sharpening, then a lesson about packing packs and rolling the old-style cotton-duff sleeping bags tightly. "Keep the soft stuff against your back! Put the raincoat in a place where you can yank it out fast without messing up everything else." And then the cabin was ready for an overnight hike.

The plan was to take every cabin out on this adventure in the course of the summer and since they'd all learn the skills in roughly age group order, over the weeks everybody got to go, even the youngest for whom the basic square knot was a skill they'd have to master *next* summer. Even they would get to go maybe 200 yards from their wooden bunkhouses and roll out sleeping bags under the stars.

As for the older cabins, we'd trudge them over the stone dam that bridged the lake, down some backcountry roads and then along a short trail into a pine-needle-carpeted forest wonderland. Some of the city-bred or even suburban kids thought we must've gone on a safari to the furthest reaches of the alpine tundra. And though it wasn't so, from inside the forest it certainly looked remote.

We cooked up easy campfire dinners, made 'banana boats'—an upgraded version of S'mores. We played Capture The Flag In The Woods, and then on to campfire games and stories.

The Banana Boat Recipe
Ingredients:
One banana
One medium bar of chocolate
Two marshmallows
One square of aluminum foil

Hold the banana in front of you, corners up (so that it looks like a boat) and carefully with your penknife make two cuts through the skin and into the banana lengthwise from tip to tip on what would be the deck of the boat, that is, the inside of the curved part. These cuts should meet at the center of the banana and should slice out a long, v-shaped sector the length of the fruit.

Remove the v-shaped piece from the rest of the banana and peel just the long slice you've removed and *eat that slice of banana*. Keep the long piece of the peel!

Now take your marshmallows. *Eat one*, and take the other and pull it apart into smaller pieces. Lay these pieces carefully in the empty space of the vee that has been removed from the banana, filling up that space evenly.

Next, unwrap your chocolate bar and break it in half. *Eat one of the halves*. Break the other half into smaller bits like little tiles and place these on top of the marshmallow covering the marshmallow with a neat layer of chocolate.

Replace the piece of banana peel on top of the chocolate and marshmallow, right back where it came from.

Now place the boat upright on the square of aluminum foil, with its tips pointed at two opposite corners of the square. Take the other two corners and bring them up to meet each other at the top—above the banana. Gently press the lower part of the foil around the banana so the banana is enclosed in the foil and with the two tips above pressed to each other, tightly crimp or roll their edges together, so that overall the top part forms what looks to be a silver "sail" rising from a silver boat.

For this next part you will need a lit outdoor campfire, preferably with well-developed ember beds. Take the banana boat by the sail, or poke gently through it with a fork prong or thin stick and place it down onto the glowing embers. Look at the fleet of silver boats sailing through the fire!

Wait a few minutes. Pull one of the boats from the embers by using the stick or fork. Set it down carefully. It's very hot. Slowly open the foil, and then if the marshmallow and the chocolate have melted and the banana has become soft, *it is ready to eat* with your spoon. Nothing like it.

Toward the end of the season I took a selection of the most able campers from different cabins out on a three day hike—well, actually one whole day flanked by two nights, an afternoon and a morning. We made one of our meals using some wild foods, took a day hike away from our little encampment and called the whole thing a 'survival hike.' Modest as this adventure was, for youngsters from the modern American way, I think it steered us toward a closeness with the natural world.

Still, there was more going on than any of us understood.

Picture this: Canopies of sugar maple and birch leaves, long-needled white pine (the American Revolutionists' icon of resistance to the oppression of the British Crown) poking their spires through and above the green arbors into a robin's egg sky and the sun beaming illuminated shafts down through the openings in the leaves, and below: midsummer wildflowers yellow and blue swaying slightly, clothed in their royal raiment of sunlight; to the sides: the soft swoosh of canoes coming to the sandy mud at the shore, stands of sedges and reeds and milkweed harboring gamebirds who take flight fluttering low over the water, trails whose boundaries are thick with ripe berries, and as evening's sky darkens this paradise, hear the whoops and crackles of laughter, and above: an owl and the stars, the first invisible, hidden amongst the branches, and the others visible, sparkling in the heavens.

No worries, no conflicts, no problems, no hassles, no pain, no regrets.

We were in the treasure box and didn't know it.

10. Jimmy and Jimi's Stories

During the winter break in December of 1967 I got a call from Jimmy Diamond. Jimmy was one of my longtime Camp Wamsutta companions. We'd been in the same cabin for as long as either of us could remember. At the same time I started teaching woodlore, Jimmy became baseball counselor.

Now he was on the phone wanting to come into the city to catch a particular musical act. Of course, I encouraged him. There was easily room at my Grandmother's (where I was staying) for the both of us.

So there we were: Jimmy, 'Jimbo,' Jimmy Diamond and I smoking pot into the early morning hours and laughing and laughing. We laughed so hard at some picture of a guy eating peas that we thought we were both going to pee ourselves.

The holiday week had been sparklingly clear. The short days were bright and chilly in the sunlight—but beautiful—as the slanting rays beat against the architecture. The busy New York hive hummed with shopping, play going, celebrating and dining.

Then the weather changed and the town was slammed by a bitter wet ice storm. Why go anywhere? Everyone had been holiday partying for a week anyway. The wind tore from the west off the Hudson and down along the streets; and from the East River bringing the wet cold of the harbor down our avenues. And then the sky dropped sleet, which froze on the pavement. And anybody with any sense stayed home.

Not us.

We were going to see Tim Hardin. Tim was the folksinger that Jimmy had been raving about. He just had a new album out and maybe now at last he was going to have the hit he always deserved.

Born and raised in Eugene, Oregon, Hardin was one of a

number of true folk minstrels who all came to the cities and recording studios of America at about the same time: Dave Van Ronk, Tim Buckley, Tom Paxton, Eric Anderson, Tom Rush, Phil Ochs and of course, Bob Dylan. They were—all of them—great poets, minstrels of love and sorrow and truth and glory. They all sang original *and* old folk tunes lauding the downtrodden and suppressed. They all sang ballads of love and freedom. But America, with its radio play format could only manage one heroic folkie at a time, and though each of these sang the wistful and grand melodies of our very own times, the laurel and the spotlight went to Dylan. And the others? Well they kept on singing and strumming and penning more songs. And if you, dear Reader, have had the luck to listen to any of these folkies pick out a tune, count yourselves among the fortunate for having heard.

Tim Hardin's one well-known song, his one hit song, *If I Were a Carpenter*, is a simple ballad of love that Bobby Darin, Johnny Cash, the Four Tops and many others covered and although it's a widely known song to this day, everyone thinks it's one of those uncopyrightable Olde English melodies like *Greensleeves* or *Scarborough Faire*.

Tim was performing at New York's Greenwich Village Café Wha? following the release of his newest album. One of its tracks, *The Lady Came from Baltimore* had been getting airplay and James D. Diamond had come to New York to hear his man play.

We were heading downtown no matter how icy the streets got. Hats. Scarves. Boots. We bundled up and out onto near-empty slippery-to-walk avenues. The heated subways were empty too—for a holiday eve—and we stepped out in the blinking lights of Greenwich Village, holding ourselves steady from slipping on the ice-coated sidewalks as we worked our way down nearly-deserted MacDougal Street.

From the chrome yellow front of the Café Wha? with its big black round-edged letters **"W-H-A-?"** an entryway led to the downstairs playhouse. We happily paid our admission, entered, bought drinks and settled ourselves in the middle of the small auditorium in time for the start of the first show. There must've been another twenty or so brave souls or devoted fans who shuffled in kicking the ice off their boots, welcoming the warmth of the place, removing mittens and taking seats.

At the front of the small stage a knee-high wrought iron fence with a few iron curlicues made a slight separation between the audience and performers who would soon enter from the wooden backstage door off to the left.

There was first an opening act. A sweet combo: banjo, guitar and keyboard, and they entertained us and we clapped for them as if we were hundreds. After a very short break the lights dimmed and Tim Hardin came out into the solo spotlight.

He opened with a traditional ballad, then played from his new work, then sang us *If I were a Carpenter.* I was enchanted. He played as though every twang and note counted, as though we twenty were an audience in a packed concert hall. Somewhere swept by the music, I remember toward the end of his set he sang *Blacksheep Boy*, the tender tune about the outcast for whom life has cast a sad fortune. Next to me Jimmy Diamond turned his head to wipe a tear. We applauded madly.

Then up came the lights, Tim went backstage and out sprang the house manager inviting the 'crowd' to stay on if we liked—for free—for the second set. He encouraged us all to buy at least another drink, but stay if we liked anyway he implored, "Because, honestly on a night like this there isn't going to be much more of a crowd coming in. So if you like the music and want to keep out of the cold, just stick around, buy a drink if you like, and we'll be happy to have you stay on."

For us that was just fine. We'd hear the second show, even if it was the same show, even the same exact show. So we bought two more drinks and situated ourselves in the front row this time resting our feet against the iron railing.

When the second set started up, the opening band came

onstage, looked around at the maybe ten people in the audience and as they began their guitar player thanked us "all for coming, actually for *staying* and since I know you're here really to see Tim, we're going to keep our part of the bargain short tonight. But we hope to warm you up a bit."

And with that they led off with a rousing run of country folk tunes, one melody bridging into the next. Latecomers, probably delayed by the weather straggled into the café and there was the shuffle and bump of people finally getting settled.

Jimmy elbows me, and when I lean toward him he whispers, "Don't look now but the guy who just came in, sittin' a few rows back, it's Hendrix."

So I wait watching the band for a couple of verses, and turn abruptly looking toward the back door as if expecting friends, checking quickly to see if they've arrived. There are four newcomers sitting in the seats a few rows back, the seats we'd been occupying during the earlier set.

I lean over to James slowly and whisper in *his* ear, "You are so full of crap. You just think Every Black Guy With An Afro is Hendrix."

The band quieted down from their fast-paced medley as their lead played his signature song and after that they thanked us for enjoying, and retired into the one-room dressing area and performers' lounge. From our first-row vantage point we could see past the door into the tiny space, all strewn with instrument cases and winter coats.

A minute later Tim Hardin emerged again and without a word slid his guitar on and began playing one of his ballads. At the end of that he paused, shaded his eyes from the fresnel stage lighting so he could see out into the sparse audience and said, "Looks like most of you were here for my earlier show so I hope you won't mind if I invite a good friend to c'mon up here and join me."

A few rows back there was a rustle in the audience and a man stood up moving toward the aisle, pulling his guitar case from behind the seats at his feet. Holy Smokes!! It *was* Hendrix.

He came down the aisle silently, opened up his case, flashed his white electric guitar in the lights so it spangled itself in the audience's eyes, plugged his cord into the amplifier Hardin pointed at, and nodded to Tim.

Tim began playing and, like a harpsichordist backing up the weightier organ, Hendrix spun a web of highlighted notes around Tim's strumming. Hendrix stood to the side, leaning back, near the door. Hardin was in center-stage. He sang *If I Were a Carpenter and You Were a Lady* and Hendrix wove gossamer lines of musical light, clothing the song in gold and silver threaded garments of sound. I never knew Hendrix played such beautiful stuff, or that a guitar itself could let go such celestial delights.

After a few more songs, Tim informed the audience, "We're just going to jam. Most of you heard all the songs earlier this evening anyway. So we're just going to play."

Face to face, playing each others riffs back to each other like tides rolling between two moons; highwaymen in the night, scattering jewels of sound along the roadside, scattering gleaming jewels as though there was no end to them: and blurs of fingers, slowly Hardin steps aside, and nods at Jimi as if to say, "Go, You do it." So Hendrix puts a foot up on the railing and plays, pushing the sound out directly toward one, then another, presenting each audience member with a crown of sound.

He holds his guitar up for a couple of moments very still, while the tones reverberate and he bows his own head for a moment as if in homage, in awe of the beauty of the notes and chords, a vassal before the Muse: Terpsichore, Goddess of Sound.

Then he's playing very sweetly, soothingly, stepping back and turning to Tim (who's been watching all this along with the rest of us) and intros one of Tim's own ballads which raised Tim out of *his* reverie and in another moment Tim was singing his lead back in center-stage while Jimi was leaning by the door, backing him up.

They finished and went quickly backstage, closing the small door. James and I waited in the café. After a time the backstage door opens. The musicians from the opening band were all in there too. We went inside and James went right up to Tim and Jimi and he says, "I just want to shake the hands that played those sounds."

Tim puts his hand forward. Shakes. Jimi puts his big hand forward and uses a phrase popular in those times, "Keep the Faith, baby," he says. I put my hand forward too. Tim shakes, and Jimi shakes my hand too, saying quietly again, "Keep the Faith."

Soon after, we were out on the blustery, slippery, freezing cold streets. The wind chills through our scarves. Two street 'kids' maybe our own age, but they seemed younger, less protected, panhandled us for spare change. James reaches in his pocket. I'm still standing there. James looks at me as he fishes out coins, "Whaddya you got?" I pass my change along too.

With my teeth chattering as we walked through the winter-bound city streets, I was thinking that these kinds of interactions were just going to become regular stuff in the new hip culture fusion that was growing around us. Little did we kids know how rare and un-plannable these experiences are. Again, we were in the treasure box and barely knew it.

PART THREE

Higher Learning

(1967–1969)

The New World Culture begins to unify and multiply into the realms of organic foods, effective & positive protests, psychedelics, community organizing, yoga, and non-religious spirituality. And the lesson is brought home that higher learning might not be available within the established institutions.

11. On the Quays of Paris

In the chill air of a 1967 summer night I land at Paris' Orly airport. School is out and I am returning to Europe to catch up with the vagabond theatre troupe. On Rue Troyon, just a couple of blocks from the great Parisian arch, I find Julian now long-haired—still bald on top of course—but his locks streaming down onto his shoulders, and Judith ready any day to give birth to my sister, Isha.

Paris is vibrant in the summer. Nights upon the steps of Sacre Coeur Church, hundreds gathering each evening, guitar friends, people sharing food, joints, laughter, watching the sunset over the city fabulous. No focused movement, no stage, no speakers, no one handing out handbills—just the pulse of people beating together, feeling feelings together, strangers safe, together, immersed in the beauty of the city below and the sky and the sweetness of camaraderie.

I tell you these moments aren't dreams. They are normal when people are free of fear, free of fear of each other, then the great bear and lion come down from the stars and walk among the spirit of the people, and the natural forces—locked in the civilized separations of family, class, race, language, religion—come out of the dungeons and under the sky and stars, breathing into the nostrils a spell of love sweeter than the sweetest incense, emboldening hearts to believe that truth and beauty can appear for real in this world. Truth hands beauty a half-opened orange. Beauty takes a piece and passes it along to you.

So night after night I took the Metro up the Right Bank to Montmartre and walked past the brightly lit night life and up up the winding streets coming around at last to the great overlooking steps to join this peaceful melange of souls and savor the evening for as long as I could.

Rumors had it that Folkies and Rockers of the time passed through the crowd and sat on the huge crowded expanse of steps; Donovan, Lennon, strummed their guitars, noticed but only by those just right around them, and then moved on. But the scene held a hint of one of the great Sixties mysteries, that everyone was a star of this show, that everyone had the secret magic key, that everyone was one of the beautiful people....

And in the afternoons I traveled a different way. Down along the riverbanks of the Seine (the river which bisects Paris into its Right and Left halves) are the 'quays': stone and paved embankments, lower than the streets and traffic of the city, but meters above the river level with its tourist boats, pleasure craft and working barges. At some points the stone quays are still used as docks and long ago that was their major purpose, but now, along the quays, and under the shade or shelter of the many bridges, these walkways serve as a promenade, a place where Parisians are strolling, watching their river meander, and sitting on a public bench reading the paper or a paperback from one of the booksellers' stalls which line the streets just above.

And in the warm days of the Summer of Love the quays are lined with bell-bottomed, bleu-jeaned flower children, backpacks thrown against the trees, benches and the big stone stairs. Beneath the bridges, blankets are unfurled marking the sleeping quarters of many of these vagabonds, hitch-hikers and stoned-out souls.

There is nothing to do here but watch the endless river roll by and philosophize about the Why and Way of the World. Unless there's a joint. Then there is smoking to be done and catch-your-breath silence as the pot comes on strong and you know you're jumping out of just whatever you were thinking about, and into just slightly new ways of looking at things, considering things, and then the talking and talking in so many languages, French and English, German and Dutch, the Scandinavian voices, the Arab, the Israeli—all yakking with each other in expression of ideas and laughter, all of different minds about almost everything, but all opposed to the war, wars, the divisions among people, the barriers, the classes, the separation of races—dissolved for a breath here on the quay.

Then I'm hungry and people are reaching into backsacks and coming out with cheeses and breads and we eat, and watch the river roll endlessly by.

I hear people fresh back from India and Nepal talking about the monasteries with sects thousands of years old, living close to the earth, practicing yogas, filled with secret knowledges about the breath, the patterns of thought, people who did week-long meditations, leaving their bodies behind and exploring realms unrealized by the rest of us. I heard Scots talking about a community just formed, still forming really, dedicated to plant communication, and growing the hugest vegetables, and using natural energies: the wind, the sun for power. People were being invited to Findhorn gardens to participate.

I met people my own age from Cuba. Young people growing up in the US of A, never had the possibility of meeting other young people from modern Cuba. These folks weren't exactly fans of the regime there, but none of us on the quays were fans of our countries' authorities.

I met soldiers AWOL from Vietnam who told the most hair-raising bizarre stories—even I had a hard time believing. They were never going to go back.

I met a couple of friends from high school. The last time I'd seen them was in the halls on their way to classes. Now they were living out of their backpacks under the bridges, and they weren't on their way to somewhere or on some quest, no, right here was quite good enough.

There was a relaxed feel to this scene that felt something, that sensed something and slowed down long enough, and that stopped from the rush-about of daily life long enough to dwell in a place where the eternal moment ruled the hour, where the eternal moment held us in its gracious palm, where we could look out over the edge at the river rolling endlessly by and where we could listen to all the sounds of the city wafting over the embankment down toward us, but where we were immune to all that busy-ness, just partners in the living breathing of the universe, and there wasn't anywhere else to go, or anything else to attain to, or any other need but to hang out and appreciate this wonderful beautiful cosmos.

Just downstream there'd been a building built to worship the Diety inside. They put big pointed stone towers on top of it, put big colored windows in its walls, called it Notre Dame, and thousands of people came to see it, or worship inside it every day, but God was here, everywhere, around us right now. Maybe they put the stone towers on to point to the beautiful sky and clouds and rain and sun. I think they put the big windows in to make glorious patterns of light, but if the people inside could look outside, they'd have found what we were finding, the glory and living light were all around us, but you had to slow down and get out of the blinding pace of modern life to sense it so.

Then the sirens came. Woooo-Whhhho-Woooo-Whhhho. And in many languages I heard, "Run! Run!" "Les Flics!" "The Cops!"

People scampered down along the quays, grabbed their backpacks, looked for stairs up to the street that the cops weren't running down, and disappeared into Paris' daily life.

Those who were accosted by the police were searched, questioned, had to produce identity papers, passport, and even so were sometimes taken in for further questioning. We never found out about for what; or if their papers weren't in order, visa expired or not enough currency; they were detained further and then shipped back to from where they came.

Still every day the people would re-assemble on the quays, or creep back in the darkening of the evening to sleep peacefully along the riverside, and still every other day or so, the police would sweep through, harassing, dragging people away up the stairs of the quays and across the curb and into the waiting police wagons.

And there arrived on the quays a couple of travelers from California, from San Francisco, telling tales of Haight Street and people living in Golden Gate Park. A fellow from Australia said, "Things are never going to be the same."

12. War, War, What's it For?

September 1967. Up all night with my friend Jeremy Lawrence. He is reading from a handful of papers clutched in one hand, and pacing forth and back, gesturing broadly with the other hand, his lead finger cutting upward spirals in the air. Slightly stocky with a round cherubic face, he stands himself up on a chair for even further emphasis. He is reading me a draft of his play, *Goldteeth*. Goldteeth is chewing up the world now, or at least aiming to, unimpeded he devours media. Unchecked and unholy he creates the alliance of capitalism, communism and money-of-any-persuasion in a banker's gleeful delight at success. Opposition tumbles away before him.

We are trying to pack for college. Jeremy tosses another sweater at his luggage. He tears himself away from his reading, "We won't be needing sweaters when old Goldteeth's running things. No, there'll be climate bubbles and everyone'll be happy and comfortable!" Another grand sweep of his hand (the hand clutching the playscript) arcs over him as though to indicate the bubble above us. What we really need is to finish our packing in time for morning departure to Portland, Oregon.

In the airport, bleary-eyed we are met by Catwoman who slinks up to us and asks, "Heading off to Reed College, eh?" Caught off guard by her foreknowledge, we mumble something and she leads us to the cocktail lounge where Catwoman slugs down successive bourbon shots and tells us, "Reedies just know things. You'll find out...but you haven't got there yet. I'm your last warning. You can still leave before the plane takes off." She throws her head back, shakes her hair and laughs and laughs.

Jeremy and I look at each other. Clearly this college stuff is going to be different from high school. Only later we realize that a visible copy of Lattimore's translation of Homer—a Reed freshman's standard—had tipped our hands.

At Reed College's idyllic, canyon-cut campus, broad lawns are set with stolid red-brick and fieldstone buildings. Huge shade trees line paths, and we attend freshman orientation. Some really cool guy with a beard is explaining how campus life *really* works, when a lanky fellow comes traipsing down the aisle, arms flapping, paying the speaker no attention. His sailor hat reads, 'H.M.S. Titanic.' He's down with the ship, on his own mission. He's waving to different people in the audience. I'm watching him amble happily, myself becoming distracted from the words of the speaker. I smile. He waves.

Later, over lunch on the lawn we meet. He's Paul Rosenberg and he explains, "Oh, anybody can figure out how a campus works. Or how classes work. The interesting thing here is the other people. I mean, if you can't figure out the orientation stuff, maybe you're not as smart as they thought you were when they let you in this place."

And Paul begins a litany of the independent oddballs, eccentric freelance freethinkers who have convinced the admissions staff here that they are sane enough to attend.

Actually there is a very scholarly element here at this school, and a very sciency one, too. And although there is a balance here between conservatives and radicals, even the conservatives seem to enjoy letting the radical minorities be who we are. That gave a great sense of the beauty of academic freedom, but I had only seen the cover of the book.

As the pages of the season turned I ploughed through the humanitarian classics—Homer, Plato, Aristotle, Aquinas—and met among the Reedies a number of friends and beloveds with whom I am still 'in touch,' 'associated,' 'in cahoots,' and even now, 'related.'

Karen McPherson became my girlfriend there. We met through Janis Olson, Paul's romantic partner. Out on the lawn over lunch between classes we all sat down together. Karen was one of Janis' roommates. Karen was studying literature, poetry, film, writing. She was tall and graceful with long straight flaxen hair that practically covered her back. Her features were soft and gentle while her light blue eyes were sharp and inquisitive. She had the remarkable habit of listening carefully *before* she spoke up. We would become each other's first lovers.

Their third roommate, Mimi Leland, a petite, dark-haired, brilliantly-quick thinker and free-spirit par excellence, I met the very first morning of orientation week, as she blithely stepped from the darkly lit chamber of one of my own roommates.

We all go to Beaver Hall in the old town district of Portland where the favorite hometown band, The Portland Zoo, is playing its legendary long sweet psychedelic musical riffs. Janis' golden wavy locks swash to and fro. Karen's long, long, soft, light golden brown straight hair slowly swirls around her as she moves slower than the music. We dance with arms flailing, out-of-rhythm with any known dance steps, but in a rhythm that is an each-to-their-own kind of rhythm, except that we are all in it *together* somehow spinning and floating in space on this dance floor *together*. It is a different kind of dance from the high school 'spring fling.'

Janis and Paul lead us over to the Crystal Ballroom: the old upstairs dance hall, long-neglected, now being cleaned up for rock n' roll. And we dance there, under the mirror ball and the oil oozey pulse of the light show on the walls.

The Summer of Love has left its mark here, and in some ways the Goose Hollow neighborhood of Portland has taken less heat than its San Francisco counterpart. Way less heat; but the reality is that all the cities on that route north from The Bay had funky old gingerbread house neighborhoods like unto the very Haight-Ashbury of world renown and these neighborhoods were suffused with the unabashed glories of young hippiedom. Eureka, Ashland, Eugene, Portland, Olympia, Seattle, Bellingham. And none of these had to put up with the impossible march of media and touristas and profiteers through the flower beds of their daily minds.

No, although much smaller than the capital, Haight-Ashbury, these little neighborhoods survived the fall of the Summer of Love with a great deal of beauty and community intact.

But behind the soft glow of the summer sun on brightly painted wood railings, behind the porches and window sills of the Portland hippie neighborhoods, over the high fir-capped hills that ridge the western edge of the city, over the coast range and the beach, yes, right in that direction, over there, over that tremendous ocean ran amok a war, a jungle war sucking boys from these streets, these highschools' freshly graduated young men, into a swamp dragon's mouth: bones and remains being spit out and shipped back here in boxes for burial.

And for what and for who?

The nation we were backing had been run by a corrupt succession of totalitarian dictators. They lived the high-life themselves, while the mass of population was not merely impoverished but denied the right to elections, free speech, or a free press. The opportunities to create opposition political parties, or even to speak out about social ills, economic injustice or political crimes weren't allowed. The people of that country wanted no more of the oppresssive (you can hear the hisss) the oppresssive military-backed ruling class.

If we really believe in all this Democracy stuff, and this equal justice stuff, and all the stuff about the value of the rights to free expression, then we should have been backing *the rebels* from the get-go. But no, the rulers of that country have been cutting us sweetheart deals—selling national resources to corporate capitalism, and then re-investing the mounds of money they made right into our own stock market. Isn't that nice! No telling if the rebels are going to let us have at their rubber tree forests and their tin and their minerals.

The rebels were being supported by the Communists to the north and our American Republic was asking its young to fight for the power of the dictators, to support a regime that had never honored the principles of Democracy, nor of Freedom nor Justice. Still, the rationale was that this had to be a bulkhead against the spread of Communism. Communism had spread—as they explained it—from Russia into China, then down into Korea, and now into North Vietnam. If we let it continue to spread the countries would fall like 'dominoes' right up to our own doors. And that was a convincing argument for many.

It never seemed to me that supporting wicked totalitarianism would show the people of that country how much better our political system was.

It never seemed to me that supporting wicked totalitarianism was a convincing way to make a case for free-market economy over state-controlled economy. If we want to make a case for a certain economic way, then make it economically, in that way, and not by warring on those who wish to do differently.

Besides, the urban areas of that country were backed up by a long-established network of jungle and mountain villages with their villagers, and fishing and coastal villages with their villagers, and these people didn't want us there. What business had we coming there and telling them what to do? Go home! Get out of our country! We were not popular over there and they were skilled in mountainous living, and rainforest maneuvering, and they had fought the colonial French before us and driven them out of the country....

It seemed like a lousy place to make a courageous stand against Communism. And it seemed like a lousy place to send young American men.

For what and for who? There really wasn't much to be fighting for over there. Unless you were the American cement company that got the contract to pour the huge landing area at the military port being built. Unless you were a helicopter manufacturer, or a petroleum company who knew the vast quantities of fuel used to sustain an active ground force. Or unless you had shares in companies that held mining rights or offshore drilling rights in that country. Or unless you held stock in a sewing machine company which had found its most profitable products to be its line of electric eye sighting tools for weapons systems. Or if you just plain old manufactured bullets, and guns and bombs then this war was good for you, and if you could convince enough of the American people that this was so, why there's no telling how much money you might make.

And a lot of people just believed in America. That this country and its leaders wouldn't lead us into some horrible mistake of a war. They were supposed to be good people, there in Washington, and despite a few bad apples the people who devoted their lives to running this country knew what they were doing far better than a bunch of green-behind-the-ears students and a few red-around-the-edges protestors.

We protesters—maybe forty or more of us—are meeting in Reed's Student Union basement, planning about participating in the Portland activities of 'Anti-Draft' week being held nationwide at an urban center near you. There's going to be a week-long series of protests around the nation leading up to a massive demonstration in Washington, D. C.

The Portland area peace groups have scheduled a mid-week march and protest at the draft board, the Selective Service (euphemism for The Draft) headquarters in a Federal Building that is shared with the Oregon State Fish and Game Department.

We are meeting to discuss how we can add to the demonstration constructively or creatively and the idea is being bandied about of actually invading the draft board. Some people will be back soon with detailed floorplans of the building. The regular demonstration is going to be held out front, along the avenue, but the building has many entrances, side doors and routes into Fish and Game that connect on the interior to the Draft Board side of the facility.

Of course there's lots of concern about what happens once we're inside. What're we goin' to do? Everyone contemplated arrest, and an experienced demonstrator, a long-bearded one, attired in farmer-style coveralls, named Asparagus, at least that's what he called himself, is explaining that no one should get arrested who's been busted before. All first timers; and no destruction of property. We're all aware of the 'Destroying Federal Property' charges that have been leveled against protesters at other sites. So the plan is that we are just going to invade, sit on desks, be disruptive, actually discontinue the drafting process for as long as we can until they arrest us. At least, thinks this group, we shall actually be slowing down or impeding the murder process.

I am amazed to be in the presence of so many dedicated, thoughtful student peaceniks. Obviously the group that had been active on this campus the semester past was eager to be back together again…and joined in its ranks by many of us from the freshman class.

Maps arrive and in short order we have self-organized into small groups who will enter at each of the doors—simultaneously! None of us will go to the actual demonstration, at first. We plan to meet up on the main level of the shopping plaza just a few blocks away and there to synchronize our watches; then our seven groups will each arrive at the exact same minute at each of the seven doors. We figure that the group that attempts to go up the main steps, directly in front of the public street demonstration, will be stopped from entering, but the rest of us should get inside before anyone knows what's happening.

When the day of the demonstration comes round we are ready. Everyone is briefed about the principles of non-violence, which we plan to adhere to. We have all checked ourselves to see that we aren't carrying any sharp objects that might be construed as weapons. None of us is carrying any marijuana, drugs or paraphernalia.

At the appointed time we meet at Lloyd Center shopping mall to synchronize our watches, all 35 of us, and off we go in our groups, by our different routes, ambling along, heading toward the various sides of the building.

My own group sidles around the corner and crosses the street. The coast is clear. We can see the edge of the demonstration down at the far corner of the avenue, and there's our door, just as on the map, right on the side of the building. We are walking, looking just as normal as we know how to look, and turning abruptly, my hand is on the dark brass knob of the door, opening it and there are about a half dozen guys right inside the doorway all wearing dark jackets, open collars, American flag lapel pins, and matching shiny black FBI shoes.

"Is there anything we can do for you today?" asks the one in front.

"Er, no," I stammer.

"How about letting us inside?" asks one of my fellow would-be invaders.

"No," answers The Man, "If you want to come inside today, you'll have to go around by the front."

We all knew the front entrance would be heavily policed. But what were we to do but head down the block toward the rest of the demonstrators? Rounding the corner we could see one of the other of our groups, the group had gone to the front of Fish and Game and had also been turned back, as had—of course—the group that had tried to go up the Draft Board's own front steps, and slowly as the speakers spoke at the demonstration and the crowd marched up and down the street, the other groups arrived all and each turned back by packs of FBI or whoever-they-were blocking each of the ways in.

At least we swelled the ranks of the marchers.

Between speakers, the crowd—clergy and students and housewives and elderly people and office workers out on lunch break—chanted slogans, "End The War in Vietnam! Bring The Troops Home," and the hateful epithet addressed to the ears of our President, "Hey! Hey! LBJ! How Many Kids Did You Kill Today?"

In a pauseful moment, Karen shouted out, "War, War, What's it For?" and I, walking beside her, echoed her call, "War, War,

What's it For?" and the crowd echoed us both, chanting and repeating over and over again, "War, War, What's it For? War, War, What's it For?" At least if we weren't inside the building, we were asking the right question and we were making ourselves heard. And at least no one was arrested, and no one was hurt.

Later that evening in the basement of the Student Union we were watching the news and reflecting on our miserable attempt to impede the selective service process. The anchorman was recounting the day's anti-draft events around the nation showing vivid pictures of draft card burnings in Boston and miles-long marches in San Francisco. Then he blithely commented, "But here in Portland, only a small orderly rally outside Selective Service headquarters," and turning to his co-anchor continued, "I guess here in Oregon, there just aren't very many people against the war."

I was so mad. Everyone there in the Student Union was fuming over the newscasts. We knew that a large number of Oregonians were actually very much opposed to the war, but we couldn't bring the dialogue into the public. Why? Because we hadn't found the way to bring out mass numbers of people into the streets? Because our tactics had failed that afternoon? Because we hadn't found the way to catch the eye, the ear or the imagination of the public?

Asparagus said, "Well, it's pretty obvious they were here at our meetings, listening to us plan." We were sitting on the benches at the edge of the Student Union building and there were groups of students still shouting at the one big TV. They were switching channels to get different newscasts. Some were talking already about planning another demonstration for the weekend, trying to bring a larger march together. "They're listening in right now," Asparagus continued, "We're so open. Why shouldn't the cops send someone over to Reed to listen in on the anti-war meetings?"

A few minutes later we were outside on the wood steps and wood-decked terrace, just us, planning together. The next day a couple of people went and made measurements. We got the supplies we wanted. And the next day....

Shortly after dawn a vending machine service vehicle pulled up right outside the Draft Board and out the back of the van came six of us already chained together securely by heavy logging chain, and marched up the steps of the building and locked one end of the chain around the front door handles and the other around the base of the flagpole holding us chained neatly in a row between them.

The streets were quiet, the October sun glinting golden through the turning leaves. It was very peaceful as the Servomation van sped off in the distance. A few friends and supporters gathered by us. They put up our sign (beautifully calligraphed in the classic Reedie style) over the Draft Board door: "Conscription Is Slavery." That was the message.

So we waited. Paul and Karen and myself and my roommate Ron Anderson and Janis and Dick Coffin, another Reedie radical, were what later became known in Portland as the 'Chain-In.' Mimi Leland and David Sweet, our good friends, were the support and press communications team. They were the ones who would later call the press with details—and handle the bail money. One supporter wore an army helmet and looked menacing as if we were preparing to be attacked. David went to find a pay phone to call in the 'News Tip of the Month' to the radio stations. We sipped hot chocolate. A few cars, the early ones of the morning rush hour zipped by. Then a police car came driving along, the officers turning their heads to look as they drove by. Suddenly the officers' car slams on the breaks, and those two policemen turn their heads to look at us, eyes *very* wide, blinking in the morning light.

Soon police backup arrived; the workaday traffic in front of us inched along as news radio told the story. The night watchman inside the building even woke up. He came and unlocked the front door from the inside and opened it. When the door was open wide, we stood evenly spread across the front entranceway's top step. It was a well-measured plan.

The police closed off the sidewalk and while a cluster of

Figure 18. October 19, 1967. "Reed College Students protested the draft by blocking the entrance to Selective Service headquarters in Portland, Ore., by chaining themselves to the main door. The students, shouting "Hell No, We Won't Go," were hauled away in a police wagon after officers removed the chain with cutting tools." (Bettmann: Getty Images, 1967)

men-in-suits looked on, a couple of office workers walked up to the steps as though to enter the building. We were silent. They could've crawled under the chain between us, I suppose, to get to work. But they turned around and left; then a Sheriff came up to us with some deputies and in a low, confiding voice said, "Lookit. I know you're here because you believe in what you are doing. But if you will just undo all this and go home, we'll just let that be that, and there won't be any trouble or problem with that." We were silent. His deputies were examining the big locks on the ends of the chain, with the already rock-hard metal epoxy dried in their keyholes. Then they were looking at the lock similarly set around our waists. "Or I can inform you that this is an illegal thing to do." He continued, "And then I'll have to arrest you." We were silent. So they read us the chapter and verse of what we were doing wrong. And they pronounced us arrested. And they read us our rights. And they brought two guys with a two-man reticulated bolt cutter and they cut the chain and hauled us down the steps, pausing in the street to cut the chain apart when they realized they had to separate the boys from the girls for different police wagons. We began chanting "Hell no! We won't go!" over and over. Supporters on the sidewalk joined in. Even though we were definitely 'going' as the police hauled the tangled mess of people and chains across the sidewalk and into the waiting wagons. No one was hurt. It was a spectacular scene.

Later when we were bailed out we each had a one-liner, a pithy idea to say if the press or media asked us anything. Today they call that a 'sound bite,' but we were just trying to distill the ideas to help communicate them. Below the banner photographs of the 'Chain-In' the Portland press quoted Paul, "That was why my grandparents fled Russia, because the Czar wanted to draft them into his army to burn peasant villages. That was why my grandparents came to America, so they wouldn't have to do horrible things like that."

It was a sentiment the people of Oregon could relate to.

13. Sanctuary

Back on campus, we arrestees had bright new high-profile identities. We were part of The Chain-In, the demonstration Portland was still talking about. We were invited to every meeting, every panel discussion, every activist committee. And what did we think of this? Would we support that? Was this a good idea? A good strategy?

On one hand I did have a certain amount of experience in these strategic things; on the other neither I nor the other Chain-In members had any constituent group, any bunch of people who really listened to us. Again, on the one hand, I was being introduced to all the people of the Reed College and the Portland groups and grouplets who altogether comprised the Anti-War movement there; and on the other I was completely unschooled in the complicated politics between all these groups. On the one hand it was a sudden honor to be accorded respect by people who'd been working on that playing field for years; on the other I knew how little I really knew about organizing and coalition-building.

I found out also that the right-wingers on campus were similarly busy organizing, and becoming less tolerant of the left. In the arena where administration and faculty hold forth, among their array of committees, boards, and regents, a certain commission called simply 'The Faculty Advisory Board' issued notice that no faculty were to sign any public letter or declaration against the war. The reason was given that as an educational institution Reed would take no stand on matters of public debatable policy and the professors, assistant professors, etc. were warned against attaching Reed's good name to any such documents.

This was commanded in a season when such letters were regularly being circulated, signed, or printed in whole page ads in America's newspapers and magazines. These were important letters at that time because of two related effects. One was how widespread opposition was to the war: doctors, scientists, teachers from all fields were speaking out and this gave a feeling to individuals in all walks of life that they were not alone if they too spoke up. The other effect was that these letters spoke directly to the students, letting us know that the people whose classes and schools we had struggled to gain admission to, that these respected people were voicing their voices, and that gave legitimacy and support to our own expressions.

Still, this was Reed—a bastion of the precious rights of thought and expression. This was the college that had famously not fired those teachers singled out by the McCarthyism Red-Scare of the 1950s, whose policy then had been to allow the faculty to stand up against that sort of wrong-headed government bullying. Why were they not allowing their faculty this right today?

On the student front there was not directly much that the right-wing war supporters could focus on. But as their coalitions emerged they began moving toward a new focus called 'Law and Order.' I was surprised by this then, but I have seen it repeat as a process in succeeding decades. When the rightist movements cannot effectively focus on proposals of merit or action, they tend to lean toward the more generalized 'issues' given such names as 'Law and Order,' or 'Family Values,' or 'Love your Country.'

'Law and Order' had been taken as a rallying cry by those opposed to all the demonstrations that were becoming a regular part of American life. That is in part because it was hard for the right wing to argue in favor of the war. There were just too many sound arguments against it; and worse, so many things our government had put forward were being found out as lies: the commitment of US troops was finally publicly exposed; the Pentagon Papers exposé openly revealed that the government knew they were embarked on losing policies and strategies; the Gulf of Tonkin caper—that resulted in the very first resolution by

Congress to commit to the war turned out to be a manufactured fraud—an invented event to sell the war to the Americans back home; the succession of one buffoon after another as the titular head of Vietnam following the murder of Diem resulted in ex-heroin smuggler Vice Air Marshall Nugen Ky attaining his country's dubious leadership, and so on down the corpse-ridden path to war where (as Socrates *and* the outspoken Oregon Senator-Against-the-War, Wayne Morse, both said), "Truth is always the first casualty."

So the right wing pronounced all these unruly demonstrations full of people chanting slogans, filling streets, waving banners and even getting arrested—as showing how we had no respect for the rules of society. Why, we demonstrators were against Law and Order!

"We oughta round 'em all up and ship 'em to Russia. Yessiree that'd teach 'em a lesson." We heard these rants over and over again.

For two generations since Reed's founding, the campus had been governed by an Honor Code. This code stated that no member of the Reed community (and this included students faculty and staff) shall do anything "Which causes embarrassment, discomfort or injury to other individuals or to the community as a whole" or "In violation of specific rules that have been developed over the years to meet special conditions in the community." This was one of the really attractive things about the college for many of the students and professors: the idea that there actually could be, in this fierce and modern world, a sense of real honor left to abide by in a world gone astray from such principles.

Doors were regularly left unlocked, cars regularly left with the keys on the dash. Exams were given unproctored, in fact, exams—even 'closed-book' exams—regularly were picked up in the exam hall, brought to the privacy of the student's home or dorm room, completed in the required time and then returned *later* for grading. Meal tickets weren't checked at the dining halls, library books from Reed's awesome collection were just walked out of the library stacks, and on and on would go the examples of a policy that imbued each person there with a sense of honor themselves.

Until a group of students from what (for lack of a better term) I must call the right wing; that is the crowd that despised the marijuana smoking on campus, that abhorred the endless 'radical' meetings to organize events all over the fair city of Portland, that was against the 'biker' element (leather-dressed motorcyclists) that had for ages been a part of Reed life. So the rightists set themselves toward installing their clique's people on one of the guiding bodies of Reed Life: the Reed College Community Senate.

The Community Senate was a faculty/student mixed body that was given a number of responsibilities. It had administered general campus policies and most of the extracurricular activities at the school, as well as parking and traffic, allotment of space for different groups, as well as general student body funds for an amazing number of programs: poetry and jazz fests, film series, visiting campus speakers and so on. It also had oversight over the school's Judicial Board, which was the body that reviewed offenses to the Honor System.

So the Righties began to campaign, through the normal campus voting process to install its own people on the Senate. This hardly caught my attention until I heard they were debating for passage a renewed version of the Honor System to make The Code *merely a guideline* for following the rules and regulations of campus life, instead of the other way around...which is how it had been since the dawn of the College.

The opposition was firm in its view: if you wanted to live by the code you just had to follow the various rules and you would be doing exactly what was right; but that the Code wasn't going to be misused as an excuse for not following the rules. Something in this didn't sound right to me. I couldn't quite fathom it at the time, but I sensed a power play here that would rear its ugly head sooner or later as this intrusive idea of the hierarchy of codes and rules might begin to be applied.

It was sooner rather than later that the example came to light. One of the artsy biker types had gently ridden his motorcycle across a part of a campus lawn. He'd been ticketed by the campus traffic patrol and had his case brought before the Judicial Board. At the J-board he argued that a) he hadn't hurt the lawn in the slightest and b) no one had been inconvenienced, endangered, or dishonored by his action. The Opposition countered that if everyone did that, the lawn would soon be destroyed. He re-countered that 'everyone' in this case was a mythological figment that didn't exist and since nobody else had done any such thing, and since the lawn hadn't been damaged—that he was innocent and couldn't be held guilty for the non-crimes of some imaginary 'nobody-else.'

The J-board found in his favor, gave him a warning as a slap on the wrist and the Righties on the Senate renewed their campaign for changing the order of the Honor System, waving the case of this unrepentant biker as their flag. "Just look at the abuse of Order and Law this fellow is encouraging. He's masking complete disregard for the beauty of this campus, for the tranquility of students reading and studying on the lawns; he's hiding behind the veil of the Honor System because it suits his lawless, reckless purpose."

It was an argument whose echoes I would hear again decades later in discussion of our American Constitution's high-minded Free Expression clauses versus Departmental Regulations that would attempt to corral those expressions onto smaller ground.

The case of the motorcyclist and the arguments it engendered prompted me to come forward in September of 1968 to attempt to gain a seat on the College Senate. It was a successful campaign, but it marked the beginning of the end of my life as a student.

In November of 1968 The Living Theatre returned to the United States after four continuous years touring on the other side of the Atlantic. They brought four plays in a thunderous charge across the continent. They played New York, Boston, Chicago, San Francisco and L.A., and a score or more campuses, almost entirely sold out shows, extra audience let in through fire escapes and rooftops (that old trick!). I went to visit them during Thanksgiving break at the modern-arched playhouse at the Massachusetts Institute of Technology.

The campus is austere; its science and administration buildings solid along the Charles River. It is the preeminent school for learning the hard sciences of modern industry. Still we are sold out, and students, anti-war activists, artists from all over Boston are coming.

The set is going up for *Frankenstein*—The Living Theatre's adaptation of Shelley's grand novel of the Monster made by science…the innocent Creature who cannot fit in to the world he has been created into. It's the most complex of the plays technically: three stories high—the whole visage represents the Monster's head; and there are fold down parts that become the laboratory and giant cables from which victims are hung, and arenas of light where sequences of the Witch of Endor, the enlightenment of the Sun Buddha, the failure of the New Age-ers to levitate their friend are all enacted like a palimpsest of visions cascading one after the other…and eventually the Monster takes over the police force and puts the whole audience in jail.

But the next Living Theatre show of that Thanksgiving 1968 weekend was *Paradise Now*. A piece of interactive theatre arts that truly leapt into new territory, taking the audience, the critics, the building custodians, and often much of the neighborhood with them into a new kind of relation between each other. The play played on basic challenges to the systems of government, economics, race, and consciousness—and then opened the challenges to the real lives of the audience, inviting answers, dialogue, arguing, debating, storytelling, speechmaking, screaming. People came prepared with theatre pieces of their own; people came totally unprepared; people left after a few minutes; people stayed through the night. It was a different play each night, based on who was there doing what, but it was held together through a series of ritual actions and ceremonia that brought the chaos back into focus and clarity. It was live art if there ever was such.

There are many other accounts of those shows, and my intention isn't to re-cap the performances.

Often during the swell of energy during *Paradise Now* people would rise to speak asking us to tone it down: because there were people swirling about in the streets outside; because the rafters couldn't take any more weight of people; because the college's regents may be offended by the nudity; or because the theatre department that had so kindly invited us here and were paying us to perform would surely get into big trouble 'cause of our carrying on; because the noise, the overcrowding might lead to the police being called; and think of the disaster that might become...etc., etc.... We thought we'd already heard all of that, but comes now this bellowing man, a number of the campus folk there seemed to know him, a Professor Lettvin and he's calling on us, exhorting us, pleading with us to rein it in...because the

Figure 19. *Paradise Now*, The Living Theatre cast and audience enact ritual ceremonia onstage. (Marty Topp: From the film, *Paradise Now*, 1968)

police might be called onto campus...and next door there's a draft resistor, actually an AWOL from the Vietnam war holed up in the Student Union building seeking sanctuary. The bellowing professor is afraid that all this crowd and noise will cause a police action and bring the heat down on Mike in the building next door. And the debate is on...."Let Mike come over here."—"No, let's all go over there!"—"No, we should all get back inside and quiet down."—"Don't be afraid of the State!"—"They want to see us get fired up, so they can cause another riot!"—"Why don't we just get on with the play?"—"We are getting on with the play."—" This is the play!"—"Is there really somebody AWOL next door?"—"Are the police looking for him?"—Some other theatre group starts unfurling long silky banners near downstage left and soon they are playing their mini-play to an interested crowd in that section of the theatre. The filmmaker Kenneth Anger is strutting around brandishing a long jagged glass tube. I walk slowly up the crowded aisle and into the lobby where the overwrought filmmaker soon appears and lets himself cool off in the night air streaming through the open doors of the auditorium. We talk. About the play. About Peace and Violence. About Art. He heads back into the fray. And I walk softly outside into the night.

Ahead of me looms the Student Union.

What a difference a few steps can make.

The Student Union was actually calm compared to the crowded theatre across the walk. Students entered carrying books and Chinese take-out, as though nothing in the world was askew. In the most central room of the ground floor off on one side was a table with a few folks sitting about and a collection of flyers in a small stack if perchance anyone might saunter by and pick one up.

I looked about, to note if somehow I was missing some hubbub of 'political' activity. No, only a few students giggling on their way upstairs. I strolled over to the table and while reading over the flyers about resistance to the war, I began talking with the people there and—when asked—introduced myself as a member of the anti-war movement from Portland, Oregon. I asked, "How're things going here?"

They all piped up that it seemed tonight "All the action was at the theatre across the way."

"Yeah, I know. I've been at the play, but I thought I'd come over here and see what was going on with Mike."

"He's just hanging out quietly talking with a few friends. There're a couple of lawyers here too, but they're asleep somewhere."

"Do you think the hoopla at the theatre's goin' to cause Mike any trouble?" ask I.

"No." "Nah." "Not really." They answer.

"The Boston Police, and the M.P.s—they're going to do what they want. We think they want to catch Mike with the least fuss and press attention and the least public uproar as they can."

"Uh-huh, the quieter the better for them. Of course, you never know....Who are we to know how *they* think!"

"It's been pretty quiet here so most of us have been getting away for a few minutes, maybe half an hour to go check the play out."

"It's an amazing scene over there."

"It doesn't matter where you come in, does it?"

"What were they doing when you left?"

"It does help," says I, "if you can stay for the whole show. But any part of it you see is interesting, gets the point across. Of course each piece of it is so different...."

"What were they up to just now?"

"Oh, when I last looked back into the theatre, the hall was darkened and in a rosy blue light the actors had linked themselves into a form like a compass needle and they were swinging slowly like a pendulum through the audience...."

"Cool."

"Well," says I, "Cool is what's happening over here. Are you sure there isn't something I could do to help?"

"No, like we say, there isn't much to do here."

"Well, he could help on one of the later shifts. Can you stay late?" One of them chimes in.

"Sure," I say.

A while later a couple of sanctuary supporters come downstairs saying the guys up top are ready for the next shift, and soon I'm stationed by a roof window with another supporter explaining to me how the citizens band radio works. Our simple mission is to keep watch down the avenue, and if and when we see some obvious invader type activity—"You know like a bunch of police cars, or some army rigs, or even what looks to you like a bunch of undercover cars, or anything like that, then press this button and say it like you see it."

Otherwise we're just supposed to check in every fifteen minutes to let 'em know we're on the air.

"Where're we checking in to?"

"Somewhere."

As the night wore on we kept to the post and nothing happened. But I did understand that there was an array of people watching from other positions, all in support of this one young man fleeing from the terrible war, all watching into the night. Maybe many of us didn't even know each other. Maybe, and more likely, I was one of the few persons helping who didn't know most of the others, but I was part of a group of people whose mission wasn't to attack or even defend against any invaders, but to pass the word, to wake the lawyers, to roust the news media, to call what public attention could be called, to shed light, if you will, on a scene that the forces of the war wanted kept in the dark.

And even more deeply, I knew that this group was self-organized, that it had commitments based on trust and action, and that it wasn't a part of any regiment or corporation. We belonged to no one. But our belief in freedom, wanting this one man to be free, brought us to belong to each other.

I never really recovered from that experience.

14. Something New

Back on the West Coast it seemed that events and people began to stream by, as thoughts and actions rolled out of the rut, and beyond the normal course of events with increasing velocity and momentum.

The forces at play generated demonstrations, leading into wilderness retreats, leading into politically charged meetings, leading back into Beaver Hall and The Crystal Palace, the two rocking dance halls of Portland.

On the political page, Hubert Humphrey, the good guy liberal, running now for President, had sadly become the flag-bearer for the Democrats' support for the Vietnam War. He came to campaign. Demonstrations filled the streets. Later he lost the election to Richard Nixon.

Nixon's Vice President Spiro Agnew came to town. He was the loudest spokesman in the administration's support for the Vietnam War. Demonstrations filled the streets. Later in a No-Contest plea for accepting racetrack bribes, he resigned in disgrace.

We made picnics in the parks of the Portland hills. We blew bubbles and played flutes. We wore scarves and lace and flew kites.

The Free Clinic, 'Outside In' opened up at the edge of downtown.

Koinonia House, Portland U's Christian Community Center opened its doors to anti-draft counseling and helped shelter runaways from the war.

Goose Hollow flourished like a Haight Ashbury of the north, without all the hype and media bombardment.

The Psychedelic Supermarket, our local 'head shop,' sold small brass hookahs, and showed furry flocked blacklight posters in its gallery room, already starting (little did we see it coming!) to commemorate the Blasted-Through-the-Looking-Glass experience we were in the midst of having.

Swami Satchitananda, the modern leader of the Integral Yoga Movement, Yogi Bajan, the current Grand Marshal of Kundalini Yoga, Dadaji from India's Ananda Marga all cruised into the Rose City in their flowing robes and their turbans and set up classes, lectures, ceremonies, ashrams, and initiations—all, all of them pointing to another way that existed outside the course of American Business Politics, and though these yoga practices and breathing practices and meditation practices were as far from what we knew as the Inner State was from the Interstate, we went to these lectures, we read the texts, we started getting up early for meditations, we cut back on our dope-smoking, we learned as much of the stuff as we could devour. And many of us drifted or slammed into full-time participation in these sects, adopting Hindi names, moving into the ashrams, finding in these communities maybe not The Answer to: How do we end human misery? but at least the answer to: How can someone full of visions of Peace and Co-operation live in a world gone mad?

Film fests showed a new breed of movie: foreign arts fare flavored with the wackiest multi-imaged (hardly plot-driven) feasts of sound, light and color.

And with all these new-found expressions of culture and idealism blossoming around us, *and around similar groups* of young people in a hundred or more cities from Maine to San Diego, what did the press and the media have to say about it? Simple, they gave us a demeaning name. They put a name on us that was meant to make all this sound and seem childish, goofy, and unimportant: "Hippies." The mainstream press found this word so very attractive because it pigeon-holed all this brand new idealism and all these brand-new effects into an easy-to-minimize, easy-to-make-fun-of, easy-to-discount, no-account, low-account fashion.

None of us, not in any of the enclaves of communalism, not in any of the food co-ops, not in any of the anti-war activism groups, not in any of the arts collectives, not in any of the psychedelic contingents, not in any of the widespread underground newspapers, not in any of the just-starting back-to-the-land communities, not in any of the yoga or meditative associations, not in any of the newly-founded environmental groups, *none of us* called ourselves Hippies. And none of us liked that term. We all knew it had been adopted by the mainstream media because it simplified their task so that they wouldn't have to look at what was happening with any seriousness.

But sooner or later, we knew we were stuck with the term. I think it was at the second of our Be-ins in Portland when people were driving in and hiking up to the top of Mount Tabor Park asking for and looking for 'The Hippies' that I surrendered and said, "This is us, we are 'the Hippies' you are looking for...come join the fun!"

Once, we ate this pure THC powder—the essence of the essence of Delta-9-tetra-hydro-cannabinol, the essence of marijuana. We'd gotten it a few weeks before on a jaunt into the California hills where an old friend's connection showed up with a huge amount of LSD-25 and my friend, Andy, turned to us, travellers from the north, to assay the material, which we did, eating the small blue pills and not long thereafter advising our curious host to "Get all you can of this stuff, this is the real deal, the holy moly, the rock of very sunlight itself." And so he did. And the dealer whose product we had so full-heartedly endorsed rewarded us with these THC capsules, saying, "Here try these. This stuff'll never be on the market. It's too expensive to make. I know. I'm in the business. Highs hafta be inexpensive to make so by the time a whole series of people has bought and passed them along to each other they're still affordable. This stuff costs me five, sometimes six bucks apiece just to concoct. So there's no way to make it affordable to market. So I just have them made for myself, or friends or for gifts. Enjoy 'em."

And enjoy 'em we did. It's a special place. Kenny, my longtime friend visiting from back east, said it was like smoking 10,000 joints. I felt the fluidity of all motion, from the turning of the earth itself to the blood in my veins to the smooth flowing of thoughts in ceaseless fountains. Walking was a slow motion rubbery affair, long catlegs stretching out to the next step sleekly bringing the body forward, smoothly striding into the next step. Mind you, nothing really out of the ordinary here, just noticing in so much, *so much* more detail.

So one time I ate this stuff and went to a Fellini movie, the oddball Italian director who put a vigorously-stirred mixture of symbolism and reality onto his screen, and I noticed how as the story line—which was somewhat apparent at the beginning of the movie—as it progressed there were more and more symbols brought out and the movie evolved into symbolism telling the story instead of narrative action telling the story. Finally just the black and white patterns on the silver screen became the story. Fellini was taking us into the realm where the flicker and flash of light was really what the plot was about. Then it got bright…very bright and the screen stayed bright and then the usher was saying, "Hey the movie's over, time to go home."

It was a time when we were discovering that the drugs we were taking were not a means to get *away* from a dull reality, but a means to gain awareness and insight. Yes the experiences were fun, but way beyond that, the psychedelic experiences were leading us to a full participation in life, in being fully-endowed players on the field and not just students or extras or members of a herd.

And art. Art stopped being something in the museums. Art became a block of wood cut (sculpted is the correct term, I suppose) with kitchen implements into the shape of a prehistoric human. Art was a set of new Rapidograph ink pens running their careful even width lines over the fabulous textures of watercolor paper. Art was Dr. P. H. Martin's Radiant Watercolor Dyes poured (!) onto gigantic paper, folded once down the middle (Kenny encouraging us to use *all* the colors) and both sides pressed smoothly together on the floor by many hands, smooshing the inks into each other and then the masterwork being opened up and spread wide as a giant Rorschach—blinding colorful—radiant with the unrepeatable colors of mixed inks, exhibiting a billion and one images and patterns—even to the unstoned eye—there as tall and wide as two people, now being hung with push tacks as the centerpice of the living room wall.

There was a lot going on.

It was hard for classes about the dynamics of ancient Grecian societies or Victorian literature, no matter how well taught to compete for our interest. Even if the dynamics of the art and politics of some ancient society were full of models for us to learn from, Hey! those dynamics were expressing themselves in our everyday lives in the most dynamic ways imaginable: the art was changing, the politics were changing, the culture was changing and we seemed in the midst of helping to make those changes happen. How could classes about some other time or some other set of lessons capture our attention in the face of the moment-to-moment arc of creativity that was sweeping between the youth and society in general like a gigantic welding spark crashing from one pole to the other, illuminating the spot behind our eyes.

AWOL's—that's Absent Without Official Leave—from the war came through bearing stories horrible, on their way to Canada and out out out of here.

Chemists from San Francisco and Boston came through bearing elixirs potent and experimental, on our way to innerspace and out out out of here.

A couple of very collegiate looking 'students' arrive visiting the campus 'from the east' they say. Harvard. They come bearing sugarcubes laced with some stuff they call Seranol or Sernyl. "Just eat one," they advise us.

Supposedly they are emissaries from the Boston group that was wildly experimenting in the aftermath of Drs. Leary and

Alpert's cavalcade of sugarcubes. Who the heck knows what this stuff is, but we get some and Karen and I and several friends all eat one and wander through the playing fields, each few steps the landscape changing around us. It has a somewhat numbing effect, as Soren, Karen's young aspiring-novelist friend who is also visiting, finds out when he cuts his bare foot on a small piece of glass and we all sit around watching his foot bleed. He's smiling, "Doesn't really hurt at all," he says, looking up at us.

We're all looking now. Not that it seems dangerous at all really, but we're just watching the whole of his body doing that bleeding thing: pulses and pauses and throbs of life, beautiful really. After a bit Karen says, looking incredulous at her friend, "I don't know about you, but I feel the pain." So we wrap a sock tightly around it and walk on down our merry way to the Rhododendron Garden by the lake just below us. Swans and geese pirouette on the lake surface in a ballet dance that they must have practiced since the dawn of their species.

For a while this stuff, then that stuff, then some other stuff floated through our grasp. Where was it all coming from, and where were we all going?

Hiya, another Reed student, and I decided to try that Sernyl again, so we ate it on the way to a psychology class that was going to be discussing Brainwave Changes During Emotional Experiences. The professor shows up gleefully waving a tape recording he says is much more interesting. He says it's some kind of brainwashing tape from North Korea. This doesn't sound at all as pleasant as the slides of the Grand Canyon or Vivaldi's concertos, which had been on the lesson plan.

He just pops it into the player and these grotesque sounds start emanating, like some deep foreboding version of fingernails on chalkboard. I look around and I can tell I'm not the only one trying to keep from getting queasy. The tape goes on and on, louder and louder and its swirling cacophonous grinding is getting to all of us. I see Hiya trying to write me a note from across the room. Then I see him laboring to read what he's written. He looks puzzled. We look at each other, and I tell you he might as well have been a thousand miles away, there was so much space between us, eddies of winds and whole canyons of breezes swirled between us, a hundred zillion molecules of air, whole islands of now visible bacteria, like little worlds floated by. It took telescopic powers of eyesight to see that great distance, and now the sounds of the tape player were coming from far, far away, maybe rebounding from off the walls of the room, themselves an unreachable distance. We were so small in this immense universe, and then, then it started to turn. I felt each breath filling me, my limbs gaining solidity, the floor beneath my feet suddenly right there where I could push against it, all the room now much smaller, almost too small for all of us, if we stood or moved with any degree of freedom we'd all be crashing and busting into each other. I looked at Hiya again, it hardly seemed you could fit the two of us in the same room, our eyesight beams cludging into each other, palpable, feelable, our breaths curling and roiling out of our mouths pushing into each others, a big tangle of breathy air hardly enough room in the world, my shoulders pressing with each breath against my shirtback, ready to burst the seam.

Then the class is done, and the students pick up their books, filing out of the seminar. Hiya and I are stragglers, still recovering. "Pretty good tape, eh, boys?" asks the prof as we sit there still nailed to our chairs.

Then another couple of travelers, this time from Vancouver, Canada, breeze through Portland with still another heralded elixir. These guys don't want to be anywhere near the college campus. "Too hot," they say. "This stuff is too good, and the law is on the lookout for us."

Their concoction didn't come in a pill. It was a smelly, oily, crumbly, orange crystal that you weren't supposed to eat. No, you smoked it.

They said it turned browner as it oxidized, and we had to keep it from air, so they wrapped it up tightly in aluminum foil, and told us, "It comes on quick, don't be driving in your car. Get seated, and smoke a piece about the size of a match head in one puff. That'll do it."

So we hurried back to the big house on 26th Street, Beanbat, as it was nicknamed, the big pink house, and in the white-walled living room opened our new-found treasure and smoked it up.

I'd inhaled the smells-like-burning-plastic stuff and was just thinking after a few seconds that this doesn't come on anywhere near as fast a—when my thought dis-integrated in mid-moment and the room and my eyesight and the blank white walls opened up in a fountain of color that made fireworks look like black and white, and the swirling pulsating mandalas of color got so thick one spiral on top of a barrage of emanating beams and clusters of baroque crystaling patterns, I could hardly see Karen and Kelly and Jonas and Jerianna across the room...they were still lighting and passing the pipes...and looking toward me to see if I'd had any effects start yet, but I couldn't find the words to talk, only blips of thought that maybe I'd taken way, waaaaay too much this time and I knew that every immediate moment was the original Creation re-creating itself, and we, we were just momentary creatures ourselves, and, and, and the thoughts swept over me like a huge tide and were gone...there was a hallowed place, still and precious. No thoughts bothered to knock at these doors. The doors and windows of perception themselves, just tiny parts of some disintegrating house way below us, like some secret, majestic temple that had always been here, just hidden from us by our own incessant thinking and scheming, and now free of those chains of verbal thought we drift, unchained at last, free, high, buoyant, floating on the shifting atoms of our chairs, slowly, slowly already drifting back down, now the walls painted with every changing image, faces and geometries, like an open book of symbolic wisdom, delivering lessons per second, I peer across at Jonas whose serene face yields a small childlike smile, and at Karen, still deeply drifting in the inner space, her hands gently resting on her lap, palms up, one on top of each other, at peace.

And they called that stuff DMT.

We trotted back to see those guys the next day and bought all we could afford.

Back on campus the posse of pals went to the biggest dorm room we had available and sat down in a big ring and we got out all the pipes and we went around the room and filled them one after the other and we blasted off off off this plane into that space again.... And for some it was a rapture and for others it was an agonizing revelation.... The illusions of our own small beliefs fade rapidly under the glare of the psychedelic eye.... The shortness of life, the delicate veil of this living moment being all that stands between us and the vast vast unknown of whatever may—or may not—lie beyond. Give up the momentary challenges, get carried by creation's wave, filled and unfilled and filled again with whatever array of images and imaginings the overflowing moment gives us....

These days weren't all just filled with short-lived events. The People's Food Co-op got founded in an old warehouse on the Eastside. It taught people a cooperative method of doing things, really essential things like food distribution and public hygiene. It taught this to thousands of American kids, weaned in the previous decades when the United States had gotten away from a hands-on connection to its food sources and supplies. Our grandparents' generation had almost universally a closer connection to the rural farms supplying fresh foods and grains to the cities' populations. So here's a whole new generation of young people totally removed from this rural-to-urban food connection suddenly (for what reason?) interested in and participating in their own food supply and providing it into the community, actually making foodstuffs available in truckload quantity and dividing it up through shared labor.

Suddenly there's an interest in 'organics.' Maybe all those people high on acid could actually see the chemical residues on the supermarket foods! Maybe they could actually feel the oily residues of pesticides when their senses of touch were enthralled with psychedelic materials. Maybe science and sensible understanding finally collided, but agribiz and its investors couldn't see the advantage of making better healthier food, only more profitable food as though the pure amount of money gained were the measure of the quality of the mouthful.

Around the corner from Beaver Hall, the Isis pottery shop opened and next door to that sat The Wayfarer, a macrobiotic-type restaurant. We hung out there eating bowls of rice and veggies, sippin' spice and herb teas after a hard day of making what we believed was called a revolution.

We passed books around that mapped out the terrain: *Silent Spring*, Rachel Carson's door-opening treatise on the poisoning of our environment; Franz Fanon's *The Wretched of the Earth*, the true horror of post-colonial exploitation; George Leonard's *Education and Ecstasy*, the revelation that the education system was gearing toward mass monotony and consumerist economy, while true learning triggers an ecstatic delight with us; Paul Goodman's *People or Personnel* and *Growing Up Absurd*, illuminating the ideals and absurdities of who we were making ourselves into and Helen and Scott Nearing's accounts of living close to the earth in Maine. We read and passed books and more books around our circle: Herman Hesse's *Magister Ludi, Steppenwolf, Narcissus and Goldmund*, and *Siddhartha*; Marshal McLuhan's *Understanding Media* and *The Medium is the Message*; John Cage's awesome opus, *Silence*; the science fiction masterpieces: Frank Herbert's *Dune* and Piers Anthony's *Macroscope*; the astonishing *Autobiography of Malcolm X* and the unsung heroic novel of those times: Richard Fariña's *Been Down So Long it Looks Like Up to Me*.

And Abbie Hoffman, the original Yippie! protestor cranked out *Revolution for the Hell of It*, a manifesto of outrageous, way over-the-top ideas about transforming society, but backed with very serious ideas about injustice, poverty, exploitation, warfare and money.

And Leary, Dr. Timothy Leary, touched his finger to the cave walls of our time and marked in glyphic letters there: *High Priest* and *Psychedelic Prayers* urging us not just to 'Turn on, Tune in and Drop out' but actually encouraging us to eat psychedelic substances and see for ourselves! And even Leary wasn't just concerned with getting high, but with reducing prisoner populations, healing psychotic illnesses, liberating exploited peoples from their hardships, enhancing education and scientific research. But even worse, in the eyes of the ruling class powers, he was encouraging the idea that you, yes you, that you could have a genuine religious revelation, made of the same stuff, the very same stuff as the Great Buddha's revelation, or St. Augustine's revelation, or the revelations of Ezekiel or St. John the Divine's, right there in the comfort of your own backyard. This had to be blasphemy! This can't happen in our well-ordered modern society! A regimented social system just could not accept that an ordinary individual—like you or me—could have an experience that would knock us out of our shoes and socks and onto barefooted holy ground in awe before the presence of the Eternal Living One!

Why, this could disrupt whatever plan the powers of Business and its servant The State have up their sleazy sleeves! And what might that be? Who knows for sure, but maybe it's some unplanned plan for everyone to work for just a few humongous companies? But whatever the franchise capitalists may have had in mind, this psychedelic stuff wasn't part of the bargain they bargained for.

And that's not the whole of it either…we were busy discovering that sex, yes of all things, Sex was just awesome under the psychedelic influence.

15. The Ivory Tower Crumbles

The Student Body President at Reed College had been a positive influence between the expanded minds and ideas of the students and the traditional minds and ideas of the administration.

Then he and his girlfriend separated. Well these things happen, and as the song says, "Breaking up is hard to do." So he brings an Honor Code violation up against her. For what? For having a member of the opposite sex in her room overnight. What?? Weren't we all doing that? Wasn't every dorm pretty much in fact co-ed? Wasn't most of the student population sleeping regularly with their beloved or beloveds? Even if the campus guidebook said: No opposite sexes sleeping in the dorms.

Remember, this bed of the latter 1960s had no known uncurable sex diseases. This era of the late 1960s had the first generation pretty much fully protected from pregnancy by The Pill, and although it wasn't as if we threw caution to the winds, or just slept about aimlessly, still we were under the pounding influences of teenage desires without the apparent dangers of pregnancy or disease. Further, we had no roadmaps of this terrain from any previous generation's behavior. There wasn't some collective decision to experiment with 'free love.' It was just there for the generation to try.

Given the circumstances we were rather traditional. That's because the power of love in all its tenderness was (and I think still is) the most compelling force in the world. So we were drawn naturally to emotional and passionate relationships. And we were totally unprepared for how much these ties could pull, swing, lift and drop us.

Karen and I clung to each other and yearned at the same time to touch others. We cascaded through a series of multiple romances, returning to each other both giddy and bruised. Love at this rate was a painful process.

Then came this bully of a guy wanting his ex thrown out of the college because she's bedded some other dude in her own dorm room.

The Judicial Board met and gave the poor girl a stern warning—and that shoulda been that.

But the Law and Order-ites on the Senate (the Senate that I'm a student rep on) wanted to reconsider and make a harsher example of her by suspending her from the school.

By one vote the liberals won out. But we had to compromise and add an additional 'punishment' of social probation. That meant she's not to go to any campus movies and social music events, and must stay out of the pool hall and coffeeshop in the commons for the semester.

So it goes to rest.

No.

The following September *a few days before the new semester starts up* The Biology Senior, eats a cheeseburger in the coffee shop and now she's painted by the so-called Conservatives as purposefully showing the most blatant disregard for the rules of the campus. She is the modern equivalent of Chaos! And needs to be expelled from the college...which for a senior honors biology student might as well have been being burned at the stake, career-wise.

Here are these lauded scholars of the humanities, students and professors all, of Aristotle, Homer, Pericles, Seneca, Plato and the quest for truth and civilization buying into this nonsense that this young woman was somehow subverting the high ideals of the esteemed institution by quietly ordering lunch at the coffee shop. This was nuts. My opinion of the school and its scholarly aptitude plummeted.

After seemingly endless debate she was narrowly acquitted.

Then the college deans scheduled an opportunity to address the still smoldering issue of opposite sexes overnighting in the dorms.

Didn't they have the faintest idea about what was going on?

My own dorm, freshman year, had one shower area on one of the floors which was where the women went to shower. It just was that way. It didn't seem like some controversial big deal. It wasn't written anywhere that that was how it was supposed to be; it just worked well and it seemed like a reasonable way for a group of young people to associate.

The thought of protesting during the deans' speeches is intriguing. Besides, maybe they really need to know about the unabashed intramural copulation the student population was practicing.

And no matter how we discussed it, it was a lighter, more delightful topic for demonstration than the grisly war.

We made plans and decided to hold a meeting—at our house a couple of miles from the campus—the one with the long wood-floored living room. A rehearsal for the proposed demonstration.

People came. People came knowing the topic was provocative. The politics of love held us in its grip. Private passions and public policy touch, momentarily, sometimes, and the warmth is feel-able.

People came who were in our close circle of friends. People came who were disenchanted with the angry direction of war protests, and who felt the joy of protesting on behalf of something lovely.

We cleared the space and sat around comfortably discussing the senate meeting, how it worked, where people could sit, stand. And the suggestion was made that we should simply attend the meeting and those of us who wanted to, at some given signal would disrobe and enact whatever naked paradisial, beautiful scene inspired us.

Well, that simple suggestion turned into a lot of people expressing that that seemed like a wonderful plan.

People could dance.

Hold hands, hug.

Make love if they wanted to.

Or kind of rock or sway standing together.

No words. No 'statement' other than the bodies, at ease with their nakedness, comfortable with each other, unafraid.

It was a utopian image: entering the debate with no clothes on.

So the plan was approved.

Still, "How comfortable are we really, ourselves, with our nakedness in public? This isn't something we do every day," asked a wise voice from the floor.

"Or even comfortable with ourselves, each other, naked, for that matter," pronounced another.

After the next few suggestions we were all disrobing, untying shoes. And the space of the long room was transformed as if a veil was lifted. We were all the same people, but suddenly it was different, as though we'd crossed all at once some invisible taboo bridge.

No one knew what if anything to say or do. We hadn't exactly gotten undressed in the heat of passion. Passion for an ideal maybe, but passion in the erotic sensual sense, no. Slowly people touched, massaged each other. Someone turned down the lights, brought in candles. Someone put jazz and blues records on in long succession through the next hours. And people talked softly leaning into each other in small groups, or reclined arms over shoulders. A couple of people lazily passed a joint, and from the kitchen came giggles and the sound of a wine cork opening.

Then one lifted a partner up, standing up, lifted her facing him, up onto his shoulders, sitting her there on his shoulders, still facing each other, and then higher, he raising his upper arms and shoulders, she raising her arms up toward the ceiling, her waist and belly and then sex pressing against his mouth.

Because they were standing right in the middle of the room, and the rest of everyone was lounging about at floor or cushion level, no one couldn't notice.

She began swaying and m-m-m-mmming and he kept careful balance, but seemed to be concentrating on his tongue and her sexual resonances.

That put a change in the temperature and the breathing rates in the room.

Many people were just relaxed, laughing talking, almost ignoring the intensity of the goings on about them. Others had a variety of sexual encounters. One couple banged so hard in the corner that the stereo across the room began to skip, it's needle zzzipping across the grooves. Some couples retired to other rooms...upstairs.

Overall it was a very good spirited scene. Innocence and Lust embraced for a few hours there. No one was filming. No one was getting paid. This was part of neither the sex industry nor of the oldest profession.

One fellow arrived late. He stood in the doorway eyes wide, mouth open, taking it all in. Some of his friends arose, and gently induced him into the event.

In the early morning hours we concluded we were ready to face the public.

16. In the Labyrinth

In the austere Faculty Office Building, where the Reed Senate was meeting, a history professor rose and blathered about responsibility and collegiate behavior.

Then the Dean of Students, a good man—a kind man—a liberal minded man, but his exhortations toward 'decency' and 'a learning environment' just missed the point.

Our cue was to wait until some Law-and-Orderite spouted some dark ages nonsense about sexuality being out of place in a learning environment like a college, or some reactionary moralistic bunk about the social disorders that stem from promiscuity.

But Dean Dudman was talking about protecting the campus from irate parents by not taking a census of who's sleeping where, and though I thought he was making a fair bit of sense in his speech, apparently others in our group took the cue as they felt it and began disrobing rapidly and then entering the open central area between the broad tables that we Senate 'delegates' were seated around.

Some disrobed protestors began climbing slowly over these tables between the seated, startled, head-shaking delegates. The room erupted in sound and commotion. "Join us!, Join us!" called the Naked Demonstrators, now cavorting, offering hands out to the assembly as they moved slowly, gracefully through the chamber.

Another line of bare supporters snaked through the now-standing, mouth-dropped spectators and entered the central arena as well. I was standing, too, my clothes dropping to my feet. Dancing in a sweet, soft rhythmic swirl, arms, torsos touching we slid next to each other. It was very slow, very slow, as though the dedication and the focus to get into a place like that had to censor out all the rest of the room's reactions and just be in the contact of that touch and that rhythm. It was a long, slow chain of moments…

and then I heard the history professor banging his gavel over and over, saying, "This meeting is adjourned. This meeting is adjourned. This meeting is adjourned!" Until (because although everybody could hear him, nobody was paying him any attention—and nobody was going anywhere) he announced, "Well, I've had enough. I'm leaving." and off he went.

Some of the Naked Demonstrators were leapfrogging and the crowd was clearing a path so as not to be in their way. Others had formed a hand-to-hand chain and were winding their way like a maypole dance through the crowd. I looked out at it all and there, seated in his chair, mouth dropped, legs crossed, utterly astonished, dumbstruck if you will, sat the College President.

I walked over and as clearly and to the point as I could I explained the real standards of life in his on-campus dorms, the injustice being done by application of The Policy by the law-an'-order factions on a prejudicial basis, and how rules anywhere that go against the vast majority's will—or delight—were doomed.

He looked absolutely terrified. I put my hand out to his shoulder. I think that frightened him even more. I started to explain that there were a generation of students that thought nudity wasn't evil itself, that there could be innocence and beauty in the naked form, and we knew it, his own students knew it, and so did the great Greeks whose naked sculpture and naked pottery and naked friezes we were studying.

I was trying to say too much in too little time and he got up and shook his head like an animal winging water off its head, like a big shiver and he turned around, clutching his bag of papers and walked straight out.

A few minutes later we were re-clothed and walking in small groups across the campus pathways toward the coffee shop. The paths were crowded with students hurrying over toward the faculty building. Excited, they must've heard something. "Garrick," calls a friend from a group of passersby, "C'mon over to the faculty building. They're doing it on the floor!"

"Doing what?" I ask.

"Doing it, you know. Balling! Screwing! Having sex!" Already he was turning hurrying on with his friends, "Don't miss this. You, you oughta be there."

Karen and I entered the coffee shop and the catacomb of its booths. I had my usual: yogurt, grilled cheese and a cherry cola.

In the following days, weeks, months, the college's administration was mum on the subject. There was no disciplinary action, no 'honor' case brought against any of us. It was as though it never had happened.

But one thing leads to another and like turns in a labyrinth where you don't quite know for sure where the way may lead, you make choices and follow the path that seems the most promising. In quick succession a dozen or more turns or choices have been made and YOU can never get back to where you were before.

A Reed Forum—a public meeting designed to air issues of community was going to be held on the topic of The War and the Effect of The War on the Campus. It seemed everyone was planning to attend: hawks, doves, the silent majority (as Vice President Agnew had already named it) the unsilent minority (as we peaceniks in counterpoint referred to ourselves), faculty, even trustees. It was a well-publicized debate type format.

Leading the team favoring our involvement in Vietnam—and supporting the Faculty Advisory Board's ban on faculty publicly speaking out against the war—stood the head of the Faculty Advisory Board, a philosophy professor. And against, stood activists including myself.

The hall was packed. People in the back passed out flyers. One gigantic guy wore a Nixon mask and kept waving to the crowd. The right-wingers from the physics department had clipboards with petitions about preserving our 'nuclear shield.'

The philosophy professor got off to a good start. He argued that the people who were staging this military effort were the experts in the field, and that we, we students all of us, in the face of these complicated situations should trust our own leadership in matters as profound and difficult as warfare. The overall cause was the containment of Communism, as true an enemy as we could actually have. We needed to give our support and our well wishes to the boys—our student's peers—who were carrying our flag. Even if the goal was muddied by the strains of politics here at home, we needed to support them with all our strength, because this was a pivotal engagement on the field of history's battle between the opposing Cold War Giants.

My turn.

Although I was well-prepped with the history of Indochina's struggle to be free from colonial domination, and the long list of lies our government had told us, and the corruption of the South Vietnamese government we were supporting, I skipped all that and went directly to the issue at hand.

Reed had been transferring its endowment funds into war profiteering corporations.

"And that is why The Board is denying the right of any educator here to sign any petitions against the war. That is what has happened to your alumni contributions, that is where your payments to the school are funneled: into the jaws of the bloody war machine. Those who profit from the wars—under pretense of patriotism or whatever—are the true villains of history.

"It can't be covered up with fancy phrases about victory over communism or any other smokescreen. The war is a moneymaker and this college has been shifting its endowment funds into it."

I read them a list of investment changes, showing money moved into the likes of Rayethon, Bechtel, nuclear manufacturing, munitions production, the companies that built the military bases, supplied the fuels and so on.

I had caught the opposition off guard.

In the course of the evening the tide never turned.

Whatever opposing speakers said, arguing over the rightness or wrongness of the war, I kept coming back to the issue that the college had been betrayed in all its higher-minded principles by trustees and administrators who had sold our soul to the big secure money of military investment.

Instead of being able to be the free-thinkers that a truly wise society needs, we had institutional interest in seeing this war happen, and in seeing it supported by the home front—that meant the college employees especially—and keeping dissent on campus down to a minimum.

The strategy of exposing compromised morals because of money's grip made sense to the crowd then, and will often make clear the motives that slogans and fancy language try to mask.

This argument about the money is one of the keys to understanding why institutions do what they do.

A decade and a half later we would see this same strategy put into dramatic practice—in the divestment from South Africa's apartheid policy on account of students sitting in at college offices all over the nation demanding that the money that their universities' endowment funds had sunk into South African companies be pulled out, until South Africa divested itself of its abhorrent policies.

No, I didn't organize sit-ins to demand the college pull its money out of the war stocks. All I did was shine a light on a hidden story.

Coming off the podium to hugs and backslaps of support, and despite my own ego inflation from a relatively victorious debate, I couldn't help thinking that there was something missing here, something I wasn't getting quite figured out. A missing piece or pieces, or maybe amid all the hoopla of the debate I wasn't finding the real path out of the maze.

17. Looking for Answers in a Mad, Mad World

I was standing, talking with Karen on the pathway outside the student dorm called Doyle, one of the venerable keystones of the ivy-style college quad. It was bedecked with genuine stone gargoyles, griffins, owls—in fact the Doyle Owl (all hundred and fifty pounds of it) had been lifted from the building earlier in the decade and had ever since been the quest of rival student and alumnae groups to steal/reclaim/capture and then greedily possess it as sort of a monster size secret charm, hidden in basements, closets, and taken out by design and then revealed on campus during the most inappropriate times—during finals, the graduation march, etc.—leaving chaos in its wake as rival on-the-spot alliances tugged and rampaged to obtain the oversized talisman.

Suddenly now, running full-tilt, with the great, wide, old-wood door slamming behind him, comes Memphis Chuck, sort of like a live owl, though an unknown figure to me at the time, speeding as if any moment we would see who's chasing him come flinging the door open in pursuit, and this little guy in a striped prisoner's shirt and a flattened top hat is racing past myself and Karen precisely chucking a plump half lit joint into the place where our hands would bobble it to catch it, and turning his head as he goes calls, "Hold this!" and receeeeding down the sidewalk, hollers, "I'll be riiiight back!"

This wasn't going to be the first time he disappeared without further notice. No one came out the door following him.

Later I came to meet the fellow-who-was-living-in-a-closet, who'd run from the Memphis high schools, who was engaging the best minds of the campus with quick-witted multi-layered symbolic conversation, at any number of inspired soirees or parties. Chuck. Chuck

Yellin. The kid from Memphis. He talked to Admissions and with favorable recommendations from faculty and the passage of an equivalency course at Portland State, he entered the realm of academe.

It didn't last long. On the first morning of classes, lecture number one —in the Humanities course that everyone was required to take—an unfortunate professor is droning on in a slow monotone thumpita thumpita thumpita beat with a low voice, something about dee-tails of com-par-ative an-cient cul-tures and the ti-ny diff-er-ences which we can, yes, to-day, ob-serve in tra-ces left be-hind that some-how in-di-cate the de-tails of ad-vance-ments of cul-tures in these an-cient so-ci-et-ies and on and on and students are scribbling notes in notebooks trying to get every precious word as though their lives depended on it, and Chuck is looking around bewildered by all this seriousness.

None of this is doing Chuck any good, and in an unparalleled fit of intellectual openness, he stands up briefly addressing the whole crowd, "I don't understand why he's telling us all this. It doesn't make any sense to our lives—or my life. And I don't understand why it's so important to all of you, taking so many notes. I must be in the wrong school."

And hefting his textbooks, he walks out of the lecture hall, over to the dean's office and drops out.

He stayed around the scene and we became allies in the adventures that surrounded us.

Mostly we were trying to figure out what made sense in a world gone wrong.

We looked at Bucky Fuller's stuff: the domes, the hepta-flexagons, the trim tab theory (that a very small effort, in just the right place, can move vast objects—or social systems—just as the trim tab, a very small piece of hinged metal, on the rudder of a huge boat, maneuvers the entire vessel.)

We looked at Salvador Dali's paintings: the image of a man, upside down in a swimming pool world of images reflecting moving images: the imagination turned inside out on the real world. Plenty of mindscape here, but no real exits or solutions, only instructions to look into the molecules of the paint.

We looked at psychology, supposedly the science of mind. Most of the college's professors in that discipline offered us glimpses at statistics, oddities, Skinnerian justifications for behavior and how and why it could or should do something or other...but in return they wanted mostly the students' mescaline, the students' acid, the students' mushrooms, and as for real solutions to our time's problems...well, they were pretty busy arguing with themselves about miniature theories.

We looked at R.D. Laing and his psyched-out idea that madness was a kind of healing process that we had to let play through, go the whole route to complete the healing of a fractured soul in order to return to the wholeness of health. He had his own clue that the psychedelics we used gave us a taste of that madness, and brought us back to this realm healthier and more wholly able to go forward. Hmmm, maybe some insight here.

This Caribbean guy, Arthur, shows up on campus with tales of a place in Central America where learned folks like these are going to set up a summer school, and teach the real stuff...the likes of Laing, Franz Fanon, Pete Seeger, some of the Esalen people are going to create a curriculum of Art, Science, Wisdom, Psychedelia, and Social Solutions all rolled into an eight-week summer course.

And with his broad grin and notoriously short buzzed hair, and amazing tales of how this school is being built as we speak, he attracts us and our companions. Several want to leave now and go help build it, but Arti says patiently that what's really needed is students to enroll this summer, to pay the tuition for the courses and several of our friends have the bucks and plan to attend.

And others mull over how to raise the three thousand dollar tuition for the opening semester. Soon, and only because he's moved by the intensity of how attractive and important to them this creative new school is, Arti decides to help them raise the money...through a friend of his in the Naval Air Force, a colonel, who runs bricks of pot in his plane up from Central to North America, landing under cover of his military status. These scholars-to-be get money together in support for this plan: one friend puts up his four-wheel drive Jeep as collateral on a loan to contribute—of course everyone who puts in is going to profit, and the five students most of all because the profit from the turnaround will pay the whole summer's expenses.

Our Caribbean guide helps them rent a truck and they scope out the back area gates of the Portland airport where the truck will drive in and transfer the load from the plane.

The whole plan is set and Arti goes into the Portland Airport by the main front entry to meet up with the colonel who's landing in half an hour, and carrying the whole sixteen thousand dollars—we never see him again, and there isn't going to be anyone at the back gate and the truck and anxious scholars wait there till dawn and dawn dawns on them the idea that the con had gone.

So not all the adventures were pleasant.

After everybody got over losing the money, and some wiser friends commented, "So what, he picked on some rich white kids, sussed out their soft spot, told the tales, and stole the cash. Who's really hurt?"—after that I knew the other hurt was that there really wasn't any school being built where the forefront thinkers of Education and the Philosophy of Life were going to be setting up shop on terms we could relate to...no, t'was but a dream and when it evaporated there we were on the asphalt, still looking around for what made sense.

Next, The Living Theatre's US tour rolled through Oregon. Radical Theater Repertory under the direction of kindly wooly-bearded Saul Gottleib and my hard-working, keen-minded, handsome contemporary Mark Amitin made sure that Reed was one of its Oregon stops. When they'd played their first USA college at Yale, half the drama department—including Tom Walker and Hanon Reznikov—dropped out to follow the magic circus, or at least follow its free-striving ideas to some other creative stage. Tom and Hanon would stay permanently with The Living Theatre touring the world and playing the pantheon of heroes and villains that great playwriting *and* collective creation can give us.

Each college stop opened with a different choice of the four plays and then ran all or some of them in different order, so that at the more conservative Southern Oregon College in Ashland, *Antigone* was the opener of choice—the ancient Greek war's traditional storyline mimicking the United States' involvement in Southeast Asia; and at the venerable University of Chicago, *Frankenstein*, The Living Theatre's version in which the monster of The State imprisons the world; but at Reed, supposedly the radical free-thinking, high-minded colloquium, the opening production would be *Paradise Now*, the grand symphonic piece of the tour, the truly free-form play, guided through the evening by rites and rituals.

While the auditorium was filling up, there's Memphis Chuck already on the stage, throwing his clothes out to the audience. The audience loved it, though some were shocked to see the naked young man astride the platforms. "No, no," he shouted, "I'm not even part of the play. I'm not an actor. This is just me in real life." The audience would not be convinced that this wasn't the opening of the play.

Soon it started. Demonstrators in the back were handing out flyers for some other production. The actors milling through the audience whispering into the ears of the spectators, "I'm not allowed to travel without a passport." Then louder and louder the complaint against national borders filled the high-ceilinged hall, loud in crescendo ending in a scream and then suddenly silent, until the whispers of the next complaint against the empire quietly began.

How different every *Paradise Now* performance was, depending on the reaction of the crowd.

How disappointed I would be by the bland reactions and uncomfortable responses of my fellows at Reed.

I'd rather expected a harmony of solidarity and support but I saw countless interactions of doubt, bewilderment and I wondered: Why so? Because of: (and I could see it right there) the impotence of the locked-in-studies, stuck-in-the-schools students who were just not able to do something instantly in real life to make a dram of change in any part of our confused world.

So how else could the students respond to the exhortations and imploring by the play's cast and theme to do something real to make things in this world better?

Most of them expected a psychedelic entertainment or a radical political drama, and not a call and a challenge *personally* to speak up about what to do and how, and to band together, form cells of social activists, artists, scientists, thinkers, information whizzes, to form clusters not tomorrow or after some graduation ceremony years hence to do something valuable—but to begin tonight!

Well, it was asking a lot and I felt my usual joy at being a part of this peer group of intelligent young people beginning to collapse like a parade float with the air being let out of it, crumpling in on itself.

In the aftermath, Karen dropped out of the college, realizing way ahead of me that what we wanted and needed wasn't going to be found there. She embarked on writing, journaling and chronicling the times, and on a novel of a world that mirrored our own. I doggedly held on in classes unable to commit to any course of study, bouncing from major to major hoping one of them would give me the secret magic key.

Chuck changed his name to Kaushal ("Ko-shawl") and said he was going to Europe. Paul Breslin, an awesome local musician had a gig with his guitar at a rock 'n roll studio in Paris. With his swashbuckler pirate's thick mustache and long wavy black hair, he stood solidly, over six feet tall, his feet spread wide apart wailing on the guitar. Chords melding with chords, fingers blurred in the harmonies, and Kaushal, refusing to commit to a drum set, sitting off to the side on the floor, pounding the most intricate two-handed rhythms on Paul's guitar case. They played and played, and the wooden timber of the big Portland houses shook in symphony.

Europe beckoned them. I said to Kaushal, "If you go, with the rate things are changing around us, we may never see you again. You know how way leads on to way. We are going to lose track and next thing it'll be a dozen years from now and you will have vanished into the ether of the other side of the world."

"No," he says, "Come to Your-ope. Meet us there."

"Yeah, well Europe is a big place."

He says, "OK then. Under the Eiffel Tower. You can't miss that. Under the Eiffel Tower, say…at dawn. You know it'll be beautiful there at dawn. No! Yes!!" (he's starting to get excited now) "At dawn under the Eiffel Tower—on Bastille Day! That way you can't possibly forget it, and neither will I."

That was still months away, and way outside of Reed's schedule, so we planned the date. He said that because there would be such crowds there on Bastille Day morning that he'd have balloons, so we could find him.

Someone brought a bunch of peyote up from the Southwest. I knew it was supposed to taste awful, but I didn't know that the plastic bag it was wrapped it in had caused it to rot, not just go a little rank or bad, but really rotten, so when they opened it and it was sickeningly putrid we ate it anyway, and we got sick…but we didn't get high.

Then another bundle of buttons arrived. It was like a wave of peyote, the all-hallowed cactus of mescaline's father and mother rolled into a button and so many people crowded into the house, so eager, so pushy, we didn't have a plan, a ritual, no we just cooked a thick tea and by the time some sixty people had drunk what should have done for fifteen nobody got off and nobody was any wiser and nobody understood why not.

Kaushal had told us about an 'open' house across town where entry was by password and word was passed among friends to get in. So Karen and I dropped by to visit, and knocking on the wide wooden door, said the password "Let's eat again, real soon!" to the kindly fellow who opened up for us.

And he opened the door wider and welcomed us in. Did we need a place to sleep? Some food perhaps? Or were we there to see the peyote? This was a very different, a very beautiful, a serene vibe. On the basement floor were yoga mats. The big community kitchen was stocked with vibrant vegetables, and whole grains filled big gallon jars, with handwritten labels and names I'd never heard of: Bulghur, Buckwheat, Alfalfa Seeds, Brown Rice, Millet and on and on in shelves along an open-cupboarded pantry. And in a softly lit room, arranged in a gigantic mandala were a thousand fresh peyote buttons arranged with care, as though each button mattered, drying peacefully. Flute music rose from downstairs. That was Gai. She taught the yoga classes, and her friends were carpenters and potters and cooks. It was a beautiful house, not because of its architecture or fanciness, but because of what and who it held inside.

Karen and I went with Gai, and Dana Gottlieb and Peggy Morrison to one of the great beaches of Oregon and with the roll of the surf before us, and the tall, forested cliffs behind us. Karen and I ate a dozen or so buttons. We climbed the steep cliff toward the sunset and watched the grand pattern of mother ocean spread out below like a window in the side of time and we climbed through into the storybook of life and back down onto the beach where with driftlogs we made a fire that lasted till dawn's rosy cheeks blew brightness back into the sky. We made prayers and dances around the blazing logs. We called out the names of the sea in languages of ancient wonder. We nestled in each other arms as the moon shone sparkling arrows of reflected sunlight in radiant streams and if you had a question about life, death or yourself you could see the answers in the patterns of the breeze or the shapes in the foam left by the waves.

Clearly there were answers to be found inside ourselves, but that didn't answer the quest for what to do with our lives in this dis-unified, dysfunctional world. What on earth can we do, or find to do that can make a difference in this mad, mad, world?

PART FOUR

Live Alive

(1969–1970)

In which pioneers of the New World Culture begin actively to seek a direction to follow to guide ourselves out of the maze of the mess that the mainstream has made, and pointers—or clues—to this direction are found in the instincts and desire of people to share together in community experiences.

18. Clues & Keys

Karen and I departed for Europe. Taking a cheap student charter flight, we touched down in London. We saw The Rolling Stones and King Crimson at the colossal open concert in Hyde Park. We saw The Who's spectacular concert at the Royal Albert Hall. We meandered through Chelsea and Chalk Farm. I acquired a small supply of lovely little blue LSD pills. We met a friend, Johan, with a Morris Mini Minor, perhaps the world's smallest automobile, and each of us ate one of those little blue barrels. Then we drove along the edge of Sherwood Forest, climbed among the ruins of Tintern Abbey, and rode in the next morning's eerie dawn mists up the tiny one lane road to the top of Symond's Yat overlooking the counties of Wales spread out beneath us. On the way back down the rocky mount we encountered a huge Rolls Royce limousine coming up as we were driving down and it had royal crests on top of its front grille and we realized it was the Prince of Wales heading up to look over his kingdom since he had just had his investiture and Johan is saying "Let them back up!" and "We're anarchists!" as we laughed hysterically. But then *we* backed up and let them pass. We drove on to the coast of Cornwall and their Garden of the Gods looking out from atop the high cliffs down to the Lilliputian fishing boats on the patterned waves below.

In the next weeks, Karen and I hitchhiked across Scotland with lorry drivers whose brogues were so thick we couldna unnastan a whirrd. Then onto the outer isles, meeting youngsters our own age, among the sheep farms. Some of them had only once been as far away from home as the town thirty miles past the ferry's pier on the other side of the bay. That, at least, gave some perspective as to the riches of experience and choices we'd been handed on an unsupervised platter. And what oh what were we doing with this platter of gifts? Merely touring? To pass some pleasant summer time? Or was there more, perhaps, some signpost pointing somewhere meaningful.

Suddenly it occurred to us that Bastille Day was just two days away and here we were on the beaches of the coast of Scotland, wading across barnacled rocks at low tide to get to this deserted ruin of Castle Tioram, exploring the ancient dungeons, and half-toppled parapets, no one else there, and the tide swooshing back in, and we are over our knees in the rising waters, holding hands and finding the footing to get back to the mainland shore. But the fallen down castle reminded us of the razing of the Bastille and our pledge to meet up with Kaushal in Paris.

We'd already taken the ferry from the outer isles back to the mainland when we'd stumbled on this eye-popping ruin—so now we clambered back to the road, hitched-hiked to the train, changed to another train, then onto the hovercraft, then another train, and we arrived exhausted just before midnight in Paris, the legendary City of Light.

As we walked out into Paris' streets, the clocks struck twelve and all the madness of celebration broke out across the city, horns honking, confetti and garbage tossed from windows and roofs. We ducked inside a pensione and spent the night under the comfort of European down comforters as the city celebrated outside.

In the first cracks of dawn we rousted ourselves and proceeded by foot to the grand esplanade where stands Le Tour Eiffel. Quiet it was. Very quiet. Not a boisterous crowd there at all. Not even a crowd. And not Kaushal. But…there was a fellow with a couple of balloons.

"Bonjour," we spoke to him, "Nous cherchons Kaushal—We are looking for Kaushal."

"Yes, yes," replied Mo, "He is fast asleep after last night's partying, but—since I was still wide awake, he insisted that I come here to find you. Frankly I didn't believe him, but he gave me these balloons, and you must be Karen and Garrick."

So he led us to a modern apartment building at the edge of the city, where Kaushal and Guitar Paul and about twenty other young French people were crashing out in Pasqual's 17th floor apartment. Actually Pasqual's parents' apartment. But they, photojournalists, were out on assignment and he had invited his many friends to his coolest pad to enjoy the summer in the luxury of the modern high rise.

And enjoy it they did: They were eating, or had eaten (by the time we got there) all the food in the house; the young ladies were experimenting voluptuously with Pasqual's mother's make up, and perfumes; the lovers in their various turns were trying out all the couches, spare beds and—in the dark of night—the luxurious carpets; one fellow was trying to fry the bird seed to see if it was edible; and the place was a wreck of linens, clothes being tried on and discarded; and amid this quiet chaos, of which Pasqual was the benevolent giver of what was not really his to give, amid this land of inventive make believe, in a large walk-in closet, soundly slept Kaushal. Paul was sprawled beneath some blankets at the edge of a sumptuous Persian rug. It was both a splendid and a chilling scene.

Later that morning we arose from our own sleep and with Paul and Kaushal both, we set out across Paris, toward breakfast of scrumptious bread and delicious cheese, and toward the American Express office, where USA-ers could, in those days, have mail delivered and picked up.

The streets were bursting with sunshine. The noise of the city on holiday surrounded us and we decided to stroll across the Seine to the Left Bank, but here comes a small crowded car, a little Fiat, filled with young travelers, their gear and their backpacks and it stops at the red traffic light at the curb in front of us. The windows are down in the summer heat, and a couple of voices from inside the car call out to us, "Hey, any of you want to go to Turkey? We're on our way and we have room for one more!"

Kaushal snaps his finger, points at the car, and looking at us says, "That's my ride!"

And he's opening the car door, stuffing himself in, and they're all busy welcoming him, and making introductions. The light changes. The car starts to drive off. Paul stammers, "What about all your stuff?"

"I'll write you at American Express. You can have it shipped." Kaushal's head is now out the window looking back at us. And the car is moving off into the traffic. Gone. Leaving us standing there open-mouthed, wondering what to do next.

Close to the riverbank, Shakespeare and Co.—the old English language bookstore of Paris—rested itself serenely near a small park. There I learned one of life's traveling lessons: Don't try to travel with contraband luminents. Whatever goodie you want will be there on the other side of the border. And here's this mellow dude offering to sell us LSD in that charming park.

So the next day Karen and I went tripping with poor Pasqual to the Paris zoologic park. And days later tripping again with a selection of his houseguests we travelled to the Forest of Fontainebleau. On the dry craggy rocks Paul lullabyed, laced, lambasted, and lassooed us with his guitar as the Apollo opened its hatch and the first of our kind stepped out onto the moon. We sat in meditation, touching down on the moon's dusty surface ourselves, and then in the twilight back to the Left Bank and cold baths.

The 'Cold Bath' apartment was in the heart of Paris' Left Bank nightlife. The son of the French Assembly's President had this second floor digs, and in the spirit of the times, opened it to the travelers 'on the road.' We called up to an open window from the bustling street below, and they threw the key down to us. Spacious and bright and lined with sleeping pads, couches, blankets tucked in corners. The sparse bathroom housed a large square tub (with—of course!—only cold water) and the place rang with multi-language storytelling. There wasn't much quiet there, and the constant entry of newcomers with their adventures to tell made sleeping difficult.

Back at Pasqual's we scrubbed the kitchen and did the laundry. Some of the 'guests' got the idea and helped but it wasn't enough in the face of the tornado all his friends were making.

Karen and I heard of a squatter's building. You entered the locked up place after dark only through the side alley. Then up the five flights of stairs to the top floor. That's the only safe floor. All the others are fallen through, planks missing, boards loose and out…but up at the top, there were places to sleep. And sure enough it was just like that. Scrambling up the creaking old stairs in the darkness, I knew Karen and I were out of time with the ordinary world. Collapsed railings and old carved wooden moldings showed in the matchlight that we used to see. This was not corporate America. This felt like a portal into a place of far-be-gone legends and myths.

And at the top of the stairs, people were really sleeping. By the time one found oneself there, sleep must have been what you wanted, else why climb the spooky stairs?

In the morning we were up and gone. That was enough.

Pasqual's liberal, actually radical, parents returned and had a fit. They threw everybody out and stood there amazed at the whirlwind of experimental young culture that had destroyed their house. Pasqual was lamely trying to describe its benefits and beauties. They were furious.

At the Rock 'n Roll Circus disco bar, air conditioned vents poured cool air onto the slick wood dance floor. Tiny lights in the floorboards twinkled in rhythm to the music. Older businessmen brought their trophy wives or trollops to dance and drink and party. In an effort to bring live wild youngsters and their vibrant vibrating vibes, wild hair and colorful clothes, and to mix us in with the straighter crowd that could afford the steep admission and expensive drinks, the club gave nightly passes to the dancers from the musical *Hair*, another stage production about the blossoming flower culture (now opened in a Paris in a French-language version) so they could come whatever nights they wanted and bring their friends. Friends of a couple of the dancers we were, and so we went.

In a booth at the edge of the club's dance floor, the Baron de Lima introduced himself. His old hands wore many rings. His sharp craggy features were topped with a dapper broad brimmed hat. He had as an entourage a crowd of young artists that he was apparently befriending.

The old Baron claimed to have a castle, "Not far from heeer." and offered to give us lodging for the night. "Do you think that weell be okay?" he half asks of his friends, for their approval in judging us.

"Yes, mais oui, of course!" they reply. And in the wee hours we are scurrying through the winding streets, down toward the river.

"My chateau," he is explaining, in an experienced storyteller's tone, as though he has said this many times, "My chateau, it is ve-ry old. Older than much of the city that surrounds it. Slowly over the past centuries the city has built itself up, and now my castle can scarcely be seen. Each wall, each tower is aside much more modern buildings, but it is there, hiding…hidden."

And in moments we are entering the gate, set into big, old stones, rising upward and to both sides, snudged up next to warehouse buildings that obscure all but the gate area and portal door.

Inside the rooms are small but elegant. He said it was a castle, not a palace. We sit in a small parlor. There are Victorian era books and statues. Balloons made of animal bladders dot the carpet and we chatter with the 'beautiful people' while the Baron enters carrying a bottle of wine with a hand-inked label dated 1899. The wine is still good, and the Baron says, again addressing his group with a question, although the answer was already foretold, "We should give our young guests, the tower suite, oui?" And they all assent, so after more chatter and goodnights, Karen and I are led up a circling staircase all built of stone blocks, up, up to a large wooden door at the top of the stairs, which the Baron unlocks with a large skeleton key and gestures us inside. There a quilt-covered brass bed occupies most of the circular stone room. Intricate stained glass windows are fortified inside with a lattice of metal work.

"It is not every night that one gets to spend in the Baron's tower, so please, please," he emphasizes, "enjoy yourselves." The door closes, the key turns, and the footsteps return downstairs. There are candles, there are chamber pots. The bed is beautifully made. There isn't any way out.

We make love long into the night. It is an erotic haven.

We do wonder whether we have made an awful mistake, but in the morning the Baron's key turns in the keyhole and he appears on the steps below us, with a handsome olive skinned young man at his side, both dressed in the briefest of underwear. "Ah, good morning, good morning. I trust you have slept well. It is time now to get up and I am taking you all to breakfast. Venez, venez! We shall meet you downstairs soon, yes?" He beams.

"Yes, soon," we say, and he leaves the door swung open above the spiral stairs.

Breakfast is a delight as well, but I think we have exhausted the Paris experience.

The Living Theatre was in Morocco beginning rehearsals for the next piece. We decided to go there.

19. To the End of the World

In the coastal town of Essaouira, Morocco we found a room in the old covered sector of the walled city, the true casbah, with its winding streets so close together that the second or third stories of the houses simply were built bridging over the streets below, creating a network of enclosed winding passageways. An old Jewish house-finder made us a deal with the Moroccan washerwoman whose worldly wealth consisted of the upstairs rooms he rented out for her. The balcony looked out over an open courtyard and birds sang and nested in its eaves.

Outside the walled city, the French sector extended along the white sand beach to the far fortress that once guarded this port when it was in the hands of the Portuguese and known then as Mogador. The French still vacation in its coastal pleasures, and Le Living (as the French called the theatre company) set up in a series of whitewashed houses along the beach.

Each day the company would meet in a large tile-floored room for afternoon discourse about the 'next' production. Already I could see the toll the US tour had taken. The unity that came before, of storming the heaven of America with new ideas, had been met with such divergent responses: the spiritual wanted spiritual answers; the angry wanted violent answers; the stoned wanted drugs for everyone; the organic mechanics wanted the end of industrial warfare on the planet and a synthesis of new earthlovin' values; the new breed of commies wanted a new version of Maoism and nobody could agree. These divergent attitudes had sunk into the theatre members' own philosophies, or perhaps opened themselves up to them, revealing in each what had been deeply ingrained already and bringing it to the surface.

So there we were each day in these group conferences—the beginnings of collective creation of the theatre's pieces, going nowhere, going round in circles, the same volatile different arguments being heard and re-heard.

Carl Einhorn is talking about at least being connected to the armed love movements, the third world struggles in our plays, even if we're the gentlest end of that spectrum. Jimmy Anderson is mapping out strategies for bringing the hippie-style co-ops to the inner cities through our street theatre. Nona Howard is talking about arts for children, plays where parents bring children to make artwork; Rufus Collins wants to go to India, give ourselves a chance to learn something instead of thinking we know it all and *we're* supposed to be teaching it. Jenny Hecht talks about Self knowing Self through sign language and touch more than spoken words; Gene Gordon is preparing for a much more repressive State and a world ridden with plagues; Steve Ben Israel is talking about a Mandala City, a play that begins the process of building a beautiful living city-of-the-future. Henry Howard listens, shaking his head. He says what we need is a Play. Julian and Judith listen, taking notes.

Mousa, a friend we met in the casbah, brought us a bag, a huge shopping bag full of cut pot leaves. He said it was the stuff they threw away. That they used only the tops of the plants for making the kief to smoke. Well, we thought this was a fabulous gift. Good pungent leaf. He brought us kief too, in folded up in packets of Moroccan newspaper. It was gold-colored chopped up buds, mixed with a thick chopped up black tobacco, and the tobacco made our gums tingle as we got high. I still yearn for that rich sweet spicy taste.

With the leaf, he taught us to make majoun, the pot butter candy that we ate way too much of. It made our whole bodies tingle. First the pot leaves were simmered in butter; then strained while still hot and the remainder squeezed through a fine cloth. Into that oily residue we stirred carob and ground up nuts, dates and figs from the market. It was sweet and gooey and we ate it by the fingerful. When you'd had enough you could tell because

Figure 20. Morocco, 1969. The author at the Living Theatre's collective creation discussions, high on majoun, in the big whitewashed rehearsal room. (Photographer unknown: Collection of the author, 1969)

the tingles started and as they came on stronger, you'd feel released from the floor, from the ordinary aspects of touch, so that you'd feel you were floating, up, up off the floor and free, weightless, high. This was a wonderful place to spend the summer, but always, slowly though, we came gently down, back into rational thoughts, and our solid bodies.

There was so much pot growing then in Morocco that illegalizing it was impossible, but the black tobacco, that was another story. The government had made possession or growing the pungent tobacco highly illegal instead, and that was how they hoped to steer their young people away from the 'backward' notions of their ancestors and into the modern world. The traditional dress was also frowned upon. Men were suddenly supposed to wear slacks or blue jeans, and women conservative European style long dresses and blouses, instead of the traditional robes. We went to the souk market and bought Jalabas—the long flowing robes with the hoods to keep out the sandy wind.

Mousa brought us to the club where he and his friends hung out and listened to Western rock and roll. We had brought a 'rare' prize with us: the double disc vinyl set of The Who's *Tommy*, in the spectacular fold-out album cover. Into the evening Karen and I hung with these young Arabic people, listening to the glistening guitar chords and smoking the kief from long stemmed hookahs nailed to the floor, while they pored in wonder over the Western technology that could produce such surreal album cover art. Little did we know that Karen was the first woman in that club space since it was built, probably hundreds of years ago. Everyone knew times and the order of things were changing though no one was sure just where it was going to go.

Each morning we walked to a tiny shop where a dairyman had prepared tiny cups of yogurt, which we ate with tiny spoons in the shade outside his blue wooden gates. Perhaps he made thirty cups a day, and when these were sold, he closed shop, latched the blue doors and went home. We shopped in the local souks for fresh fruits, and our washerwoman landlady laughed and laughed at our attempts to do the hand laundry. She had an array of buckets and grabbed our clothing bags away from us, flashing her broad grin, she went about the job on the courtyard tiles one big bucket next to the other in a semi-circle around her, and her arms like propellers guiding the soiled clothes of our adventures from one tub to the next, then rung out, all in a series of balanced fast-paced motions like a strong adept ballet dancer, ending with the pinned garments drying in the sun on lines that crisscrossed the open, sun-filled courtyard. And with us as wide-eyed audience, she smiled her broad grin again, saying in Arabic: Now, that's the way you do it!

One day meandering along the corridors of the covered city, we saw a somewhat familiar face. Ronnie (R.D.) Laing, our admired British author and psychedelic pioneer stood looking rather blankly into the door of one of Essouira's banks. We introduced ourselves as having read several of his books, and offered to be of whatever help we could.

Simply he was trying to receive a money wire, and speaking no French—and no Arabic—was having a difficult time of it. Another bank had referred him here, and as this was a simple office in a remote town to begin with, it hardly looked like a bank at all anyway, so he was staring trying to figure out if this was indeed the right place. We aided and abetted his efforts with our French and shortly he had received his cash and was on his way with us back to the Theatre's domains and dinner at Julian and Judith's apartment.

Among the company were several excellent chefs, including one runaway from the hothouse of four-star professional French cuisine, who had joined with the company and found his talents appreciated by the mostly vegetarian entourage. So Adrien cooked exotic northern Sahara vegetables for us and Ronnie regaled us with stories of his tour of the world.

What with things heating up politically in Great Britain for him, he had decided to take a sabbatical around the world, heading eastward across Europe, then Turkey, India, and Japan. From thence across the Pacific to Mexico and onward, eastward to Morocco, stopping in each place to meet with other scientists, doctors, therapists and social visionaries to discuss the art of recovery from madness and the use of these new psychedelic tools. We heard stories from the madhouses of Japan and the monasteries of India, the Mayan temples of Mexico and on and on, around the world. He and his little bottle—ah the little bottle—of acid, traveling together, sharing the elixir of enlightenment with the wise and weary alike.

But who had he come to see here in Morocco? Julian asked him.

"No one." He said it was his last stop before heading home and he thought he would just free-form explore before heading back to the rigors of professional life in the British Isles. Besides, here he was with us, so this must be his appointed connection on the Moroccan shore.

He had a brilliant speaking manner, captivating with storyteller's twists, uplifting with the lessons learned—and then clearly communicated, and frightening for moments as he rose from the dinner table explaining how every intellectual likes to talk about madness but push it just a little over the edge and everyone recoils, as he starts getting a bit more incoherent as though a trance was a'comin' over him and his voice changing, he staggers a few steps, bumps into whatever's there, gurgles a bit, spits out a few grams of food and wild eyed now accuses of...of...there, there, he's calming down now and resuming his seat, says (perfectly politely) "See what I mean?"

And besides all that, his little bottle is now empty. So it must be time to go home. In fact he was attempting to get the money for his last tickets when we ran into him...his final travel and flight back to London. "But here," he hands us the empty brown glass vial," it may look empty, but you know the LSD crystals stick to the sides of the vial, so fill it with a bit of water, or gin, and enjoy yourselves." He hands the bottle toward the center of the table, and with my parents looking quite content not to take it, Rod and Mary Mary—longtime Le Living members –apprehend the bottle.

Later, downstairs in one of the Theatre's kitchens, the vial is filled with water and shaken hard. Karen and I are too tired from a long day to want to stay up all night, but several are eager and try a big drop onto a sugarcube. A few wander off to their own abodes and Adrien, our chef, reports that the walls are waving in and out with each breath he takes, and soon he's pretty incoherent, lying down on a cot talking babytalk. Now he's using mostly sign language, and we, his friends are sign languaging him back to come walk out of this food smelly kitchen and under the starry sky, so soon we are strolling along the roadway above the beach all exhilarated in the cool night breezes.

A couple of days later Karen and I take a very measured dose out of the bottle and walk to the beach where, in the broad sweet daylight I find my thoughts coming faster than I can say them or even think them at once...and the waves of light in the reflections from the ocean waves are startlingly real. The sand my bare foot moves is falling in precise geogravitational patterns, each boulder of crystaline sand resting against the next, all its tiny weight held in perfect place as though this were the moment written in the sands of time, and then another shift of the foot and a new pouring of sand grains stack up in another perfectly balanced array of crystal silica.

The Perfection of the Universe seems Overwhelming. We sit to meditate, but we end half sprawled gazing oceanwards, hardly able to keep memory or anticipation from invading the meditative space. People walking along the beach leave trails: the several recollected images of their movement like streamers behind them... or is it the anticipated movements of where they're going as well?

We stand and walk slowly down the long beach to the abandoned, tilted fortress past where the sands curve toward the point. Rocks lead to it at low tide, and they are barnacle or anemone covered so it's hard to walk out among them through the pools and exposed rocks. But we scramble up onto a low corner of the old fort, and then no further. This is enough. The panoramas of imagined history: ships of war, centuries of maintenance of this place, flags, anchors, chains, now all old—tilted unevenly, away from the sea, urchin encrusted, the hulk of maritime conquests and human subjugation from ages ago, here lost slogging in the tides, a relic. We scramble back to the shore, and much more composed wander back along the shore and sit, finally watching the sun touch down its orange globe on the cusp of the sea and then set below it, the blue darkening sky with hints of green, the glow from the sea, and out come the first stars twinkling behind us and overhead.

Most of the rest of the night we huddled together back on the rooftop, watching the Perseids meteor show burst bolides and meteors in brilliantly colored firetrails across the deep night sky.

A few days later we set out with Julian, Judith and my sister Isha, along with many company members on a jaunt past Telouet toward the Sahara's edge.

Telouet was a mystery. A true labyrinth. A house in the side of the hill, with rooms dug in such vast array and depth and winding chambers beneath the earth that people still got lost and never came out, or so they said. We could, with the aid of a guide, wander some of the courtyards, with their moorish interlocking patterned carvings, even the rooms on the surface were a maze, doorways into doorways of similar carving, turning at angles, and back around again. The fellow who gave the tour was himself born a slave, since although Morocco had 'outlawed' slavery in the 1920s, it was not until its independence in the 1950s that slavery truly came to an end. He remembers a different time, before he was a tourguide, when he was a slave here.

Julian asks if the rooms are still being dug. "Oh no, not officially. This is a public monument now, and we are not authorized to make changes to the architecture. But," he adds," there is often work going on here that we do not know about."

Isha takes ill as we travel through the heat and refuses her food. We know we have to find something she can keep down. At an unnamed village we stop and find the local version of Atlas Mountain bananas, which we mash up and she nibbles at last from the edge of a spoon or a finger.

On we travel over the Atlas Mountains, past all the agricultural preserves, toward a high mountain souk. Here is the market in all its original meaning.

Donkeys bray among the camels parked on one side of the series of tents. Aisles of tables covered with blankets, and blankets spread out on the ground. The smells of foods, fruits, birds cawed, children ran about. We were a spectacle in our automobiles. Children ran after us. We were Westerners, foreigners, Europeans, we must be rich. They begged, they hawked wares at us mercilessly. Surely we would be the ones to throw fistfuls of currency, there would be plenty for everyone.

It was awkward walking through the remote souk. These people didn't speak any French. There was no way to say: We are artists. We are not rich tourists. Karen and I were surrounded by hawkers when Adrien comes and finds us, "C'mon." he says, "Steve's figured it out." And Steve Ben, another of the great Living Theatre mainstays, *had* figured it out. At the side of an old wall, partly in the shade, sat a group of old men. They were playing ouds and reed flute instruments. Some had tambours and tambourine like instruments. Steve was there clack clacking with his tongue in time and rhythm to their melodies. A couple of the other actors and actresses had joined in. A few had odd instruments in the cars and went to get them. I was drumming on my sketch pad, sitting way in the background. Karen chimed with her bell. We all played for a long long time. The caravaner merchants from the souk stopped by to listen. Children watched, respectful. Oh, these people are artists, musicians, trance makers maybe, from their own country.

As evening cooled the rocks and sand we strolled through the market again. We were shown fine loomed fabrics, unusual sweet dried desert fruits, toys, hats. We bought some yarns, some silverwork.

These souks are temporary. A few times a year the tribespeople come together in such or other place to trade goods and stories, to let each others' children meet, and to let the old old men play music in the shade.

Our own caravan moved on.

In these outreaches of North Africa the great desert is mostly rock. Hard packed ground and no water. Farther away are the sand dunes, the picture book desert of endless hills of sand shifting in the hot winds. Fingers of these dunes reach toward the mountains. And there is our destination. The end of the world. The end of the habitable world, anyway.

Sitting on rock ledges, with rock and hardpack stretching far and away from us, Karen and I might as well be at the edge of some impassable wall. You can only walk out there as far as you have water to carry. There aren't any roads. And off in the distance are the fingers of the dunes, an even farther no person's land...where legends live, perhaps, but people don't.

Behind us in increasing intensity reaches all of civilization. There wasn't anyplace else to go, and there hadn't been much in the way of answers to my questions on the way here. Glimpses of good ideas, notions, a few insights of wisdom maybe, but no trumpet blast from anywhere or anyone signaling Big Truth about how to live in a society at war with itself, poisoning itself, quashing itself, and only these faraway dunes, a hint maybe of what the world could all come to with enough ecologic degradation, with misuse of water, misplacement of chemicals...gasses...waste.

If people just worked all together for each other, above and beyond the divisions we are chained to, even these rocky valleys could have water in them again.

I pictured the broad view below me slowly greening up, and perhaps it was the sun's lower angle now, but I could see that there were two valleys, two rocky valleys running downhill, joining becoming one valley and I could see them now running with a little water, then more, then lush torrents cascading together, and the valley's ochre brown cast overlaid with plants, soil, cool breezes, fruit trees. Farther where the rocky-bottomed mountains spread out into rocky plains, there could be fields of grain, orchards, out as far as the dunes, green and greenery, even growing up over the dunes, turning them to grassy hills. White puffy clouds saunter across the blue sky and occasional dark rain clouds dispense precious water drops over the hillsides.

There at the edge of the lowlands, right where the rivers meet a band of people are walking along, a few grownups talking with a group of youngsters, explaining to them how this wasn't always a lush fertile valley, and even though I picture them tiny, very far away, small figures I'm just barely able to see in the distance, I can hear their voices,

"These hills were once just barren rocks,"

"And these streams, only sandbottomed for *centuries*."

"And these fields," he takes his hands and places the palms together in front of him, spreads them apart slowly, emphasizing the whole area he's looking at, "were just endless hot sands and stone."

"And you," (I'm not sure if he's talking to the children walking alongside him—or to me), "It's up to you to find the others who will make it green like you see it now."

I take my own palms and press them together, then spread them out, my arms widening slowly, but below and before me there is only desert as far as an eye can see. Are these visions merely pleasures of my imagination or are they clues & signposts that I will need to find my way?

It's time to go. Evening comes swiftly in the mountains. Karen gets up from our meditative perch, and I follow.

In the following weeks we drift back through Casablanca toward Europe, then to America and driving across from New York to the West Coast, going back to Portland but still not sure where we were really heading.

20. Familiar Musing

"When You Awake" by The Band was playing and everyone I know is trying to figure out what the lyrics mean. We were trying to get The Real Clues from the most prominent spokespeople of our generation: the bands, waiting apprehensively for the next album by The Beatles, The Band, Dylan, The Stones, The Airplane, over and again listening to each line trying to get the message. But these songs didn't have any more answers than we did...or maybe there really were clues in the verses we were all listening to.

Kenn Kushner comes out again to visit from Northern New Jersey. All this exciting talk of the demonstrations and the intellectual peer group of activist artists has stirred his brain, and he comes to visit us. It doesn't take long before he tells us what he thinks of the droning monotonous lectures about dead European cultures with their microscopically examined 'periods' of sculpture and architecture. He says art is doing everything beautifully as his long straight light brown hair dances in the breeze.

He uses watercolor paper, heavy paper to draw on with Rapidographs, draughtsmen's pens that produced fine or broad even-width lines. Shapes appear on the paper that form the background for other shapes, and images get inscribed within images. I look over his shoulder as the creative process slithers out of his pen and forms permanent indelible characters on the page. Bubbles lend dimension and distance and world after world float out of those thin stream lines and emerge, two dimensional but real enough. He says I should learn to draw. "At least take some classes. You <u>are</u> in school aren't you?"

But drawing like that seems more like magic than something you could just learn.

Figure 21. Mandala. (Kenn Kushner: 1969)

He's designing a wooden table with Rorschach-like sides that show the matching grain of the wood against its opposite, making a symmetrical tabletop—and the fine furniture store downtown says they'll buy them. Still, he's on a low budget and needs to get the materials. He comes back to our place one night handing me a package, "Here I bought these for you," he says.

I open the bag and find a set of Rapidographs.

"You're going to have to get your own paper."

I was still struggling to make sense of a college education in the midst of all these esoteric, artistic and perspective-changing experiences.

There was another big on-campus demonstration—one in a string of causes: anti-war, anti-draft, Black students' history classes, endowment investments, marijuana prohibitions. And afterwards I found myself in a cluster of activists all urging each other on, to go and sit in *on*, and 'capture' the campus' nuclear reactor. "That'll get their attention!" said one voice. "Yes, let's take the reactor!" said another. And eyes turned to me, activist that I am, for support or encouragement. In that moment I knew that none of what was happening on campus was going in the direction I wanted to go, not the classes, not the protests; none of it. I waved the group aside saying that taking the nuclear reactor wasn't going to do anyone any good. And I headed over to Eliot Hall, the administration's main building, to drop out.

After I left Reed College I was suddenly able to immerse myself in a cavalcade of events, which were ripe for happening in the Portland scene. I felt I had stepped outside and the weather was changing in rapid succession like a blowing wind, then high storm clouds, then thunder, then lightning, then rain, then mists rising softly, then a flock of geese, and sunlight streaming under the evening canopy, brilliant golden light flooding everything.

My friend Dana Gottlieb, moves off campus to a room by the railroad tracks where the boxcar rumble and the coupling of trains in the night is an ever present reminder of the goods and transport of the world. Ruggedly handsome and robust with a grin that makes everyone around him smile too, he is living on a straw mat, with his clothes all in his backpack hung on the wall. A few candles in brass holders and the classic texts of Taoist philosophy sit austerely on a small table. He is cutting out all the extra stuff and living, he says, "simply." He starts eating 'organic' foods, foods without pesticide residue on them. He puts a calligraphed version of Gary Snyder's poem, *Smokey the Bear Sutra* on his wall and reads it aloud to whosoever will listen.

Doug and Charley and Mark and Gunga-dar, also 'members' of that Bush Street house and community play rapid-chorded music on western *and* Indian instruments in the big open livingroom/kitchen. Later they would depart to apprentice with Ali Akbar Kahn at his College of Music in California. Paul and Kaushal, both now back from their European adventures, join them with Paul on guitar and Kaushal—as always—drumming on Paul's guitar case.

Kevin and Alice move out to Bridal Veil, to a cabin at this old pioneer town just above this phenomenal waterfall. It's upriver from Multnomah Falls, the towering tourist attraction falls on the Columbia River, but Bridal Veil is the quieter sister falls, though awesome in its splendor, it is the hidden place, the one suited for refuge and meditation.

Jonas and Jerianna are living upstairs in the big bedroom of the Beanbat house. They are fed up and bored with higher education's offerings. They want to start a theatre troupe. They want to teach live participatory theatre to audiences in the streets. They want to do plays that will change the way people see and feel about the world.

I'm from a theatre family. I see the merit in what they want to do, but I don't want to go back to do that. I want to go forward to something new, but I haven't the faintest idea what.

Laurie is living in the other upstairs bedroom. She is more sophisticated by far than I am about the ways of the world and love and politics. She adds a measured sense of reasonableness to our ensemble.

We brought the Be-In idea to life in Portland. We printed banana day-glo flyers that invited people to make peace and just "Be" together. We handed them out at Portland State, and Lewis and Clark College, among the boutiques of Goose Hollow, and at a dozen high schools in the Portland area. People came from all over the city. We met at Washington Park, overlooking the city's Rose Garden. We brought mountains of popcorn. People spread out quilted blankets, shared food, played acoustic guitars, and tourists came to gawk and ask if Jerry Rubin or Abbie Hoffman— the most prominent characters of the freek freely movements— would be there to talk, or show off or whatever. We told 'em those guys had been here earlier and had left already, or we pointed over into another part of the crowd and said, yeah, they're here, look over by those folk, I think they went thata way. But it was apparent to me how much people depended on personalities for leadership, even in the most freeform of movements.

The second Be-In happened a month later at Mt. Tabor Park on the side of a dormant cinder volcano cone, but still within the city limits. It was an eerie gray day and fewer people came than before. I ate mushroom powder and swayed in the breezes like a living statue riveted at the feet to the lawns of the park, the somber weather keeping me earthbound.

We had in our hands one of the keys to unraveling the problems of our time, our people, our species: making beautiful sharing experiences happen. But how do we bring the people together to share what already seemed so clear? How?

We were all making beautiful everyday objects all the time, as part of a creative lifestyle: candles (of course) but also clothes, weavings, cushions, drawings, watercolors, paintings and frames, wooden toys, boxes, beadwork, and jewelry—so we decide to open a small crafts and consignment store in Gladstone just outside the city limits. We rented from a kindly cookie salesman who was pleased to see some of the counter culture trying to get a foot into the commercial world. We named the store: Familiar Musing.

Sometimes we spelled it: 'Famili are Mu*sing.' It meant thinking in a familiar way. It meant our family was singing like the Zen mystery word: Mu! It meant pondering on some thought one had thought about before, perhaps with amusement or delight, and then one finds oneself thinking about the same again, and remembering the delightful chain of thoughts that had led one here before, to this same puzzle, or same poetic insight, or same remembrance, perhaps that all thoughts are part of the most wondrous process, the process of consciousness, spinning itself and ourselves with it, through the ages, even from the bodies of one generation to the next, like the waterfalls, or tides. Hmmmm.

How often do our own daydreams spiral in on this kind of thinking? Rounding some un-addressed corner within our brains, light shimmers forth from the Royal Spirit sitting at the core of each of us, the light shines, beaming on us and we can see that we have been here before, many times, and what is there to do but to give proper respect and praise to the Originator of Thought, the endless chain of light and imagination that our bodies surround with their casing of bone and muscle. A familiar musing, ay?

We set up a stained-glass workshop in our basement and put lamps and window mandalas in the store. Friends contribute home sewn clothes, gowns, hats, pouches, bags. We carry pottery and some old-fashioned home-sewn dolls. All our friends want to give us bongs, elaborate water pipes, and roach clips to sell. Reluctantly we carry those too. We stash them in a corner. The front window shows the lamps and the dresses. The whole place is done up in neo-ethnic-space-angel motif…meaning we just decorated it with all sorts of stuff…not a single stylistic theme in sight.

We were gently flamboyant.

There was an endless small stream of people, who came on in, and we talked, chatted and met the neighbors. There were a few sales. Sometimes to gift hunters looking for something crafted. Sometimes to neighbors who wanted to see the little store succeed. Sometimes to friends, or friends of friends.

Then there were the people from the halfway house just a block away. We had opened up on the route between that facility and the corner store where the residents of the house could go on occasion to buy cigarettes or a newspaper. These were probationary walks where they (the half-released inmates) could take a timed but unsupervised stroll to the store and back. Slowly they began to saunter in, check us out. Even more slowly we heard their stories. Usually they just came in for a minute, browsed and left. But slowly the whole picture came clear. They were already out from jail, were working some kind of supervised jobs, lived dormitory style, and were supposed to be getting re-acquainted with the normal world.

There were among them some convicted robbers, some in for fraud, a few for crimes of violence, but for the first time I met people who had been imprisoned for dodging the war. These people were already on their way out of prison. They'd already served their time. The war'd been slogging on so long that men who'd dodged the draft, and had somehow got caught, been convicted, sentenced, and done their time were now in a halfway house in a mellow outskirts-of-Portland neighborhood.

And still the war ate new souls.

We met Davison from the halfway house. He'd served a little over two years in an Oregon prison. He'd been driving from California toward Washington State and he'd picked up a hitchhiker. They were having a good time driving, listening to his car radio, so he offered to scrape a pipeful of pot together from this baggie of seeds and stems...which his companion politely declined...and then at the end of his hitched ride into southern Oregon, the hitchhiker reports Davison and his car description to the state police who bust him and he ends up serving two plus years, "For sticks and stems!" he fumes.

It's hard to believe: here we are smokin' up a storm in private, or in the parks, or outside the movies, or at the ski lodge, or in bed, or on the beach, for the past two plus years. And here's Davison just getting out now. Just still finishing that ride north to Washington.

But it was through these guys that we made connections that would later serve to connect the underground railroad that spirited people out of harm's way, people sought by the war machine: AWOLS, dodgers, resistors, wanted protestors—all up to Canada through a series of safe houses, good rides, protected identity and safe passage out of this 'Land of the Free' and into another country.

In the quiet of Familiar Musing's neighborhood we made friends with these semi-prisoners, then friends with their administrators and then, in an amazing stroke of good timing and good fortune the inmates made arrangements to have a halfway house/craftspeoples softball game in a nearby park during one of their days-off outings. We choose up sides, with mixed teams from both groups. The administrators watched bemused, pleased even, though there were worries about what might be in the sandwiches we brought. But everyone played OK softball so I guess they figured the food wasn't laced. Altogether it was a really nice scene. And of all the bumbles and jumbles that the Sixties mosaic was made of, this was a clear picture of the magic at play.

21. Renaissance Faire

In the *Willamette Bridge*—the nearest thing Portland had to a community newspaper—a weekly that was trying to be an arts and culture magazine, a political voice and psychedelic beacon all rolled into one—there appeared a notice about a Renaissance Faire going to be held outside Eugene, Oregon about a hundred miles to our south. Little did we know this was going to be the first of an unbroken chain of events, Renaissance Faires, lasting on into the next century.

A few years later the Eugene Renaissance Faire got sued over its name by some other organization and lost, and changed its name to the name still used today: The Oregon Country Faire. The events occur on a yearly basis, though in the beginning there were two each year and the first one was in the fall of 1969....

In Portland we readied our crafts, our tents for camping, and blankets to spread on the ground for display. There was a buzz in the air—not just a feeling of anticipation but an actual buzz of people talking to each other about the upcoming faire and getting ready.

We put a poem in the *Willamette Bridge* about it. Well, the poem wasn't specifically about the Renaissance Faire. No, it was more a poem 'for' the faire. But it ran intriguingly in the paper inside a box with a contact phone number and the simple statement, "Come to the Renaissance Faire."

> Mirror, mirror on the bear,
> You've got hippies in your hair,
> π eye sky to the sunset x,
> Sleep on the ship with the wobbly decks.
> Here's what ourglass sailors say about sailboats...
> The universe rings an empty bell.

Kenny's girlfriend Carol, smiling, wise, and with a well of good nature had just arrived now from the East Coast. We sit up one endless night eating purple double dome acids and watching the *endless* patterns our eyes and the walls and the stars all make. I read out loud from Margaret Wise Brown's children's book, *The Color Kittens*. Karen and Carol design tiny lanterns. Kenny draws.

A few days later they accompany Karen and me on the drive from the big city to the first Oregon Renaissance Faire which was nestled in the meadow and woodlands just to the west of the southern end of the Willamette Valley. We drove down the long highway skirting the river's edge from Portland where the Willamette deltas itself into the great Columbia, south through the fertile expanse of rich topsoil now in warm September lushness of fruits and grains, south following the distant two ridges of thickly forested Douglas fir, the two long ridge tops running north/south: to our right the Coast Range; and to our left the foothills of the high Cascades along whose length there would periodically arise a snow-topped wonder of a mountain.

We had packed our camping gear and an odd assortment of crafted goodies: candles, woven belts, scarves, dipped candles, wood sculptures and carvings, sand candles, molded candles, poured candles. Candles were simple to make...and seemed so appropriate as a symbol for the moment.

Robin and Ron Ulrich had secured the property for the event and Bill and Cindy Wooten, owners of The Odyssey coffee shop, had publicized the Faire throughout their community network of friends and family. Everybody in the Eugene community knew Bill and Cindy and so the word had spread.

We wound our way up to Hawkin's Heights off West 18th Street at the far end of town where the streets of Eugene seem to meander into the forest that surrounds it.

Parking was on either side of a graveled road and through a natural break in a hedge led a pathway into The Faire. We found a couple of people with clip boards, paid a tiny 'booth' fee and were directed to set up anywhere on the downhill side of the field along the one circular pathway that ran around the whole meadow. Scattered runs of trees and islands of brush separated different areas from one another and all along the perimeter of the circle people were pitching tents and shelters. Alongside the pathway itself folks were lining up tables and blankets and setting out wares for sale.

A few people were dressed up in medieval style and other courtly attire, but most of us were there in our flagrant multi-colored bellbottoms, broad sleeved shirts, long homemade dresses, India print cotton headbands, bells, beads, bangles, fringes, cloaks, scarves, swashbuckles, braids, feathers, sandals, and patchwork. A gorgeous sunset filled the sky and from each of the small campfires came flutes and laughter, songs and sweet notes of folk guitar. It was a very pretty sight.

We set our own camp, and strolled along past the pottery, weavings, children's toys, clothing displays already set up—some so exquisite, some even more beginner's work than our own. And then settled in for sweet night's sleep in the deep forest of our own kind.

The daylight awakened us, and we spread out our wares. The selling part was at best only a modest success. I don't think we took into account quite how many of these people, these people out here in the country, were already making their own candles. As the afternoon rolled on, I took a go-round of the full pathway of the faire...up through the arch of trees into the upper meadow and around past the tethered horses, and down around the far side where a hay wagon rested and against it leaned a man, a minstrel, plucking a strange twannginging instrument. As the people walked by he sang each a verse, a rhyme, a clever wordplay couplet linked to the bright spirit of the moment and perhaps to whatever the minstrel saw in the face or demeanor or clothing of his passersby. He sang me a verse as I drew close, and since his tune was simple, as he kept strumming I sang him a verse in return. I leaned against the hay wagon, and watched and listened as he minstreled to the strolling fairegoers.

There were other wandering performers, dressed in period costumes with lute-like instruments, playing mostly well-rehearsed 'renaissance fare,' and there was a fabulous dulcimer workshop—instruments for sale, lessons, performances, and a group of academic musicologists who played woodwind flute or clarinet Tudor-style melodies.

Saturday night, as the darkness fell again, and the public commerce subsided, people drifted about visiting each other's camps—there was no stage or central performance area—making friends, laughing, listening to each other's tales. One larger fire circle on the uphill meadow became a magnet for people to sit together, and slowly the camp wandered by, sat and watched as larger wood was piled and the warmth and light of the fire illuminated first a banjo player, then a zither-wielding velvet-dressed angel came and sang us a song, then a couple of Oregon cowboys sang a hilarious country duet—but each performer was quick to do their piece and get on with it, so's the next eager participant could do their song too. There's a modesty and excellence in these fresh creative moments when everyone knows there is something new and everyone wants to give everyone the chance to make it the best. It was that kind of circle. It would drift in and out of melody, into conversations and laughter, into silence.

Karen and I look at each other and say "Let's do a Chord." That can be our little group's contribution to this circle. We whisper to Kenny and Carol about it. We know there are other people in this circle who've been to some of the street theatre pieces we've done in Portland where The Chord was part of the play. We start softly, lowly, quietly enough so that only people near us hear and slowly let it grow, the sound filling our voices and the area. People's heads are starting to turn hearing it. Ahhhhhh-hhh....We stand up, holding each other's hands. Ohhmmmmmmmm.....We can see some people looking toward us confused, as this is something clearly different, and some people nodding appreciatively, knowing already that this is a vibrational sound, a harmony of primal tones. Aaaaaaahhhhooooooom-mmmmmm....But are they going to join in? Or are we going to be doing this little omm performance for their benefit as spectators to the sound, and across the circle I see someone else standing up, resonating the sound, echoing the sound, holding up people's hands next to him. It's the *minstrel* from the hay wagon, and the people by him stand up alongside him and there are people standing all around the circle now, arms over shoulders, or holding hands, or just standing, or still seated facing the fire, all omming and ahhhing and hmmmming in voices as clear as the night sky. The stars were sparkling above us and the glow of the fire was in front of us, and then the sound quieted down and we got really still and then softly someone's instrument played crystalline notes and a sweet voice sang the next song.

That was the way it was: 1969.

I remember some time later reading Stephen Gaskin's classic books, *Monday Night Class*, and *Caravan*, (both products of that same season) where Stephen writes about how one of the problems with our developing culture is that we envision Perfect World Peace but the high point of our technology seems to be candles and scarves. I thought back to that first Renaissance Faire and maybe it was because the ground under our blankets was a little uneven, or maybe it was a reminder about what beginners we really were, but our candles leaked wax on our blankets and we used the scarves we'd brought to sell to keep ourselves warm at night.

Still it was becoming clear to me that the message of demonstrations or the meaning of events was more in the community that existed during the event than anything else. We had been a little village at that first Oregon Country Faire, and we had made that village appear for those few days. There was something going on here that was more than marketing a few wares.

22. The Turning Point

Sometimes events just roll on along as though on curved tracks made of time, powered by the force of the moment's ideas and coupled to the force of everything that's gone before, propelling us from one event into the next. Only when we get a hind-looking perspective afforded by turning around to observe what we've traversed can we see the bumps and dips in the roads we've traveled; and sometimes, even, from afar we can see back to the points where the compass bearing we were following found new directions.

Karen and I rolled north from Portland to a camp that Kenny and Carol had set up on the beach along the Olympic Peninsula, at the edge of the gigantic rain forests, which populate that corner of the continent. Portland town and the college seemed way far behind us. Before dropping out I had been trying to keep attention on classes by taking the most fascinating courses I could. I enrolled with this brilliantly wild English Professor on a study of the mad and marvelous in Victorian literature; and a course on calligraphy, really a course on the advancement of human ideas through the medium of writing, and took classes with the most progressive political science professors, but how could these studies compare to the vistas looking up these trunks of immense towering cedars straight up, up to the sun-filled blue sky, and hiking up the slippery terrain along waterfall-filled cascading rivers (the lush brush alone was twenty feet tall) and then back down again along the loop trail further north, the orange sunshine acid we'd dropped now digesting in our stomachs, reading the signs of life in the glyphs on the patterns of the great trees' bark, we follow the trail down toward the ocean shore, traipsing on the sand among the driftwood giants, some of them pieces of old ships, storm-smashed and floated up here still with iron rings and hardware riveted on, and then with the sun dipping into the green-blue sea and the sky all aglow we gathered the fire wood and sank into reverie in the comforting glow of this small controllable source of warmth and light.

And then Kenny reaches into his pack and pulls out this statue of a man, an Atlas-like man, arms extended, strong, solidly built which he'd carved from a block of wood, sculpted himself. Maybe it was an unfinished piece, and he's going to work on it. Anyway, it was one of the pieces that didn't sell at the faire, and he just puts it in the middle of the fire. Nobly placed, the flames race up and down his wooden arms. We're stunned. It's a beautiful sculpture. It's just starting to burn. We look at Kenny in amazed surprise. Doesn't he want us to stop his burning? Or?

"No," says Kenny, "Just watch him burn. He's only going to do it once."

How can you learn this stuff in a classroom??

Back in Portland, the community as we know it thrives. Portland State holds Teach-ins on The War, and Reed Professors attend—because The Board at our oh-so-liberal institution has prohibited such stuff from going on at our own hallowed halls. Academic freedom doesn't count for nuthin' when your employers are invested, heavily invested in the war products, and the associated industrial supply line of war materials, scientists, chemical weaponeers, missile guidance experts, strategists, nuclear ballistics designers—who were, after all, one of the most highly valued products of the Reed Institution—out of the classrooms and up the ass-embly line of graduate studies and then into the arms of the well-paying warmaker machine whose bloody profits were in turn donated by thankful graduates back into the endowment of the school.

So the Teach-Ins go on at the downtown college. Wayne Morse—one of only two votes in the U.S. Senate against the fraudulent Gulf of Tonkin resolution boldly speaks about the crime of this call-to-war. Of course it turns out (years later wouldn'tcha know it?) that that Senatorial Gulf of Tonkin resolution passed *en masse* by our august national body, that resolution committing U.S. troops to the Southeast Asian War was based entirely on a fraudulently concocted story about the attack on a U.S. Naval Vessel—a story concocted by design to swing the votes and hearts of our countrymen—and that it did, and did well, consigning us in a hell-bound handbasket on the basis of true red white and blue propaganda, made-up stories of the commie bogeyman to woo our good souls into a bloody war.

Wayne spoke, and teachers spoke and students spoke with the idea of educating the public to news we wouldn't get on TV... and there came to speak, also, returnees from the battleground with stories so sickening that no ears should ever have to hear things like these.

At a fancy fundraiser for one of the political parties (it hardly matters which, they were both waving the bloody flag) Holly Hart from the protesters' scene from Reed, and Kaushal (now back from Europe) both manage to 'sneak' in. Holly dresses up in a black gown and has a friend purchase her a ticket. Kaushal gets in in a waiter's jacket through the service entrance of the hotel. And then in the middle of some muckamuck's speech Holly stands up screaming and pours blood all over herself. She's dragged out of the ballroom and Kaushal, chanting anti-war slogans, is similarly removed from the premises.

There are more parts to the movement than we can keep track of. Underground presses crank out broadsides. Leafleteers pamphlet the downtown. Demonstrations are becoming regular events. The Goose Hollow psychedelic neighborhood of old Victorian turreted houses, blessed with views of the Willamette River and the backdrop of the Portland hills is scheduled for demolition to make way for new freeways. Church pastors are speaking out at Sunday sermons and sheltering AWOL soldiers on their way to Canada. One of the people's presses prints our flyers aimed at the High School students and we pass these out at the end of the schooldays at the biggest Portland high school campuses.

"Warning: The Country You Love is about to Take Your Life!!" reads one of these scary handbills.

And the rumor spreads among the city's anti-war protesters that some heiress, from some agribiz family has given money, big bucks, to help fund a demonstration, a national-scale demonstration, a Major Demonstration, right here in the Rose City, our own hometown.

There's a meeting to be held to discuss apportioning the money for the demonstration and its plans. Word of mouth is spreading the news. We show up, The Black Panthers show up, dozens of groups and individuals: groups from Portland State, Lewis and Clark, the other colleges; Goose Hollow people, Marxists and clergy.

The meeting's held in the Centenary Wilber Community Church on old Burnside Avenue. We walked down the stairs to a big linoleum-floored basement. Short, wide windows ringed the top of the room, letting the early evening's sunlight pour down onto us.

There were tables arranged in a big rectangle and people were invited to sit. We preferred to stand. There were a lot of people there and the basement was crowded. There were a lot of people there I didn't know. At one side of the table a group of four people sitting side by side began with remarks, one after the other, enthusiastically describing the strength of the community here united against the war, and of the need to bring people together here from all over the country to express our beliefs in unison.

There was a lot of nodding in agreement from people listening. But as the talk wore on, there was another strain of ideas coming from these four and their friends. One was describing how Portland was seen by a lot of radicals in other parts of the country as just too 'it's ok, we're an easygoing kind of a place.' In other parts of the country people are seizing the streets, putting themselves in front of the cops. Not letting them pass!

A woman to his right proclaimed, "We need to make Portland the next Chicago." To which her friends and supporters around the room nodded approvingly. She was of course referring to the Chicago 1968 Democratic Convention demonstrations and police riots.

Another fellow went on about how long it had already been since Chicago, and how we could mobilize that kind of action. "We can tell the country that there isn't going to be Business As Usual for the Capitalist class while this war is on. We can close the downtown of this city."

None of this sounded so appealing to me. A few people spoke about the need to demonstrate in a non-violent way, and the folks at the front answered that that stuff had been tried already and again and again, and "Look, things are only worse today. The war is more enormous than ever."

That was a tough argument to counter. People were saying that the time for peaceful resistance was at its end. Not that there was something bad or wrong about having protested peacefully, but that those tactics hadn't succeeded.

I was speaking, explaining that what was developing already here in Portland was a set of tactics that really was the solution. And that we needed to *demonstrate* those. We needed to bring together and demonstrate the positive alternatives that we as a culture were in the midst of developing. And bring these together in a demonstration, "Like the," I was looking about the room at the faces listening to me, "Pancake breakfasts the Panthers serve, like the free schools and universities that are forming from the dropped out students and teachers from Reed and Portland State, like the yoga and spiritual groups, and their meditations, like the whole healthy foods we're eating, like our free-wheeling music and the songs that really have a message. We need a festival that brings all of these together and demonstrates what kind of a whole, healthy community we are moving towards."

"But that isn't going to end the war," said one of the guys who'd been describing the fires in the streets.

"Well, we need to show that Peace isn't just corporate commerce as usual," I paused. "We need to show something more than our anger and our rage. We need to create something beautiful if we're going to win over the rest of our generation."

Now lots of people were talking. For and against. A clear-voiced black man from the front and center group urged everyone to speak one at a time and to listen to each other.

A clergyman spoke about the need to keep in the tradition of non-violence.

One guy called out, "Just burn the banks and get it over with!"

Several young women spoke about how the dialectic of imperialism was making this violence happen and the response to it was inevitable.

A Black Panther, in 'uniform' supported the idea of a demonstration that showed our best stuff, our best community stuff. "You don't get it," he said. "You go downtown, breaking glass and burning and you are going to get beat. Not just beaten. Beat. They will take you apart."

Kaushal spoke up, his arms dancing in front of him, "Sure let's bring people in from all over the country. Let's make that happen. It wants to happen. The time is ripe for that, and there's a lot going on here and a lot out there that wants to spiral in around us. And we should help that happen, but what the world needs right now is a dose of light and beauty, not just more hatred and destruction."

Lines were being drawn. People were choosing sides in their minds.

"You people are just wishy-washy drug heads who want to pretend that everything's alright when it isn't," said a guy in a button down shirt with a fatigue jacket over it, pointing his finger sharply at each of us.

Karen was speaking now, "I think some of these things you're talking about are just plain scary. Closing businesses or burning banks isn't going to change anything. Riots and firebombs aren't going to make them go away. If we want to show people that the money system isn't The Answer then we need to show that. Have a Free Festival, a demonstration where we show how if people get along in Peace and share resources, teach and share our talents we can get along outside the money system. That would *really* demonstrate something."

"You're dreaming," came the reply.

I wanted to know what was the story with the money supposed to be earmarked for supporting this event. Who had it? Was it real? Who's deciding how it gets used? Palms up, shoulders slightly shrugged, I ask, "What's the deal?"

The next thing I know several people are telling me where to get off.

"Oh you're just here for the money are you?"

"We wouldn't tell you if our lives depended on it."

"Just know that the money's really there, and there is going to be a demonstration. And we are going to make Portland the next Chicago. And if you don't like it, you must be at the wrong meeting."

"Yeah let's get on with the meeting. We have a lot to plan. So you've had your say, now let the rest of us continue."

There was nowhere else to go but up the stairs and out the door and onto the green grass of the church's lawn. As we left there were jeers behind us, "That's it, just leave. If you don't get your way just leave."

"Let the radicals plot the revolution."

But there were a fair number of people who also exited up those stairs. And out on the lawn in the next few moments standing in the slanted rays of the evening sun, we all said to each other we were going to make that positive demonstration happen. That was the thing to do. That was the right thing to do.

One guy said he would talk it up among the hip and organic restaurants in town to get support for the food provision. Richard said he knew most of the local Rock 'n Roll bands and he would round up musicians. Big name stars he didn't know, but local talent he was sure of and he would start talking it up and getting the bands together. We were talking in a hubbub and exchanging phone numbers and names.

I was exhausted. That kind of thing wrings the oomph out of me. It was a very hard moment, because even though I was sure we were onto something valuable, still I'd left friends and anti-war associates down in that basement and I didn't see how we'd get it back together.

PART FIVE

Toad Hall and Beyond

(1970)

In which the people of the emerging New World Culture begin to come together to express the hope we have for humanity's future. It feels as though powerful forces are moving us toward one another to bridge the gaps that have separated segments of the peace, ecology, civil rights, and spiritual movements for years in the past. The infamous Vortex Festival and the ongoing Rainbow Gatherings have their root in these moments

23. Kaushal Puts his Finger on It

Kaushal and Karen and I and Jonas and Jerrianna are sitting in the big room of the 'Beanbat' house. Dawn is creeping in at one side of the windows, like a far beacon signaling just faintly from one side of a dark night. I'm looking at a pile of trinkets on the end table next to the old, plush blue sofa...an unusual bottle-cap, a piece of iridescent shell, a twist of wire in the shape of a star, pulled from my pocket earlier in the night, but under the glare of our psychedelic ((yellow double-dome)) moment-to-momentness, and the brilliance of mere air and the awesome powers of sight, the trinkets themselves seem useless.

Jonas was saying how, "We spend valuable enlightened minutes encased in these boxes that we've built or rented, these houses, to conceal from us the elementals that we're made of, that run through us like blood and water and electricity."

And at Jerriana and Karen's suggestions we are all off for a walk through our tranquil neighborhood. Outside in the just dawning light we encounter the marvelous foliage the gardeners of Portland have cultivated: succulents in starburst patterns, spikey things whose tendrils reached out bobbing in the air, evergreens of many species—one a deeper, darker green than all the others—each of these alive, breathing as are we, sensitive to the dawn light as are we, surging with electrolite fluids as are we.

How wondrous was this natural world! How beautiful. How full of peace and grace.

The day is cloudy gray, and the air seems to reflect the greenness of the plants, like a green fog that softens all the brilliant now-fading-from-view mandalas of the night before.

I see no place for me, for any of us to fit in this world. Sure there's the quiet world, shielded from the frightening challenges of trying to reform a paradise corrupted. Sure there are the sleepyheaded denizens of this town, sure there's that kind of peace, the peace of the sleepyheaded. But how can we—with this vision of beauty and harmony, these ideals that we ourselves, if only briefly, but truly nonetheless, can touch and experience—how do we blend into this world they're offering us, a world of corporate commerce? And if we're really good boys and girls a nice sleepyheaded house in a nice sleepyheaded suburb, with a nice gleaming gas guzzling car and all removed from the pain and starvation and oppression of most of the world, and that's the reward if we don't stand up and shriek out about the misery, which doesn't have to be.

My mulling turns to talking, and I say out loud, "No. I don't see any way for us, for me at least, to fit into this world." I am gesturing with a sweeping arm toward the downtown and Portland below us.

"Just enjoy the walk," says Jonas who points toward these bulbous flower buds which look comically like they are about to bust right open in front of us, and we do enjoy the rest of the walk and sweet fronds and ferns and fabulous foliaged features of the fresh, free, fruit-bearing forms of life.

Back up the stairs and inside, as we unwind about the table, shoes and sweaters coming off, Jonas expounds further on the subject of us not fitting into the molds that society has ready. He says there are other models of social order. He brings us some of the societal experiments: New Harmony Indiana of the 1840's; the horse-and-buggy-using Mennonites; tribal societies of olden times. He is warming to a point, and the sunlight breaks a shaft through the gray outside and into our big front window and over Jonas' shoulder (these natural additions have a way of influencing our thoughts) and now Jonas is talking about the Communes of Mao's China and the Kibbutzes of modern Israel. How they're onto the right idea: getting people out of the cities, back to the land, in touch with the natural forces, the forces that really shape the world: water, weather, land, minerals, plants, and bring together the ideas of cooperation for the common benefit of everyone... only, over here we need to do it without the government, without the red party, or the red, white and blue party; no, as free and independent people to join together and....Go Back To The Land, make a commune, a free commune, one where people don't have to have all the same ideas, or wear the same uniform, but where everyone's working with the earth and each other for the common good. That's how to produce for prosperity and happiness.

I'm liking what I'm hearing. There may be possibilities for us in this world after all.

Karen is speaking up about gardening, and putting food by, and pioneer crafts and quilting bees, building barns and weaving cloth, and how, "These things aren't lost arts...yet. But if we don't keep them alive, who will? And these are the know-how, the knowledge that sustained our forebears, and we could sustain ourselves, grow food, keep warm, build shelters."

Jerrianna answers in poetry, spoken slowly while slowly the city woke up around us, about the links between the young and the growing forces of nature and the need for people, all people, *we people* to learn the skills of working and playing together.

Jonas continues, sunlight now beaming in toward all of us, "The model of corporate and industrial hierarchy and military hierarchy and political hierarchy might not be the best one for our race's, the human race's future." He pauses and smiles a quiet knowing smile.

These were enchanted moments.

"I'm all for it," I'm blurting out. "Let's go. Out of the city. Try something new. I don't know anything about gardening, farming, building, but I could learn, couldn't I?" I was a bit giddy. Sure there was novelty and camaraderie in good lively conversation, but I had been in a spiral over what really did make sense to pursue, and the options that seemed open at the end of college had become less vital with each passing contemplation on the matter, and here's Jonas, happily pointing out the window, over the imagined hills and forests and into some other part of this reality, this real earth, pointing out what seemed to me to be an appealing and intelligent option...coming from nowhere, it seemed, but from our own accumulated ideas and insights.

There were some bellweather groups already off in that direction. I'd seen photos in the New York underground press about New Buffalo and some of the other clans in Northern New Mexico, and somewhere in Colorado a group out in the countryside experimenting with collective lifestyle and geodesic domes made of welded old car bodies.... So there were some other travelers out ahead along this way already.

Now we were all talking at once, toast and tea were toasted and brewed, and Jonas set down an atlas in front of us and said, "So where do we want to go?"

"Oregon." "Oregon," we chimed in. All of us coming from other places and naively, though earnestly, enamoured of this lush green place, this emerald city of parks, this first home for all of us away from home.

Oregon. So Jonas opens the big atlas to Oregon and Kaushal, his palms forward, is waving his hands back and forth, "Wait. wait. wait," he says emphatically, his hands criss-crossing each other in front of him. (Kaushal's been right with us all through the nightlong event, but in the background, maybe a bit morose, thoughtful, observing quietly.)

Now he jumps to the middle, "If we're going to do this we might as well do this right," he announces.

He lifts one hand high in the air, retracts all the fingers but the thumb which he begins to move in a circle, a spiral in front of him around and around, we are all following what he's doing and with firmness and not a moment of attention to any of the details on the open page below him, he lands his thumb firmly down on the map. We all get up to see where it's pressed down on the page. We gather round. Kaushal says, "This is where we should go," and with the rest of the group hunched around and looking carefully, he slowly rolls back his thumb like from the making of a careful finger imprint, and there, there exactly is the word "Rainbow."

It's the name of a small town along one of those splashing rushing rivers that runs from the crest of the Cascade mountain peaks down to the slower larger Willamette River in the valley below.

We resolve to go there soon.

And as the day warms the big room, lightheadedness overtakes us and we converse, laugh, and grow sleepy. I think though, that the relaxation that overcame us, the satisfying feeling in the now warm morning came mostly from having solved one of life's puzzles, answering that *it is possible* in a dangerously crazy world to find choices, alternative ways that can make good sense.

In the weeks that followed we made several ventures. The first (of course) was to that town named Rainbow. It was a quaint, quiet community stretched alongside its rushing river, and nearby were vacation homes, cabins, lodges. We met with a real estate guy and his sister. They were level-headed old timers. Explained about this being the vacation and touristy side of the valley and we needing to be in the more remote, less expensive other side of the valley, over in the coast range or in those foothills. They were very nice to us. I know they thought we were a little strange. Maybe they were trying to steer us as far away from themselves as they could point us; but I think they were just steering us right.

We made many other drives through the backways of Western Oregon. We were looking for a place where there was fertile land for growing food; wood for building and for fuel; water for drinking and for irrigation. And it was clear to us that the town, Rainbow, was more like a signpost along the way than the particular town we were supposed to settle in...but when we were talking about the place, the land, the farm, or the idea of what we were looking for we called it Rainbow. When friends asked what on earth we were up to, what *were* we doing?—we had at least, at last, an idea, a vision, a mission, a plan to fulfill.

In the midst of these explorations, in early May, 1970 the National Guardsmen shot dead four non-violent student protestors in Ohio. That made our quest for a way out of the system seem even more urgent.

24. Toad Hall and Beyond

May 1970. In the flower-studded springtime brightness we drove north to Bellingham, Washington where Western Washington State College hosted its annual art event. The Bellingham Arts Fair had been a regional 'happening' for years.

In addition to its usual roster of art and crafts, speakers and poets, sculpture and painting exhibitions, the Arts Faire decided (fully in the best spirit of these times) to add a multi-media three-ring show audaciously named Dr. P. H. Martin's Magical Medicine Show and Traveling Tranquility Circus. It came complete with acrobats, dancers, magicians, clowns, comedians, and (wouldn'tcha know it?) rock n' roll.

The circus troupe was home-based in Portland. Through the Goose Hollow neighborhood we knew several of the show's performers, many of the stage techies, and even ultra-brilliant, dour, Gary Ewing, the producer. So did everybody else in town. We got in touch to see if we could help out with the show. So had everybody else. Performing in a giant commissioned inflatable (inflatable!) tent, the circus was just too good a gig, too much fun, not to try to be part of. But Gary and The Circus were deluged with requests, and just couldn't hand out an okay to everyone who begged begged begged to be included.

So we pulled our crafts together: the candles, the wooden children's toys, the weavings, the stained glass lanterns and signed up for a crafts booth to exhibit our wares. We packed sleeping gear, and our display set-ups and drove north through metro Portland and across the Columbia River where lush forests girded both sides of the road, up past Olympia, past Seattle and on to the arts and college town of Bellingham.

After we'd registered for our booth space at the Art Fair's office we let on that we were also here as 'additional help' for the circus's 'road crew.' So we were directed toward both Red Square where the outdoor booths were going to be, and toward the free food being supplied for crews and worker/participants at a restaurant called Toad Hall.

We headed first to Red Square, a huge open Quad, like an Italian Piazza, with a fountain, room easily enough for the giant inflatable circus, as well as the crafts and arts exhibits. It was paved with red, vivid red, paving blocks.

We tied colorful ribbons to the poles that bounded our display space, and set off toward Toad Hall.

Down a flight of stairs we found ourselves in this college-scene restaurant whose decor and hand-painted olde-timey signs were meant to be reminiscent of *The Wind In The Willows'* infamous meeting place. There were meals being served to the crews doing set up, sound or lights, and also to the visiting poets, writers and speakers who were part of the five-day festivity. Windows along one wall let the light shine in from above.

The sweet smell of fresh baked breads and spicy pastries mixed with aromas of stews and curries and vegetables. The free food line switch-backed toward the front door and then curved around the side of the big room; strangers and old friends talking and enjoying the camaraderie and the anticipation of the events coming up. We found a table and draped jackets on chairs. Some of the circus crew is there, eating already and they are frankly glad to see us. We represent good help for the big work ahead and they encourage us to go eat.

Approaching the rear of the line I saw the minstrel fellow I'd met the previous September at The Renaissance Faire , Barry Adams. He's still got his home-made two-stringed instrument over his shoulder. We greet and introduce the folks we are each traveling with to each other: Chuck Mills, Karen, Dana, Rob Roy Rowley, Linda, Kaushal, each is greeting and meeting, talking about the fair, the circus. It seems we're traveling in clans now, as groups of like-minded adventurers meeting each other. Clans meeting clans.

I talk with Barry about the Free Store the Portland community has just opened in a little storefront right near the downtown, a place to bring, give, and share goods, outside the money system as much as possible. We've found a place for it, donations to open it...."Even if it lasts just a short while it's an amazing thing." I talk about the yet-unnamed effort the community groups of Portland are planning as a different kind of demonstration; and about Familiar Musing, the crafts store. And I mention, thinking of our plans to 'land on the land' that we are heading toward something else, something earthy and more long-lasting. There's a lot going on that we are in the middle of.

He's listening carefully. His reddish hair curls playfully alongside his face. Light skinned and lightly freckled he nods and smiles. He's dressed part cowboy and part hippie. Chaps (those are leather overpants cowpokes wear for riding) and a hat loaded with colorful pins and buttons. His fringed jacket looks like it came from both Haight-Ashbury *and* Western Montana.

I ask what he's up to. "Well," he says, turning his head a little to the side and then straight ahead at me, "A Gathering."

He pauses.

"A Gathering for everybody," he goes on, "For all people. For everybody to get together...in Peace. All the different kinds of people, to show that it can be done, that people can get together, be together in Peace. And for free. No money. And out in the mountains. No roads, no electricity, just people and earth and sky." His hands move outward, then upward, indicating slightly the natural elements he's referring to.

"No big stage with paid performers, but (listen!)" he turns his head slightly as if listening, "music everywhere and circles of people," he glances and motions about the room, "with their arts, sculptures, plays." His voice drops a bit, almost whispering, "And outside that circles of schools, teachers teaching what they know, workshops on a hundred, hundreds of subjects, people learning from each other, sharing, everyone welcome, healing areas for the sick, children's areas for the little ones." He's motioning with his hand, showing rings within rings, "And at the edges, gates with greeters welcoming people home, and beyond that circles for parking, and for horses and beyond that the mountains, wild and free and beautiful."

It seems like he's trying to tell it all at once.

"This *is* original." I tell him. I can see the rings within rings and how the whole event radiates outward. "But what," I ask, "What's really at the center?"

Barry draws his lips together and looks up for a moment, finding the words, "At the center, in the middle of the time of The Gathering, we all sit down together, in a huge circle, quietly, in *silence*, in Peace." And he stops and smiles.

This *is* creative. It's just a direct, simple, original idea for what to do. It's open to the potential of showing the positive sides of human experience. "You're describing a kind of mandala of people in nature," say I. "Bringing together the families, the clans, the tribes, our movements, the parts of our culture—bringing these all together with a Silence, a meditation at its center."

"Yeah," he says smiling, "A silence, a meditation, a prayer, call it whatever you like, but all of us together at once in Peace. Invite everyone in the world. Be open for *everybody*."

I'm seeing the coordination of community needed to create this—and also how a Gathering like this can bring forward many pieces of the emerging, diverging new culture. This is good; this is very good.

I say, "Let's do it."

It seems as simple as can be...at first. Just people together. It could be a taste of the antidote to the ills of the world; a little like what Steve Ben from The Living Theatre called "A Vision of Mandala City"; what Julian and Judith referred to as a joy play, a festival of joy, where the stars would be everyone.

Or a place where making a sharing and functioning community *outside* the commercial systems could instill a kind of independence; and the unassuming grand center, the Silence. Something that could be shared equally by all...that no one can know or do any better than anyone else...could bestow a kind of grace.

A chance to listen—or to pray—or contemplate—or meditate, and which (I already knew) could withstand the rigors of the most psychedelic scrutiny, whose strengths and blessing would only be magnified in the psychedelic light.

The food line is moving verrrrry slowly. Chuck Mills, another long-haired Montanan is talking now, telling me about their camp in the mountains, up the Skagit River and how they're going to be moving deeper into the mountains come the warmer weather.

Barry is continuing on about the schools and workshops of the Gathering. I'm standing on the line next to Chuck—he's their driver. The Marblemount Rider Clan is who 'they' are, down from their base in the Cascades, from the camp they call Love 2, and they're all traveling in Chuck's van. "Yeah," he says, sorta drawling—just a bit—"Gathering, it's a good thing. We're doing it already, at our camp." He's tall, wiry and muscular. Dressed in jeans, a shirt patterned with zizzy lines like an old blanket, topped with a worn cowboy hat with a long feather along one side, he describes the encampment up above Marblemount, Washington: the river to cross, the diamond-shaped mountains up above, the kitchen built in the woodlands. "It's the Spirit, that's who wants us to do this. We're just tools for what the Spirit wants."

We were talking about bringing together all the clans, the collectives, the communities, the cells, all the *families*.

I'm talking about community processes (instead of paid service workers) where people work together to park the cars, prepare the food, provide the healthcare, cleanup (we'd all seen the photos of the mountains of trash left behind at Rock Fests) and now we're talking about bringing together many of the different splintered groups of the peace culture in one show of togetherness and practicality and something spiritual as well.

It seemed an opportunity to create something new and beautiful; something I already knew lots of people were searching for.

It also seemed like a good answer to some of the political questions that nagged the conscience of our times: was it even possible for people to exist in a peaceful society?? If you don't like the political system as it exists around you, what other or different or better examples do you have?? Can there be a functioning society without money exchange or competitive economic classes??

At least for a brief spell of time "The World Family Gathering" as Barry called it might show such things were possible.

And the way for showing—for making briefly real—these political answers comes to us in a spiritual unity found in the equality of the silent meditation. And that peaceful community could express itself by providing the physical logistics of Gathering. And that could stand as an example expressing political and social hope for humans-at-large.

The chow line is only slowly creeping ahead.

It was easy for many of us to talk at once adding ideas and 'pieces of the vision': public forums for communicating, pageants and celebrations; cooking and baking; medical and healing arts areas; nature education for young people—and the old people—quiet areas for simplicity and retreat; drum circles and torch lit night-time performance areas. Barry is talking about old timers from the mountains, from the indigenous tribes coming to talk to us, to teach us. We're picturing people coming from around the world each bringing a piece of their culture.

And a harmony with the land: a cleanup that would rid the woods of years of previously-left garbage; footpaths vanished; kitchen and camp areas disappeared, the whole area naturalized carefully. Hands-on effort gently restores the land. What a learning experience for everyone who participates.

This vision for Gathering seemed to tie together answers to political puzzles with the spiritual quests for peace and love in nature.

Toad Hall faded into the background. That place right there

felt like the crossroads of the earth. There was a light off in the distance and we could start moving toward it, or point in that direction, or tell others…and see if others saw the same hope in the same idea.

Barry's talking on about mythic and mystical relations of events like these through the long history of our species. He's reckoning this with past and predicted gatherings both mythic and real: Camelot and Atlantis; the Ghost Dance, the New Jerusalem.

I'm talking about our trips into wild lands: the dunes, the coast, the bays, the hot springs, the waterfalls. How at each of these places we make our camp. Then hike to some overlook or secluded shore to do our practice, our meditations and thanksgivings.

Chuck and Barry smile knowingly. Others are smiling too. Yeah, brother, sister, yeah, this is where it is at.

Now Chuck starts explaining how the Love 2 camp is a long-term venture, and when Harold—The Old Man, or Poppa Harold, he calls him all of those—gets there with the horses they are going to go into the deep wilderness packing their camp with them and enter the seclusion of the mountains…and, "Make the camp we're gonna call Love 3 and stay holed up there, just livin' the righteous life…for a year or more. Maybe up until the very time of the Gathering."

"July 1972," Barry chimes in "is just a little more than two years from now." To twenty-something-year-olds, two plus years is a long time. I think it's about the amount of time we're going to need.

I'm asking if Love 2 or Love 3 or maybe Love 4 is where we're inviting all these people to?

"No," Barry goes on, "that's too small up there. We need somewhere in the middle of the continent, somewhere everyone can get to, somewhere up in the Rocky mountains, in Colorado."

Barry is talking about 144,000 or more people like in the Book of Revelations at the End of Days in the Bible. And he's talking about helping to fulfill those Prophecies.

I consider myself a political realist and I know that the visions and dreams of a people keep us going through the roughest times. Still, I am getting a little less easy here. First, a really brilliant idea; then a story about Old Man Harold who's supposed to show up with these horses; now a rap about Christian Revelations.

I want to know who *else* is involved and where this is coming from. My concern is that he's maybe getting this from someone who has their own other motives and I want to know, "Just who started this?"

Barry looks down, then way up, then level at me and says, "Jesus Christ is who told me about it. But I think everyone who gets told gets told in a way that they themselves can best understand."

His seriousness of belief is absolute.

Still on topic, he starts telling a story.

He puts his hands together in front of him, and slowly folds them open like leaves of a book and then draws them gently apart. He says, "Picture a place where two valleys become one valley. At first there's only rock and dust and stone. And then children come, many children, and they do all kinds of good things to restore the earth. And the waters come back to the valleys so the hills and valley floors grow green and lush." His hands make the motion of waters flowing together toward each other and then they close back together as in prayer.

These are universal images. I recall sitting at the edge of the African desert looking over vast dry riverbeds and sands 'seeing' the dry valleys green up and the place turn fertile and the streams and rivers start to flow.

I continue as I saw it, "So years later when the valleys are flourishing and ripe with fruit, and the rock slopes are rich with trees, the Old Wise walk with the Youngsters pointing out all the beauty of the land, and explaining to them that all this" (I'm using some hand motions to portray the scene) "was once hard and rocky and bare...until the Children came and helped make it green."

"Yeah, you got it," says Barry smiling.

It was then. Exactly then, that I knew that Shared Vision was a part of our time. And I knew for certain that to help this plan happen *we had to find the others*, other people who had seen this dream or been touched by this dream, and bring us together, to Gather. I knew that there would be clues, like signs, like the image of the two valleys becoming one valley and the barren areas growing lush, that would be *shared images* and that these would be like keys that would tell us: yes Brother, yes Sister, this is a dream that belongs to all of us.

The rest of the Bellingham Arts Fair was marvelous, but nothing as absolutely inspiring as that scene at Toad Hall.

Dr. P. H. Martin's Traveling Tranquility Circus got set up in the big Red Square; the acrobats, dancers, and musicians jammed under the huge inflatable tent as the grease gun mob on stage performed its attack on the innocent. In a finale, a late afternoon encore performance, the cast of the musical *Hair*, on tour from Seattle joined the Circus and altogether both choruses sang "Let the Sun Shine In" from the *Hair* musical, and in the heat of the afternoon with the bright sun shining, the now over-inflated tent burst at the top and oh-so-beautifully came wafting down floating side to side like the hugest imaginable deflating marshmallow finally covering everybody in the folds of its lightweight fabric as the choruses finished their ensemble song in magnificent disarray.

The craftspeople made a thriving marketplace; we sold our candles, our toys, our lamps; Chuck put up a tipi in the Red Square right near our crafts display.

Poets Gary Snyder and Ken Kesey read in packed auditoriums; fairegoers danced naked through the plaza's fountain; and on the late shift, from the balcony of a big gymnasium, we watched The Portland Zoo—surely the favorite band of the Portland psychedelic rock n' roll scene—blaze through a pantheon of their melodic rolling rock n' roll songs including an endless (so it seemed at the time) version of their signature piece: "Meditation."

But nothing as absolutely inspiring as that meeting at Toad Hall.

25. Festival Summer

Like a cavalcade, like a mountain stream pouring unstoppable from one churning pool through waterfalls to the next, in rapid succession the summer of 1970 inundated us with a series of Convocations, Congresses, Comings-together—call 'em what you like—each of a very different style.

Each one drew us in, taught us, made us part of its energy and in turn let us become an essential part of its own operations—and be able to add our own expressions to its wholeness.

Since the dawn of recorded time, the comings-together have been for us humans a means of advancing our ideas. Trade routes of ancient days with their caravans and camps: traders and artisans, politicians and idealogues, young lovers and old adventurers, all congregating at the grand markets along the route...watching the entertainments, bargaining for goods and treasures, learning, apprenticing, cooking, washing, living, falling in love, listening to the preaching of sages and fanatics, learning to exist as a temporary, a seasonal, human community at the edge of the desert, or along a lush riverside, a place where the tribes and the people can talk, laugh, meet each other, expose each other to their many different ideas that make up their cultures and tell the tales of their adventures and their mythologies.

Next up on the roster of these happenings (after returning from the Bellingham Arts Fair), we planned to attend the second Eugene Renaissance Faire at the end of May, just two weeks away. We eagerly invited the Marblemount Riders to come join us and do the Renaissance Faire thing together.

The second Faire was set in a new location and the Wootens (Bill and Cindy)—prime organizers of so much that was going on in the emerging Eugene Community—have found us a place with a big loop through the forests instead of around a meadow...much better...it gave the sense of wandering through an enchanted forest past the elvin booths and alongside strolling puffy-sleeved musicians.

Yes there were bikers, and wild-west-types...the Merry Pranksters set up a silver pyramid...and a tribal family calling itself The Family of the Mystic Arts installed a cider press and served burritos (a mucho original menu at the time) in such a coordinated operation that I just had to look on in wonder. Here was a communal group that had the step-up of having been together already several years: they had their natural coordination figured out. They had equipment, a pickup truck, a flatbed truck, ovens and wood-burning stoves that they offloaded into the forest, which they used to prep the meals they sold. They had scarves and robes and weird musical instruments, and velvet hats and straw hats and sashes and buckles, and beautiful olde hand-cranked apple crushers and cider mills.

I could see there was something evolving here. Our own crafts were becoming more advanced in art and style; but more telling, we were involved in a collective that was linking clans and communes and collectives in what seemed to be a thriving economic base. Of course we were often selling back and forth to each other, but there were tourists, and thousands of day-visitors who passed through and bought the arts and the burritos.

We set up a quiet space, a massage zone as a free service for craftspeople and cooks. In fact anyone was welcome to lie down on the colorful blankets and relax or receive a massage. As the afternoon wore on more and more talented massagers from different schools of technique came by, intrigued, and soon there were so many people giving and receiving massages...mostly given by people who knew considerably more about the healing art of massage than we did.... The entire affair was running on its own... without us.

So we, Temple Tribe craftspeople from Alder Street in Portland, Oregon and the Marblemount Riders from Love 2 Camp in the Skagit Valley, Washington ambled up to the junction of the two ends of the loop and lashed together a raised log platform about six feet high and did a piece originally from The Living Theatre's *Paradise Now* production: *Flying*.

This is a careful and sophisticated piece of acrobatics where two lines of people face each other, extend their arms in a very particular interlaced arrangement and stand in a double row beginning at the base of the platform and extending straight away from it, pointing in this case toward the sun. An individual stands up on the platform, toes to the edge, and with a slow count of three breaths, leaps upward from the platform toward the sun, arms extended out and up, and lands—usually gracefully—in the supportive arms of the lines of people below.

Then slowly the person who has just 'flown' is gently rolled over and placed on his or her back on the ground.

There is a lot of guidance to doing this right. First members of the group who are acquainted with the procedure do it, then in turn each one of the 'catchers' from the two rows, then—well by then we were surrounded by hordes of amazed faire-goers, and for the rest of the afternoon we 'flew' people. A tremendous act of faith it is to do this...it looks so graceful and exquisite, and as people line up to take their turn, a guide at the base of the platform helps them remove belt buckles, rings, keys and holds these hard or breakable objects securely for them to be picked up later. Then at the back of the platform after the person has climbed up, another guide explains about taking the three breaths, while the crowd coaxes, "Breathe, breathe," and on the third breath, "Fly!" and aiming just as high up toward the sun as one can, one springs out and upward.

All that is easy compared with the moment of standing there, looking down at these people none of whom you've ever met before, don't know their names or nuthin' and there you are about to leap upwards into space and six feet from your toes to the ground, maybe ten feet from your eye level seems suddenly like a perilous distance...but there is a moment aloft, maybe only a moment, but a long, long moment it is, when the upward soaring thrust of all your muscles and the downward pulling of the gravity of the earth are just equal, and that cusp between the motions is truly suspended, 'flying' in space and sunlight.

Our clans were learning to work together with the highest degrees of trust. After the Faire we returned north to Portland, partying out at our Alder Street Temple and at Lila's in North Portland. And whatdya think? The Marblemounters are all leaning on us to come north to the Skagit River Valley, to Love 2.

We make plans to visit in June.

Again the journey across the Columbia past Seattle and this time eastward into the high Cascades.

We have to follow our map along the winding valley to the big cabin at the Family of the Three Lights commune. They're busy removing a new well pump from the back of their truck and lugging it to the well of the cabin. Our crew—about eight of us in two cars—is welcome, but even more welcome when they find out we're heading out soon to the Love 2 base camp upriver.

One of the founders of that community (another Chuck—a *different* Chuck from Chuck Mills who I'd met at Bellingham) explains how it's a lot to maintain an open door and be expected in a communal sort of way to have, or get, food ready for whoever shows up for dinner. And even when willing folks show up, eager to help with whatever tasks are at hand, it's so often so much easier to wish they (in this case *we*) weren't there, so the crew that already knows each other can work together to get the job-at-hand done, instead of interacting with some newcomers (that'd be us) and trying to teach us both the techniques of the job at hand, and how to work with them. This was a momentary peek at a natural reality of collective life that I would see repeated many times.

Duke, Chuck Mills' son, a young teenager, knows the way to Love 2 and can use a ride from the commune upriver toward the camp where his dad is. So we pile back in the rigs and follow the route deeper into the mountains. There's a turn in the road and a wide shoulder where the road cuts right, and Duke says, "We park here."

We gather our backpacks and head down a path and as we approach the river we begin to hear the cascade, a deep rumbling sound that doesn't quit. Then there it is. Raging. Torrential. White splashes of foam frothing and splashing everywhere. All the spring snowmelt thundering downward. The river is one continuous mass of surging, raging waterfalls.

And there's a big arching log over the river, low at the start on our side and then rising higher and higher to the further bank. I ask Duke, "How far is the next way across? The next crossing?"

"There isn't any next crossing. Maybe miles and miles. Maybe."

"Well," I say, looking at our well-packed and well-balanced backpacks, looking at our good hiking shoes, "We've got this under control."

"You don't have the river under control," says Duke.

By now people on the other side have noticed we're here. They're looking across at all of us gawking at the powerful water in front of us, and from the far bank they're shouting instructions. "Look at the log, not at the water!" Several people are shouting the exact same thing, so it's some kind of very important message about how safely to traverse the log bridge.

And traverse it we do. Slowly, carefully, looking at the big log beneath our feet and not, not at the moving swirling surge of water below us. And step-by-step we cross the river. Except for Rain who got off balance toward the end of the log at the high-above-the-water part, and toppled off and fell in, and Glen—her boyfriend—runs back out onto the log bridge and dives into the water after her. They get whooshed downstream feet first together through several cascades and then we see them scrambling out onto shore further downstream. Someone from the camp goes to check on them, and returns a while later saying, "They must be alright, by the time I got there they were already making love on the riverbank."

In the flat of the woods above the river was a most beautiful camp. It was as serene as the river was wild. Tall fir, hemlock, spruce and lush undergrowth, soft forest floor and the shafts of sunlight mingled with bird calls.

There was a kitchen built of strong lashed-together poles and strung overhead with tarpaulins. The rustic shelving was all of smooth peeled parallel poles set crosswise with trimmed branches cross-laced all right next to each other to make a flat surface. There were tables for food preparation, extra sheltered places for storage, a flat plyboard for rolling out bread dough. The big pots and pans, and mixing bowls and utensils hung from wooden S-hooks. On the downhill side was a wash area: water containers, tubs, scrubbers and a rock-lined runoff area for gray water.

At the center of this was a cooking fire, and off just a little ways was another fire pit for warmth, eating around and evening campfire delights.

I knew, amazed, I was looking at a model for a very different kind of encampment. This was structurally very different from backpack adventuring, even several day campouts, where we had set our food and gear together. We were still essentially living out of our backpacks with some extra supplies lugged in from the car. This was a different sort of thing. And here I saw what appeared to be the apparent model for how the planned Gathering would and could set itself up. Chuck was the obvious architect, but clearly Conga Tom, Lila along with her two children, and Laika, Duke, Barry and others had helped. It had all the field marks of a group process...lots of different styles.

We set up our own tents, brought our food to the kitchen, filled our water containers from the spring up above and joined these Marblemount mountain people for a week at Love 2.

A few days after arrival we take a group journey up the side of the hill, which adjoined the camp. Up the hill, which turns into a steep craggy incline, which continues upward, turning into what we would call in English, a mountain. There are limits to what we can do without topo maps and climbing gear; somewhere high above the Skagit River below a huge diamond-shaped rock face we can go no further, so we position ourselves on these various ledges overlooking the sprawling forests below us and we sit. Time and timelessness pass by and rest a while with us. The meditation cradles us here, high above the known world, and we sit peacefully, each in our own thoughts or prayers or contemplations, breezes blowing gently against us, afternoon's orange sunshine radiating on us and reflecting back at us from the rock faces. Then, only slowly as the sun's arc brings the shadows from the side and the temperature begins to drop and the breezes of early evening begin to cool us, do we start the return down the mountain, back to Love 2. But it was there, sitting together on the ledges of that mountainside that I knew that these people, the marblemountaineers were on the same wavelength as our clan that had traveled north to be here together; that the meditative space we were seeking was the same space; and most of all, that these were people with whom we could make the shared vision of the World Family Gathering come true.

It was hard leaving. The scene was so together: the camaraderie so easy, the food so good, the weather so nice, the stories and music around the fires at night so entertaining, the working together on the chores of the camp so hand-in-hand. But the folks there were still waiting on Harold to show up with the horses to go deeper into the wilderness.

We had a crafts store *and* a free store to get back to. Even with collective partnerships there is only so much time off you can take without things coming apart behind you.

We sat and jabbered together at length, shaping the ideas for The Gathering, imaging, and imagining and discussing...and we left with the possibility in mind that these folk might be up in these here hills for the next coupla years and we, leaving Love 2, would be left with the task of spreading the word about The Gathering to come, and come 1972 they'd ride out of the mountains on horseback and rejoin all the rest of us.

What a plan! Little did we know how things change and grow.

Back at the Alder Street house in Portland we are taking in 'referrals' from Outside In, the Portland area free clinic. That meant that people hitchhiking into Portland, or traveling, driving through might find their way to the community center that really was the clinic and get referred to us as a potential place to spend a night. This was not only fun but also sort of crazy. We met all kinds of folk. Mostly though, people who were on the road were seeking something…maybe something spiritual, maybe something political…they didn't know, we didn't know. But from this pool of people we found folks keen to help with the craftswork, with the freestore, with the peoples' food co-op. Basically folks who had a destination came, spent the night and we talked and cooked and ate and partied together…and come morning they'd pack up and with a good hug, leave for the road ahead. But those sans destination, just on the road, we often were able to channel into the Portland community scene in some positive way to help the evolving culture grow.

The Bellingham Arts Fair, having been so close to the Canadian border, was full of whispers about AWOLs (absent without official leave) from the armed forces—as was all the peace culture up in northern Washington State. So through these connections—and the free clinic—our house on Alder Street became a safe house on the underground railroad for draft resisters and war refusers—usually the latter landed fresh back from the battlefields of Nam at one of the California bases, then sought advice from friends, or peace action groups and through the evolving underground network got steered north up the I-5 corridor en route to peaceful Canada who was accepting many of the USA's best, recognizing these talented young people as an asset to their nation.

But in the USA this was a very hush-hush thing. AWOLs and draft refusers were being hunted for. People were being busted for aiding and abetting 'criminals.' But what could anyone of morals do, but help a person escape from a war they considered without merit, without morals, and without meaning? So help them we did.

Karen was just magnificent in all this. She was the supreme hostess. Gracious. Always overwhelmed by the stream of people, meals, dishes, places to arrange the backpacks and lie down, bedding to lie down on, laundry, and advice. Always the comforter, the rational, carefully thought-through idealist, giving sound counsel to so many bewildered travelers, runaways, stoned-out, spaced-out ones. Her mix of inspiration and practicality navigated the way for us through so many of these undefined projects: the Free Store, Famili(are) Mu*sing (the arts and craftstore), the Alder Street house, and from that we became at least a little better prepared for what was yet to come.

And to everyone, *everyone*, we talked about the Gathering, and about the free fest we Portlanders were planning for the end of the summer. The energies and the people were spiraling in, just as Kaushal had said they would, and the "Vortex" was beginning to form. Portland in the summer of '70 was vibrant, a throbbing amalgam of community-spirited adventurers on a true course toward…we weren't quite sure what, but a true course that we all believed in even if we didn't know the name of the destination.

Then we heard about the Buffalo Party.

The way we heard it, the nephew of a ranch owner outside Eatonville, Washington was planning a three-day rock n' roll concert on his uncle's ranch. The uncle thought it was a pretty good idea, probably a money-maker, and a chance for him to have a good ol' fun time over the Fourth of July weekend.

But Washington State, like so many states, had recently passed what were known as "Woodstock Laws." That is, laws designed to make it impossibly difficult to hold large outdoor concert-type events. These laws were passed frankly as a reaction to the culture that these Woodstock-like festivals might be celebrating—or even worse (!) *spawning*.

But this old-timey rancher thought the government had no business saying what he could or could not do on his own land. He was a born and bred American, that was all. And he had a lifetime's worth of friends in his surrounding community, so in reaction to the State government's notifying his nephew that this 'event' was prohibited by law, he announced that he was just having some of his friends over for the weekend—for a pig roast!

Well, bureaucratic governments don't take kindly to being end run, so they still told him No Go. So, he got with his old buddy Graham Green of the Flying Saucer Clubs of America (a UFO-interested group) and they concocted a plan. And the old farmer announced to the media, that they was holdin' a Politcal Convention for the Buffalo Party and they were goin' to be nominatin' Mr. Green for President of the United States of America—and anyone who wanted to run against him for the nomination was welcome to come too—and the people a-comin' were all going to be the official delegates, and the bands were the hired entertainment for the delegates, and any politician who didn't believe in the land of the free, and the people's right to participate in the American election process should just pack their bags an' move over there to Russia.

And the Buffalo Party was going therefore to be a free event. People could just donate freely to the cause as they came in.

So on we went. Once again across the Columbia River and northwards into the hills of lush green Washington. "The Buffalo Party and Pig Roast" was an amazing scene. When we arrived at the entrance we were ushered over a makeshift road across a ravine. Nearby was a regular wooden and steel bridge that no one was using. It seems the County Sheriff had come out and warned these folks that the event was illegal…and hundreds of the farmer's friends visited the Sheriff to tell him, come November he was going to be voted out of his job. So the Sheriff decided just to patrol the county roads for unsafe drivers instead of harassing the Party. Then the State Police had come and blocked one of the entryways, so the farmer took his Caterpillar tractor and bulldozed right through his own forest a couple of other roads. At the best way in he made a smaller (one lane only) ravine crossing and began bringing cars in and out in groups, first one direction then the other. And at the big bridge he installed dynamite explosives and made known that if any, any, any vehicle came across that bridge onto his land he would blow his bridge up and anything on it. He posted a notice: "Bridge scheduled for immediate demolition, cross at your own risk."

Inside, the site was like a big amphitheatre bowl—*ideal* outdoor acoustics. Parking was on one side, concessions next to stage left, and a whole huge hillside for sleeping out under the stars and watching the stage below you with its towers of speakers and colored lights.

Maybe 20 or 30 thousand people showed up. All of the local bands played. On Saturday night the flying saucer guy gave a rousing speech. He talked about our brother and sister starbeings who wish us well. He proclaimed he was running on a platform of Intergalactic Peace. The crowd went wild with cheering. The announcer said we were going to try to nominate him by acclamation. So at his word everyone made an affirmative cheer and he received the Buffalo Party's nomination for President.

All the while tens of thousands of people have been subsisting for two whole days, some for three days now on a steady diet of cold sodas, ice cream, and candy or snack foods. We took inspiration from the spectacular free kitchen put together at Woodstock by the Hog Farm and Friends—and decided on having a Sunday morning pancake breakfast.

With the (amazing isn't it) instant approval of the farmer's nephew we were able to make an announcement from the stage, and pass hats for donations through the packed amphitheatre and bring vans to Seattle to score colossal amounts of pancake ingredients. We returned exhausted to get a few hours of sleep before dawn.

Come early light we stake out a space about three-quarters of the way up the bowl from the stage. The sleeping crowd is thinned out enough to yield the space. I start digging a small fire pit, and with some of the musicians from the Bush Street house in Portland, and Glen and Karen we soon have a small frypan going with some batter sizzling, cooking away.

Up the hill, dreamily, strolls a young couple. "Hey, good morning. Would you like some pancakes?" I ask.

"No," and "No," they answer. "We're gonna wait for the big pancake breakfast later on."

"This is the 'big pancake breakfast.' At least the start of it." I reply.

"You're kidding." she says.

"No," I respond, " This is the beginning. We'll just have to hope it grows."

"Good luck," he says, " We'll be down later to help...after we get some sleep," and they wander up the hill.

The next people wandering by stopped to help. And we dug the second small fire pit next to our first. Soon there was a row of small cookfires, and a number of camping stoves making a curved arc facing the stage and all the sleeping people below us.

As it grew and more and more people came we began mixing the batter in buckets and then in a couple of new 'garbage' cans. Some guy brought his canoe paddles to stir with. By late morning there was an endless stream of people walking up the hillside toward the breakfast, and a long graceful line of cookfires and volunteers cooking, measuring, mixing, cleaning. Everyone happy, being fed. It was really beautiful.

There are people I met that morning who are Best Friends For Life. Joanee Freedom showed up, on the road far from her native Jersey shore, her old man still asleep in her travel-trailer, her wavy hair sticking out from under her floppy hat, and here she is flipping flapjacks, serving the people, same as she ever does.

From a campsite nearby Terri Faires wakes up, sees the evolving crescent of pancake makers and happy eaters. She explains, "You're who I want to be working with," and she pitches in all day…and for decades to come.

Just when we thought it couldn't have gotten any nicer, a full band comes onstage and begins to play. Melodious rock 'n roll music fills the whole valley. People are dancing. The weather is sparklingly clear. The 'breakfast' goes on long into the afternoon. And it takes us another day and a half to clean the 'kitchen' all up. But there was a joy in the freedom of that Buffalo Party that won't ever go away. Just ask anyone who was there.

26. Emerald Lakes

A small packet arrived by courier—by india-print-shirted bell-bottom-trousered courier—at the Alder Street house where the carved wood sign over the door read simply, "Temple Tribe." The packet contained an invitation and a marvelous hand-drawn map to The Emerald Lakes Gathering, located in The Three Sisters Wilderness Area, scheduled for the third weekend of August, 1970.

We already had a lot going on: the Free Store in downtown Portland was in its final hour; we were still looking for a land base to land on; we had a stained glass lamp shop set up in the basement and a weaving room upstairs where we could craft artful items to bring to the crafts store. Plus we were working with people all over the city on what was now becoming known as the Vortex Festival.

The People's Army Jamboree was also organizing and mapping out plans for its rally, its concert and its marches. There was huge discussion going on citywide about the dual events: both set for Labor Day weekend, both drawing huge numbers of supporters from all sides of the youth culture. And both sides utterly convinced that the 'other' choice was simply the wrong thing to do.

We spent a lot of the summer looking for a land base to settle on, driving through the Coast Range, camping en route, practically living on blackberries, the grandly abundant and so thoroughly satisfying berry of the Oregon countryside. On the one side of the coast range the streams run down to the broad Willamette Valley, but over the ridge to the west, they flow in tight twisty canyons of green foliage, over-towered by immense firs and hemlock and cedar, as they burble through steep shady drops and occasionally open out into small valleys rich with topsoil.

We looked in such areas for available land, maybe with a barn or old building on it to help us get started.

Back in Portland we tended the crafts store, and met with so many folks about Vortex: Glen Swift, a wiry, frizzle-haired soft-spoken wizard-type from the Isis Pottery shop and gallery next to The Wayfarer restaurant gave us intros to many of downtown's alternate culture merchants along with sage advice on how the intensity of putting together this festival needed "To come from an inner place of serenity and sureness of doing what was right and good." The Wayfarer eatery was an outpost for the teachings of Meher Baba, a Hindu avatar, which is where we met the restaurant's owner, Ben Wright, the coolest of the cool Portland entrepreneurs who guided us to many of the other counterculture restaurant owners and cooks. These people would be the Vortex chefs. We met up with Bobbie Wehe and Seth Booky, organizers extraordinaire and merchants of Nepalese, Tibetan and Indian textiles, art and incense through The Good Earth, their clothing and accessories store. They were able to bring together the people who could install and manage the stage and sound system. Richard was, in fact scheduling all the local talent, the bands who would provide the free music. Dan Galusha, a long red-haired, freckled and bespectacled philosopher who was living part time in the basement of a church (another temple janitor), brought us in touch with some amazing mystic Christians, from Koinonia House, wholly against the war, and wholly in favor of a peaceful expression of human community. They gave us use of office space—at least for address and phone, and most crucial, use of their meeting hall. All these people would be at the crux of the multi-intentional effort that Vortex was becoming.

The news media was largely focused on the threatened 'anti-Vietnam riots' they portrayed as the agenda of the People's Army Jamboree. And even though those people told the press over and over again that their agenda was to mobilize people power for social justice and to enlighten the rest of our country to the plight of Third World nations being used by the West for a kind of economic serfdom, still, the image the press gave the citizenry of Portland was of mayhem in the streets, and pitched battles between the angry protestors and the American Legionnaires, whose highly politicized convention was occurring at the same time and whose delegates would be roaming the same Rose City streets.

And periodically we'd meet someone who had also gotten an invitation to the Emerald Lakes Gathering. The mysterious hand-drawn lettering was intriguing with notations about a birthday celebration for a 21st orbit around the sun, and a planned collective 'celestial' ascent of the South Sister mountain peak. We looked at maps and found no such "Emerald" lakes, but a small cluster of mountain ponds whose printed name was "Green" Lakes. That was the place. They were snuggled at the base of the Three Sisters mountain peaks inside a true wilderness zone. The map's mysterious details and arcane penmanship beckoned us. The route in by either a north or south trail was a seven or nine mile hike. The south way was longer but the northern trail led over a pass. Either route was a long way from a parked car.

Posted flyers announced a Vortex community meeting at Koinonia House and their hall was packed. Some of the pacifist Christians chaired the meeting, and speaker after speaker from the floor offered support: the restaurants would provide cooks and servers; Richard had lined up (it seemed) every active band in the city and came with a long list of groups who'd participate for free: rock n' rollers mostly, but folk music too, and R 'n B and fiddle-playin' mountain bands. Some people said they'd work to attract a couple of big-name bands—maybe bands whose tours brought them near—who could be persuaded to play. Carpenters spoke up about plans to build temporary facilities and a stage. Electricians spoke up about wiring. The Beaver Hall people had sound equipment. An Explorer Scout group had Native American style tipi lodges we could use.

There was a surge of goodwill toward the Vortex plan, and a fair share of it was coming from an attitude of "We've got to do something to save our fair city from the angry and violent mobs that are headed here...and if that means lending support to this flower power rock n' roll show, then so be it."

There was a lot of fear already planted.

And it was strange to have so many solid-citizen types onboard for such a free-form event.

Someone spoke up about the American Legion and the envisioned conflicts with that group. I responded by suggesting that we communicate with them about the nature of the event we were producing, and invite them to come visit Vortex, and see that not all the counterculture, not all the protestors were hateful, angry or destructive. I volunteered to write letters and communicate with the American Legion on a friendly positive note, and to communicate this intention and invitation to the press as well.

When someone questioned "What about medical needs?" doctors and nurses, (even a couple of medics recently returned from Vietnam) stood up volunteering services. A further question arose about drug problems, especially the 'bad trips' that everyone had seen portrayed in the press from other festivals and in many of the images surrounding the rock party scene.

And Kaushal Yellin, from our own clan was speaking up, telling how he'd just come back from the Atlanta Pop Festival which had drawn over 300,000 people, and where there'd been lots of problems with that. He's explaining to everyone that they had tried alternative as well as standard medical treatment (which meant treating these people as temporarily insane, restraining them, shooting them up with Thorazine or some kind of come-down pills) which resulted in several medical tents looking like casualty zones, full of screaming hysterical people and doctors at a loss about how to control the scene. Instead they also had a place where people could come and get some gentle re-assurance and hand holding, and soft words of advice.

"And that's what we should do here," he concluded, from the front of the hall, "Use a couple of those tipis for Rainbow Tipis where if someone's having a hard time or is spaced out on hallucinogens they can be brought to us and we can softly guide them through it."

"What do you mean 'Rainbow Tipis'?" asked the next questioner.

"Well," Kaushal said, raising his eyebrows up for an instant, "Somebody's got rainbows pouring out of their eyes and ears. They're seeing rainbows splattered all over the walls, their friend's faces, and they've never seen anything like this before, and they're rightfully freaked out, and their friends can bring them over to these tipis, these Rainbow tents, and we'll be there, I'll be there," (he says, volunteering) "to walk them talk them along gently until they come back down into their own familiar bodies and minds."

Later we came to understand that while some of all that dis-association was due to people misjudging dosages of very tiny material, much more came from people tripping for the first time among friends who had never tripped at all, and having a hard time communicating or receiving support or comfort from their own circle of friends and becoming distrustful, paranoid, and disoriented as a result.

The public discussion moved on to other topics and I whisper to Kaushal, "That's a big job, a round-the-clock job you've volunteered for."

"Well, somebody's got to do it. Besides, half this hall is freaked out about people freakin' out, and now they trust us to take care of it."

"Us?"

As the meeting wound down we talked about where, where exactly, to place this Vortex on the ground. What was the location to be? There were several suggestions and one group of friends volunteered to check out suggested sites and return with opinions.

We turned our attention southward with another journey into the coast range still looking for forest and farmland to call home.

Two weeks later back in Portland we found out that Bobbie Wehe and Seth Booky, having determined that McIver State Park, twenty minutes east of Portland along the Clackamas river, was an ideal place to land Vortex, had communicated with Salem and with Governor Tom McCall about using the park for the festival. McCall was called a 'maverick.' He had been a newscaster who felt he was better qualified for public office than any of the officials he interviewed, so he ran for Governor—as an independent—and won. He approved the plan.

Meanwhile, The People's Army Jamboree had negotiated with the City of Portland for use of Delta Park—a large flat park, bordering the Columbia River to the north and pretty much out of the way of the downtown parts of the city, but a place to set up a speaker's stage, and to camp out while mounting the daytime protests downtown.

Still another Pacific Northwest tribal group was the Sky River Family. They were neither loudly political, nor loudly social-activist. They were just loudly classic psychedelic rock 'n rollers. A year before they had hosted a small but wonderful rock concert in the Washington woods, and they had just announced and publicized with posters that they were going to hold another one: Sky River II—the same weekend as both Vortex and People's Army.

It was time to go to Emerald Lakes.

We had heard also that folks from Marblemount were on their way down there too. What? They were supposed to be en route into the deep woods to make winter camp. But as the weeks had worn on and August had begun to turn its season's face toward winter, and still no Harold, and no horses, the clan decided to head south to Emerald Lakes instead.

After parking at the northern entranceway to the wilderness, along with another carload of travelers whose timing had brought them through our Portland house, we—Glen and Rain and Kaushal and Karen and I—all loaded up our backpacks and set off into a land of awesome grace and beauty.

This was the best.

The hike was huge. Over the pass and the last staggering hill climb, below us the southernmost of the Emerald lakes is revealed with the clans camped up from the lakeside below the towering peaks of the Three Sisters.

In the evening light and coolness coming over the last ridge, heated and sweaty from the hot afternoon's haul, striding down the hillside, offloading packs, stripping down and heading to the water; cries behind us of "It's mighty cold in there" so easily ignored in the refreshing need of a cool plunge. We are splashing ahead into the lake. THIS IS GLACIAL WATER! It is ICE COLD!! And we are splashing out of there as fast as we can. Standing around the already orange-flamed fire in the now blue-darkening light.

Images: Rock outcroppings silhouetted against a sky bearing its evening stars. Music of guitars and flutes strumming and fluttering across the lake. Lapping water against the rocks and sand at the lake's edge. Drums up on the high side. People coming slowly toward the fire. Hands passing around home-baked breads while pies bake in Dutch ovens by the fireside.

In the morning light, patches of flowers wave at us, laughter peals, children toddle on the green green grasses of the Emerald lakeside. Birds caw from the forest, soar overhead, plunge to catch fish. We are in a Natural Paradise.

The Marblemounters are there: Barry Adams, Chuck Mills, now called "Windsong," Tom "Rob Roy" Rowley, Laika, Terry Faires, Lila Rain and the "Old Man" Harold—why he must've been at least 40. So are the folks from the Mendo Zendo (the Zen Buddhism center of Mendocino, California), gnarly wise man Baba, and dobro player Mitch Mitchell. I re-meet David Lescht aka Davy Light, his gracious wife Ellen and their good friend Jim Robinson whose 21st birthday it is. It turns out he's the one who actually penned and sent out those invitation packets. I had met Davy and Ellen a summer ago in their lushly overgrown house in Eugene's student district. The Phantom Feeders (a group that fed on-the-spot meals to the homeless and street people) are there in force, plus sundry accomplices of the various communes and communities that stretched along The Fertile Crescent from Northern California through Southern Oregon in a continuing swath across Washington State and through a band of Idaho and on into Montana. There assembled: a hundred people all told.

We are camped in a broad semi-circle along the tree line at the southern lake's northern edge and we lay plans for an ascent of the South Sister. A fiddle plays haunting melodies from some unseen place. Puppies run happily about, playing with my longtime companion cat Sesame who has hiked in here on his own four legs along with us. Well, he hiked most of the way. We did carry him when he meowed loudly enough.

In the early morning a long strip of LSD's is passed around. They're blue dots on a single long curlicue of paper. Never seen 'em like that before—or since. "How many do we take?" someone asks. "Two? Three?" the roll gets passed around and we begin the ascent. The cairn-marked trail leads up to the high glacial snowfields. These are glorious moments. Don't you believe for a second that the Hippie Dream never existed. The snow is all crystalline sparkling. The sunlight shimmers onto us like the flow of photons that it truly is. The rocks are colossal jewels and we climb among them each one helping the other along.

At the top we are all present and accounted for. Despite our free-spirited nature, many of us are skilled—even professionally trained—guides and outdoorspersons. From the top we can see forever. But it's time to go down. We glissade down the melted snowpacks, skimming along on the heels of our boots. And it's easy to see the green lakes far below us. There, the Family has made hot dinner for us and by darktime everyone's back along the shore of the lake.

The next days are as peaceful as it gets. People sitting in meditation, the sounds of axes splitting wood, couples walking holding hands, everyone in harmony.

27. V is for Vortex

We arrived at the gates of McIver Park just as the event was beginning to construct itself.

Out from Portland, up the well-maintained state highway along the Clackamas River and coming up a long country road flanked by farms suddenly there was the turn into the park. Already folks from Green Lakes were laying out parking zones well beyond the usual designated State Park lots. They motioned us on down the hill.

At the next downhill level toward the river lay a big field and at the far end of that a cluster of people stood talking; we drove along the field's perimeter over toward them and found they were the crew assembling to assemble the stage. Trucks stood next to them with unloaded piles of lumber and timber. The circle was discussing general construction plans: the log beams up front to give the most rustic and natural look while the joists and posts stood behind giving solidity and strength.

Figure 22. Building the Vortex Stage, McIver Park, Oregon (i). (Lee Meier: 1970)

Figure 23. Building the Vortex Stage, McIver Park, Oregon (ii). (Lee Meier: 1970)

Figure 24. Building the Vortex Stage, McIver Park, Oregon (iii). (Glenn Davis: The Far Out Story of Vortex 1, 1970)

Figure 25. Building the Vortex Stage, McIver Park, Oregon (iv). (Glenn Davis: The Far Out Story of Vortex 1, 1970)

Figure 26. Building the Vortex Stage, McIver Park, Oregon (v). (Clackamas County Sheriff's Office: The Far Out Story of Vortex 1, 1970)

A dozen of the crew had been up at Green Lakes. They hinted to us that this team would have the stage up in plenty of time; we'd be better to head down farther toward the river where the village was just starting to get together. So on we went, down the winding park drive to the village below: crews unloading restaurant gear, electric hook ups; tarps set between park trees to cover supplies.

We found a shaded area behind a large opening in the trees and set up camp. Then the troop of Explorer Scouts showed up. They were donating the tipis that we could use to help center the living village in whatever way seemed appropriate to us.

I asked if they had people or scouts or visitors who planned on staying in these tipis also.

"No," said one of the Explorer leaders, "We'll just need one of the tipis so we can drop in or stay over if we like. We'll probably use just one, maybe two, at most. There're thirteen lodges. In a way we're here to give the troop practice at setting them up."

The scouts have already noticed the meadow next to our camp area. "Yeah, that'd be a great place to put them," volunteer I.

In very little time the first lodge is set up. And I'm learning from these folks about the tradition of the horseshoe of tipis oriented in relation to the sun and away from the wind. Each lodge had its purpose or its family. Things were oriented certain ways for certain reasons. And in moments a couple of us are in the middle of the mix setting up the lodges along with the Explorers.

When we're mostly done they again make clear to us that they don't—absolutely don't—want to watch over these tipis during the event.

"That's your part of the bargain. Take good care of them," says the troop leader, and putting some of their gear in a lodge on the river side of the u-shaped arrangement, off they go.

We designate two of the tipis Rainbow tipis—one on each side near the center of the crescent; another tipi for Lost Children or child-care needs; one fills up with dry firewood; one becomes a Volunteer Center where people who are here to help set up—or just here for the weekend—can come and be steered toward Things They Can Do To Help. Such as parking or serving and preparing food, or stage crew.

Figure 27. Joseph set up a battleship's array of steam kettles, Vortex 1, September, 1970. (Glenn Davis: The Far Out Story of Vortex 1, 1970)

Figure 28. Vortexers chopping vegetables in front of Joseph's deisel-powered boiler, Vortex 1, September, 1970. (Clackamas County Sheriff's Office: The Far Out Story of Vortex 1, 1970)

Nearby the community kitchen stands one of McIver Park's brick washhouses. It has excellent water faucets, drains, lines for hose connections and it becomes the main food preparation area. Next to it an old-timer from the Portland Gray Panthers, Joseph, is setting up a battleship's array of steam kettles. These are gas powered, and he's got a trailer that's pulled the whole thing here and a trailer for the fuel supply.

Figure 29. Shoveling rice from Joseph's amazing 'kettle drum' cookers to feed tens of thousands of people. Vortex 1, September 1970. (Gerry Lewin: 1970)

Joseph and Bobby Wehe had rounded it up at Zidell's scrapyard. It's the kind of thing they used on 6000-person battleships to feed *their* crew. Lines of pipe connect these stainless steel kettles. Each holds 250 gallons. There are ten of them. They look like a giant line of kettledrums. He's busy hooking up burner parts under each of the kettles. And hoping to get the thing running.

People are busy everywhere and as we're walking about, people are flashing each other the 'peace sign': first and second fingers held up in a 'V". For years that handsign was used as an indicator meaning "For Peace" and/or "Against the War." But today people were bopping up and down the parkland paths flashing the 'peace sign' and calling out, "V is for Vortex!"

It's a bit of a blur to me as to when the 'set up' of the event turned into the actual event itself...partly because the whole thing was free so there wasn't a day or an hour when the 'gate' began charging money or collecting tickets to get in. No, the whole thing just grew, starting from whenever *you* got there.

Vortex 1 A Biodegradable Festival of Life. What does that really mean? What does it look like? Pictures from the Exhibition:

everywhere tents are springing up, families unpacking. I wander up toward the upper field and see the stage rising. Large tents and tarps are going up behind the structure. A driveway is roped off along the field edge to separate traffic from people, trucks are using the drive, depositing equipment and materials by the stage. I hike farther uphill. By now there is a parking pattern. Vehicles being directed toward nearest parking first and lanes roped off for conduits from the main entrance to the parking areas farther away. Like a hive in full swing of late summer (which it is) we are preparing for what lies ahead. But already ahead is a line of cars approaching the park gates, full of people who have heard the news and have somehow decided to attend.

Shuttles are running from the top (parking) to the village, and back again up the hill. People coming in are brought with their camping gear down to the bottom near the riverside, and then after they set up house, it's just a walk up to the stage.

At the kitchen, service has already begun. Teams are working as servers, cooks, washers, and preps. Ben Wright from The Wayfarer Café is in the midst of this activity like a walking talking signpost, gently giving directions, answering a question for someone, pointing toward something for another. Selmah, whom I had met at the Kozmos House (another amazing community dwelling) in Portland, was mixing pancake batter in brand new 30-gallon plastic garbage cans.

Joseph has got one of the burners cooking. Behind the brick washhouse a group of folks are unloading cardboard boxes full of frozen burgers. They're stacking bagged blocks of ice between the rows of stacked burger boxes to keep them cold. It's a gift from a coalition of downtown independent restaurants doing their 'civic duty' thing and helping what they hope will keep the Labor Day weekend peaceful in their downtown.

We carefully dig a firepit in the center of the crescent of tipis, line it with rocks and, to preserve the sod for replanting later, we set it carefully in a shady place and water it regularly to keep its

Figure 30. Vortex 1: The line of cars stretched for miles. (Oregon State Parks: The Far Out Story of Vortex 1, 1970)

Figure 31. Bathers and sunbathers at the Clackamas River. (Kerry Haas: The Far Out Story of Vortex 1, 1970)

biology alive. We drag firewood from the park's farthest reaches along the embankment that drops off toward the river. By the flowing Clackamas there are already sunbathers, swimmers and waders all enjoying the beautiful late afternoon. Across the river and up the embankment there stand a few State Police watching, protecting no doubt the wealthy estates that line the opposite shore.

After dark and dinner Tom Rowley brings his congas out to the fire and sets up a beat, a couple of other drummers join him, then more. The stage-building crew comes trooping down the hill, weary from a long day's work in the sun, and they see the glow from the village, people dancing under the stars, the fire illuminating the circle of lodges. It is the village at peace, enjoy it, by tomorrow night the stage will be 'on' and who knows how many more thousands of people will have arrived.

Vortex held true to its name: a swirling mass of experiences.

And the space between the masses...mysterious as spirals and cascades of light and sound.

The next afternoon I'm wandering back up the crowded trails toward the upper roadway and the stage. There are throngs of people celebrating. Celebrating whatever could be celebrated. And I see up ahead on the trail there's a crowd surrounding a voice. A voice speaking in preacher-like tones of authority. And I hear the words, over the heads of the knot of people, "Yessirree brothers and sisters! We are here to celebrate! That's right celebrate! Celebrate the Birth of the Lord! Celebrate the Birth of Love. Yes! Love in your hearts Sisters and Brothers! Now, Who here can tell us what else we're here to celebrate?"

He pauses and I draw closer. Close enough to look through the standing bodies and catch a glimpse of a short animated black man in the circle's center. And then a young lady's voice pipes up, "We're here to celebrate Peace with each other."

"Right you are pretty little Lady," sweet talks the black man in the tan shorts. "Right you are, now come up here and claim your prize!"

She ventures forward and receives into her hand some small objects that he describes as, "Two of the prettiest little Mescaline capsules ever put together." He goes on, "Next on our little givaway we have four, count them four, small blue flats of Check-o-slovac acid. Made just a few short years ago in the liberated territory of Check-o-slo-va-kia, be-fore the Russian tanks moved in. This is the real thing, my dears." He pauses and looks down touching his palms to the sides of this head. Everyone's watching while he seems to take a moment to think. He lifts his head up. "Ok, this little answer and question is about Life. Why is it sacred? Why must we protect it??" His voice is rising again, "What do the holy books and prophets say about it? Any answers? Any answers?"

And a young man's voice in the crowd says, "Well, it says, 'Choose life'—that's in the Old Testament—and I guess that means, sometimes we have to make decisions between things like war and, you know, not war."

"Right you are!" exclaims the man in the middle. "Come right up here young mister and claim your prize!" The young man steps forward and is given the four blue flats.

I'm fascinated by this one man wondershow. I see him fumble about in his shorts pockets. "Aha!....I thought this game was maybe going to have to come to an end, but no. Right here, Right here in my hands I have several more treats and sacraments for you all! Alrighty," (He rolls along in his rap seamlessly) "Alrighty, now I want to talk to you about Lib-er-a-tion! We hear talk about Black Liberation. About Women's Liberation. About the liberation of the empire's colonies, and about liberation of the mind. Well let me tell you, brothers and sisters, what we need is pimply-faced boy liberation and fat girl liberation. We need liberation so every god-given person on earth can walk around with respect."

I am continuing to head up the path, his voice trailing off behind me, "Brothers and Sisters, I tell you, you know how we treat some poor boy with a pimple problem, or some poor girl with a weighty problem. Well the time is going to come when every man, boy, girl and woman is going to be able to walk this earth with respect, isn't it? And when tell me, who will tell me, who can tell me? When is that time to be?"

The paths are full of people just getting here, heading down to the village to set up their camps. And I'm continuing on my hike uphill.

Up at the stage area, the sight takes my breath away. There are thousands and thousands of people and the music hasn't even started yet. And the thousands of people are moving, most of them moving, it's hard to figure just where. Kind of like in a big wheel of people or a great herd of elk circling.

And then at one side of the field I see this huge god's eye, a criss-cross of two poles wound 'round with colored yarns in a gigantic mandala pattern. This god's eye cross is being carried around the

Figure 32. Looking out from the stage, Vortex 1, September 1970. (Gerry Lewin: 1970)

huge field and people are following it, like some colossal totem, and as it moves through the field or, as I figured out, had been moving in a great circle around the field for a while now and was now heading in toward the stage with the vortex of people turning behind it. It's carried up onto the stage, and people are following, bringing a whole arm of the public up onto the stage, and there's a man, speaking out to the crowd. No one can hear him, the mics aren't turned on. It's Old Man Harold. Barry's near him, and they're making a prayer, an invocation I guess. And then the cross is moving again, off the stage and the swarm of people moving up the ramp to the stage behind them, bringing the whole circle, maybe even most of the whole field of people up onto and across the stage. It's like a giant parade moving across the stage and back down onto the field level. Everyone there early enough had a chance to be up on the stage—and to see for themselves the whole view out overlooking the assembled crowds below. No other rock festival had done anything like that before.

After that, the bands opened up and the music played for free for the next four days.

28. Calm in the Storm

All the same long Labor Day Weekend, the American Legion's convention is ongoing in Portland. The People's Army Jamboree is marching in the downtown streets, The Sky River rock festival is happening in Washington State just to our north, and today, two buses of Legionnaires are en route toward Vortex.

At the front entranceway the buses are offloading dozens of rowdy, some drunken, and a few curious members of the Right Wing veteran's organization: The American Legion. Most of these guys are in their mid-thirties or early forties, veterans of 1950's Cold War conflict: Korea.

Inside the park word has passed through the Vortex that these buses are up by front gate, and I'm there in a few minutes. The Legionnaires are clustered by their buses on the shoulder across the highway. Young longhairs are on the park side of the road gathering, curious, too. The guys from the buses are holding beers and sipping Jack Daniel's whiskey and a few of them start to holler, "Why don't you cut your hair, you look like a little girlie!" and "God Bless America!"

The longhairs aren't just keeping their mouths shut either. "If you don't like us, go away!" and "God ain't blessing your war!"

The few State Troopers sitting in their cars by the Gate were very uncomfortable.

"Get a job!" "Grow up and defend your country!" holler the voices from across the road.

When all of a sudden over one of the sawhorse barricades that channeled traffic, leaps a man dressed only in bathing shorts. He's barefoot and striding across the highway toward the busses. His shoulder-length blond hair flops behind him. He's beautifully handsome. His muscles and hair shine in the sun. He approaches the Legionnaires and throws his arms up into the air. "Welcome,

Brothers!" He calls out so everyone can hear.

"You're Not *my* Brother!" call back several voices.

"That's what you think," he answers. "I'm two weeks back from active duty." He gives his rank and unit number. "And I fought for my country so that festivals like *this* could happen. They don't have festivals like this in Communist countries do they?" He has everyone's attention. And he walks into their midst and just starts talking quietly with them.

Figure 33. Chuck 'Windsong' Mills (center) playing drums at the tipi circle, Vortex 1. (Gerry Lewin: 1970)

I am amazed. The whole scene breathes a collective sigh of relief. It turns out that some of the Legionnaires want to come in, look around, enjoy the show, and that most of the others just want to hang at the gate for a while and then go back to Portland, having visited "The Vortex." So one bus slowly loads with its passengers, and the other waits for a few hours while the guys go inside to walk around.

Down below the stage in the village, the tipis are all functioning as though we had been doing this for years. There are lost children brought to the lost

Figure 34. Shanti Sena tipi and volunteer peacekeepers, Vortex 1. (Gerry Lewin: 1970)

children's & lost-and-found tipi and lost parents are coming to be re-united with them. There's a medical lodge for first aid, mostly scrapes, stings, minor burns...the usual mishaps of camping excursions. There's a tipi where volunteers have brought firewood.

There's a Shanti Sena Tipi, which is our first effort to find a way to PeaceKeep ourselves. The idea came from the Sanskrit words meaning Peace Scenes, and Glen Swift, from the Isis Gallery, explained that only people who are genuinely peaceful themselves can be a peacekeeping force in a community. It all seemed so obvious and so new all at once.

Figure 35. One of the Rainbow tipis at Vortex 1. (Gerry Lewin: 1970)

Our "Rainbow" Tipis were full. Full of people who had taken LSD, or Psilocybin or Some Other Psychedelic for the first time. Mostly these folks were the pioneering member of a group of friends, trying this stuff out, getting less easily communicative as the drug came on, and then brought to us by concerned friends who'd never heard this pal of theirs saying things like "Oh My God! Everything Is...Everything!!!" So they'd bring 'em by the Rainbow Tipis, where we sit 'em down, be generally quiet, let the flow of the Time Being roll easily around us, and tell their friends that he—or she—would be just fine in a few hours. Just let them relax here in this safe space, and check back later. We'd softly offer water, warm tea, cushions, sometimes quiet music, or, as appropriate, poems, stories, readings, even discussions as folks drifted back into verbal communications.

One time a couple of professionals from the Portland

psychiatric community came to the tipis. I was in the middle of telling a tale about White Rabbit Meets Br'er Rabbit and these professionals got into it, listened, joined in the process for the night, watched as we served tea, watched folks come in, find some calm in the storm, and then move on.

Sometimes it wasn't so easy. Some tripsters were tremendously disoriented. One man seemed beset by devils. He saw everyone as a devil: no disguise: tails, horns. He was really freaked out. He kept saying he wanted a car. Not these "devil's footsoldiers." So we brought a car over. And he saw it was the devil's car! No, he was torn. He wanted to get in a car. He said if he was in a car, he'd be outta this horrible place. But whoa! The car that got sent was the devil's car! So we got him a different car. He wasn't so sure about the second car either. Finally he got in the car. Just sitting there. And he chilled out, and got calm, and came to grips with whatever was inside him. And a couple of hours later, he just thanked us so much for bringing this car over, so he could sit in it. I guess he just needed a car, not a tipi.

Another frightening experience was 'Love, Peace and Happiness.' She began screaming and running in the dark of night. Through the camp. Suddenly, the scream, "Love, Peace and Happiness!" would erupt at top shrieking volume and then she'd come running in some direction straight as an arrow, completely naked, barreling through the crowded part of the sleeping camp, through tents, branches, gear, at full speed and then out of sight and completely quiet. Time would pass, and then again, just as suddenly, her shriek, Love! Peeeeace, and Haaaaaappinessssss! would tear through the night, followed by her. She did this over and over. Running at top speed, out of nowhere and back into the expansive shadows of the park.

We searched for her between the screams. We called her Love Peace and Happiness.

But the scary part was the cliffs. Alongside that part of the encampment, on the riverside, were steep rock cliffs. It was easy to find the broad pathways down them in the daytime, or really even at night...if you were looking. Harold came and said that the cliffs were the problem, that we had to get near the cliffs, to keep her from hurting herself. So a few of us spaced ourselves along the cliff tops facing inward, listening for signs of the midnight screamer. At the same time others went searching for the woman. Harold is holding his head looking downward with his thumb and index finger at the bridge of his nose. I ask what he's doing and he tells me, "I'm meditating on that girl's safety."

Another half hour, and several screaming runs later, here she comes full speed—straight toward the cliff. I'm much too far away to stop her. And like that! She stops. Just freezes, each muscle like a statue's. Harold is just still as can be, too. In that same meditating position.

I walk toward her slowly, but in a moment she's taken off again, with another brain-curdling scream, "Lovvvvvvve! Peeeeee-ace Aaaaaaaannnd Haaaaaapiiiiiiineeeeeesssssss!" She's run off, away from the cliff and back into the darkness of the park.

Another couple of hours and I'm ready for bed, exhausted. I heard that toward dawn someone found her sleeping, curled up; and gently set a blanket upon her. Watchers kept a protective eye on her and in the morning, her friends came back from the music up at the stage, and after she awoke they led her gently back to her own camp.

Kaushal is up by the side of the stage with another tipi. He's got it set up as one of the Rainbow Tipis where anyone can come and get some peaceful time.

But not far away, and on the same side of the stage, there was a medical tent set up by—was it volunteers?— or was it Portland City Medical?—or County?—Or State?—or What?

Inside under fluorescent light doctors and nurses treated many of the common hazards of outdoor public assemblage: scrapes, sprains, sunburn. But to the matter of psychedelic overdoses, these 'professionals' had a different style.

Kaushal described a fellow held down, strapped down to a table, flailing about wildly, making animal-like noises while the doctors struggled to administer a hypodermic shot.

"Horrible," says Kaushal.

"Yeah, his friends brought him to the wrong tent," I reply.

Down below in the village, in the night hours, in the center of the horseshoe of tipis, played the drums. Many more drums than I'd ever seen together before. Conga Tom—aka Rob Roy—had definitely been right. These *were* the hand-held messengers of the meeting of old and new civilizations.

As the show at the upper stage wound down, down the hill came folks: audience, crew, musicians, and the circle at the tipis intensified. More wood on the fire, more people dancing, more drums, flutes, shakers, rattlers, rollers. There is a beat thumping between Earth and Sky.

I'm already exhausted, sitting as I still do: leaned back against the side of the lodge, my daypack as a sort of cushion, just watching, enjoying it all, but way too tired to get up and join the fray.

The drums crescendo: someone rings chimes, and the beating subsides into one of the quiet moments between the rushes. A woman's voice calls out "We Are!" Just like that. Into the Moment. And another voice responds, not missing tempo, "The Rainbow!" "Family!!" exclaims another. "Of Living Light!!" echoes a deep baritone. And there's almost another silent moment. But a half of a moment—much less time than it takes to read this—later, just a half of a moment later, someone cheers, someone cheers and throws a hat in the air, and everyone is cheering and there are lots of hats and headbands being tossed high above us.

It was a nice moment. We were finding identity as a People. It seemed more like a spontaneous expression of awareness and delight than a naming ceremony. I hardly thought I'd hear that phrase again. And I don't know who hollered the words. But the name, Rainbow Family of Living Light, has stuck and wisely so.

PART SIX

Into the Woods

(1970–1971)

In which young people of the generation of the New World Culture take to the hills in order to discover and learn the essential lessons of nature, outside the boundaries of the corporations and the banks. And in which these visionary young people co-mingle both with each other and also with the rural old-timers who still hold the wisdom of the pioneer spirit.

29. How the Whole Thing Works

Water rains down from the sky, touches the earth, and begins to flow along farther and downward into the earth, emerging as tiny rivulets, then streams and rivers, and eventually simultaneously emptying into and filling the ocean.

Along the way, we enter the flow, tapping its courses for drinking water, agriculture, cleanliness and recreation. Who controls the faucet controls the human world: where people will go, what we will do, how we will fare. Political power comes out of the water faucet. Although Mao Tse-tung said it comes from the barrel of a gun, the guns, the oil, the machinery of State are all vested in the fundamental outflowing of drinking-quality and irrigation-quality water.

Civilizations have risen and fallen on the tides of their own water systems. There's an argument to be made that our humanity's first cities were the results of dam builders and water channelers, whose work along the Tigris and Euphrates rivers became the first walled villages.

Eight hundred years ago the largest city on Earth rested along the Missouri River where the Mound Builders flourished. More than 125,000 persons dwelt there. Gone. Disappeared; not by war. Today's science thinks they fouled their water supply.

In mid-September 1970 shortly after Vortex, Karen and I rendezvoused with friends from Reed, companions from the Alder Street house and other members of the anti-war Portland community and headed into the Oregon Coast Range. We had found a place in a mountain valley where water flowed out from the hillsides' natural spring formations.

At the bottom of that valley a small river ran in the shadow of a towering, deeply-forested north-facing hillside above it. Water above, and water below. The image of a small farm nested in a huge forest. Greenery. And wood for lumber and fuel. An old, funky, unfinished cabin, a fallen down barn and an ancient overgrown orchard all graced the property. A winding mountainous road a dozen miles long separated us from the rest of so-called civilization.

And the river just keeps flowing down to the sea. Here, the river is mostly ankle-deep or knee-deep at most. But it does gather steam as all these side creeks sleek their way in through the trees. Through 80 miles of backwoods, and a huge old burned area, over a broad falls that the salmon leap during the torrents of winter, and then into the salty estuary of its much larger sister river, the Umpqua, where they mix their waters for the last several miles before joining the Pacific Ocean.

We packed our gear, a dozen or more of us, and left Portland and unpacked ourselves a half day later on the dirt flat in front of the old unfinished cabin.

Figure 36. The Hippies have landed! Top row, from the left: Heath, Bear, Teri, Dana, Terri, Maggie, Laika and Rob Roy. Front row, from the left: Garrick, Karen, Major and John. (Photographer unknown: Collection of the author, 1970)

Figure 37. It was a joyous occasion. (Photographer unknown: Collection of the author, 1970)

Karen and I put up our white and golden tent between the cabin and the trees. Others set up in different clearings—sites of potential homes and houses. No one camped out in the common space, the cabin, soon-to-be-called Main House.

We'd found a hidden valley suited to a life close to the earth, the soil, the rains, the woods, the natural forces of growing plants, which after all had nurtured our ancestors since time had begun being kept track of. And which could surely now nurture us as well, despite our brief interlude (as playwright Bertholt Brecht called it) in The Jungle of Cities—despite our generation's parents and grandparents who inhabited the concrete canyons, despite our entire lives' dependence on supermarketed food supplies and push button energy sources—off we went, full of what? Vision! And enthusiasm into the Great North Woods.

This farm had been settled by homesteaders in the early years of the 1900's, and then logged and re-logged leaving a stand of baby trees re-growing where once the giant fir, cedar and hemlock had stood. These young trees, mostly three or four inches in diameter crowded the hillside thick as green fur, so we cut trails through them, forging fence posts and rails from their green timber.

I could afford a part of the 160 acres from monies Irving Beck, my grandfather-in-the-auto-parts-business, had earmarked for the remainder of my college education. Four months earlier I turned twenty-one and had access to these dollars, which I retrieved and immediately put into this land. Well, part of it. The land I couldn't afford I took options on, to acquire at the same rate within a future time period. And that's what happened. There were others who came up that road who understood what we were doing and who had the funds to purchase—in three separate parcels—the rest of the 160 acres. As a result, the whole of the 'commune' as we called it then wasn't in any one person's hands, but spread out among several instigators.

Back in Portland, Karen and I had been busy making sets of dome hubs. We'd cut and drilled three full sets with the idea that we could set up at least three geodesic structures. We'd worked in Gary Bickford's family's machine shop, where he had grown up learning the use of these industrial grade cutters, drill presses, etc. He'd been one of the great techies of the P. H. Martin Medicine show back at the Bellingham Arts Fair and he was also one of the keys to the building and construction at Vortex. He showed us how to cut the pipe, and most importantly—fabricate a jig that would put pairs of holes into the steel pipe at the angles required by the geodesic geometry. That was an eye opener—seeing how the industrial tools could make the parts we needed for these thin membranes between ourselves and the winter cold.

We selected a level spot on the hillside above the old orchard for the first of these.

Rob Roy and Laika, from the Marblemount Outlaws found a place to build their 'Tower' and encamped there. They planned a hexagon defined by six huge pillars, cut from on-site timber.

Bear, Michael Bear, the largest man among us, part Minnesota

Potawatomi Indian, described plans for a log cabin. But said he, he was going to get to work on the firewood supply instead, and just stay on that for right now. At least some of us had some practical sense. He and his sweetie, Teri, would camp out under a leanto in the woods not far up the hill from Main House.

Dana, our photographer friend from Reed and Portland's 'Bush Street House' set up his ultra-light camp and helped with everything.

Mike, another Reedie, came down from Portland with his Land Rover full of tools—not, he said, to live at the farm but just as a 'technical advisor.' He seemed to have a lot of tool and building experience. His friend Russel showed up with his son Christopher. Russel was an actual skilled carpenter.

The fallen-down barn with its great gray wood near the front entrance was already slanting when we got there. By the time we had pulled a few boards off, it was starting to collapse, so a posse was organized to tear the whole thing down carefully and use all of it. After that, the remains of another decayed old homestead dwelling got carefully pulled apart, de-nailed and stacked to make ready for re-use. It was hard to picture what it had looked like because it was already just a heap. Paul Breslin, the guitarist, worked relentlessly pulling nails and sawing off the rotted ends of the old boards.

Selmah, from Chile originally, joined us and after a few nights in the Main House moved to the small shed at the edge of the old orchard. She and Kaushal cleaned up the Main House attic to get it ready for winter habitation. They found a huge old dead rat under the eaves and Selmah removed what was left of the beast—after Kaushal convinced her it was okay to pick it up because it was 'organic.' Selmah trotted around the farm in a pair of silver shoes and a purple velvet coat embroidered with rainbows and mushrooms. Early each morning she would go down to the river to bathe and come back up the hill to start cooking breakfast for everyone.

We were not your typical farmers in coveralls and dungarees. Nope. We were bell-bottomed, embroidered, patchwork-sewn, multi-colored, scarf-wearing, ruffle-shirted, head-banded, orgy-sandaled, peasant-skirted, barefooted, and sometimes even just marvelously and completely naked.

Annie, another broad-smiling California Girl, moved into the remains of an old chicken coop also at the orchard's edge.

Peggy Morrison, a wavy-haired ex-Reed student, moves down from Portland and is good at everything: gardening, wood chopping, orchard-pruning, fence-mending… and she has people skills, to help with the endless small-scale fusses that arose among us.

Auggie, fresh from the legendary Haight-Ashbury scene arrived and became best of friends with Terri Faires. They and Peggy sewed hats in the upstairs of the main house cabin for selling at the Eugene crafts markets. Auggie ground flour in our hand grinder. That was an endless job. And she made endless pots of tea.

Terri Faires said that she would build a dwelling made of all the remnants, the remainders, all the extra and unused pieces and parts from each of the other cabins we were going to build. All the odd flats of wood and boards—the House of Twelve it would later be called, because of its twelve sides.

There we were. Actually and at last, and at *a beginning*. We had stepped forward into our own brave new uncharted world, and we felt like muscle-men lifting a ton, like guitarists thwanging a reverberating chord, like children in paradise: there we were, upon The Land, with the tools and energy and gung ho attitudes that could (we were sure) move mountains if need be. It was an exhilarating time, cut loose really from the mainstream and watching pilgrims of great talents (and no talents) come over that winding pass and down into this valley of green. There was enough water for a multitude, fuel a' plenty, and fields with deep topsoil that could feed a village of families at least. For those moments we felt we had set our feet upon miraculous ground.

Figure 38. In the lower field we fenced two acres and grew all manner of vegetables and greens. (Garrick Beck: 1974)

After the September sun sweetened and ripened the colossal blackberries, shady October arrived and the apples, pears and plums in the heritage orchard yielded their fruit. Then the rains descended. The perennial rains, the constant misty damps, the relentless showers, the gray gray skies of the coastal clouds, the pelting storms, the weeks on end of droplets suspended in the air were upon us and the axes sank and stuck in the damp wood. Twine strung across the ceilings was hung with more socks than we could count. We lived in our wool shirts, our wool jackshirts, and our damp wool caps. These are the reasons the University of Oregon teams are named "Ducks." The gray days of fall stretch endlessly—seamlessly—into the gray days of winter, and then, yes even then, into the long gray days of early and even mid-spring. It's like one huge long gray day that gets dark at night.

Long before the calendar pages had turned from that first September to the month of Thanksgiving, we had, all of us, moved into the attic of the main house.

Well, almost all of us. Laika laid out a massive tarot card reading in the downstairs room off the kitchen, and she and Rob Roy moved into that one private room, along with the cards... and they kept the downstairs fire going at night.

Mike and Russel and Christopher stayed in their rigs or drove back and forth to Portland to dry themselves out, returning for work parties aimed at specific projects.

But the rest of us moved ourselves into the cramped upstairs. We nailed one-by-twelves up against the exposed insulation and followed Bear and Teri's advice and hung cloths to make separate rooms for ourselves.

Each night as we blew out the yellow flames from the olde-farm kerosene lanterns that lit our evening world and said our good nights, Bear and Teri began their regular ritual of nightly sex. As I said he was a huge man and while I have no idea how tiny Teri survived under him, I do know that at first just the attic floor, and as-s-s-s-s they got-t-t-t-t into it—the whole house would shake to the ka-umphing of their banging rhythm. Bear was trying to be quiet (he said) but while he umphed and gr-r-r-r-d himself along, she positively squeeeeled with delight. For the rest of us, this every-nightly routine became an expected event, and liberal, even extraordinarily liberal as we were, the sound of it, actually the immediacy with which they went at it—was intense enough to have a bit of an effect on everyone else. While it was difficult to concentrate on one's own romantic passions with the physical effects of the whole house quivering, still on occasion, the soft cuddled sounds of other lovemakers would waft among the attic beams. And there were the wonderful occasions where the rains pounded big drops down on the roof just over our heads, and the winds whistled their long whines, then it was hard to hear the banging and the cooing through the thin cloths And those of us lucky enough to be in couples could all find the privacy to be passionate. The whole house shook, itself a force of nature containing like a seed contains—or a herd of bison contains—the youthful forces of sexuality at play.

Each morning we were up and about for a healthy country breakfast. The open double room of the downstairs of the cabin was becoming more and more the center of our activity. We'd be gathering there while sizzling pancakes were coming off the woodstove's grill. And hot teas and fruits and oatmeals were dispensed from big bubbling kettlepots. And then we'd meet to plan and briefly discuss the priorities of the day—and pass the morning pipe to 'blast off' before heading out to the day's work.

We built a workshop slanting off one side of the House—which by springtime could be turned into a greenhouse. We put up coldframes and planted fall greens. We read all the giant Rodale gardening books. We filled one downstairs room of the cabin with 30-gallon cans full of grains, flours and beans, like a mini granary. We stocked tins of cooking oil and honey, and tamari—the soy sauce of choice. We turned the old hen house behind Main House into a tool shop and everyone put their tools there. We built workbenches and installed grinders and vises.

The old orchard yielded fruits and Karen had some knowledge from her New England country upbringing about how to make preserves. So we bought canning pots and jars and lids and jar racks. We built deep shelves in the cabin's back room, now renamed the pantry and loaded them full day by day with pears and apples, pie fillings, and late season berries, sauces, and jams and all manner of Mason and Ball jars now colorfully full and bright as Christmas ornaments.

These were rich times, filled with the newness of our adventure and the boldness each of us felt in making this idea real.

Figure 39. The main house cabin at the Rainbow Farm with new porch, cedar shake roofing and greenhouse made of recycled windows. (Garrick Beck: 1974)

And rich also in the realm of sensate experiences: the smells of the ever-active community kitchen; the turning colors of the alders as their yellow fingers reached down through the hillsides of dark green fir; the hearty laughter of our own selves in the evenings' kerosene lamplights. Jack Armstrong, up from Santa Monica, having heard about our venture down there, began making candles by setting up bicycle wheels from which hung many wicks. Each one was dunked into vats of hot wax, and then the wheels turned and with each go-round the wax thickened on the cords.

I don't think we were striving to be 'self-sufficient' in the sense of being able to do without the 'outside' world. Often authors wrote about the back-to-the-land movement and its wish to leave or abandon society, "to become 'self-sufficient'." These absolute ideals are a myth, put out by journalists who could only see or imagine an absolute goal instead of the complex interactive thinking of most of the communal efforts of that era. We were hoping to keep as close as possible to direct contact between our own efforts and the forces of nature and bounty of the earth. We were trying to live more simply, but we weren't trying to live up to anybody's defined standard about how separate or independent from the rest of the world we were supposed to be. We weren't trying to grow all our own food in order to meet somebody else's ideal of being 100% free. No, it was more of an experiment, an attempt to find a lifestyle to satisfy our souls.

Still, leaning away from dependence on petroleum, we went about the business of gathering a winter wood supply without the benefit of gas-powered chain saws. They were, after all, the central symbol of the logger's trade, the clearcutter's weapon of choice, the leading edge in the scalping of the forests. So we used the old-style, two-person (yep, that'd be 'two-person' not 'two-man') cross cut saws to cut the logs and spars we dragged down from the hillsides. Luckily for us, the loggers who had clearcut these hills a decade and a half before left an enormous waste behind them: whole trees cut and left behind—unthinkable today!—left perhaps because the truck was already full and it was the end of the day, or the job had moved onto some other hillside, or just because there was sooooo much wood—or so it seemed, sooooo much wood—so much that it would never end—so much that what was wasted seemed insignificant compared to what remained. The woods then seemed limitless, so much that hunks of trees five feet in diameter and forty or even sixty feet long were left, just left to rot on the forest floor. That's the way logging used to be.

We slowly cut those remaindered giants apart, then sliced and split and wheelbarrowed the pieces down the hill to make a winter's worth of firey warmth. We were ant-like scavengers bringing splinters to our fireboxes. We installed a wood-burning cook stove and lined its firebox with copper pipe. We ran water from the uphill spring into the pipe and ran the pipe to the shower. So when the cooking was 'a cookin' the shower was full of scalding hot water.

We had the electric company come out and yank out the power poles that loused up our unobstructed views of the valley.

But although we had obtained a series of building permits, clearly with the rains upon us the building of homes would have to wait until spring. In the meantime we made plans and selected the building sites. These we were able to clear and level while we waited for the end of the endless rains, the pause of the perpetual mists, and the drying up of skies that you could squeeze like a sponge.

Along with our regular dedicated crew, there was an ever-changing parade of people passing through, or dropping by. They were moving in 'forever,' and moving out days later in an unending cavalcade of faces and names. Slowly at first, only slowly, but as word of this commune—in 1970 and 1971—spread through what was surely the afterglow of the Sixties Counterculture, people who hadn't quite found what they were looking for began showing up.

In the newness of the experience I believed that where we were going the world would surely follow. I felt certain that enormous numbers of people were going to leave the cities, seeking a cleaner more-connected-with-the-earth lifestyle. I felt certain that resources were going to pour into valleys like these from Maine to Southern California. And in some ways we could actually see that happening. Stories in the alternative press carried pictures of communes in New Mexico, land trusts in Vermont, yoga centers in Florida, while hitchhikers told us of God's Lands in California, and collective lands in Missouri. People drove in in droves! From every kind of community stop on the road.

In the evenings in good weather we would gather in a big circle on the lawn in front of the main house and hold hands for a grace before meals. First we'd do an Ommm. A long Ommm sometimes ten, fifteen minutes. So what if the food labored on all day was getting cold! Then prayers, then invocations, then chanting, then maybe another Ommmm. It would start getting dark! But so what—that's what we were here for: a deeper spiritual experience, right?

Oh how little actual knowledge comes with vision.

How little we really knew about growing or preserving food. How little about even the basics of firewood and woodland tools. How little about the tilling of soil or the machines that centuries of civilization had developed for that purpose, or the use of those machines that our civilized culture had left to decreasing, aging populations of country folk. Oh! How little we knew about building or construction; about foundations and insulation and the complex tricks of roof joinery and 'flashing' that prevented leakage—or even torrential entry of water into the living spaces. Oh how little we knew; truly babes in the woods.

But even more telling: how little we knew about the dynamics of people living together. The shared houses of the Portland scene we were leaving behind had all the respites of other friends nearby, of entertainments, of numerous and diverse activities that could balance whatever stresses life in an urban collective presented. But here 12 miles up the river road, 14 miles over the mountains from an itty bitty town of eleven hundred people, with ourselves alone, and with us alone as our peers, our personal challenges soon began to multiply.

Still we had managed to insert ourselves into the flow between the water coming down the hill and the water flowing to the sea in the river below us. I was seeing how all of humanity does this; in fact has to do this in order to survive. Yes, of course everyone knows we need water…but seeing this close up—and here you could see it close up—in the immediate geography right in front of our eyes, and how we were part of it was a clear revelation in miniature of how civilization really works.

30. Frank and Lois' Story

Up and down the river from us lived a series of remarkable people. In the view of America they were just oldtimers, folks who kept to the old ways living the rural life. So maybe they didn't seem remarkable...to an outsider.

But to ourselves, newcomers from the cities, we saw these folks whose families were descendants of the homesteaders, or who had come to the valley in the Great Depression when land was cheap—these people were pillars of common sense and American wisdom.

All of their own children had departed to the cities, lured to the modern metropolitan zones with all those conveniences and all those entertainments. No need to chop wood to keep warm. No need to drive 12 miles just to go to the store. No need to boil big soup pots for a winter's worth of tomato sauce. No need for such intimacy with the dampness of the weather.

So these folks grew old like the trees in the valley, tending the orchards, logging the trees, raising cows and dogs.

Ma Beebe lived up by the head of the valley near where the river was so small you could leap over it. Round-bellied she hobbled about her property, swaying from side to side. I never saw her go anywhere without a tool in her hands: a trowel for transplanting strawberries, a rake for the leaves, a spoon for stirring sauces. And a big floppy rainhat.

She homesteaded with her husband just after The Great War (as she called WW1). And now here she was half a century later explaining the basics of strawberry cultivation to us wide-eyed kids. She said, "Nature'll teach ya."

We heard that some years after the Beebes built their beautiful log cabin, the "govment" men came and surveyed the place. It seemed the old lines run by the homesteaders with wire and compass were off course. Further downstream the families were off by only a little bit, but up here, away from everybody else, they'd plumb missed by enough to put the cabin and the cleared land and the gardens off the property. The 'govment' men got them an eviction notice. When the day came for the Beebes to be moved out, all the folks from the logger camps up and down the valley came over to Ma Beebe's for breakfast. When the Federal Land people showed up, there were about seventy-five men there awaitin' for em. The loggers explained that if the Bebee's lines weren't right, then it was the public oh-fishals job to put the lines right. Right around the Beebe's house and property. The 'govment' men went away and Ma Beebe and her cabin stayed right there, beautiful, at the head of the valley.

Shortly after we arrived in the valley we baked up a selection of pies made from the various fall fruits and berries. A delegation from our farm went to each of the neighbors and introduced ourselves and brought them each a pie. It seemed like a good thing to do. At least it was a chance to meet our neighbors and show ourselves in a friendly way. Pretty much everybody was pleasant, cordial and at least willing to give us half a chance despite our outrageous freeflagflying hippie attire.

There was Johnny Gunter, who at eighty was still hanging his handwash clothes out on lines to dry in the wind; The Harrises, who had been logging this valley a little bit at a time forever; The Leslies who had an authentic Ford Woodie in mint condition in their old garage.

Mrs. Knight lived way further down the road, but we came to know her through shoveling manure from her stable of Saint Bernards. She had begun raising the Saints decades ago, and had even been a guest on the 1950s television program, *What's My Line?*—where celebrities have twenty questions to figure out the contestant's line of work. But a farm full of Saints is more like a ranch than a kennel. So we hauled off the manure and put it to compost.

The neighbors didn't judge us by our hair, or our clothes, or our ideas about the world. If we were going to come into this valley and plant fruit trees, and grow gardens, and cut firewood, and do all the vegetable farming we said we were going to do and do all the labor it takes just to live out here, then they would give us a fair, unprejudiced chance. They'd seen ne'erdo-wells and slouchers before and they saw in us some kinship in love-of-the-land that let them see past the weird look, and past—at least on a trial basis—all the crazy press about the hippies.

Ma Bebee's cows came down river and we learned about the hazards of Open Range country, which is where if you don't want the animals in your gardens or your fields or your orchards You Fence Them Out. Or you have trampled gardens, stompled wheat fields and half drunk bovines munching on fermented apples from the old overgrown fallen-over apple trees and stumbling off, hither and yon as they please. So first we shoo the cows on downriver and then Ma Beebe comes and enlists us in her quest to round up her 'got away' herd. And here are we vegetarians helping her round up her winter income. What do you make of it?

Our nearest neighbors were the Carpenters. They'd wagoned in over a northerly route where the largest trees in valley once stood, and come upriver to settle on a gentle south-facing slope. Now the Carpenter grandchildren were themselves senior citizens. We brought each of them a pie. At one of the elderly brother's homes, he came slowly to the screen door, opened it and listened quietly while we made our 'Hello Pitch' and offered him the pie. He said quietly, "So you want to be good neighbors?"

"Uh-huh, yes," we answered.

"Then you leave me alone and I'll leave you alone." And he pulled the screen door shut and turned around and walked back into the shadows of his house. For the next seven years not a whisper passed between us.

Their family held a reunion of sorts on one of their adjacent properties and I was invited. Amid all these people chit-chatting and reminiscing, someone asked that same Mr. Carpenter (who was sitting off by himself) just how he liked "being right next to all them..." (I could see she was reaching for the word) "you know, hippie-types."

"Best damn neighbors I ever had," he said and then shut his mouth. He'd just asked us for something straight up, and we'd given it to him. I could see how he must've asked the same from everybody. Just to be left alone. And I guess we did a good job at that.

The Gatchells moved here about seven years before us. Frank and Lois had been schoolteachers in the north of the state, a little ways outside Portland. They moved out here with their two sons because (as Frank put it), "There's something not altogether right with the ways the cities are growing, with the ways people are learning to live. They're *missing* something." So he and Lois and their sons moved out here and began their gardens, their vineyard, their firewood piles and putting their foods up for winter storage. They held jobs in town, but built a modern sort of homestead during every free waking hour. They keep a fleet of old Volkswagons that they swapped parts to and from and kept them running year after year. They knew about machinery and saving seed stocks and sheltering tools from rust. They had garden fences tall enough to keep out the deer. They knew about moles and gophers and civit cats. They knew about the damp and the damper and the dampest damn weather on land anywhere. They knew about wool clothes, and rubber boots.

And they were willing to share these tidbits of knowledge with us. Little snippets of How To Do It Right that altogether made a body of knowledge. Frank showed us how to turn the earth with a hand shovel in an elegant three-part move that put the topsoil on the bottom, deftly separated it from the clod below, and chopped the upside of the downfacing clod neatly into bits. Those could then be easily hoed and raked to form neat garden beds, squash beds or vegetable rows. All the while he's explaining how this decomposing soil is turning into nutrient for the micro bacteria and the worms and beetles and ants even as we speak. He's still holding the shovel, and rocking his foot on the knurled back edge of the spade. "Here, you try it," he says.

Jerry, his son, has work helping with the pack animals on wilderness hunting expeditions through the Northern Idaho and Montana snowfields. Martha, Jerry's wife, comes from a background of theatre…as a theatre arts student and as an actress in her own right. The Living Theatre is no stranger to her education.

Terry, their other son, comes over with his dad, for the umpteenth time in answer to one of our ignorances about mechanics. How little did I realize how much of farming —even the most basic farming—relies on endless machinery: pickup trucks and flatbeds, water pumps and sprinklers; winches and hoists; trailers and balers; couplings and discs; plows and harrows; rotavators and seed sowers. And all of these have parts that endlessly wear out, or break (meaning they can be repaired) or bust completely (meaning they can't be repaired).

But first, before you can fix or replace anything you've got to get it apart. Even if you can see what's wrong, you have to be able to take it out of the iron and rust and paint and screw threads it's put together with. And sometimes…sometimes you try all day to get that part off and it just won't budge. Even WD-40, the cure-all lubricant won't do it. Banging on it from the side with a five-pound mallet won't do it; pulling and pushing and grabbing and straining and the thing hasn't moved a hair. Call the Gatchells. And Frank and Terry come on over. Frank's chewin' his tobacco. He takes a look and smiles. Terry smiles too. They put their hands on the rotator we've been trying to loosen and Frank gives it a rockin' motion while Terry holds onto the shaft behind. It doesn't budge at all. "Yep, says Frank, what you need is a gear puller." Pretty soon we're down at his house and he's explaining that in order to get these gears on and off, people have also invented machines just to get the machines apart. And he introduces us to the world of gear pullers: three armed contraptions of different sizes that fit over the round gears or clutches or flywheels and then screw a point down onto the middle of the shaft and then... Wham! You hit the blunt back end of the device with a small sledgehammer, and bang-o with a ringing sound the clutch or flyheel or gear or whatever pops off or at least loose of the shaft it's been on.

Wow. What an insight into the way things work. Every machine's got these. The whole mechanical matrix uses these. How little did we know. How unschooled in the valuable arts were we! Supposedly soooo educated, but without the rudimentary knowledge of the most crucial machines: the ones that grow the food and pump the water onto the seeded crops and thereby feed the world.

Frank and his son Terry came back over and brought their gear pullers, showing us how to undo the gear mechanisms of the pumps and tractor's innards. They were both chewing tobacco, helping us struggle with our own machinery. But instead of struggling and getting nowhere, we were struggling and getting the gear 'popped,' removed, and the broken piece replaced.

So here is a guy who can show us, and is willing to show us, how these things go together—and come apart.

Ruth Stout wrote her garden handbooks a dozen years ago. The Rodales compended the small scale farming data of the American Generations into three hand-held Encyclopedias. Helen and Scott Nearing's chronicle of their return to New England homestead-style farming, Eric Partridge's marvelous books on the awesome wonder of hand-held homesteader's tools (*profusely* illustrated by that author)—these all came a decade or more before our own time's publications like *Mother Earth News*, or *The Whole Earth Catalog*.

The Stouts and the Rodales, the Partridges and Nearings were writing for these earlier modern homesteaders. People whose models weren't the way-out beatniks (though they have read their books), people whose heads weren't spun by psychedelia (though they were tolerant toward others' right to experiment), people whose reasoning didn't include fleeing from a war (though they were keenly opposed to it). For the sanest of reasons they had moved out to the land and set up shop…years ahead of us. These originals—not us—were pioneers of the Back to the Land Movement. And they didn't make a big deal of it. They just did it and they did it well.

Nor were they descendants of the homesteader breed. They'd seen this course of action before the hippies made their way to the woods. Lois and Frank moved to the place where the livable countryside meets the edge of true wildlands. They made a life that included pantries of jellies and sauce; that had rows and rows of firewood decked up under the roof; that maintained its own machines; and that enjoyed the sun and the rain.

Lois shows Karen, Peggy, Auggie and our Terri how to collect flower seeds from both cultivated and wildflowers. And how to start the tiniest and slowest-germinating seeds between two damp pieces of paper. And hot canning? Putting food 'by' in glass jars with screwcaps and gasket-lined lids to preserve it? It's one thing to read about the steps in a manual, and another to have Lois show the process in action. The preparing, cooking, jar-filling, liquid-adding, capping, boiling-in-submerged-racks process… whew! It's got timing and movement, and heavy hot wet racks of jars to maneuver. But once you learn it, you hold another key to the chain.

31. Equinox

In the Oregon Coast Range, the first sign of spring is that the rains turn warmer.

We've made it through our first cold winter and we decide to hold a Spring Equinox Celebration. All of the communes along the wet backbone of Oregon's coast range must be feeling as pent in and pent up as we are. Since we're the newly landed ones, we figure it's our time to invite everyone over to the Rainbow Farm to celebrate the Equinox of Spring.

Bear says he'll build an open-air kitchen down in the lower field not far from the river. Auggie helps him set it up and they plan to crank out huge stainless pots full of lentils, green split peas (can't stop stirring that one or it'll burn on the bottom), brown rice and chai tea.

With all the people traffic that's been wandering through the farm it's not hard to put out the word by word-of-mouth. Sensibly we decide to park all the cars on the dry upper slope and lay out a softball diamond in the lower field. We figure we'll gain some help with various farm projects, meet the folks from the other landed communities and have a grand time of it. The Rainbow House in town helps spread the message.

People start arriving and tents spring up throughout the woods and across the meadows. The CRO (Cro Research Organization) farmers from Veneta arrive. They've been on the land for years already and they chuckle at all our beginner ways. The Lorien people travel from near the California border and the street people come from Eugene. From San Francisco comes the Medical Opera—a free clinic clan and midwifing center. Lots of individual travelers, hitchhikers, a few old friends, but lots of young travelers 'on the road' arrive. A woman and her boyfriend show up—he's just helped her 'escape'—walked her away—from the State mental hospital outside Salem. And the STP family show up—known widely as bikers without bikes. They want to know where they can party in their own rowdy style, so we show them to a place between two fallen over apple trees where they can make their own kitchen. The whole place is dotted with cars and people.

I decide to build a small log platform from which we can do the ritualistic 'flying' sequence from the Living Theatre's *Paradise Now*. Just as we had done at the Eugene Renaissance Faire, two lines of catchers stand opposite each other with everyone's forearms extended in a supportive pattern that we have learned from the theatre and practiced before. Behind the platform helpers make sure the next flyer has removed their shoes and all objects from their pockets. Then the flyer climbs the platform and after three slow breaths leaps—with arms extended—upward toward the sun. There is a moment between the leaping up and the

Figure 40. Barry 'Plunker' Adams 'flying' at the Spring Equinox Celebration, Rainbow Farm, Drain, Oregon. (Photographer unknown: Collection of the author, 1971)

inevitable pull of gravity back down, just a moment at the cusp between those forces when it really feels—it really *is*—suspension in mid-air.

Lots of people from town show up. Most don't want to join the party—they just want to watch. So they park along the road. The region's Sheriff, Charlie Orr, arrives. He asks, "How're things going?" and we tell him "Just fine." A man is staring with binoculars at the nekkid people down by the river. He complains to the Sheriff about the "indecent exposure goin' on up here," and Charlie tells him that he better put those binoculars away or he's gonna come under the Peeping Tom ordinances, and what would *his* wife say to that? So he just keeps on watchin' and passing the binoculars around without making any more complaints. They see some of their friends down there, a makin' pals with them Hippies.

Barry says we oughta hold a Council so people can talk together, listen together and find out what we are really all about. "Cause it ain't just a party in the woods, is it? No," he says cocking his head slightly, "these people here have a lot going on during the rest of the year. And we should use this equinox to hear what everyone's doing and what all these people are really thinking about."

A couple shows up with a bag full of 'green flat' LSD's. She's raising money for some medical operation and wants to sell these to raise the cash. Some rich hippie steps up and buys them all, and then just gives them away.

Then five burly loggers arrive and they *do* want to party. I recognize these guys from some other scenes in town where they terrorized a couple of blithe freaks just a few months ago. Busted some poor hitchhiker's teeth. They come on over to the Main House askin' where the party *really* is, and one of 'em says, "I heard there was gonna be a drinkin' contest. Now where's *that* gonna be at?"

I can see they're carrying liquor bottles. I'm trying to think fast on my feet, "Sure, c'mon with me. I'll take you right to it." And I walk them down to the lower field being just as friendly as I can. I bring 'em over to the STP camp and they come in loud and ready for I'm not sure what, but when one of 'em starts up with, "So is this where the Hippie's drinking contest is?" up staggers January, a longtime STP'er. He's been lying down half-past passed out, and he rises to his feet already pretty loaded, and he hollers back, "Yeah Brothers this IS the place, ain't it now?" He's wobblin' a bit and he turns open the metal cap from a gallon jug of one of those Gallo wines and while he's got everyone's attention he starts chuggin' it, chugga lugglin' it and we're all watching and the bottle is getting emptier and emptier and No One can drink that much. He's got it tipped into his mouth from the side, kinda hunched over a bit to get below it, one finger through the glass finger hole, not missing a drop. And now the whole damn thing's empty. He tosses the bottle heroically up end over end high into the air.

Still hunching over he looks slowly around at everyone—who's been watching him in disbelief. Half growling and half asking he bellows, "What do I win?"

I left those loggers right there figuring they'd about come to the place they'd been looking for.

Bear's kitchen is cranking out hot stew and tea and cider and salads. We hold a huge circle for grace and dinner. Rob Roy has his drums out and echoes of drums and people and sweet melodies fill the valley through the night.

The next day we hold the softball game: choose-up sides just like in any sandlot. At the same time there's a sweatlodge going on down by the river, and later in the day it's time for the Council. I'm a little uncertain about this. We've never had a 'Council' before. I'm not sure how it should work, or whether it'll be interesting or what. So a few of us talk about how we should do this. Barry suggests we all just sit in a circle and see what happens. We blow conch shells to get everyone's attention and so folks come together. We're at the end of the field where the tall grasses are. When people have had a chance to meander over I explain that it's time for a Council amongst us. "This is a chance for everyone or anyone to speak while we others listen. And if anyone doesn't want to stay or listen or talk that's okay, but we're going to try to get started with a circle," which we do—one of our long Ommmmmm circles—and then everyone sits down.

I stand back up and begin speaking. "Hopefully everyone is going to get a chance to talk about whatever you want, and the hope is to go around the circle." I encourage everyone: "Say a few, just a few words about what you're doing, what you're up to: your projects, your farms, your communities. And if you don't want to say anything, that's fine, just pass, or offer a poem, or a prayer, or a thought, or, or whatever you like. And we'll see where we are when we've gotten around the circle." I talk briefly about the Rainbow Farm, and what we're hoping to do right there. And I finish and pass to the person by my side.

One by one people stand to speak. The seriousness with which the hundred or more people took this first try was so completely sincere. And for the next couple of hours everyone listened to everyone's trips: there were people who spoke about a Free University in Eugene, about a collective orchard in Hood River, about the Oregon Renaissance Faire, about a people's publication center that was buying an old comic book printing press. There were midwives who spoke about home birthing, farmers who talked about growing organic vegetables and grains. People talked about psychedelics and political visions; people told stories and recited poems; many people just passed, and waved. I just sat and listened and watched. The cornucopia of the culture had a lot to show to itself. When it got just about half way around the circle (that's where Barry was sitting) he spoke at length about the Gathering upcoming in July of 1972 (now about a year and a quarter away) and he spoke about there being councils daily at that gathering, not unlike this one here.

We were beginning 'to council' together. Not just go to *a* council. Not just *hold* a council—but counciling together as way of communicating in our community, as a participatory experience. Counciling was becoming a verb, becoming something we did—and still do—and not just a thing. We don't just go to a council, *we council.*

When the speaking had come full circle, I put my hands and arms toward the people next to me, and we all stood up and did another closing Ommmmmmmm.

That night fires sparkled among the campsites. Equinoxers strolled from one campfire to the next. Tim played his banjo while Rod played violin. Drums sounded from below, by the river. It was a sweet night to equinox on.

The next day, after we picked ourselves up and headed to the field kitchen for breakfast, Auggie spoke up saying, "We haven't had a Tug of War yet!"

"What Tug of War?"

"Between who?"

"What are the sides?"

"Choose ups? Like the softball game?"

"No, let's do Drinkers versus Smokers."

"Yeah, that oughta be good."

"And How about over the slough!"

There was a small ditch filled with muddy water between the upper part of the lower field and the lower part of the lower field. A trickle of water from one of the uphill springs kept it full of muck with just a little water on top. Someone went to get the biggest rope and everyone was gathering friends and getting on either side of the muddy divide. The two sides looked pretty equal, maybe forty or so people on each end. Big ones, slender ones, barefooters and big booters. Someone got a whistle and the biggest guys on either side were tied onto the ends of the rope. There were plenty of spectators to root and cheer. I was on the Smokers side of things. And some people swapped sides to make sure there were about a fair number on each end of the rope. The CRO's and STPer's (with some exceptions, of course) were pretty much on the Drinkers side, and the

Rainbows, and the Tree Planters and the communards from places with Middle Earth names pretty much on the tokers' end. There was a piercing whistle and the tug began. For a good quarter hour no side could budge the other. The tokers were toking and the drinkers were drinking and everyone was hollering and heave-ho!-ing. And then I felt my foot slip a bit forward, and the tug was pulling us toward the other side. It still went on for a long time, but we were slowly, inexorably being pulled to the slough, and of course it dawned on everyone that losing meant you got pulled right on through the mud and there were feet slipping now into the muck, and up to our knees, people falling down in it, everyone cheering and finally that was it, the drinkers had won fair and square and pulled us all through the muddy mire. Gawd, it was a mess.

The Equinox Celebration put us on the map, as though we didn't have enough activity already. It let other communes and communities send their overdose of visitors over to us. The next months were a whirlwind made of faces.

Teenage runaways. Forty year-old runaways. College kids doing 'research' for a course; carloads of inner city kids for whom this was the first time they'd ever *ever* been outside the concrete matrix of the city; patchwork-clothed wandering minstrels already well-schooled in the arts of the Hippie culture; roadies lacking a band who wanted to pitch into the emerging counterculture in whatever way they could; groupies without a tour who just wanted to ball and show off about it; still more war evaders heading north to Canada escaping from the Army; children of wealth escaping the system to get a good look at what else might matter; religious believers of every imaginable yoga, guru, avatar or cult.

A red-headed barefoot flute player arrived with "Lemurian Scrolls" which purport to portray the subatomic energy fields that powered ancient civilizations and that could power ours—in the future of course.

One night a guy appears at the Main House door—he's walked in from the other side of the mountain where his last ride left him. He's standing there in a long tan robe, handsome, bearded, longhaired, a striking figure. I ask his name and he tells us he's "Messiah, Son of God, but you can call me whatever you want." He makes a beautiful open-handed gesture. To our silence he replies, "I'm back."

I ask him if he could wave one of his hands and turn all the tanks into tractors. Or doing that without waving his hands would be just as good.

"Oh you of little faith," he replies, "Always asking for a miracle. Always asking for proof instead of trusting your eyes and your head and your heart."

I'm explaining, "It's not a matter of not believing, it's just that the Scrip on this situation is that we're counting on a Thousand Years of Peace. So I figure that turning all the tanks into tractors would be a good place to start. I mean if that's what you're here to do, let's get on with it!"

He's looking a little bewildered.

"If you're actually taking orders from On High—like many of us—c'mon in. You're welcome here. We're off to till soil for planting grapes in the morning so we figure that's part of *preparation* for the Messiah. It's the best we can do. On the other hand, if we find out tomorrow morning that all the tanks have been turned to tractors, then I think you'll find we're all Your eager disciples."

"Here, here!" and many cheers to that come from the around the room.

Later in the springtime a group of Native Americans from the Warm Springs Reservation visits and we establish friendships and begin a fairly regular set of softball games.

Some hunters show up from Washington State and wonder if they can co-exist with this strong vegetarian presence.

A couple of cocaine dealing hotshots cruise in from Florida and lay out the lines for everyone for days.

A television crew from Portland arrives. They want us all to come to their studios in Portland and fake a Thanksgiving meal so they can record How The Hippies Do It.

A Russian naval vessel has mechanical troubles off the coast of Southern Oregon, and while it's receiving parts from onshore a Russian sailor skips out, sticks out his thumb on the coastal highway and a few rides later he's standing at the Rainbow Farm. He's traded his camera and rifle for American money and we are figuring him as a candidate for 'passenger' on the next ride going up to Canada.

A broad-bellied, big-bearded, party animal shows up blaring his Led Zeppelin into the garden's pre-dawn hours. Hollering, "Where's the Party???!!! Get out of Bed!!! What are you doing asleep at a gorgeous time like this???? You should be out here tripping!!!!" He's got his car's speakers out on wires now and he's setting them up on the roof of his van.

Turns out he'd been deported from Nepal for leading a group of café lifestyle Hippies out onto some mountainside and re-structuring the blocks of an old deconstructed temple into a real live open-to-anyone LSD temple, right there in the High Himalayas. Now he's *our* guest. Every couple of weeks he gets a package from home. Sits down by the mailbox waiting for it. And it's full of money. Just wrapped up cash. He's a modern day Remittance Man. A guy from a wealthy family whose family sends him plain old money just to keep him away.

And he's ready to put it to use here.

In another week he's got a group of the most lost youngsters teamed up and they're going to build a bunkhouse up the hill, nestled under a canopy of fir trees. He's buying boxes full of tools, lumber, glass. At the same time he's coming back from town with a truckload of tomatoes or corn or greenbeans. He's bought out some farmer at a roadside market! It's all we can handle to preserve, dry, can, and cook all the food we're growing, let alone all this. He's hollering, "Just cook it, Feed the People! Give it away!" And he's gone up the hill to continue with the construction. So why bother working so hard with hand tools in the gardens when this guy'll just buy it all for us?

When the fall rains hit and it began to get cold again and damp all the time, the Fat City crew—that's what became the bunkhouse's name—they ran out of stovewood one rainy night, "What the heck, let's just use the hammer handles." "They're already just about the exact right size for the stove's firebox." "And they're dry already." "Yeah good oak wood." So they burned a whole box of hammers.

From Philadelphia came first a couple of brave souls, out of the poor white neighborhoods there. And they grew strong in the strong country ways, and soon brought back a crew of their friends from the city's streets.

A runaway from the nearby town had settled in; got a girlfriend and wouldn't come home. So his brothers, all five of them (well, maybe a couple of 'em were his cousins) all loggers, came up to bring him home. We formed a big circle outside in front of the porch. We clearly outnumbered them. And we were strong in our beliefs, and tough in our own way. And they were tough too. Everyone was a little worried about the outcome of this confrontation. They were firm the little brother had to come home.

There was a long argument about whether he was eighteen or not, because at eighteen he was an adult who could make his own decisions. Seems he'd been seventeen when he left home and he was eighteen now. I knew, at least what with all the talking, that at least the potential for violence was averted. Still, at the end he got up, walked across the circle and went home with his brothers.

Pepe and Artie and Carol and White Light and Sebastapol and Katchina and Peacock—the Pride Family—arrived in their white breadtruck traveling from Bolinas, California. They brought know-how, fine tools, and a sense of stoned ceremony that embedded itself in our mix. Later they would land and lodge at New Buffalo, one of the ongoing communes outside Taos, New Mexico.

Living Theatre members going up or down the West Coast visited.

Reedies came by, I think more amazed at how far out, "far out" really could get. We ourselves at the core of this could hardly see the lasting image for the swirl of individually colored moments that were spinning before our eyes.

And parents came. Terri had been building the House of Twelve at the edge of the yard. It was the cutest, zaniest 12-sided one-room cabin. And her parents were coming to see what had become of their daughter. So they drive up in their shiny new car, and Terri and Karen give them the tour: gardens, orchards, kitchens, the dome, outdoor cannery, building sites.

It's all going along pretty well when the Remittance Man pulls

Figure 41. Building the dome: Leonce (who came with the Medical Opera from San Francisco and helped midwife for Karen and my daughter, Eden), with David and Marco cinching the bolts that hold the framework of the dome together. (Garrick Beck: 1971)

up with a Department Store truck with gigantic freezers on it. We don't even have any electricity. There's a huge commotion. Everybody wants to get involved. "Just unload them." "No! Take them back." "We don't want them." "But they're paid for already. If you don't want to keep them just re-sell them." "No! We don't want the tentacles of industry creeping into our pure world."

The truck drivers have a stunned bewildered look. The arguments are engulfing the truck. Sixty people in patchwork and tie-dye and country-dirty work clothes are all hollering at each other. Terri turns to her parents (visiting from Seattle) who are drop-mouthed staring at all of this, and she says, waving her hand at the spectacle, "Well, that's the New Age for you."

The whole idea of us, city kids, trying to make a communal life in among nature may have really been vastly beyond our abilities, or maybe just a couple of dozen—or even a hundred—years ahead of its time. Still, flute music drifted up and down the

Figure 42. The dome at Rainbow Farm. (Garrick Beck, 1981)

valley at dusk, guitars rang in the firelight, racks of fresh canned tomatoes were cooling in the pantries, huge communal meals got cooked, served and washed up after, people were housed and fed and cared for, children were born, skills were learned and taught, crops were grown, fences were stretched, fruit trees were planted and pruned, 'trash' was recycled, foundations were laid, buildings were built, fuelwood was harvested, seeds were saved, and most of the folks who traveled in and out of our lives were glad to pitch in to help make it all happen.

32. Christmas 1971

The nearest small city to our back-to-the-land community was Eugene, which is where we went for building supplies or whatever else wasn't available at our tiny town in the Coast Range. One day we stopped to visit at the somewhat-associated Rainbow House in town. Sitting around talking we came up with an idea. The proposal was that come Christmastime the Eugene community could use a Happy Birthday Jesus party, sort of a new take on an old celebration.

In the weeks that followed we visited each of the Eugene area's health food stores, told 'em our plan and asked for contributions toward The Cake. Everyplace we went contributed something. We just asked for whatever they felt good about giving. Of course, most of them knew us as regular customers. We visited the Willamette People's Co-op, The Kiva, Sundance Natural Foods, several of the homespun organic restaurants, even the conservative old-timey healthnut stores. Everyone gave something. One gave honey, one gave eggs, one fruit, another nuts, many contributed sacks of flour. And we invited the folks from each of these to meet us at the north end of the Eugene mall at dusk on Christmas Eve.

Of course, we visited the Health Food and Pool Store, just over the bridge into neighboring Springfield. It's run by Merry Prankster—and renowned author—Ken Kesey's brother Chuck and his wife Sue. It serves as the headquarters outlet for Nancy's Yogurt and the other fine Springfield Creamery products. They called it the Health Food and Pool Store because in the midst of the racks and shelves of edibles stood a log and beam structure upon which was set a regulation pool table, so naturally, you could shop for your granola and organic lettuce and shoot a few racks of pool while you were at it.

When we pulled up there, the Merry Prankster's team was in the middle of their own goings on. They had two huge used pizza ovens coming in by truck. One of the Pranksters was radioing to the truck on a CB, the others were clearing the way from the driveway inside to where the ovens would rest. Ken was there and Chuck, Sue, Bobby Skye, Ken Babbs and a half dozen more, all sleeves rolled up, ready as the truck came in. They were not at all interested in what we were up to unless it was either to get out of the way, or to help carry the ovens—which we did, and verily verily these were heavy ovens and all of us, grunting step by step until we were setting them down in the appointed space. Babbs was pointing and directing, announcing at last as we wiggled them into position, "This is, this is where we want them."

In the catching-our-breath aftermath, they heard our plot and kicked in a large tin of bulk raisins.

In the days before Christmas the farm on Smith River was a beehive of activity. There was all the usual gift making and the holiday meal preparations, as well as the huge round-the-clock job of baking the cake. Cakes is more like it, since in the two wood cookstove ovens we were using every baking pan we had to crank out cake after cake. Rob Roy Rowley and I were building a three-part plywood and two-by-four platform to carry the thing on. Dominic LaGrasta was supervising the wheat grinding in the two flour mills. Major Petersen, Annie, Auggie and Karen were in the middle of the baking marathon. Laika and Terri were testing icing recipes. Jack Armstrong and Howdy Johnson had started making two thousand little pink birthday candles. They had their bicycle-wheel candle-dipping operation going full blast.

The plan was to assemble the cake piece by piece like a mosaic, with a hollow cross-shaped space right in the middle. So it went, on into the night, assembling the pieces, icing the cake and setting the rows of candles in place. By the mid-morning before Christmas Eve the whole thing was ready. Well, there were maybe only 800 or so candles done, but it sure looked like 2000. Then, we disassembled the gigantic cake into its three parts, so we could get it out the door and into the vehicles. A few hours later some forty of us packed ourselves into our vans, and off we went toward the Eugene mall.

The mall itself was a recent creation of the city council, which had (in a long-fought move) closed the city's central streets to vehicular traffic and built and landscaped a dramatic public pedestrian mall. At the furthest north end we found parking and unloaded the cake parts. The light from the shops and department store windows was already shining brightly out onto the darkening, shopper-filled streets. The place was bustling with last minute gift buyers.

Other friends who'd planned to meet us were there and we were meeting and greeting and simultaneously trying to get the cake together. The three wooden parts were designed to be nailed one to the other with a series of pole handles so it could be lifted and carried along.

At this point I'm trying carefully to tap one of the big nails in when I hear a deep voice behind me, "Don'tcha think you're choking up a bit too much on the hammer?"

Of course I was. I look up over my shoulder. It's Kesey. I was trying not to take high strong swings with all that crowd around. But the nail wasn't going in either. He grins, and tilts his head sorta sideways shrugging one shoulder, as if to say: Hey, it's your show, do it any way you want. So I bring my hand down to the hammer's grip and with a couple of manly shots the platforms start solidly coming together.

In a few more minutes we've successfully lifted the cake and about a dozen of us are holding the handles comfortably at waist height. Someone has placed a big Bible in the hollow cross, and a couple of votive candles, and now someone's set a small Oregon grape and fir bough wreath into it.

And off we go. Slowly, the whole lot of us is parading south toward the center of the mall singing the songs of tidings and good cheer. We'd alternate the serious religious carols with secular songs, all of them in the wonderful enthused harmonies of the season. "Oh Come all Ye Faithful" and then "White Christmas;" "Rudolph the Red Nosed Reindeer" and then "Silent Night;" and of course, wouldn't you know it, what with the cake and all: Happy Birthday! Dear Jesus, Ha-ppy Birth-day to Youuuu!

It was wonderful. People and more people came over. This was something different. Something interesting. And we told them we were celebrating Jesus' birth in the most popular, joyous way we could imagine. People joined for a bit, sang along and then mostly went on their own merry elvish ways finishing off their Christmas shopping. But some stayed with the parade, charmed by the innocence and expression of joy as we wound our way slowly down the mall. The center of the cake was filling up. People were putting all kinds of stuff in the empty space of the cross: flowers, incense, peppermint canes, small wrapped up gifts, pine cones, more Bibles. Many of the parading company were holding candles, a couple were ringing bells. It was a beautiful sight.

But when we came to the center of the mall where the two largest streets used to cross we met another group of Christmas spirits. It was the Jesus Freaks. And they were angry. They were on the mall that night too, handing out flyers urging people to boycott the money-spending frenzy of commercialism that had overtaken Christmas.

It was easy to understand what they were protesting. But their handouts were scary, telling folks they were being used by the Devil to subvert the meaning of God's Son, that every dollar they spent on so-called gifts was another dollar going to The False Prophet of Materiality.

And when they saw us, they began a mighty wailing. "Beware lest you become like these Children of Satan!" they called out pointing at us. "See how far from the truth Satan has taken them! They make a mockery of our Lord and Savior!" Some of the folks on the parade went over and suggested they join our celebration as this obviously was not a commercial hype but a simple outpouring of joy and thanks. But they'd have none of it. And on we went singing and strolling, and on they went haranguing the crowds.

A few robust, song-filled city blocks later we arrived at the quieter south end of the mall, where a gentle slope of still-green grass led up to a merchant association's manger and creche scene—with the statues of the Holy Family, and the Shepherds, and the Lambs and the Kings. We set the cake down at last, and with a hundred hands to help, lit as quickly as we could manage, all the eight hundred candles.

There, under the star-twinkling sky we joined arms over shoulders in a big circle, many layers of people deep with the rest of the crowd standing, watching from all around. And softly, so gently we intoned a long sweet Ommm. As the harmony of the Ommm ended a woman's voice slowly began, "Our Father Who art in Heaven...." And the crowd picked it up and recited the prayer, and the breeze picked up and rippled gently across us and blew out the candles.

It was a very quiet moment after that.

And a small voice somewhere to my right spoke up, asking, "Does anybody want any LSD?"

Even in 1971 only months really after the Sixties had ended; even in Eugene, Oregon, deep behind The Granola Curtain; even ten years before 'They' began the War on Drugs; even then, that was an outrageous question to ask in public.

My old Reedie friend, Hiya, turned to Kesey—who had been the one asking the question—and he said to Ken, "I thought you'd graduated from that," referring of course to the infamous Acid Test Graduation.

Ken smiled, looked right at him, and said, "I decided to re-enroll for my doctorate."

Hiya had his mouth open in no time, urging the kind provider not to be sparing with the material. Myself and dozens of others joined in line, getting dosed on the tongue.

We proceeded with our plan, saddling up the giant cake and walking and singing again back into the center of the mall. We set it down on a low wide wall that was part of the walkway's architecture and singing one last rousing round of Happy Birthday, we proceeded to cut the cake and each eat a piece. It was quite delicious.

Even with everyone who had joined us in the celebration eating a piece, still we had only dented a corner of the confection, and as planned, we began to hand out the cake to all the passersby and all the shoppers.

Jack and I and Karen were cutting the cake and everyone else was taking two or three pieces to share with the crowds. Pretty soon most of our friends were coming back saying it wasn't so easy to give that cake away.

The folks who knew us or who'd paraded with us, all gladly ate their fill, but when they were done and departed there we were with a huge amount of cake left trying to explain to total strangers who hadn't seen the show, who hadn't seen the parade what this was all about. People were in a hurry to get their shopping done, and not so interested in stopping for a piece of some strange kind of cake.

We kept trying to give it out, but the longer we tried, and the more people turned it down and turned away, the more awkward the whole effort began to seem.

By then the Jesus Freaks across the street had started to notice our problem and they began coming closer, handing out their flyers nearer and nearer to us.

I'm coming on to the acid. I can feel that taste in my mouth and my thoughts catching up to each other. The whole scene seems to be taking a turn in an unexpected and uncomfortable direction. A couple of folks are arguing with the Jesus Freaks now, and more and more friends are coming back disappointed from up and down the mall with the cake pieces still in their hands. I'm not quite sure what to do.

I'm looking around trying to gather my thoughts and there's Kesey coming out of the brightlit front doors of the Five and Dime store. He's headed toward us, his big head festooned with three, no maybe four or five, colored pointy party hats. The elastics are all under his chin. He's wobbling slightly, carrying a couple of big shopping bags, and now he's blowing one of those unrolling party horns. The kind that goes, Phew-eeee! as the colored paper unrolls like a color-striped lizard's tongue. He's got three of these in his mouth. He's blowing one then the next, "Phew-eeeee! Phew-eeeee!" One in one direction and then one in another. "Phew-eeeee! Phew-eeeee!"

I feel like I'm seeing him moving in triplicate, what with the three horns blowing, and he's rocking slightly back and forth as he walks, and the multiple pointy party hats only add to the illusion.

Now he's standing right in front of us. Smiling. Beaming.

"Ken," I say, a bit soberly, "Do you really think this is what we need right now?"

He looks at me again with that big questioning smile then hands me the shopping bags and says only, "It's for communication." Then he turns right around and heads off into our own crowd removing the party hats one at a time and giving them away.

I look into one of the shopping bags. There's another set of those same colored foil cone hats, and a plastic package of blowers. I take these out wondering if I can bring myself to feel any more foolish or do any more birthday partying. And there, under the blowers and under the hats are packages and packages of cocktail napkins. I am struck as by a sphere of Light. Merry Christmas, Happy Anniversary, Happy Birthday, all different kinds of cocktail napkins. Disney characters, Charlie Brown, even Happy Hanukkah, dozens of cellophane wrapped packages.

In a fraction of a moment I am unwrapping the packages. I slide a napkin under each of the pieces of cake in one person's hands. Everyone is getting the picture fast. Everyone's helping place the cut cake pieces onto the holiday napkins. Karen, Jack and I and everybody are all trying again, walking up to strangers on the mall, in the midst of Christmas shopping frenzy, asking if they'd like a piece of Happy Birthday Jesus cake, and watching them take the napkin and the cake and walk off saying things like, "Thank you, what a lovely idea, What a lovely way to celebrate Christmas."

Over the next hour we gave out all the cake. Every last piece. All eight hundred of them.

The Jesus Freaks slunk back to their other corner of the mall where they could preach their brand of religion without the interference of our joy.

The Pranksters had already headed on home to their own pleasant hills. But Kesey was always like that. He seemed to have the gift of insight and the bravery to take reality by the hand and lead it along.

The stars were twinkling in the clear night sky, as they sometimes do in rainy Eugene, and we bundled ourselves up and into our vans, and drove on back to our mountain homes.

PART SEVEN

On the Trail with the Rainbow Rock

(1971–1972)

Where the patchwork pieces and the threads of the New World Culture begin to fit and weave together in a way that we can start to see patterns that show our place in the evolution of human history. The fabric reveals images of past, present and future societies while the patchwork nature of the assembly indicates social forms that herald a future where people come together despite their differences.

33. The Hopi, The Hippies, The Missing Tablet and The Beautiful Blue Corn

Part 1

Over the hilltop and down into our almost-hidden valley in the winter of early 1971 rolled a deep-purple square-backed truck containing a small clan on their way north. They had been on the road trading. They said they didn't want to use any money so they had adopted the trading lifestyle. They had a truckful of good stuff: tools, blankets, books, toys, candles, rope, clothes, stuff we could use. It was fun to go to their big purple truck and trade.

Right before they departed they gave us a pouch of Hopi corn seed. They said it was a gift really for the nice welcome they'd been given. And with the seed they gave us planting instructions for the traditional way to plant the corn.

A few months later spring sprang, the soggy Oregon ground dried out, and we turned the soil in the lower field. First we planted the frost hardy greens, then the transplants from the cold frame greenhouses we'd built, followed a few weeks later by plantings of corn and beans.

We brought everyone together by blowing the conch shell. We re-told about the way of planting where the man with a stick goes ahead, poking the holes and the woman follows behind planting the seeds, dropping them into the holes the man has made. But in the discussion, seeking balance, people wanted to do it both ways, with both men and women each taking turns with the sticks and the seeds.

It was beautiful. All done in silence. The corn pouch was passed with reverence for the life inside it. As we planted, the afternoon began to cloud over and a light rain started to fall. In the end we held hands in our OM circle as the clouds burst over us and wetted down the valley. The sun dipped under the clouds filling the forested hills with golden misty light and a rainbow rose up from the river and arced down—I thought it was going to land on where we'd just planted the corn. But no, it touched instead on the godseye standing in the center of the garden. The whole scene was dazzling. The sun, the mist, the rainbow, the new planted deep brown earth, us a part of it all.

Then someone's small voice said, "Why don't we go up the hill to the meditation place to take this all in?" Single file we went up the trail, a flute casting slow notes across the valley. As we get to the prayer platform—a wood platform we'd built overlooking the valley—someone notices a rock nestled in the decay of a giant cedar stump. But it's only after we've risen from sitting in meditation that we look it over, passing the carved stone among us. We leave it set in the stump as it was.

Over a joyful, noisy dinner, amid many other topics, the rock is mentioned. "Did anybody see that carved rock out by the prayer platform?" asks one of the corn planters.

Nobody else seemed to know anything about it.

For most of the next year the stone sat where it was. The rock itself was carved on one side with images that were themselves made up of smaller images, figures and faces, and within those smaller signs, figures, designs, until smaller than that it was hard to tell where the carving left off and the natural pattern of the rock began.

The following winter Karen and I left Oregon for the East Coast to visit my grandmother and her father and mother. But along the route we made stops passing out invitations to The Gathering next July. The invitations were printed and posted, but wherever possible it was given by word of mouth, in coffee houses, yoga centers, community newspapers, laundromats, street corners, on campuses, at rock 'n roll shows, places of worship...wherever, whenever. And myself and Karen were not the only ones out doing this. There were other carfulls traveling criss-cross the countryside meeting people and spreading the invitation.

One set of travelers went through the American Southwest and then eastward and up the coast to where we met up in New York. We were planning a trip to Washington, D.C. to distribute invitations and we traded tales of where we'd been. One of their stops had been in the Hopi Lands where they'd heard the yearly ceremonial telling of the Hopi histories and prophecies. Our southern traveling companions, Michael 'Bear' Pizer and Barry 'Plunker' Adams, retold the part of the story about the times yet to be, where people called the Warriors of the Rainbow would come and somehow set things right in this troubled world…and they would come bearing a rock, a carved rock that would signal to the Hopi that these were the people of their prophecies.

A rock? A carved, inscribed-type tablet rock? I recounted the tale of our corn-planting and we made plans to go back to Oregon and bring this stone down to the Hopi for their examination. First I got on the phone to Kaushal back in Oregon and asked him to go get the rock and hold onto it, protect it. Returning west later that spring, we found the tablet now in Kaushal and his partner Sihu's care. Sihu is angelic, dark-haired, sparkling-eyed. She moves elegantly, carefully and hands us the tablet, now wrapped in a soft white woven baby blanket and tied with a coiled cord.

We loaded up two cars and a van with fourteen of us and headed toward the southwest. Close to our destination we stopped at Jacques and Ella Seronde's place on a remote mesa. He'd been living there for years, acquainted with the Hopi and Navaho peoples. "You gotta purify yourselves, make yourselves ready," he told us. And we followed his advice, taking time to fast, bathe ourselves, meditate and wrap up our hair as a sign of respect.

Then we went, early in the morning, to the Hopi village where Mary—Skyblue Fiedler's friend—knew there was a Kiva, a prayer space that was open and where we could sit and meditate before

Figure 43. Sihu, Kaushal, and Peyto Yellin (Photographer unknown: Courtesy Sihu Yellin, 1972)

going on. An older woman met us at the door and explained that this Kiva used to be open but that too many people had come and abused the space so the Kiva wasn't open to the public anymore. On we went to the well-known Hopi Interpreter Thomas Banyaca's house. He wasn't home.

Our next stop was David Monongye's house. Already the sun was starting to bake us. People were home there, and I and Rome (the one Native American among our group of travelers) and Barry went inside. The radio was blaring loud tinny music. A woman was feeding young children. An old woman sat still on a bench at the side of the room. There were buckets of fried chicken on the table. An old man sat eating, "Come in, c'mon in boys," said the man, gesturing toward us at the door. This was David.

And in we went. "What do you want? What brings you here?" he asked over the din of the radio and the children.

"We....We bought you a stone tablet which we found," I began, getting right to the point.

"You brought a what?" he said, trying to hear over the lunchtime noise.

For a moment the possible foolishness of this whole journey flashed through my brain. "We brought you a stone tablet," I went on slowly and clearly this time, "which we found."

The younger woman's hand switched off the radio.

"Do you have it with you?" asked David.

"Yes, it's outside in one of the vans."

"Well go and get it and bring it in."

Like a curtain rising on a whole different scene the place transformed. The food was swept off the table. The children ushered out another door to play. The old woman had lit a candle and was sitting by it at an altar in the corner when we returned inside with the wrapped up stone tablet.

"Open it up," David encouraged.

We did, and he ran his fingers over it, almost more to be touching it, feeling it, than looking at it. "Well, how did you get this?" he wanted to know. And I recounted, in brief, the story I have told you here. Barry spoke about the planned Gathering that we were all working on, and Rome, as a Native American, spoke to David about the respect we young people had for the Native American ways.

David asked a few specific questions about where and when we got the rock. Then without further to-do, he wrapped it back up and getting up, said, "We'll just have to see who's here to take a look at it."

He went and spoke with his neighbor, then told us they were going to round up some of the others, that he thought there were "enough of us here to have a good look together," and that we should go to this house he gave us directions to.

We followed the directions he'd given us, which took us back to the very same place, right next to the Kiva, where we had been earlier that morning.

It was Mina Lansa's house. She was head of the Hopi Bluebird Clan and she met us at the door once again, and invited us inside. The entryway opened to a larger room and there were assembled a group of older Hopi. Seventeen I counted. I was nervous as could be. It was a humbling experience just standing there and feeling the combined weight of thousands of years of the tribe's culture.

David motioned for us to come up closer and tell our tale. As we spoke, he translated into Hopi, and there was another man there who translated. Sometimes the translation process was simple; other times the Hopi would all speak among themselves in this wonderful song-like language. David was encouraging us not to leave out details. Things that were small to us, might be important to them.

We spoke also about the vision of this Gathering, and how this was the spiritual quest that had brought us together as a clan. They talked again for a bit among themselves, and then asked a series of questions: What were the colors of the godseye in the garden? How much corn did we plant? What direction was the tablet facing when we found it? How many people had handled it, carried it since then? and so on.

In all this telling we were clear, very clear, that we made no claims whatever about what this tablet was or was not, only that all things considered—it seemed that the right thing to do was to bring this stone to them.

At last, their glances turned to Mina. And she came forward and asked us—her eyes as piercing as a night bird's eyes in the dark of the desert—she asked us to show them the rock. Without any further fuss I unwrapped it and held it toward her.

She looked and spoke with clarity and to the point. "It is not the same color, it is not of the same type of rock, nor the right shape to match the piece missing from the tablet that I have."

She turned now and was addressing not just us, her rainbow visitors, but all the people in the room. "However," she went on, "when my father gave me that tablet, and left me his instructions he told me that this world is full of illusions and we must not let our eyes be fooled. He told me then, that in a time like this I should take the rock and place it near to the tablet itself to see edge to edge if the pieces fit."

"Can you give it to me?" she asked, and without a word I held the stone out to her.

She took the rock and moved through the bunches of people toward the rear of the room and out a door at the back.

Perhaps ten minutes later she was back. When she spoke her quiet voice had clarity and strength. "It is as I thought, your rock is the wrong shape, color and size." She was shaking her head, "It does not fit as the missing piece of our tablet."

David took it from her and handed it back to us. "This is your tablet," he said as he passed it back to us.

I spoke, feeling honor at having been thoughtfully received at all by these real elders of an enduring tribe. "We are a very young tribe, like a grandchild tribe. You are a very old tribe, like a grandparent tribe. We need all the help and advice we can get from you.... And if there is anything we could do for you, let us know and we will do what we can. At least we will try."

David again translated, and from the eager responses, it seemed there was lot to be told to us. "It is clear," he began, "that you and we are working for the same Great Spirit. We all desire Peace in our lives, for our children and for everyone. Because this is what you are working for, we know that you are warriors of the rainbow, but whether you are *the* Warriors of the Rainbow that have been foretold, well that is another matter, but you are young and full of hope and there is much life stretching out in front of you."

Then the other Hopi man was translating, "If you want to know a task that we believe The Rainbow Warriors will accomplish, it is to rid the Black Mesa of the demon machines that the coal companies have put there. These are sacred lands for us and they are being destroyed for coal and the smoke in the sky that the coal brings."

Several Hopi were talking in the old tongue now all at once and the translator was trying to keep up with it. They were telling us about the strip mining. I felt in awe of their serious wisdom and their passion not for the money coal and uranium could bring, but for the safety and security of the children of our world.

Then the conversation changed tone, and now they were giving us instructions on Care of Sacred Tablets. A number of the old Hopi spoke, and they were telling us of their traditions, several of them speaking up in modern English.

"Don't take any photographs of it."

"Don't make any rubbings of it, or draw a picture of the pictures on it."

"This way, the only way to see what it looks like is to see it with your own eyes."

"Keep it wrapped up. Don't keep it open all the time on display. That way when you do open it up it is a special moment to pay attention to. Otherwise if it's open all the time on your shelf, then people will forget, and they will argue and do foolish things in front of it."

And with glad hands and many thanks we wrapped up our tablet and departed from Mina's house out under the now darkening sunset sky.

Later, back in Oregon we set the rock—carefully wrapped up—at Main House at the farm on a shelf with other ceremonial objects and instruments. We included accounts of this meeting with the Hopi in the collectively-edited and collectively-written booklet, *The Rainbow Oracle*, as well as an article about the coal company diggings at Black Mesa. Rainbow people have been volunteers trying to keep destructive forces of profitgreed from damaging Native sacred lands ever since. This is a long trail we are travelling, and the journey is far from done, but we do keep making headway and we do keep trying.

34. Kitty & Elizabeth & Another Nina

As the time for the Gathering—July of 1972—approached, more of my attention was poured toward communications for the event. We used the evening time in the attic of Main House at the farm to assemble a list of addresses on 3 x 5 cards and to prepare a mailing.

From his camp on the Feather River in California, Barry has sent us his long handwritten "Invitation" to the Gathering. It's very long. It goes on and on. But the prose is beautiful. Karen and I edit it. And we bring it to Bullfrog Information Service, which publishes a local Eugene area newsmagazine. They have the first section of the Invite scripted in beautiful calligraphy and printed in their magazine as a single-page Invitation with the rest of the longer descriptive material as one-page article facing the Invitation.

There it was in print, and beautifully so. David Zeltzer and Judy Sachter, an artist couple who had met in the orchard at the farm, ran off big silk-screened copies and we sewed them onto the backs of our jackets. We printed and re-printed as many copies of the two pages as we could continually afford to. And we began to fold these and stuff envelopes on into the middle of the night sitting cross-legged up in the attic. We gathered the mailing lists from every New Age and Hippie publication, from every anti-war directory, from every yoga and zen center listing; from people who gave us their names and from people who gave us their friends' names.

We handed out the flyers—Invitations really—at concerts, clubs, laundromats and cafes to everyone we possibly could. Friends of ours heading anywhere took a pile of the Invites and went on their ways giving them out as they went along.

Then we formulated a plan to travel back and forth across the continent to pass the word of the "World Family Gathering." One group would go south. One would go north. We'd touch paths on the Winter Solstice at the Space Arch (threading the eye of the needle of the continent!) in St. Louis on the Missouri riverbank, and then meet again on the East Coast, and then back west where the northern route would cross Canada and the southern route would dip into Mexico.

The harvests were mostly in at the farm. Storerooms of food had been put by. Firewood was abundant in the woodsheds. And folks had moved into the several half-finished (but secure enough for the winter) shelters that we had been building all summer long. The A-Frame by the river, the Dome, the Tower, Fat City, Jake's Place, the Stardome and the Troll Hut were all inhabited and casting their warm glows into the autumn mists of our second rainy season on the land.

Still it was an overwhelming task just to maintain the daily basics for everyone. Most of the stalwarts of the community's enduring projects were becoming fulltime innkeepers for the endless travelers passing through. Sure, most of these travelers were looking for a place to live, but not necessarily here. Most of the visitors were eager to help in whatever ways they could. But in the meantime this was a wonderful opportunity for folks on the road to kick back, stroll along the meadow's edge, write poetry, read under the branches of the orchard's trees, wade in the river with pants rolled up—and *then* help with whatever needed to be done. But it was a huge job to care for everyone. And there were others who showed up who were less inclined to help.

There were fusses over whether people living on the farm could take food stamps—a government dole program. "Well what's the difference if someone gets monthly support from their parents, or from some bank dividends?"

And there were fusses over diet. Vegetarians versus Meat Eaters. Fruitarians versus Sprouted Grain Breadbakers. It was nuts. Of course everyone had to learn to respect each other's diets and each other's utensils. But that isn't easy in communal kitchens. So there were endless arguments.

And there were fusses over beer and pot. Just about everyone wanted beer and everyone wanted pot. In the first years of the 1970s it was commonly considered that pot was only a tropical crop. But we found out otherwise. Still, the laws were intense, so people traipsed off the land to find 'secret' patches to grow on. And people made vats of beer. As people put more effort into the cultivation of these mild intoxicants there was less effort available for other agriculture.

What all this meant in terms of community was that a lot of people who had found us because of some quest for a visionary ideal were just plain worn out from all the meals they were serving, from all the shelters-from-the-storm they were rigging, from all the laundry they were doing, from all the vehicles they were repairing, from all the dishes they were washing—in addition to the "regular" work of agriculture and building construction. Plus, these good deeds came along with the aggravations: the arguing, the missing 'spaced out' tools, the differing levels of responsibility that people possessed, or the different levels of cleanliness. And health? Whatever drifted into the community we were all at risk to catch: colds, staph, hepatitis. So there was constant medical and health monitoring and endless concerns and discussions. Even the counciling that helped us find solutions was time consuming, very time consuming.

So a lot of people with great talent and inspiration moved on, looking elsewhere for a country community to live at. But others found that this service of cooking, sharing, giving, building, planting, growing, providing, nourishing, sustaining was very likely the goal, the dharma they had been seeking. So the balance shifted, and on the community continued.

And what else were young people going to do in the woods? Procreate! Karen and I had our baby girl Eden. She was born upstairs in the attic of the Main House. And we were not the only new-found parents. The verdant pastoral life inspired procreation. Rob Roy and Laika had Morninglory in the structure built atop the prayer platform, before the Tower got finished and became their home. Sihu and Kaushal birthed Peyto a few miles to the north in a quieter back-to-the-land scene at Lorane. Bear had split up with Terry and was now with Annie who had Michael Jr. at the Coburg Farm—one of the original settler houses in the Eugene area. Kathy and Ron had Orissa. The whole scene was vibrant with life and we were all being born into a new dream with a new generation born in the cabins of the hippie hills of Western Oregon.

Karen and Eden and I and Sihu and Kaushal and Peyto—off we went eastward along the Columbia River Gorge then down through Denver, passing out invitations all along the way. In Denver we postered the student district and the arts cafes. We were *in* Colorado... soon to be home to the Family Gathering. We met local residents, student activists and folks from Boulder. Some of them lived at a 'co-op' called the Titanic Co-op. It used to be an old, huge fraternity house and now was a people's co-operative.

Figure 44. Author, Karen McPherson and our daughter, Eden Star at the farm in Oregon. (David Roberts: 1972)

Steve Berman, one of the co-op members, said we might it use for 'staging'—a loose term for all the logistical/information/supply operations that mass events depend on.

At a gas station halfway across Kansas in the windy twilight we're gassing up, changing the diapers, and there's another station wagon unloading a car full of fringe-wearing, head-banded, beaded, long-haired travelers. We hand them an invitation and we all pause to talk at the side of the station sheltered from the wind. Before we part ways, we hold hands in a small circle, do an Ommm in the graying light, and walk back to our cars. The gas station attendant who is looking at us knows something different is moving along these roads. We leave him a couple of Invitations to share with his friends. Our new friends from the other station wagon take a stack of fliers to hand out until they can copy their own. Kaushal says as we continue down the highway, "Those are the people who are going to make this Gathering happen. It's a natural for them. They know as much about it already as we do. They've seen it in their own dreams." And that's the way it was.

Kaushal and Sihu cut south to Memphis while Karen and I went on to New York, then Washington and Florida. We meet with the Yippie! radicals in lower Manhattan and the Black Liberation movements in Harlem. We meet the Ethiopian Coptics and we hand out invitations in Washington Square Park in Greenwich Village. At the park people are handing out fliers for anti-war demonstrations, union support, bands and music gigs, and then we see there's a guy there with a big black beard and he's already handing out fliers—Invitations—for the Gathering.

This jovial man is Bo from California, on his own travels, spreading the word: Colorado July 1972. He's talking to us about food supply, food preparation and how we're gonna be able to do that. He's connected to organic vegetable and grain producing farms in California, and he's askin' us what we're working on for the Gathering. "Communications," I stammer, taken by surprise by the already-in-motion enthusiasm of this character whose path we are crossing. "Those are the people who are going to make this Gathering happen," I can hear Kaushal's voice repeating.

In New York we meet up with Bear and Barry who have traveled across the Southern U.S. along with a whole hippiebus full of Invitation-bearers. We are exchanging stories of our travels. People are diverging with the fliers: New England, the Great Lakes, Europe, Mexico. We decide we should print a booklet with contributions from the people we meet who have something to contribute: words, pictures, artwork, poems, and practical stuff about earthwise living too.

Our next stop is Washington, D. C. Karen and I and Bear and Barry head south. We go straight to the Capitol building. As we enter we ask about how we can present these Invitations to the delegations from the fifty states. The front door guards look us over and direct us around to another smaller entrance. There are the offices of the Capitol Police. They look us over while we talk plainly with them about wanting to present at least one Congressperson and Senator from each state with this Invitation to the World Family Gathering. We explain we've come from four different states to bring these Invites to the Capitol—especially to our own Senators and home district Congresspeople. But since the Invitation was for Everyone we'd like to bring them to offices from all the States. They talk among themselves and decide to bring in the Chief. He questions us briefly, looks over the Invitation and makes up his mind. "Give them two escorts. If there's any problem, yank them. If not, let them distribute the Invitations and," he says turning to us, "enjoy your time in the halls of government."

Off we go through the labyrinth of Capitol hallways. We have uniformed accompaniment. We proceed through the wings of the building. The Capitol Cop opens the door. If the office is busy, one of us hands the Invite to the receptionist and lets him or her know that the Senator and all the good people of his or her state are cordially invited to the World Family Gathering. They take the flier, thank us, and on we go.

But if the office is in a lull, the Capitol Escort announces us formally to the receptionist, "People from the Rainbow Family of Living Light come with an Invitation to the Senator and the People of the State of _____." These guys were used to this. This opening the door and announcing routine. And so were the receptionists. But it sure opened eyes wide with the appearance of four bell-bottomed, bell-clad, leather-fringed, button-festooned, mirror India-print-dressed and westernwoods-styled hipsters. Everyone was very polite to us. Often they would call in a staffer to look at the Invitation right then. Usually they'd just take it politely, but sometimes they'd ask questions and a few times the whole staff would wander in, and just enjoy themselves talking with us. We were definitely entertaining. Sometimes a staffer might ask if we'd gone to the hip scene in the college town in their home state to pass Invitations. But mostly the questions were the same old ones about "Who's backing this financially?" and "How much are tickets going to be?" and "If no one's selling any tickets, then how are you going to pay for this?" And the same disbelief that anything could happen without money paving the way. Still we brought them a glimpse of something other than their daily grind.

Eventually we went through the whole of the House and Senate offices in several buildings. We split into two groups: each with one of the Escort Guards. Even so, it took us two full days. A few Congresspeople came out to meet us. We met Senator Goldwater, the Arizona conservative. Then we dropped off Invitations at the National Archive, "Here, file this Invitation. You never know, you might be glad you have it later." And at Nixon's White House, in the White House Mailroom. And we drop one off at the Library of Congress. And hand them out along Constitution Avenue. And along side streets where very rapidly—in a short walk's distance—the white marble buildings of state seem very far from the squalor of the residences of the people. We are still handing out Invitations. Meeting the street youths. Talking about the families of the world, and the drumbeats of our world.

We stay with the people from the Yes! co-operative. It's a health food and restaurant business. They want to help. But they are going through their own collective processes: arguing among themselves about their own limits. We come onto the scene, visiting, ideal helpful guests (in our own eyes) in their collective houses. And now we're the ones being scrutinized, and being argued about by the full-time members of the collective. How long are we planning to stay? Can we come help unload the produce truck tomorrow morning? Now I'm seeing the collective process from the other side.

Through them we get in touch with Dr. Bronner, the legendary pioneer of earth friendly soaps. He asks questions about the Gathering's spiritual orientation getting to the point quickly about the silent meditation, which he likes. "Well…" he says—and there is a l-o-n-g pause (enough for a little meditation right there), "You're going to have to be very, very pure for this to work."

I hadn't really thought of myself or ourselves as "pure" exactly. But from where Dr. Bronner was coming from, there were a lot of pitfalls along spiritual roads. Pitfalls of pride and power, greed and temptations. And to him, this was his warning to us. Still, he said he would see to it that Yes! had a donation of bio-degradable soaps for the Gathering.

We went out to the hills of Virginia, by the town of Nethers, and met with the woodland clans there, made a sauna, ate morning glory seeds, watched the rocks steam and the waters hiss. In the dense dark that night I could see imprints of light made by the warmth of people.

Up and down the East Coast we pasted fliers. The yoga centers in Key West, the college taverns in Fort Lauderdale. Karen and I stopped at the Carolina oceanside ashram retreat of Meher Baba, the Hindu Avatar who came west in the 1920s. He brought messages of peace and goodwill and introduced the catch phrase "Don't Worry, Be Happy" in his teachings. We were hosted by Kitty and Elizabeth now in their *nineties*. They had fled the socialite scene before the

Great Depression when they were young wild things and had scandalously run off with this smiling Hindu monk! Now they served us tea in delicate teacups. Dressed in high-collered, lace-frilled dresses, they were as lively and bright as teenagers. They didn't have any trouble understanding how things like this Gathering could run on the input and energy of the participants instead of money. And the meditation? They said a few clear things about that. "It's always bigger than you think it is when you start," says Kitty.

"It's a way to get connected to our Creator," says Elizabeth.

They shared scrapbooks with 40- and 50-year-old pictures and clippings about their adventures—and all the terrible press about yoga as a 'hoax' or a 'hustle.' All the crude cartoons of the foreign mystic and the groupies (though the papers of that day called them 'tramps.') And the photos of the travels and ashrams and festivals and meditations.

"So don't be afraid if they call you names or don't understand what you're doing. Just keep doing what you believe in," says Elizabeth

"And if anyone tries to stop you, just keep picturing the *meditation*, because that's what you're going towards," says Kitty.

This from a couple of little old ladies!

The next morning very early they steer us toward a path that leads to the bay's edge. There's a bench just right for watching nature. Wind in the tall swaying grasses. Gentle waves lap the shore. I pray like crazy for whatever virtue it's going to take not to mess this up. Karen is sitting beside me. It's a morning of tranquility and grace.

In Baltimore we connect with the counter-culture radicals at People's Books and then travel north toward Woodstock in the Catskill Mountains of Upstate New York.

At a little restaurant just off the town square we encounter Fantuzzi sitting at one of the woodblock tables; a musician and minstrel. He's another person who recognizes this idea because he's seen it himself in his own mind. He's onboard for the adventure, and with his scarves draped about his trim body and beaming a smile he walks us down the road toward Family and Gail Varsi. Family was a drop-in center. A place for community self-help, staffed by volunteers who did medical referrals, traveler's aid, runaway and suicide hotlines, and hosted benefits for a variety of local causes. And Gail was the person at the criss-crossing of this web of light. With her long dark hair and tall slender figure she stood looking us over.

She listened carefully to our rap and said, "I figured I'd see you sooner or later." She'd already heard about the Gathering, already knew it was set for July '72 somewhere in Colorado and expected sooner or later to bump into some of the portenders of the event as they passed through Woodstock.

She suggests we make lists of what people should bring; things like food, acoustic musical instruments, warm clothes for nights high in the mountains, water containers. We start jotting notes and making lists. She already understands community and its needs.

Back in New York we talk this over with Barry and he types up a letter that starts with, "Howdy Folks." This letter contains all the additions to the information on the Invitation we can cram into one page. It's a broadening of the specifics of the Invitation and over the next months gets edited and re-edited with each new idea that just has to be included. Really all these ideas are coming from the dozens and hundreds of people we are meeting who are already on this wave. Each one contributes some key and these keys are being written up in each new *Howdy Folks*. Longer written or more complex suggestions are held onto for inclusion in the planned booklet. Meanwhile, the *Howdy Folks* letter gets pasted onto the back of the Invitation's printed copies replacing the more extensive "New Jerusalem Mandala City for All People" rap that had come from the original Bullfrog Press printing. Michael Greene, an exquisitely talented pen & ink artist from the Woodstock scene won't let these themes go, and he inks an illustration of the upcoming Gathering vision with the themes of Mandala City and New Jeruseleum (as he spells and letters it) boldly titled. We use his artwork for the booklet's cover.

Gail brings us to Nina, just outside town in a modest but exquisitely decorated home. Surrounded by artworks from all the continents resides this maîtresse of the Woodstock scene. She's really of our parents' generation, though younger by far than Kitty and Elizabeth. She's on Woodstock Family's traveler support list, so Gail gives her a call and gives us directions. Nina Graboi sits us on cushions around low tables. Round-faced and bright-eyed, she seems to twinkle as she talks. Her rooms are all bright with windows looking out at woodlands. She worked at a community college on Long Island and had—as part of a literature program—invited Zen philosopher Alan Watts to lecture and read there. He walked with her along the sands of the Long Island Sound and turned her on to marijuana.

From there she graduated to be a regular participant in the Millbrook community where Tim Leary had set up a center for his League for Spiritual Discovery. That was a place where LSD use was a regular part of life. It was disbanded by the cops under Gordon Liddy (later of Watergate notoriety) in a well-publicized raid.

Nina lets us make warm soup in her kitchen. She listens thoughtfully to our plans for the Gathering. We talk about a great range of topics. I complain of the current system of politics. "We have to find ways to move things along without political parties or corporate rulership. We chose not to work for Humphrey and now we've had four horrendous years of Nixon. What a mess!"

"Oh, you'll see," Nina answers, "Nixon too will play his part. He'll end up showing just how low he is. And the nation will be the better for it."

I couldn't swallow this optimism. But it turned out she was right.

Nina brings us to Roni's party. Located on a barge, her home, moored on the Hudson. This awesome floating multi-storied structure is host tonight to a party for I-have-no-idea-what. The place is beautiful. Shimmering lights on the Hudson. There's a fireplace onboard. And huge tapestries. And a stone Buddha that must've weighed a ton. And a hundred or more people, dancing, talking, laughing. There's a jam sesion playing music on one level. Someone is handing out clearlight windowpanes of acid. Through the night performers play jazz and rock, poets speak poems, we get to recite the Invitation and speak about the Gathering. Below deck there are rooms entirely bedecked with billowing tie-dyed fabric and soft tie-dyed furniture. Open portholes close to the waterline let in the breeze and the scent of evening on the river. We are in a real dreamworld.

In the way late hours we help bake breads and pass out hot buttered rolls and warm tea to the still-tripping partiers.

Nina is like a den mother to the pack. The psychedelic den mother, watching out for everyone, always encouraging, bringing out everyone's best. She says she'll caravan with Gail and whoever else from Woodstock to the Gathering.

35. Visionworks Press

Turning westward we traversed the continent going through Ontario—stopping in Toronto giving out Gathering Invitations at Superschool (an educational experiment where Karen's younger brother Christopher was finishing high school) and at Rochdale (a skyscraper Co-op & gigantic Free University). We crossed Manitoba and stayed at Big Mike's infamous crashpad outside Winnipeg. Then a little farther out of town we cooked for the sit-in/takeover of the regional Indian Affairs building on a Canadian Native reservation. Next we drove north to Saskatchewan where Karen's mother held a teaching post at the university and then…south to Colorado.

There we made a rendezvous with Denny who was from the Universal Life Church. That's a church, founded by Reverend Kirby Hensley, which approved of "Universal Principles" without giving those too much definition. This grew in the early 1960s from a very obscure organized religion to one that had lawfully ordained thousands of ministers many of whom used this designation to escape the draft. By the turn of the next decade the ULC was holding outdoor rallies with rock 'n roll and other festivities. Denny had helped organized last year's rally in Idaho, and after getting a Gathering Invitation, he contacted us saying he knew of a site in Colorado where the event could be held. We met him there at the foot of Table Mountain. It was a small mount really, very unremarkable compared to the splendor of the majestic snow topped peaks and valleys surrounding us. Denny said that it wasn't currently used by anybody. Since there were so many truly awesome hiking and camping areas nearby, this dusty flat-topped mesa was pretty much left to itself. He gave us the names of some young forest ranger and park ranger apprentices he'd spoken with and they'd told him us it was rugged ecologically and that for sure nothing else was going on there over the July Fourth Weekend. From its summit you could see snow-covered mountain ranges and peaks in a 360° vista. I remembered the Mishnah story about Mt. Sinai where the small mountain is chosen from among all the other larger more spectacular mountains because of its modest character. It was literally at the height of the continental divide, right on the 'spine' of the continent.

But it was dry. People would just have to learn to conserve and carry and respect water. And it was public land. National Recreation Area territory. That's land with more open public use provisions than even the National Forests. Near the mountain's base stretched a long flat where we could park all the cars. So we had found a site. I remember that evening in the chill Colorado air we had a glimpse of the Aurora Borealis.

We decided to go to Denver to visit the state's capital and invite the Governor and his staff to what we were planning. They thought we were joking or half out of our minds. Especially when we told them tens of thousands of people, maybe even a hundred and forty-four thousand people were going to show up.

We told them this event was going to happen in one way or another and we needed to be in touch with the relevant people in the government about traffic and such, and that it was just common sense and courtesy to notify public officialdom in advance. We gave them Invitations, maps, contact addresses and phone numbers. But they just couldn't bring themselves to believe us.

People are, more often than not, bound by what they already believe. And it's hard for any of us to imagine what we don't have a category for.

All anybody in those offices could relate to was "Rock and Roll Festival." Woodstock was still huge news and numerous electric music festivals had occurred during the two summers since. So when Karen, Barry, Skyblue, Mary and I walked into the Governor's office for our appointment all his aides wanted to know was: "*Who* were the backers? How much *money* did we have to produce this? What *bands* were going to be playing? Which *record labels* were behind this? What *food vendors* had we hired? Who was handling *ticket sales*? *How many* tickets were we planning to sell? and *How much* were the tickets going to be?

When we told them: there weren't going to be any ticket sales, the event was not a commercial event, and there wasn't going to be an electric stage, the Governor's aides kind of squinted at us, as if to say, "We don't quite understand? What are you trying to do?"

"It's a Spiritual <u>Gathering</u>, not a commercial <u>festival</u>," we all tried explaining.

"Would there be music?" they asked.

"Yes, but from a thousand acoustic guitars, and a thousand drums, and a thousand flutes."

"And food?"

"The people who come are going to bring the food, not vendors, not hot dogs and soda cans, good healthy food at woodland kitchens cooked by the participants."

They looked at us like maybe we didn't really know what we were doing. One asked nicely, "Are you sure that many people are interested in an idea like this? What if fewer people come? Are you sure there won't be just a few dozen of you?"

They just couldn't relate to us. I think they related to our homemade shirts, our hats with 'mojo' pins, baubles, and feathers, my crimson patchwork extra-wide bellbottom corduroys, Barry's fringed leather chaps, all of which—along with the rap about the Gathering—made us definitely a welcome break from their regular office world. They could be amused by us, but not, not as Anybodies to be taken seriously.

We invited them—and their families—to come—and to tell their friends—just the same as we had been inviting everyone else we'd met for the past two years.

After a couple more questions, one about whether we *belonged* to any religious group (we each took a crack at answering that); and How much money did we have to put this event on with? (you try explaining "Voluntary Contributions" to a roomful of State officials); they happily wished us a very good day and assured us the State of Colorado wished us all possible success with our 'festival.'

Outside in the Capitol's parking lot our station wagon had been ransacked. Nothing was taken. We had come in a clean car with no contraband. But all our stuff had been opened and thrown around. It looked as though it had been searched.

A week later back in Oregon we began to assemble all the clippings, stories, artworks, poems, cartoons, invocations, etc., etc., that had been given to us along these double figure-eight trips across the continent. Everywhere people had passed these to us for putting together a 'booklet' about the gathering to come. We had an old-style ball-head selectric typewriter with about six interchangeable font heads, and these piles and files of illustrations, and texts … and a cabin in the snow on the side of Mount Hood to work at. So about a dozen of us (Karen, Barry, Skyblue, Jack, Terry, Bry, Cathy, Denise, Bruce, Mina, children and myself) drove up through the snowbanks of the High Cascades and worked in a marvelous collective spirit to compile these into booklet form.

Over at Visionworks Press in downtown Eugene under the guidance of master printers Sean O'Reilly and Katie Jackrabbit we photographed, shrunk, enlarged, and burned the plates for the book. People slept upstairs at the Free University next door. Printing was a colossal learning experience. Katie and Sean were excellent teachers, and already well-acquainted with co-operative processes, so this tribal version of getting things done was something they were already used to. He was a member of a local band called the Lost Cactus Cowboys and had been a movement printer for the better part of a decade already. Katie came from a radical labor and radical feminist background and together they—and other friends—put together this hub of information spinning off their presses. They had already printed volumes for several different ends of the new culture: radical political stuff, health stuff, pro-marijuana stuff. They looked at us like we were just a little bit too flower power for their taste, but they dug on the cooperative aspects, the non-money-for-free aspects, the open-to-everyone approach and fact that we were bringing together many parts of the peace, social justice and spiritual scenes.

Now dozens of people were involved: cutting the paper, stacking the paper in the presses, adding the ink, using the long vacuum camera, developing the negatives, pasting them onto the yellow alignment sheets, stripping the negatives, burning the metallic plates, putting the plates on the presses and adding the ink, then actually running the presses. It was a great lesson in human cooperation and in the value of the First Amendment guarantee of Freedom of the Press.

The presses rolled and the pages were printed. The printed sheets were brought upstairs to the Free U where dozens more people folded and collated the pages, assembled the books with their saffron-colored covers and hand-sewn bindings. This wasn't just printing, this was publishing. 5000 copies. 144 pages. Colored inks. We printed text in all colors—even yellow, which was hard (nearly impossible) to read. The first half of the booklet was entirely about the Gathering, the ideas, the inspirations, the hopes, the methods, the suggestions. The second half contained all the *other* inspirations and suggestions: organic agriculture, creative educational visions, architectural models, women's rights, home birthing, political statements, the Hopi's statement about Black Mesa and the story about our visit to them with the carved rock, a drug education playscript, Quotations from General Tao, and at the end—on the last page—we put a map to Table Mountain. And the title—out of the blue as we opened the parcel with Michael Green's cover art, there it was: "The Rainbow Oracle". As for the center, the middle two pages were left blank—like the silence at the center of the Gathering—just an empty slate to write your own story on, or an open sky where anyone can dream.

As box loads of these were packed up they were shipped out with carloads of people (and stacks of the one-page invitations) to wherever that ride was going. And that's how the pilgrimage started, because from there, for most of us, after wherever we were taking the booklets to, the next stop was Colorado.

Figure 45. Artist Michael Green's cover for The Rainbow Oracle printed at Visionworks Press, Eugene, Oregon, May/June, 1972. (Michael Green: 1972)

PART EIGHT

The World Family Gathering Comes True
(1972)

Like a wish in a dream coming true, the parts and pieces of The New World Culture assemble themselves in one place, gather together and make a community that works. Food, clothing, shelter, healthcare, energy, transportation, sanitation, equal rights for all, sharing, caring, and learning from each other. It is a glimpse of what has only been imagined, but shows us that a different way of organizing human society—without banks, corporations, or governments running things—is actually possible.

36. At the Gates

Colorado was our destination. It was time to go to the Gathering. I brought boxes of *Rainbow Oracle* booklets; camping gear, bulk foods, tents, tarps, tools. Karen went back east to Woodstock to meet up with the caravan from there.

I drove down from Oregon with a carfull of Gatherers. We went directly to the Titanic Co-op in Boulder, the place that had offered space for use. What a scene! Everything was already in full swing. Cars and trucks arriving, people everywhere: gear, children, foodstuffs being unloaded and stacked, tents going up on the lawn, and the folks from the co-op looking on in amazement. Steve Berman and his best pals who'd invited us were having the best of times. But the rest of the co-op who'd happily consented were looking around in astonishment. We decided that what was needed was a good meal so we took supplies and went to the co-op's titanic kitchen and cranked out fifty or so loaves of bread. It was an activity that brought pretty much everyone together in the big cafeteria room and focused the swirl of people energy. There we learned that Table Mountain had been barbed-wired by the State Police, that the Colorado Legislature had just passed—only days ago—a 'Woodstock Law,' really an *anti*-Woodstock law that prohibited outdoor mass gatherings. Later this law would be declared unconstitutional. But today it was on the books. And Table Mountain was closed and guarded. Still people were going up there—at least to the vicinity—and camping where they could. Someone said a local resident had given us a parking lot—a field—where we could stay put. Rumors were abundant. But everyone was still coming home. Home to the Family Reunion of the Human Tribes. And just proceeding on the outrageous assumption that things would work out all right.

The press had little idea about what was going on. And it was apparent from the press that the State had no idea what was going on. They'd seen a Universal Life Church flier. The Secretary of State's office contacted Idaho authorities where the Church's picnic had been the year before and got scared right out of their wingtips by stories of naked people, rock and roll, marijuana, hallucinogens, and other earthly delights. The governor declared that this event was simply not going to come to Colorado.

We sat up late typing up a press notice. And in the morning it was hiked, biked and hitchhiked to all the Denver and Boulder area TV, newsprint and radio media calling them to a press and public meeting in the basement of the Titanic Co-op later that afternoon.

Everyone showed up. The place was packed full with cameras, lights and people. Mitch Mitchell, Skyblue Fiedler, Paterson Brown and I sat upfront. We had a beautiful banner. We handed out the *Rainbow Oracle* booklets. We read the Invitation and passed out *Howdy Folks*. We served hot buttered bread.

Then each of us made short comments covering different ground. Skyblue introduced and welcomed everyone. She spoke about not being afraid, about "People being together with people: learning from each other, sharing with each other. This is not something to be fearful of."

Mitch told the press not to be so quick to parrot the government's version of the story without looking into it themselves. That was their job: to get the real story, the whole picture. Why, here they were getting a very different view of the Gathering already, "See the equipment and the backpacks and the trucks and the buses and the people and the children. Pay attention. Come be part of the event. Come up to the mountains and Gather with us. Report the news as you see it. Gather with us and tell the public the truth about whatever you see."

Paterson talked about the spiritual side of the Gathering. He spoke eloquently about the "Cathedral of Nature" and that "prayers and meditations have taken place in such surroundings since time immemorial."

For my turn I talked about logistics, tactics, parking, food, water, medical, trying to communicate as much assurance as I could that this was going to occur with much good sense and many capable people.

Cameras rolled. There was a barrage of questions. The press could hardly believe that this wasn't a thin disguise for what would turn into a giant rock 'n roll festival in the end. We all answered as best as we could. And other people in the room—other gatherers—took questions and gave answers. There was a lot of talk about what to do about the closures the government had already put into effect.

"It will all work out."

"A way will be found."

"Don't be afraid. This is meant to happen. Just look at all the thousands of people coming here. On their way *here* traveling in this direction right now."

"The State of Colorado is over-reacting. This isn't any kind of violent demonstration. This isn't even a Protest. It's just people from all over the world coming to *these* mountains to hold hands and pray for or wish for Peace. It's not a rock festival with generators and promoters and tickets and stars with records to sell. It's just people coming to use our public lands, our Commons, for a peaceful experience."

"And on the Fourth of July, on Independence Day, what could be more suited to the Ideals of Liberty than all these free people assembling peaceably? All these different people, all these different kinds of people, all taking time to share with each other. To give an example that humanity is not so fouled up. What could be more American than that?"

A reporter asked me how we expected to dispose of human waste in the mountains. I replied that we would use slit-type trenches. She asked if that was hygienic enough for large numbers of people. I replied we got the design from the United States Marine Corps Field Manual, and that it was a tried and tested design (I had become acquainted with The Field Manual during The Living Theatre's production of *The Brig* years earlier).

We were so naïve, and so completely full of enthusiasm and faith.

But it certainly led to the press taking a more careful look at what was really happening. And some officials from the State of Colorado were there too, watching and listening. They went away with a different view than they'd come in with, too. And the Titanic Co-op folks were having a grand time touring the news crews through their own housing and food co-operative.

Like a wheel in motion with nothing to slow it events moved like a carousel—whirling and rising and falling in rapid succession. We went with a couple of the Colorado officials who brought us to the CBI Headquarters, Colorado Bureau of Investigation. John McIver was the lead officer's name and we took that to be a good sign because McIver was the name of the park back in Oregon where Vortex 1 had succeeded two summers ago. At the CBI we meet an officefull of folks who asked the most sensible questions about things like parking space and public health. They looked at the *Rainbow Oracle* booklet and thumbed through it. They took us at face value. They had figured out that we weren't a commercial operation; we weren't music promoters; we weren't selling drugs; we weren't a political demonstration. They saw us as naïve nature lovers—which was in some ways true. They told us that governmental wheels turning against us were already in motion and those might be hard to stop.

We passed another night at the Titanic Co-op and the next morning our carfull left for Granby. Granby was the Colorado town nearest to Table Mountain. The Gathering was already gathering there. Vans and people were outside the big café on Main Street and everyone was giving directions to Paul's place a little ways out of town where people were going to park.

I asked about the parking at the base of Table Mountain and people looked at me blankly then someone said, "That's all been closed off. We're parking at Paul's."

So we drove out to Paul Geisendorfer's, which was a flat field a little ways out of town. Already there were two tipis up and a big silver Airstream trailer and rows of small trucks, vans, VW vans, and tents, children, people. We pulled in and parked among them. It was about forty acres or so with a small rise toward one side. I knew only a few of the many people there and it was hard to figure what was really going on. Patrick Thompson from the farm in Oregon was already set up and he guided us to a place to encamp our own tents. He was parking cars in an organized manner, maximizing the use of the space. A big evening dinner was being put together collectively and that would be an opportunity for council and communication.

After eating we stretched out hands to start council with an Ommmm and then fifty or so folks stood together in a circle and slowly the story emerged. Yes, the State had put up a barbed wire fence along Table Mountain's base. And signs warning "No Trespassing." And there were police cars stationed at the juncture of the roads at its base. Every National Forest public campground for fifty miles was "Closed for Repairs."

Some people were really unhappy to have come all this way expecting some majestic mountain meadowland and finding themselves parked on a flat outside town. And some people were there who had been expecting a rock festival and were totally disappointed that there wasn't a stage and electric music.

I was in favor of finding a different way up Table Mountain (it's about seven miles away) and getting ourselves up there, getting on site, getting gear on site, taking the high ground. Some people were very happy right where we were. "It's beautiful here. It's not about the location, it's about the people!" A few folks said that Paul Geisendorfer—whose field we were in—had an idea about another site. I had a long discomforted sleep.

Late the next morning Paul arrives. A square-shouldered, solidly built man, short blondish wavy hair, soft kindly face, blue work shirt, jeans. And so there's another meeting. He's explaining how we need to get moving to this meadow that we can go to. It's seven miles in the *other* direction. I'm seeing that as being farther from Table Mountain, not closer. Paul is listing the virtues of the place and the lake that is there, and the forests to camp in. It's also a long haul: two and half miles of very steep uphill trail to get into it. I'm very dubious, but there are a lot of enthused folks and the suggestion is made that a carfull goes right now to take a look and come back here to tell the rest what it's really like. Others are wary that this property he wants to take us to is private land—even though the surrounding forests are all public. One person volunteers to go along with this scout party and come right back with as critical a report as possible. So off goes one truck heading toward Strawberry Lake.

They didn't get back until way late that night. Two of the folks sent a note saying it was so beautiful they were staying there and setting up camp immediately. The rest of the crew was enthusiastic about the place: vistas, water, woodlands, remoteness, mountains above and lake below. As for our critic, he said, "I think everyone should just pack all their stuff and get on up there."

I show Paul the *Oracle* booklet, give him a copy. He looks at it for a few minutes, smiles. He seems relieved to see that there must be others who have put some thought and effort into this. We decide that in the last dark nightime hours as many carloads as can will drive over to the foot of the trail that leads up to the lake, and we'll hike in with the first light of morning.

I ride with Paul. He talks on about the water that's there and how this is the key thing we need to look at, because water is the foundation of all civilization. I ask him where the water comes from and he mimes his answer: he just points his index finger straight up and smiles. As if to say both, "It comes from the sky, from the rain," or " It comes from God." He smiles, tapping his copy of the *Oracle*, "It's nice to meet more people with a strong spiritual view."

I ask him how he got inspired to be so involved with supporting this Gathering. Turns out he'd been a foot soldier in the Korean War in the 1950s, gotten captured. Escaped. Got recaptured. Escaped again, this time into the jungles. He lived for weeks on wild things. Had a vision. Of a Spiritual City. Got recaptured again. When he was released in a prisoner exchange and returned home he went about finding and buying land for this Spiritual City.

I told him, "Here we are."

He asked, "Do you think this Gathering is The City?"

I said, "I think what the whole world may learn from this Gathering will help bring the world Peace."

He nodded and smiled and kept on driving toward the trailhead. Now Paul was saying that if we were going to be utilizing the high lake for our gathering, "We'd better get all the supplies and people in just as quick as we can, because 'they' might just close some of these roads off when 'they' find out this is where we are. We have to get well supplied, and get everyone off the roads and up to the lake."

I told him I would work on that.

Figure 46. Hiking up to Strawberry Lake, Arapahoe National Forest, June, 1972. (John Papp: Courtesy Nathan Koenig and the Woodstock Museum, © White Buffalo Multimedia, Inc.: 1972)

In those exact pre-dawn and dawn hours of June 17, 1972 as we were moving in to Strawberry Lake, the Watergate burglars were being nabbed at Party Headquarters in Washington. It was a very good morning for the counterculture.

The trail was terrifically steep, switchback after switchback at 11,000 feet elevation. Whe-ew. Then a leveler area, then another ascent, finally opening onto gentle woodlands and an awesome meadow with a quarter mile lake at the far end. They said Strawberry Lake was a quarter mile long, a quarter mile wide and a quarter mile deep. It was magnificent. Above the lake and reflected in it were Rocky Mountain peaks with snowcaps. From the adjacent hills ran springs with water good enough to drink. People were kneeling and kissing the earth as we entered the meadow. Some folks were already carrying downed logs to form structures for community uses.

I set the rice I'd been carrying down next to where a kitchen was just starting to go up, and told the few folks there that I was

Figure 47. The trail was terrifically steep, switchback after switchback at 11,000 feet elevation. (John Papp: Courtesy Nathan Koenig and the Woodstock Museum, © White Buffalo Multimedia, Inc.: 1972)

going back down to the parking lot (really Paul's wheatfield) and going to round up supplies and tools and food and people and send them here.

At the parking area almost everyone is packing their gear to shuttle to Strawberry Lake. There is pretty much no parking up at the trailhead. Just offloading and turn around areas.

So we'll just park the cars back here and shuttle everyone over to the trail. Those who don't want to budge don't have to. They can just gather right here and help with the shuttling. I pass the hat for food supplies.

In Boulder I go by the Titanic Co-op, which is like a hive of hippies if there ever was one. We put up maps to Granby, the parking, and Strawberry Lake.

We take a collection for food supplies and we go to the Green Mountain Co-op and put in a giant order for grains, beans, flour, oil. We want them to deliver in their truck. They'll do it.

At a megamart in Denver we meet a young couple shopping for the Gathering. They have an empty truck—just their camping gear in the back. We buy all the megamart's potatoes and some cases of oranges and fill the truck. Off it goes toward Strawberry Lake.

The Governor is having a fit. He's calling up National Guard units and encamping them to the north preparing to defend Table Mountain from the oncoming assault by Gawd-alone-knows-who-we-are.

By the time I get back to Paul's parking lot outside Granby the roads going to Strawberry Lake have been closed from all directions. The police are letting folks into Paul's field because there isn't anywhere else for them to go. There are hundreds of people in the streets of Granby: pumping gas, eating at the cafes, buying supplies from the stores, shopping, waiting for the roads to open. There is a radio system in place at the front gate of Paul's and a table around which people are studying all kinds of maps. Vehicle after vehicle is leaving the field, loaded with people and their gear. Their own cars are safely parked at the far end of the field, and off they go to be let out at some farther destination from which they can hike around the roadblocks and onto the site.

Now the police are getting aware of this and they are tracking each car as it leaves. They have arrested some folks hiking in for trespassing on public property.

There is a plan afoot. Lots of people are getting ready with their backpacking gear. Lots of empty vehicles are readied. I'm brought to the map table and shown the plan. First one car gets loaded up and drives off in one direction toward the far roadblock. One of the police cars at the gate follows it. Then another car gets loaded up and takes off and another police car follows it. Then another car followed by another police car. When there aren't any more police cars at the gate then everyone loads up into dozens of waiting vehicles and off go all these people together in another direction, out from under the eye of the State.

It worked fine until on a back web of roads the lead driver of the caravan loops us right back near town. We are so spotlighted. Colonel Schippers and his State Patrol are right behind us now. They are ordering us to pull over on their PA horns. Lights are flashing. Sirens wr-r-ro-o-o-o-ing. Everyone pulls over. The loudspeaker horns order everyone out. People are disembarking in disarray. "Is this the place?" "Why are all these police here?" "What's going on?" Searchlights from the police cars are bathing everyone in brightness. All our vehicles are leaving so as not to get towed or impounded. People are scampering in many directions carrying children, pets, tromping through the fields heading away from the road, "Is this the way?"

There is a news crew filming and a deputy is ordering everyone to freeze or "Or what?" I holler in the pause where the deputy doesn't know exactly how his sentence ends. "Or what?"

I ask Col. Shippers. "What are you going to do, arrest all these people who don't even know where they are for trespassing?" Deputies were standing behind their cars with rifles out.

"I don't know, we'll just have to see what happens," he said slowly. I had an immediate recollection of Kent State where students protestors were killed because higherups' orders fell on a colonel's shoulders.

"Freeze!" I hollered, "Everyone freeze! His crew is aiming rifles on your backs. Stop running!" People got still really quick. Someone put their hands up and called out, "Don't shoot, we surrender!" Cameras were whirring. It was a very confusing scene.

"I'm not going to shoot anybody! Dammit," Schippers said loudly. He paused and looked around. There were people watching him from all directions and Gatherers spread out in all directions. "What are we going to do with this mess?" he asked out loud, looking at everyone around him. It was a fair question. I think he knew that if they started making arrests that everyone would flee into the night in every direction through the woods, the farms, the town, really chaotic. And besides what would anyone be arrested for?

"Well," I volunteered, "I think we need to get back to the parking field. All our vehicles are gone. Either we'll walk the four miles back to Paul's, right through town, or you can order up a couple of the buses the papers say you have at your command and give us a lift."

Some people choose to take the bus; others just walked.

In the meantime during Col. Schippers' 'raid' many vehicles left Paul's successfully, unloading their passengers in the dark and getting people and supplies through. Maybe *we* were the decoy.

By the next day though things had gotten worse. Hitchhikers along the roads were being arrested, vehicles were being stopped and impounded as unsafe for the tiniest reason (a ding in a windshield, or checking for the most worn spot on a tire, declaring it unsafe, ordering the passengers out and towing the car). The State set up a holding pen for arrestees on the grounds of the county fairgrounds. People who couldn't show the officers 'enough' money were arrested under local vagrancy laws.

All the cars they hooked were being towed to the town's airport. We told the law at the airport that just as soon as Paul's field got 'full up' we'd just send everyone right over to the airport directly. That way folks wouldn't have to get towed, save the tow fee, and just pay whatever fines. "Probably be cheaper than parking for a week in Denver."

At Paul's a sophisticated radio system was in place. Dispatch, mobile units, hand-helds. I saw that there were a lot of us with recent in-the-field military experience and that we were way ahead of the law in on-the-ground organization and training. It wasn't that we 'had' any organization, we just had the on-the-spot abilities to communicate and act together.

And there was another plan afoot for the next night. In this strategy, people arrive late at night from several directions meeting up at the edge of the railroad yards. In the shadows of the railyards we established a buddy system between groups so that two carloads or two families or two individuals were buddied together to stay with each other during the all-night hike. Then we all leaned back against a steep railroad embankment and shimmied along on our backs just out of sight of the yard's active watchtower for a couple of hundred yards to the other side of the yards where the railyard joined the forest. Once again I found myself crossing the amazing line that separates the less-free space from the more-free space. I was entering into that arena again as we slid by the watching eyes in the guard tower. Then there was only an eight-mile uphill trek with no marked trails. From the edge of the forest on, we traveled by map and compass. First we crossed a narrow strip of forested ranchland, and then navigated our way up and over a high 'saddle' formation and finally down a narrow valley that led into Strawberry Lake. We travelled with more than 150 people supplied with food, shelter, tools and willpower.

The first of us got in around dawn. I hiked with Feather Hammond, nimble and golden-haired—and helped with her duffle—while she carried her adorable daughter, Tracey aka Grasshopper. We entered the encampment of the gathering around mid-morning.

I saw people washing clothes in buckets, carefully, away from a small creek bed.

Everyone welcomed us home along the way but the 'hot' news in camp was of the people hiking over from the Boulder side, from the Titanic Co-op, crossing the Great Divide through the Indian Peaks and coming in from the other direction—a much longer and more grueling hike than ours. Another group following the same route we'd taken—a day later—was actually shot at by vigilantes, and escaped backing off slowly, hands raised, into cover of the woods.

I set to work tapping a small springhead for common use: bringing the water cleanly from the edge of its wet greenway to a rocky path where people could get to it easily while keeping the spring area protected.

Down in Grand Lake, Colorado, at the county seat, the State of Colorado brings a suit under the new Outdoor Mass Gathering Act to prohibit the event from occurring. Rainbows flock to the courthouse to represent themselves.

The parking lot at Paul's is filing up. The caravan arrives from Woodstock: 70 cars. The caravans roll in from Florida, Texas, Montana, Everywhere.

Colonel Schippers arrives up at the lake with Orders from The Court to several individuals. Ordering them To Order Everyone To Leave (myself among these individuals so ordered). He presents these to the named individuals at council. Skyblue reads her Court Order out loud to the crowd. What do they do? They cheer! They holler, "We're not moving!" "She can't order us to do anything!" "No way!"

"See," says Skyblue, "I've ordered them."

Turns out that years ago in harder times Paul took his father and his father's friend as business partners in the lake property. Paul didn't own all of it. Now they wanted us to buy it, "Just collect, you know, ten dollars, thirty dollars each from the hundred thousand you say are coming and the place is yours. Yours. All that water that The City of Denver wants," says his father's partner.

What a deal! But no one wants to turn this into a commercial event. Not even for the water. And certainly not all-of-a-sudden because here's what looks like a commercial trapdoor opening up in front of us.

So the next day the troopers return with posters signed from Paul's father and his partner declaring their property, Strawberry Lake, "Off Limits" to us, to anyone. I saw Paul at the woodland's edge. "Whatdya think we should do?" I asked.

"Just pull back off the Lake Property into the woods onto public National Forest land," he said quietly, hardly looking at me.

"....And just use the open meadowlands and the lake for day use," I add.

"Something like that," said Paul.

So we moved any tents and set-ups off the meadowlands and under the shelter of the woods.

I went to work digging latrines. We had a whole crew and a half working on slit trenches uphill from a crossways of paths. Here come a couple of guys, one's wearing a trenchcoat. He looks like a cross between Columbo and Telly Savalas. It's McIver from the Colorado Bureau of Investigation. He's here on a see-for-himself mission with his partner. "What are you doing?" he asks, pointing to our hole-in-the-ground.

"Digging latrines." I point to where some are already dug and to where we're going to dig next.

"Good," he nods.

"Do you have anything to tell us, any advice for us?" I query.

"Keep digging," he says.

In court the Judge ruled in favor of the State's law and against our Right to Assemble. On the ground over 2000 people have been arrested. The State has set up a courtroom on the fairgrounds. People are being fined, released, bailed out, given court dates, or held because of insufficient bail. I believe it was the largest number of actual arrests in a non-violent action up to that date in U.S. history.

At a meeting of State and Federal Officers some lunatic official

Figure 48. Starting to dig our first latrines, Colorado Rainbow Gathering, June, 1972. Notice the banjo player helping keep spirits high. (Photographer unknown: Collection of the author: 1972)

suggested they could just fly planes overhead and gas us. This appalled the State Forester, as well as all the National Park and National Forest Officers. McIver of the CBI spoke in our favor suggesting that working with us was by far the best solution. And the young Forest Ranger's assistant we'd met months earlier spoke favorably for us. The Arapaho National Forest people said it would be all right with them if we gathered on National Forest lands.

At Paul's the field is filled to overflowing. The State of Colorado still has the roads blockaded. A huge council is held. Paul speaks, inviting everyone to try to find their way to Strawberry Lake. Barry Adams speaks heroically and says he's going to shoulder his backpack and his plunker (his two-stringed musical instrument) and walk to the Lake, which is exactly what everyone does. Thousands of people shouldering up; gear, kids, kitchen equipment, musical instruments, tools. Beautiful.

The best route to walk is toward the road closure by the headwaters of the Colorado River just to the east of Table Mountain and

Figure 49. Paul Geisendorfer addressing the massive assembly on his land at Granby, Colorado. (John Papp: Courtesy Nathan Koenig and the Woodstock Museum, © White Buffalo Multimedia, Inc.: 1972)

Figure 50. The assembly on Paul's land right before the march to the Gathering at Strawberry Lake, June 1972. (John Papp: Courtesy Nathan Koenig and the Woodstock Museum, © White Buffalo Multimedia, Inc.: 1972)

Figure 51. Barry 'Plunker' Adams says he's going to shoulder his backpack and hike to the lake. (Photographer unknown: Collection of the author, 1972)

then turn along Grand Lake toward the trailhead. A huge column of hikers, singers, dancers and flowerbearers approaches the barricade. Paterson has gone ahead. He's at the officers' cars talking with them, as they see the 4,000 or so marchers come over the rise in the field and slowly swarm around the bewildered officers and their squad cars. The mass hiked onward to Strawberry Lake.

From then it was a continuous stream. The State still had orders to enforce the roadblock. So no *traffic* could pass. But we could walk by the blockade. So we parked the cars on the *huge* flat right where we'd originally planned to, just off to the side of Table Mountain. Then we walked the other way seven miles and after that, up the trail to the lake. Vehicles that were already 'inside' became the shuttles and maneuvered the people and equipment back and forth all gathering long.

Up at the lake there was a surge of people and supplies coming in. Everyone had a piece of the story to tell and a piece of the Peace to put together.

37. Gathering for the First Time

Awesome forestlands spread out from the top of the steep trail that had become our entryway. Light shone down through the branches of the tall spruce, pines and firs. The green and silver blue needles sparkled in the light. Just ahead one footpath crossed from north to south and the other curved around the meadow and led to the lake.

Campsites were being set up all along these routes. Spontaneously people were constructing shelters, fire rings, and kitchens in areas near to the water supplies. The water came from springs fed by the mountain snowpack above us. Kitchens with names like "Walrus Well" and "Creative," "Sweet Pea" and "Morningstar" sprang up just from the meetings of neighbors there on the site.

A kitchen named Harmony was brought intact with all its supplies by compadres and co-madres in this gathering's vision from

Figure 52. Gathering at Strawberry Lake, Colorado, July 1972. (John Papp: Courtesy Nathan Koenig and the Woodstock Museum, © White Buffalo Multimedia, Inc., 1972)

Eastern Washington. They set up at the north end of the lake and a string of cymbals hung from trees like a musical walkway for passersby to play. Two sweat lodges, the clean and the mud, stood beside the c-o-o-old water lake. Flutes echoed along the shore. The sunlight is bright and I can smell the teas brewing.

Kitchens with names like 'Rainbow' and 'Love,' hundreds of cooks stirring the broth, music and chanting as people work and play. Nobody's running anything. Everybody's helping.

Two kitchens came from Woodstock: one for healing herbs and remedies; another for food. The Woodstock Health's Angels—a medical corps from the legendary Catskill Mountain town have brought a medical center. Two M.D.'s are there along with several nurses. They are already doing triage: cuts and bruises, sprains, burns.

Farther along the trail is a junction of the two main footpaths. I hold an on-the-spot workshop on Geodesic Structures and we fashion a sturdy icosahedron out of native materials. It becomes our Information and Rumor Control station. Behind it we drape parachute cloths and open a Free Library. Just drop books off or pick them up. No signing in or out. Or just sit and read in the colorful shade.

Kitchens with names like 'The Good Earth' and 'Faith,' but it isn't about the food. These were really community centers, chakras of the mountain village. The food itself was pretty minimalist: huge pots of rice and beans and stews and porridges and wide griddles of flapjacks.

The people climbing up this mountain weren't coming here for gourmet meals in the woods. They were here for the spiritual community. Everywhere people singing, chanting, holding hands, meditating. And chanting (!)… in Sanskrit, in English, in Latin, in Japanese, in Native American languages, in Hebrew, in tongues I had never heard. One or a couple of folks would start and others would join in. There'd be dozens or hundreds of people swaying and chanting old American Shaker melodies, or Krishna melodies, or Church melodies or Native American Indian melodies, like

Figure 53. Playing the cymbals at Harmony Kitchen. (Alan Carey: 1972)

different choirs scattered in the woods. It was a new sound, a new song made of many songs. You could walk along trails and hear the changing choruses from camp to camp. The spirit of the voices seemed all like One Spirit in a delightful harmony.

Up the trail ahead there's another medical station. Already one baby has been born with its help.

At a kitchen calling itself Little Harlem a group of inner city-ites have set up a drumming circle. White bongo players from California and rock band drummers are joining African djembes and Native American drummers in some ancient drum rhythm. But an argument is developing in the cooking area and I listen in. It's the same conflict over vegetarian and non-vegetarian. I'm hearing new voices expressing the same old arguments. Shades of the farm in Oregon: I had seen how destructive that split was in that community, so I listen carefully. But I'm also hearing compromise and solutions here. People are going the extra yard—the extra inch—even a hair's breadth—to find the common ground: veggies for the veggies, meats for the meat eaters; separate veggie cookpots; everyone helps keep it clean; R-e-s-p-e-c-t for each other and all of our weird customs. One of the brothers, Louis, from Little Harlem looks over at me and says, "Hey, there's the fellah who gave me the invitation up on 125th Street. What do you think? About all this food stuff? Are we all vegetarian here? Or are we everybody? You hearin' all this? Are we all eating out of one pot, or is there some special way we're 'supposed' to do this?"

"No, I think you've got it figured out just fine." I nod and smile. We're already ahead of where we used to be. Compromise is one of the key tools of a non-violent society. And compromise means giving something, in order to meet the other side halfway.

Figure 54. Strawberry Lake. (Alan Carey: 1972)

The Love Family, a tribal group from Western Washington has set up its kitchen at the edge of the great meadow, near the entranceway. They are feeding thousands of people.

A supply depot is being fashioned out of logs and Visqueen plastic—the all-important barrier between dry food and the elements. People are sorting and distributing tools, twine, tarps and bulk foods in sacks and boxes as fast as it arrives.

And nothing commercial. No tickets, no coupons, no paying for food, medical or parking. Everybody's sharing. Everybody's brought what they could and there's enough to go around. There isn't some organization running things. There isn't an entry fee. Nobody's getting paid and the tasks of daily life are getting done anyway. And whether or not this is a harbinger of a better future time, or just a momentary madness, it is happening before our very eyes.

There's a green slope at the meadow's edge where people are gathering to listen to each other: our Council. People are speaking in poetry, in political statements, in prayers, in public with each other there to listen and share. Announcements are being made, logistical questions being raised and discussed. We are evolving a process that is almost as old as these hills. Forever humans have

Figure 55. Author speaking in Council, Strawberry Lake, Colorado, July 1972. (Nathan Koenig: Courtesy Nathan Koenig and the Woodstock Museum, © White Buffalo Multimedia, Inc., 1972)

tried to figure out how to manage ourselves without tyranny. Here is a public forum in its origins finding out how to let each voice be heard. First a staff was passed from speaker to speaker; then after much objection the staff was replaced by a bowl; and then by a feather. The feather had the vibe. The council went on for days.

Right after breakfasts people would begin to gather on the slope by the meadow's edge and blow conch shell horns while people assembled. It was important for us to get to listen to each other: to our ideas, our dreams, our hopes, our personal tales, our causes. We were so utterly new at this. And the chance to hear our ideas expressed so freely, one by one, felt valuable even if it was preachin' to the choir.

Announcements were made about events and classes. People spoke about community needs. Ideas like our community fire agreements were discussed and consensed to. People offered prayers, and led chants and told stories. People spoke about communities around the world: Findhorn in Scotland, The Farm in Tennessee; hideaways in Central America; communes in Mao's China; kibbutzes in Israel; communes in Northern California and on and on. The counciling was going on and on. No one knew where it was going, but it was sure enough happening. People drifted in and out, maybe staying to listen for a couple of hours, then speak, then listen some more, then move on to some other part of the Gathering.

Look across the meadow after dusk: firelights flicker in an arc across the landscape. Paths are lit by candlelight. Stars twinkle above. People who were strangers now become neighbors. There is sweetness in the air and I can't tell if it's from the wild flowers or the wild flowerchildren.

There are long Ommmmms. Right in the middle of the pathway. A few people put their arms over each other's shoulders and begin to chant. Others join in and soon there's a multi-ringed chorus chanting for hours, *for hours*. People are swaying and harmonizing, rings within rings. Sounds within sound, it just won't end. You either have to walk around this humming ommmming mass or join in—you think for just a few moments—but then it's hours later—already dark and you're still there. Unbeliveable. But true.

And the Drums. Like a freed being, out at last under the natural sky—circles within circles of dancers and drummers in unrestrained motion. At night bodies dancing in the firelight reflect red yellow orange surrounded by rings of drummers indigo violet and then more dancers, clappers, stompers on the outer edges infrared ultramarine. The sound is *mountainous*. The earth seems to throb in response. It's like a huge pulsating single lifeform; breathing, pounding, dancing.

Figure 56. Omming at the first Gathering. (Alan Carey: 1972)

Political pamphleteers from the Yippie! Nation pass out leaflets inviting us to the ruling party's political convention.

Saddhus from India sit silent in saffron along the trailside.

Someone has reprinted *The Rainbow Oracle*. I see a second printing, with a lighter colored cover passed around. There's a stack of them at Information and Rumor Control.

All this is going on at the speed of imagination. One new thing after another. And one thing is for sure: we never did anything like this before.

The mountaintops glisten with melting snowfields. One takes the shape of a giant white bison hurtling across the purple-blue rockytops.

Still the Fourth of July looms ahead of us. People are continuing to arrive streaming into the encampment from it seems like the seven corners of the Earth.

A discussion is emerging in Council about where we are going to gather for The Fourth of July. Are we going to sit and do the Meditation and Prayer here or are we going to go to Table Mountain for our Circle of Peace? There are voices speaking out on all sides.

Mostly I listen. I have done plenty of talking all along but here is a question larger than I can figure. On the one side: "Why would anyone want to leave this Paradise we are blessed with right around us? There isn't anywhere more beautiful in the whole world. *This is* the place. The door to *this* mountain has been opened up to us and we just have to open our eyes and see it all around us. Move from here?—Back down that trail and all along that seven mile road? Back into that scene with all those cars and police and craziness? No it's craziness itself to leave here. To go where? To some dry mesa top? No water up

Figure 57. Council at Strawberry Lake, July 2, 1972. (Alan Carey: 1972)

there? No way! A place that the cops have restricted, barbed-wired just for us? No way! Why try to go there and undo this beautiful Gathering?"

And on the other: "Our Meditation of Peace is all about bringing Peace to this world. It's all about going to places like Table Mountain, places where the Peace isn't allowed and bringing it there. Don't be sidetracked by these lovely meadows. The real mission is to fulfill the Silence. It's not just about having a sweet time ourselves. It's about bringing the Peace and Love from here back into the world. To help change it for the better. And that means going to Table Mountain."

Lots of people said they'd seen Table Mountain in their vision of this Gathering. And lots of people said they'd seen a meadow just like this meadow here at Strawberry Lake. It seemed like the silence was just going to have to be fulfilled in two places.

Toward midnight on July Third, people began filing down the long path toward the road below. There were thousands of flashlights and candles. The line moved slowly in the dark. It was as steep going down as it had been going up. No one knew how many people were going, how many staying. Everyone was just doing what was right for each self.

Hours later I was still on the roadside walking along Lake Granby on the winding blacktop toward Table Mountain. The sun rose, illuminating the lake. Karen and I took turns carrying Eden on our backs. We passed and were passed by old friends, friends we'd just met and so many we didn't know at all. We crossed over the headwaters of the Colorado River. Thousands of hiking boots, sneakers, moccasins, flip-flops, bare feet making the trek. Table Mountain finally revealed itself small in the distance. Small that is, until you're standing under it after hiking all night. Then it looks huge. An endless height of sagebrush outlined against a bright blue sky.

At the flat beside the lakeshore below it, stretched out a sea of cars and vans and vehicles of all description. Our parking lot,

Figure 58. Dawn, Fourth of July, 1972, from the top of Table Mountain. (John Papp: Courtesy Nathan Koenig and the Woodstock Museum, © White Buffalo Multimedia, Inc., 1972)

a sea of colored roofs filling the prairie. And there was a group of fifty National Parks Federal Marshals. All equipped to the teeth: riot gear, motor bikes, helmets, truncheons, spray canisters... all of them just relaxing, hanging out by their vehicles enjoying their morning by the lake.

"I don't know what they got so hopped up about to send us here. They told us be prepared for a riot. Everyone we've seen looks peaceful, cheerful, happy," said one blue-uniformed officer leaning on his cycle.

The bottom of Table Mountain was still barbed-wired and some folks thought that the law in blue was going to try to 'get us' on the way out. Someone had trimmed the wire down to one low strand along the stretch most used and people were helping each other over it. One after another entering again that Free Space that straddles the invisible line between worlds that are less free and worlds that are slightly freer.

While we're hiking up the mountainside and I hear behind

me a rhythmic huffing puffing sound, I turn and there's a cluster of folks carrying, literally jogging uphill carrying a wheelchair with an older man seated in it. As it comes close I put out my hand to offer help and one person drops off carrying as I grab onto their spot and up we go now almost running up the mountain. I feel propelled by the Will of it all. It's as though I'm being propelled up the mountain by the chair and the person in it and the force surrounding all of us. I look and one of the other carriers is Barry. It was the only time we saw each other on the Fourth of July. After a bit I drop off the crew and another Rainbow along the trail immediately takes my place.

Whatever dreams I had, vistas I saw, looking out from on top of Table Mountain aren't nearly as important as the experience that it was happening in the first place. Inner insights are so very personal, tailored to the makeup of each person. The Nature of The Living Spirit is revealed to each person in the way most suited to their own intelligence. Some see religion, some see science, some see politics, some see nature, some just believe what they see.

The mountaintop was covered with people silent in the brilliant sunlight. Standing, seated, holding hands, eyes closed, eyes open; in meditation, in contemplation, in prayer, in wonder, in awe, in thought, in quietude, in ecstasy and exhaustion; some already sleeping in the sunlight; some strolling, rambling through the sage philosophically observing and pondering; most sitting looking back over to the East, the way we'd come, over the lake to the peaks beyond; tripping, straight, stoned, sober, silent for hours.

Toward midday I see there is a large circle forming on the south end of the mount and I go there. A long slow sweet Ommmm is brewing and it goes on softly over the mountaintop for a long, long time.

There is huge mound of boxes of fruit. Someone has actually carried tons of fruit up this mountainside. And people are passing around grapes, melons, peaches, every kind of fruit.

Figure 59. July 4th, 1972, Silent Circle for World Peace, first Rainbow Gathering. (Alan Carey: 1972)

For many of us the silence didn't end until we were beginning to walk down the mountainside late in the afternoon.

Back at the other end of the rainbow, back at Strawberry Lake we were greeted with amazing and beautiful tales of the circle there. Everyone seemed to think they'd made the really right decision about where to be. There were a few more nights of music 'round the fires and crisp, cold mountain morning breakfasts as the encampment started packing up, folding up its stuff and going away. The first "World Family Gathering" may have come and gone but by now *everyone* had taken to calling it The Rainbow Gathering.

38. Is it the End or the Beginning of the Rainbow Trail?

At the tail end of the Gathering, as the very first cleanup crew volunteered itself, as the thousands of new-found tribal family zigged and zagged and wound their way down the switchback mountain trail, the realization of who and what and whatfor was only slowly sinking into us. And what did it mean? What did it matter? A few close friends and I spoke about camping quietly in the woods for a time, giving a chance for it all—the culmination of two and more years of activity—to flow over us.

At the start of the rainbow trail that led two-plus miles down from The Gathering at Strawberry Lake to the shore of Grand Lake—right near foot of that trail was a picnic and camping area.

Some dozen of us agreed to meet there, along the lakeshore, by the evening of the next day with all our stuff backpacked downhill and ready to go.

Karen and I took our campsite apart, helped pack trash to the trailhead and found that, between us and Eden, our almost-one-year-old daughter, with her baby gear we had just a bit too much stuff to carry all in one trip. So we stashed some bedding and a box at the top of the trail and blowing the surroundings a salutory kiss, left the meadows of Strawberry Lake, as beautiful a place as there is in the world.

At the trailhead on the way down, I meet Nathan Koenig, artist, historian and filmmaker who has his Super 8 camera rolling trying to record all these new and unique experiences. He says everywhere he looks there's more to film. Later he will found the Woodstock Museum where artifacts of these times, and this culture, are displayed for future generations to enjoy.

Below, at the foot of the Rainbow Trail, was a torrent of cars, people, packing, bundles, busses, trucks, horses, hitchhikers. It was a scene. And just down the way, the picnic area where already some of our small circle was waiting. Our friends Sunny Mason, political and social activist from Minneapolis and Reggie Soto from Oregon said they were going to look for a quieter place to spend the night, away from all this synchronized chaos, maybe on the other side of the lake. Others were still being waited for, and I went back up to retrieve the last of our gear. Karen and Eden waited by the lakeshore in the gorgeous afternoon sun.

When I returned close to two and a half hours later, Karen had a story to tell. First she explained that Sunny had found another camping spot, more remote, on the further shore, and that the rest of the clan, everyone we were expecting had shown up and followed the directions to the next place.

She had remained waiting for me. And in the meantime, "All of a sudden," Karen described, "a whole group of police cars came right into this picnic area. There were a lot of different ones: state, county, and other cars too. And they blocked this whole area off. They weren't interested in all the people over there." She pointed to the packing and loading going on at the road and trailhead. "They were looking *for us*."

"How do you know that?" I asked.

"They came around checking everyone's I.D. They had some kind of list, and they'd look at someone's drivers' license and check the name with the guy holding the list and one after another they'd shake their heads or call back to the guy holding the paper, 'No, not this one.... Not this one either.' And one of the officers was concerned asking, 'Are you sure?' "

"Garrick, they were looking for us. Someone, some spy, told them we, this bunch of us, we were going to be here."

"Whaddya do when they got to you?" I asked.

"Oh," she said calmly, "when I saw what was happening, how they were coming around I.D.-ing everybody I just started nursing Eden." She smiled with a tinge of cleverness, "and I stared off into space trying to look as slack-cheeked and spaced out as I could. It was fun. I've never *tried* to look that way before. When they asked me my name, I told 'em, speaking very sl-ow-ly, 'They call me...Sun...rise.' Then he asked to see some I.D. so I told him I'd left my purse up top and my boyfriend had gone back to look for it. 'He's been gone since early this morning. I hope he gets back before dark.' The cop looked at me like I was just the pitiful sort of Rainbow he expected to see floundering around up here." She laughed and then flashed her rich sparkling smile.

Then her face grew serious and she continued earnestly, "They stood all together talking right here. I guess they figured I was too spaced out to pay attention. They were saying things like, 'Dammit, we almost had 'em, too.' 'They must've moved on, probably trying to get out of the area.' And that was it. They got back in their cars and left. Their timing was 'perfect.' They got here right after Rob Roy and Laika and Terri took off for the other camp. And let's us get out of here too."

So we left pronto. And retold this tale carefully in the twilight with our friends at the far end of the lake around our last campfire of the 1972 Gathering.

I believe that 'they' have been trying trying trying to pin our wings ever since. The personages of the 'they' have changed over time, but the 'they,' the faceless system of Bureaucratic Regulation, just cannot stand to allow this kind of unchecked, unrestrained freedom to grow and flourish. Even if no one is hurt by it, even if no resources are damaged, even if it embodies the ideas of free assembly, free speech, free religion, free admission, 'they' just cannot imagine that such a thing can exist beyond the bounds of their authority's grip. And what is the nature of Freedom if not the ability to pray, or speak, or assemble in peace, causing no one harm, without having the tentacles of the state enwrapped about one's limbs?

That night we agreed, conceding there was no way for us to hang out all together, that the fellowship had to scatter into the wind. We planned our departure for dawn the next day.

In the chill early daylight dense summer mists rose from the lake covering everything. The maintenance ranger came by our breakfast circle. He'd come over the night before while we played tunes around the fire. "I think there were some guys here looking for you this morning." "Yeah? Who?" "You know, guys with lights on top of their cars, arm patches...shiny badges. Sounded mighty like it was folks like you were who they were lookin' for. Lucky for the mist, they couldn't see a thing. I told 'em if I see anybody like that I'd let 'em know. But if I was you...."

He could see we were already packing.

Then we circled around the picnic table, smoked, said goodbye and sang happy trails....

Sunny took off in the 1950s sedan she'd just bought for five dollars (five dollars!) with Leda and Barry and Anuha; Rob Roy and Laika and Terri headed by various routes north toward Seattle and Montana; Jaysun and Feather piled their stuff into her van and went to seek their fortunes in the Great Southwest; Chuck headed toward Cortez and Montana. Skyblue and Mary and friends headed back to Denver; Kaushal hitchhiked, trusting his fate, "only to the wind." And Karen, Eden and I drove off still undecided about which way we were going.

PART NINE

Back to the Woods

(1973–1982)

How easily the dreams can unravel in front of us. Continuing what has been started presents ongoing challenges. We are not immune to the conflicts among people; and we are not immune to the challenges that providing food, water, energy and social care have always posed for humans. Still, we find answers in the old tribal knowledge that the nation-states have tried to make disappear.

39. A Hint to the Things that Remain Hidden

After the Gathering Karen, Eden and I first took shelter with David Zeltzer and Judy Sachter, friends from our collective farm in Drain, Oregon. They had a place now outside Denver. They'd spent their entire time at the Gathering shuttling people in their VW microbus back and forth from the state's roadblock below Table Mountain to the foot of the trail up to Strawberry Lake seven miles farther along the lakefront. They never hiked up to Strawberry Lake; they never hiked up Table Mountain. The way David put it, "This was the Gathering. We saw *everybody*." And Judy explained, "Some of the parts are just like the whole."

They had silk-screened thousands of small banners with a butterfly emblem and "Rainbow Family of Living Light" in a circle around it and given them away to all their riders. That's how those little banners had been so broadly distributed. And we were coming to understand how these amalgams of experience fulfill each of us; and how each of us helps fulfill the whole. Karen and I talked about wanting to get away—really away—to kind of think over this entire effort of years of energy spent bringing this Gathering together. David suggested places along the rocky ridges of the Sangre de Cristo Mountains. Places with names like Electric Peak, Crestone Peak, Bushnell Peaks, and Mount Marcy. He says these are as wild and as remote as anywhere.

That's where we summered. We hiked high into the mountains just below Bushnell Falls at about the 11,000 ft. level. We backpacked in all the supplies we could carry and subsisted on those plus all the wild plant foods we could supplement with. It was a magnificent place: a crystal cold lake, abundant firewood, soft meadow grass and wildflowers everywhere. And a view that stretched to Pike's Peak off in the distance. As proud and stunning a vista as Earth offers.

But what could we see about ourselves? And the years of work (posters, handbills, flyers, mailings, phone calls, printing, visits to every kind of new age center, invitations, travels, announcements from stages, radio shows, etceteraaaa….) and uncountable dreams we had thrown together towards this Gathering just past? And what was it worth? And where was it going? Or where had it gone? And what, oh what, were we going to do next?

It was easier just to stay put and bask in the serene aftermath up here at the place where the rockytops met the treeline … until the first cold snap brought the reality that this too must pass. So, come the cold winds and temperature drops of September, we had no choice but to hike back down and face the basically unchanged real world.

We bought beads and strung necklaces for trade. We headed toward the still-warm coast of California and we heard rumors on the streets that all was not well back at the Farm.

In Laguna Beach we met up with the Brotherhood of Eternal Love and attended the trial of Boney Bananas—their camel—who they'd brought into their vegetarian restaurant and fed a veggie burger. They were ticketed for unsanitary conditions, to wit: having a live camel in a public eatery. They argued in the courthouse that having a live camel was far more sanitary than having a dead cow (like any ol' hamburger) and while the trial went on someone stuck up Wanted Posters for "Mr. Big" all over the courthouse bulletin boards advertising a zillion dollar reward for the apprehension and arrest of the iconic producer of the legendary Orange Sunshine LSD—said to come from these very same parts! It was nice to meet some folks more far out than we were.

Then north to Santa Barbara where friends gave us a tour of the new Bank of America recently rebuilt like a blockhouse after the highly televised burning of the bank during the recent student anti-war protests. We stayed with friends in Isla Vista and sold or traded necklaces on the beachfront.

Finally we camped out at Montaña de Oro State Park and ate the last of our morning glory seeds. The hillsides turned into curtains of interlaced Buddhas as we hiked up the mountain trails. A great, endangered California Condor fanned its vast wingspread at us and raccoons tag-teamed us to steal our food back at the camp. First one snuck up slowly toward our camp's table and I chased it away. Then stealthfully—as though pretending to sneak up—it tiptoed back toward the table so I chased it away again. Then again and again. I was trying to chop wood for our fire. Finally I thought I'd teach it a lesson it'd never forget. So I turned with a roar the next time it approached the table. I wheeled around as fiercely as I know how and brandishing my axe as any wild animal knows is a dangerous thing I made after it, wailing and swinging my weapon—with no real intent to hurt the creature—just to frighten it away for good. Well the chubby thing backs off from me looking for all it's worth just mighty terrified and backs clear back to the farthest end of the clearing. Not content with that I chase it for good measure off into the brush and catching my breath I turn round to see a good sixty feet back at the camp one very smart raccoon working busily up on the table. *Up On The Table!* Throwing, yes, throwing! my foodstuffs to the passel of *five* other raccoons down on the ground. The ringleader up top tosses our grapes, then our broccoli then the nuts, then the chocolate over the edge of the table to the others who catch them deftly in their slender paws and one by one the little culprits scamper off into the never-to-return woodlands carrying all our best foods like This Was They Way They Planned It! "Karen!" I holler, and she comes out of the tent, "You've gotta see this!" So she hollers back, "Do something!" but it's really too late, the little bandits have gotten clean away.

Still all that camping and traveling along the coast was just postponing the inevitable return to Oregon. We returned to the Farm and it had become a very different place.

First, many of the people there had left. Jack Armstrong had moved on... to an apple farm in Colorado. Major Peterson had turned Born Again Christian, moved to Cottage Grove, the next town to the north, and was working in a lumberyard. Annie had followed along with him. Rob Roy and Laika's tower structure had burned down and they'd moved back to Eugene. Bear and Annie had moved to Southern Oregon to Takilma near Harold and Jeanie's place. And the Philly Crew had brought in new pals from the streets of Philadelphia. But it wasn't just the change in personnel. It was a change in tone. Gone was the mixed-up gently anarchic playful community and in its place was a tough gun-toting wild west horse-riding league who looked down on the hippie ideology of peace and love and looked up to the protection of the rifles, the thrill of hunting and caring for one's own and the strength of their own tough-guy attitudes. Gone was the aesthetic of the gentle-spirited community and in its place stood a band of very committed, very sure of themselves, very belligerent roughnecks.

Still, there was undoubtedly a community. But in the now-falling fall rains the multitude of horses' hooves had made the front yards and hillside a slough of mud. The main house was hung with animal skins and carcasses were being smoked and cured. There were set-ups for tanning and softening hides everywhere. The artful copper-coiled hot water heater powered by the woodstove was dismantled and the coils used for a still. In the place of the hot water element was a half-indoor, half-outdoor fire-brick heater that was slowly charing its way into the back of the house. Liquor was abundant and vast quantities of pot were being grown. Rich green beer was brewing in vats which was potent enough to make someone drunk just by smelling the stuff. It was a helluva scene. It was home to a different kind of outlaw.

No wonder the hard-working gardeners had taken off. No wonder the lute players had departed. No wonder the weavers and potters and woodworkers had high-tailed to greener pastures.

Even so, there were bright lights amid the dim overview. Tim was still playing his banjo. Rome, a peyote church member, had arrived from Yakima and was teaching his strong earthy spirituality to these city wildcats. Wayne seemed to be the pillar of the community, evening out the conflicts among the drunkards and the fools. Esupé and Arupa were all cooking and baking in the kitchen feeding stews and breads to the rifle-bearing horsemen. And there were lots of new folks there drawn in by the Philly Crew, younger, older, all connected by word of mouth to come out to Oregon where there was a new free, really revolutionary life just a'waiting. Greg and Peter, Ron—who Cathy had hooked up with—another Harold, and Slim—among many others.

It was a different kind of community. There was no care, it seemed, for the sweet paintings and tapestries; there was no need for the all the books which were heaped up like so much trash; there was certainly no respect for ideals such as the Gathering. But there was an attitude of "Hey, you want freedom? Well, here it is! Enjoy it and get with it, or go back to the city and get out of the way."

On the other hand, there was a deep sweetness *within* the community. Everyone there cared for one another deeply; stood by one another. And, yes, they still blew the conch before dinner. They still circled and Omm'ed before the meal (though not everyone joined in). And they still served food freely to the still-seemingly-endless stream of people on the road, looking for shelter and community.

Some parts of this were profoundly free, profoundly connected to Nature—and other parts were just macho and destructive. It was hard for me to make out how to relate to it all. Hard? It was damn near impossible. It was easy to see why all those communitarian folks had left. But the people there claimed—and rightfully so—that they hadn't chased anyone away. Everyone had just left of their own free will.

We had long difficult discussions on the front porch, smoking huge spliffs of homegrown and arguing about what was right. There was a huge attitude about hippies who wanted to live the organic life but who didn't want to kill game and who'd rather pay some impoverished workers to pick their nicey nice avocados so they could think they were being oh-so cool, but who wouldn't or couldn't handle the power of learning to hunt, or who didn't want to fire up a chain saw in order to get out of the way of the power companies providing their winter's heat.

I tried to point out the hypocrisy in any absolutist way of thinking and the contradictions in trying to do anything right or purely. And some of this was clear enough to Rome and Wayne. But to many of the others I was just one more of the spoiled refugees from the well-off classes who couldn't face up to what real freedom looked like; who wanted it to be all prissy clean, and all neatly folded when reality was really a wild messy rough-hewn place to begin with.

There was challenge here to a lot of what I dreamed of and I had no idea how to deal with it. Some of the Philly outer circle were quick to suggest that if I wanted them to leave they could just burn the whole damn place down—"Wouldn't take but a couple of matches on a dry day with all these fir trees around"—and although the heart of that band of characters was far from such thoughts, still the expression was voiced and they didn't do much to silence it. "Frankly," said Rome, "You oughta come back here, move in with us. Live this lifestyle. You'll see it's not as bad as you think it looks."

"But don't," said Wayne, "invite us all out here to live in a free community and when it doesn't turn out just like you want it, suddenly turn into The Landlord and expect us to all take your orders." It was a profound conundrum and I couldn't see a solution.

Karen certainly wasn't going to live there. And neither was I.

We hightailed it the next fifty miles into Eugene and stayed with friends while we tried to sort out what to do. Pretty much my friends in town told us the same thing: give 'em thirty or sixty days to move out. Tell 'em the party's over and to go figure out what they want to do on their own. Then move back and carry on with your own dream. I could see the eviction shootout with the cops and the kids in my minds eye clear as a horror movie. A reckless force with nothing to lose meets the power of Property and the State—and whose side am I on?

We had to bide our time. It's a great lesson that when you're not sure of what to do—really not sure—don't go ahead with an ill-bred plan too soon, too fast. Wait your time and let new ideas come along to help guide the way.

The winter's holidays were fast approaching and Eden, Karen and I drove across Canada to visit her mother who was teaching now at the University of Saskatchewan and then to my Grandmother back in New York. Again it was a chance to obviate the imperative of dealing with the situation at The Farm and to put our attention to where we wouldn't have to think on those things.

We went downtown to eat at one of the organic style hippie food restaurants in lower Manhattan. There were two of them just a block apart on Sixth and Seventh Streets in the East Village: The Paragon and The Cauldron. In those times restaurants that catered to the organic veggie crowd were really rare. And the two were so close in looks and menu that I can't remember which one we ate at that day. But shortly after we sat down four young women sidled into the booth just behind us. Two of them were telling the other two about their road trip out west. And damned if they weren't relating their experience about showing up at The Rainbow Farm.

"... So we heard about this place connected to the Gathering out in the Oregon hills and we decided to go there next because we had this idea that that's what we really needed. Maybe communal life was for us. So we followed the map over this long winding mountain road and sure enough there's the big log mailbox and when we turn up the driveway and come up to this cabin suddenly we were surrounded by all these guys on horses—"

"With rifles" chimes in the second woman. "I mean with their rifles *out* like they were in some kind of wild west movie. And not just men. Armed women too!"

"So they surround the car and ask us, 'What do you want?' I figured we must've been in the wrong place. So I tell them 'We came to see the Rainbow Farm.' "

" 'Well, you're lookin' at it,' says this guy with a grin."

"I tell him, 'Yep, we've seen it alright. Thanks, and you all have a nice day.' And I put the car into reverse and we just backed right on outta there!"

"If that's communal life in Oregon," says the second woman, "I'd hate to see how they do it in California!" And they all laugh and move on to stories of their other adventures.

Karen was looking grim faced at the soba noodles sitting in front of her. Even if I thought the overheard story was embellished or exaggerated for emphasis and story-value, I was appalled. I knew scenes bearing even minor resemblance to that had been going on over and over. And I knew it was my responsibility to make things change. But how? That overheard conversation made clear that it wasn't really about me or my dreams; it wasn't really about the rough-cut crew at the Farm. It was about the hopes and dreams of countless young seekers of those times, questing for something outside the mainstream and what *they* might be able to find.

Karen and I returned to Oregon and took a little house in the hard-working sawmill mill town of Springfield just across the river from Eugene. We took a booth at the Saturday market and made and sold beautifully crafted wooden children's swings and toys. We talked with everyone we had any respect for about how to deal with this *without* either calling on the power of the State or giving in to the gang on the land.

We spoke with the Bill and Cindy Wooten, two of the co-founders of the Eugene Country Faire who suggested we just sell the place. "Put it on the market. Make the huge profit that has accrued on account of land values having risen so dramatically around here and let the real estate people deal with whoever's out there. Never go back. Take the money and start over. Learn from your mistakes."

We spoke with Steve Lebow, proprietor of the Giant Zucchini—a very successful veggie restaurant in town—and Sprout City—one of the country's very first commercial sprout farm businesses. "Tell 'em to go to hell. Get the hell off your land. What are you on? Some kind of God Trip? Where you've got to be Almighty kind to these assholes?"

We spoke to Kinswoman, one of the keystones of the Eugene Farmers' Market Collective and a mainstay of more of the Eugene community efforts than anyone could count. "You've got to be very clever because you don't want to compromise your non-violent principles. And you shouldn't because that's what you're about. So don't call the cops and don't let these bullies have their way. So you've got to figure out something that'll work for everybody. Good luck."

We spoke with Fred Nemo one of the early inspirators who had joined with the Farm and helped acquire the other adjacent acreage. Wild Bill Hassleback and a whole group of his friends had moved over to that side of the hill in order to be apart from the Philly Crew and still be part of the Farm. Fred said simply, "I'm at a loss. I don't know what we should do. It's a dangerous situation and we need to act only wisely."

We spoke with Medicine Story and a group of Rainbow Gathering adventurers who were on a multi-bus caravan spreading word of *future* Gatherings. Tisa Jewell, Sarra Sunshine and Story stayed at our house in Springfield and encouraged us to go back to the farm and be convincing. "Explain why this lifestyle won't work in this place," said Tisa. "Why it's agricultural land and not horse country," said Story. "And why this aggressive macho attitude won't win the day for a Peace and Love vision," said Sarra.

So Karen and I trooped back out to the Farm to explain all this to folks out there.

Things were even more difficult than before. The inner walls of the main cabin had been knocked out to make a big communal room. But those were *weight-bearing* walls and the whole roof of the house had curved itself downward and inward. They'd chainsawed logs to make an immense table and pounded it together with huge spikes. But it was so big it was almost impossible to sit around so everyone stood around it. Remember when we were children and all the tables came halfway up our chests in height? Well that was what it was like.

Everyone looked like children again in front of these humongous tables. A horse corral—it had been decided—was what was needed so one fellow had gone up the hill and chain sawed down a slew of trees, a whole huge area, all fallen and toppled into each other, a real mess to work with, and figured he'd done his part of the work all in an afternoon. So now it was up to everyone else to go and build the corral with the trees he'd cut! Two immense pigs, aptly named the Nixons (after our then President and First Lady) now inhabited the orchard. They were so tough and wild that nobody could go in the orchard anymore and a good deal of work had to be done continually just to keep these huge creatures penned in. They were rooting up the beautiful old orchard sod and getting hell-bent pig-drunk on the unharvestable fermented fallen apple crop. It was a spectacular scene.

I spent hours on the big front porch talking with everyone being as reasonable as I could. The responses ranged, as ever, from succinctly proud of the raw and no-holds-barred back-to-the-earth lifestyle to the viscerally berserk as when one fella on horseback rode around in the yard relentlessly shooting off his firearm into the air. Finally he came up to the porch and butted into the more rational conversation. "All I know is I been firin' off this rifle and this here Garrick ain't flinched a bit. So I figure he's gotta be an OK guy." In fact a couple of weeks before the guys had been sitting around on the front porch bored as heck so they started taking aim at an old hippie 'bread truck' that had been parked immobile at one corner of the yard for the past couple of years. It was pink and white, a real old-time bread delivery truck and we'd christened it the clownmobile on account of its colors. Well they decided to use it for target practice and shot out all the glass and tail lights and put holes all through it. Yeah later they realized they'd also been using it to store the big water pump we'd irrigated the field with and put bullet holes all through that too.

But a lot of the conversation was sincere, as when Tim explained, "Lookit, we're different from you. You're not goin' to change on account of anything we tell you. And neither are we goin' to change either."

I knew he was right because loopy as this scene seemed to me, there was a genuine community here even if it was light years from anything I'd ever had in mind. And these folks—wild as they were—still believed in what they were doing with the same strength of belief that I had for my dreams. I felt I was in a winless situation.

I left that evening as close to despair as I'd ever been. I had set out to change and fix the world by showing something new and beautiful and now I could hardly bear to look at what it had become. I'd left The Farm and gone off to make a Gathering to show that people were not so fouled up and here we were just about as fouled up as could be. I had to reckon with what Utopianists keep hidden behind their cosmologies and day-to-day outlooks: all the things that are the potential problems in a freer society.

In a last ditch effort to make some sense of this I tracked down the wandering Living Theatre off in some hinterlands of Europe on one more endless leg of their foreign tour. I arranged a time for a phone call with Julian and Judith. I spoke with Judith first and she quickly put me on with my father saying, "You know he's better at these things than I am. He solves all the theatre's communal problems." So I talked at great length while he listened carefully occasionally asking a question or two and I mapped out all of this in even more detail than I have here. "Uh-huh," he said over and over to indicate he was listening while I went on and on. Karen sat by me the whole time listening in too. It was as if I was telling both of them the story together. Way more than an hour into it I realized I had welled up and was streaming silent tears. Finally I was done. And Julian spoke so slowly and so very calmly.

"Well," he said "you haven't gone and made a mess you can't get out of. Because you haven't gone and made Enemies. You already realize that as much as you disagree with the principles of these people, they do have genuine principles and even if you don't share them, they *aren't* in the same camp as the military state or the capitalist corporations.

"They're rebels against the mainstream status quo just as we are. And that's why you haven't found it easy to do something rash like joining with cops to throw them off the land. And that's a good thing you'll be glad of later.

"In the meantime what you need to do is just as you have, continue to treat everyone there with respect and, *and* help find them another place to move to. That's the only way to deal with this. Otherwise you will likely—very very probably—create more violence that will hurt them and you too in the end.

"Explain to them that they have to carry on somewhere else, and that you'll help them find a place to do that, but that at this place there is going to be a different kind of community. They'll understand. It will seem like a good idea to them—and it will work because it *is* a good idea. It lets them carry on the life they want and it gets you the farm back. So take whatever resources you can muster, and whatever you can muster from the community of people that support what you're doing and help them find somewhere else to move to. That's the solution."

And that's who Julian always was; genuinely wise, and a genuinely wise father to me.

And that's the solution we began to move ahead with on the very next day. First I contacted Fred Nemo who saw the wisdom of this plan in an instant. Then we looked into alternative land possibilities and began to put the resources together to make the down payment. Then I went out to the land and spoke again with the crew there. It seemed difficult only at first. There was some skepticism but then slowly the idea sank in and the realization that they could have their *own* place to live as they chose seemed like a better and better idea. I spoke about Eastern Washington where land was less expensive, and much drier—better horse country by far, better for the horses' hooves. And much more remote, good fishing, good hunting.

There would have to be multiple expeditions to find the right place and Fred pioneered the way with this. He drove out to Eastern Washington with part of the crew, and even took a journey toward Canada—the carload never made it across the border. One customs official told them succinctly, "Come back in five years after you've rehabilitated yourselves." So Eastern Washington became the focus of our search.

How was all the stuff going to get moved? I bought a flatbed truck and gave it to them, and as to all the stuff at the farm I told them just take whatever wasn't nailed down. A lot of the stuff they didn't want to move, but some things like fencing they did, so we talked it over and 'negotiated' that they could take all the fencing, just leave all the posts. That was a good solution, and there were many more like that. I wanted them out in time for spring planting and they wanted to be landed somewhere in time for exactly the same reason. And so it was actually done.

We found a place, wild and remote. Fred, mostly, scraped together the down payment. One of the crew had an insurance settlement pending that came through and that helped them make all the early payments, so without too much enmity the Philly Crew departed for points Northeast and I and Karen and several of our friends returned to the Farm on the Smith River in time to put in crops for the spring season of 1974.

Still the place was a wreck. Everything not nailed down had been hauled away. Stuff that couldn't fit in the trucks had been left in heaps or strewn about. Broken parts, pieces everywhere. Windows missing. All the fencing cut from the posts. The roof-beam of the house sagging lower and lower without its underwalls to support it. Mud everywhere, and rats. The multitude of horses' hooves had tromped the green Oregon grasses into fields of ankle-deep thick brown clayey mud. The plumbing was taken. All the functioning tools. It was desolate.

There were some definite plusses in the positive column as well. The cabins we'd built, minus the tower which had burned, were all fortunately intact: The Dome, Jake's Place, the A-Frame, The Troll Hut, and the Stardome all still stood or leastwise crouched on the hillside. Most of the other shacks and hovels were marginal to begin with. Maybe they'd been imaginative

Figure 60. How it was left. (Garrick Beck: 1974)

summer shelters the first year but after several seasons of relentless wet winters there wasn't much left of these domiciles anyway: Fat City, the House of Twelve, Mushroom Cottage and a few other nameless hippie havens were already self-composting without needing any additional help from anyone.

The forests themselves were vibrant with growth. The lower fields were as deep with loamy soil as ever. The river was flowing just the same. The cool night air at the Farm was the same cool, fragrant night air and the cement installations (the vitally-important springboxes) were all intact.

But there was a lot of work to be done. First clearing and cleaning. *Then* rebuilding the community of people to jumpstart this all over again.

40. Forest Magnificence

Into the midst of the tall fir hillsides Karen, Eden and I returned to The Farm full of ideas about what to plant and grow. An assortment of friends—friends of the farm, friends from Eugene, and friends of the Rainbow—came to help. Sometimes staying a day, or for days, or sticking around with us and moving in as the scene began to revive.

As well as moving in, and moving ahead with the cleanup of the recent exodus, there began an immediate turning of the earth at the kitchen garden just below Main House.

This garden would continue to sprawl year after year farther down the hillside, terracing as it went and producing grape arbors, squash mounds, trellised tomatoes and peas, even lengthy asparagus beds.

Nadine, formerly Skyblue, commandeered the kitchen. Smoke

Figure 61. Karen pitching hay into the main house garden. (Garrick Beck: 1974)

and ash had left a thick greasy coating on everything. Parts of the cabin floor had rotted from wetness below leaking pipes and *that* had admitted termites. The firebox of the wood cookstove was burned-out and ash outpourings had smoldered through the linoleum. Cupboard bottoms held decaying foods. She scoured and disinfected, scraped and painted it back to life.

We hauled out the goner wood stove.

Jake, of Jake's Place, returned and moved into his old digs. He organized tools, and made lists of needs, and priorities.

Roland Hanselman, who had built the top part of the rootcellar: 'the little A-frame,' had moved in down the road, where he'd bought acreage with another old homesteader cabin on it. He worked with us to level and gravel the muddied driveways.

Ron and Tera Rutecki, of the old crew, stayed on. Ron had a horse named Bo who could plow and pull light equipment. So as the lower fields dried out, Ron and his horse, with help from David, Scottie and Baker Paul, got the furrows turned.

Tera had the green thumb of green thumbs and she grew huge heirloom vegetables.

Friends in Eugene sent us a steady trickle of volunteers who

Figure 62. Tera with cauliflower. (Garrick Beck: 1975)

Figure 63. Ron tilling the field with Bo. (Garrick Beck: 1975)

stayed sometimes for a weekend and sometimes they moved in.

We set up a small metal I-beam with a steel top-plate on a housejack and using a long-pole lever (so we could be standing *outside* the house) we raised up the roofbeam of the Main House and then inserted two hand-hewn poles to support the roof. The bent-backed roof creaked and groaned with each inch we raised it. That house made *a lot* of noise. "E-e-er-r-r-k" by "R-r-e-e-r-rk" it raised back up.

Half the chicken coop got torn down and the other half became a workshop.

Tall Paul became the community mechanic teaching everyone as he helped us fix everything. "All machines break, wear out," he explained. "How to fix them without wearing yourself out is the lesson."

Charlie Martin, from the old Rainbow House in Eugene came and showed us the art of orchard pruning. And how to graft and repair old trees.

David and Judy, now back in Eugene, visited endlessly, camping in the orchard and tending to it.

Bruce, from Southern California, became a fixture in and among the garden beds.

Another David—a superbly talented craftsman—and Sarah—the community midwife—along with their kids were down at the Heptagon house on Fred's place. They had their tipi up, too. They had weathered the whole wilding times at the Farm, holing up at the end of a long trail through head-high brambles.

The whole of the property had been clearcut in 1956. So when I first got there in the fall of 1970—way before the idea of 're-planting' had become commonplace—the trees that had naturally regrown were all about 14 years old. They were young saplings, just a couple of inches wide at most.

Each of the slopes of the hillside had been conducive to certain species' advantage. So some had patches of baby big leaf maple, some had a predominance of small chinkapin (a softer yellow oak), other areas were naturally occurring stands of young alder along with a few small clusters of thin ash and crooked madrone. Of course the big three were the conifers: hemlock, cedar and most prevalent of all: Douglas fir. I began to see that these were already existing, and could exist all intergrowing in their natural habitat like this: in a multi-species, multi-age forest. And I began to cultivate for that—for the healthiest, strongest, most vibrant version of that. Multi-age, multi-species means that each species that inhabits that hillside is growing in its optimum locations and that each species is growing in a continuum of ages from seedlings through saplings, through young trees, mature trees and eventually aged rotting trees who in turn provide habitat for other forest creatures and humus to go right back into the forest floor.

This kind of forestry takes a little more hands-on attention but the result is so abundantly productive and visually beautiful that it is hard to understand why this isn't the standard mode for forest care everywhere.

The details are many, but the concept and overall approach is basic. In each area we thinned out the thicker stands of whatever age trees were crowding each other from the sun before they

Figure 64. Diversity is the key to a healthy forest... providing habitat for zillions of creatures and forest products for people's uses. (Garrick Beck: 1976)

would die off from the crowding. *Be careful* to avoid harming the baby trees already naturally seeded and growing there. These are the future giants of their type! Protect the smaller ones that will replace today's larger ones in the future. Nature gives us, *hands us!* a continuum of self-replenishing providence. It's up to us to cultivate towards that generosity and productivity, not to cut away at its might, destroying its soil (its base) and its young (the self-seeded baby trees) as though that made any sense. Well, it makes sense if you want to harvest just as much in raw dollar value right now as you can. Then sure, go in and chop it all down and sell it all and drag everything over the ground, uprooting and breaking all the brush and all the seedlings in the process, denude the landscape, expose the tender soil to the washaways of water and wind and rain and snow, eliminate the homes of birds—who eat insects and rodents—eliminate the homes of insects who devour plants and thereby make soil droppings and mulch, eliminate the brush that shelters the tiny ground cover plants that hold soil in place and what do you have? A depleted forest with regressively lower and lower grade soil that can't produce quality timber without the use of chemical fertilizers that further poison the earth, without toxic sprays that further poison the ground waters and eventually our own drinking water—nor without toxic weed suppressants to kill (in the most hideous manner) competing weeds that will simply outgrow the baby trees given the harsh environment we've 'created' for them.

So the solution? Multi-age, multi-species forestry. In the long run—and by that I mean the run of a lifetime, not some unimaginable millennia—in the long run it gives a measurably more productive output in terms of plain old board feet than clearcutting, or even that so-called 'sustainable yield.'

In 'clearcutting' the harvester reaps the benefit all at once of all the available value of all the timber on the land—at terrific cost. Clearcutting denudes the landscape of all the trees and in the process all the brush and all the groundcover. As a result the open exposed earth is subject to tremendous runoff of soil during rains and weather. So much so that even the big-timber led legislatures have all enacted laws mandating re-planting within a certain time so that there is some chance for regrowth before too much precious soil is washed away. It takes 10,000 years or more to make an inch of soil. And if even excellent forest soil is 10 inches deep and a couple of inches are washed away in each successive clearcutting then in a very few cycles of harvesting there isn't the soil to support tree growth. And that is what is happening. That's the great cost of clearcutting: it leads us to a forest floor no longer capable of supporting trees. And that *is* what is happening.

There are other costs: there is loss of habitat for all the creatures of the forests, and on account of the muddy runoffs into the streams and rivers there is choking of aquatic life: fish, turtles, salamanders, crayfish, clams, mussels all die. All on account of the muddy residue of clearcutting.

In the meantime (and it is a mean time) the harvesters have pocketed the maximum amount of immediate money. And we'll have to wait on the average in an Oregon Douglas fir forest just about 60 years for regrowth in order to be able to clearcut mature wood again. That's a '60-year cycle.' Of course, after a few of those cycles the growth rate sloooows wayyyyy dowwwwn.

That's where the phony concept of 'sustained yield' springs from. The idea initially was to protect the forests from overcutting by mapping out areas that could be cut in rotation every 60 years. So some patches are 10 years old, some 20, some 30 and so on. Then at the 60-year mark the trees are considered mature and here come the chainsaws and the trucks. Well that plan was certainly an improvement over cutting down everything, as was done in Roman times back in the Old World leaving whole nations without trees for wood. And it was done sweeping across this continent to make room for farms and fields and dairy cattle. By the time so-called civilization reached the West Coast of North America it was finally getting figured out that having trees and wood to build with and make furnishings with continually would take some planning and not just cutting. So this effort toward 'sustained yield' was promoted by foresters and 'wise' timber managers.

But the pressure for more profits looked at that cycle and figured out how to milk it for more than it was worth. Here's how it was done: assuming the maturing tree cycle of a forest is 60 years (as it is in our example of the coast ranges in Oregon) then a certain number of board feet can be garnered every 60 years. But what if the cycle could be sped up to 58 years? Then timber could be harvested on a 58-year cycle. So lets add some chemical fertilizer to the forest and increase the rate of growth of the trees. Okay, we'll do that and now in theory there's a 58-year cycle.

And the timber interests get everyone with any say-so to agree to this. Well then, let's spray some pesticides to reduce competition for nutrients from shrubbery. Okay, that'll increase the growth rate maybe another 3 years. So now we're down to a 55-year cycle. Multiply this by thousands and thousands of acres and there is a substantial difference in how much money a harvester can rake in by raking the forest bare every 55 years instead of every 60. Well let's genetically select the fastest growing trees to begin with and just plant those. That brings the clearcutting cycle down to 50 or 52 years. And there are two direct results of this: The first is that the trees themselves grow larger with fewer years' growth rings and that means the wood itself isn't as strong. It's pithier and less hard. It won't support the same load as the slower growing wood. It won't last as long in positions of stress. It rots more easily. It's actually a lower quality product. In certain weight-bearing instances builders have to use larger boards to support the same loads as the normal growing wood. And second, the cycle in which the soil erodes down the hillsides is sped up. It gets massively washed away every 50 years instead of every 60 quickening the time until the soil can no longer nourish and support the trees. And that *is* what is happening.

On the other hand, *selectively* removing trees, beginning with overgrown saplings and broken or damaged trees, and after that, thinning poles for fencing and pole building, advancing in decades to pre-commercial thinning to, eventually, selective harvesting of mature trees in a careful and individual manner yields a continuous supply of timber *without* destroying the precious forest floor, forest soils and the rest of the environment. It means managing narrow pathways through the forest for removal of the logs. It means lopping the branches and arranging them to foster new ground cover. It means trimming the stumps near to ground level. It means people at work in the forest instead of just gigantic machinery. It also means doing without soaking the forests in chemical pesticides and chemical fertilizers. Without clogging the streams with clayey mud. Without vanishing the habitat of birds, rabbits, foxes, insects. Without making an ugly mess.

Figures 65 & 66. Perpetual yield forestry is not only productive… it's beautiful, turning forests of thin poles into stout timber while increasing birds, bees, brush and wildlife. (Garrick Beck: 1977 & 1997)

Figure 67. William horse-logging with neighbor Jim Ward's team. (Garrick Beck: 1982)

And if you count up the board feet yield, over a 60-year period there is actually considerably more wood product and considerably more money in total. But that's not the way today's economy encourages management. It's all about how much you can get Right Now. Instead of about the true value of the long-term yields. All the foresters of every stripe and rank know this, but the economic imperatives drive us in the wrong direction. We just can't bring ourselves to act in the long-term interest when all the measures are about the income this month!

In the long run multi-age multi-species forestry will be the model. It's the only way to have vibrant forests on into the future and have wood products to use as well. I call this process *perpetual yield*.

We teamed up with Jim Ward who had draft horses. He came from an old homesteader family just over the hill on the town side. With his beautiful, huge horse, Old Tom, and his old-timer's know how, we thinned out some larger close-standing trees and moved them to the road using winches and horse power.

We studied the form of the land to define trails that could serve as winding ways to slide the logs downhill. We cut only a few trees at a time felling them into the open spaces and then the beautiful horses could pull them to the landing by the road below. Then we would cut a few more and drag those. It was hard, hard work but incredibly beautiful. It's a slow careful process. The trails we made then are still in use. They're the natural ways to drag heavy things down the hillside. And the logs stacked in 'decks' could be trucked into town and returned as coin-of-the-realm.

We harvested Doug fir primarily, but also hemlock—'white wood' they call it—for sale as board feet. We pulled out big leaf maple that made outstanding birdseye boards. We stacked up alder and any broken ends for firewood. And above us the forest only grew taller and all around us the immense multitude of forest flora continued to flourish.

41. Life on the Farm

We planted the whole lower field in wheat. And harvested it with a gigantic old creaking combine.

The front of the combine—painted yellow—coming round and round pushing the wheat stalks down into the red mower blades and then up the conveyor they go into the heart of the machine where a cylinder spins them through such a small space that the seeds separate from the coats—the seed from the chaff—and plinketty plinkitty plink the grains are falling into the hopper and poured in huge numbers in front of a fan (to blow off any remaining chaff or bits of straw) and down into bags right there.

This whole gizmo rumbles across the land. It's as big as a tank. Bigger. Harvesting *and* threshing, combining the two jobs (so they called it a 'combine') all in one machine grinding its way across the contours of the field. It was beautiful. I don't see how there could be a more useful device. What is its purpose? Provision of grain, of bread: the fundamental human food.

It's the advancement from the beginning of agriculture where people flailed sticks against grain heads, then threw the loosened pieces up into the air when the winds picked up. So the chaff—which was lighter—blew away and the seeds fell back to the ground where we could scoop them up. T'was Ever Thus. And here it is in its current form: creaking slightly side to side as it performs the harvest, lumbering along, an old faithful machine.

The homesteader pear trees began to produce huge numbers of pears—after we pruned them and cut away the decades' dead wood. We built a wood-fired dryer out back and cut 1,000 pounds of splendid Comice pears in half, pitted them, put them through the dryer and brought them to one of the Pacific Northwest's Barter Fairs where we traded them easily for all sorts of tools and provisions.

We trimmed back the vast blackberry morass that was overgrowing the house and connecting it to the forest.

The attic roof was hung eave-to-eave with drying onions. We broke the stems down first so they could cure in the field, then gathered them safely under the eaves before the damps of autumn turned them mushy.

We made a bicycle-powered irrigation pump.

I collected secondhand windows and pieced them together like a stained glass mosaic to form a greenhouse. We grew plant starts for sale and trade.

Gene Grinell brought an old rolling seeder that could be horse drawn. It's astounding how much harvest a small amount of wheat will produce. Say one head of wheat has 20 wheat kernels in it. Well, that's a 20 times yield—or about 2,000%. I figure that is the maximum return on any investment it's possible to make. All the other investments of the human economy are sub-sets of this Staff of Life Equation. All the other economic activities lead to or from this activity: the harvesting of grain. It's the fundamental building block of human economy. Got grain? Then your people can eat.

This horse-drawn seeder spaces the grains or corn just the right distance apart. In a pinch a couple of strong folks could haul this contraption around by themselves. The little hoppers holding the grain going up and down as the cam-valves open and close like a big old carousel creature. So we painted it up like a carousel ride and Ron's horse, Bo, towed it on down the field sowing the seed as it went.

We sold carefully dried heirloom veggie seeds to the Territorial Co.: the cool night/hot days Willamette Tomato; the sweetest crispest Danvers Carrots; the vivid purple and white Jacob's Cattle Beans; as well as pioneer green beans and sugar snap peas.

It was huge work and we weren't mechanized for all of it. Still, from the point of view of satisfaction and lifestyle in the out-of-doors and doing something truly useful, I don't see how it can be much better.

Figure 68. Bo, the horse, pulling the carousel seeder. (Garrick Beck: 1976)

Figure 69. The seeder attached to the tractor with Kunga Tyson driving and Baker Paul following behind. (Garrick Beck: 1979)

Figure 70. Author in the carrot patch. (Photographer unknown: 1974)

Millie brought her Purple Easy-Peel garlic from her great-grandparent's stock so we planted that. Joy Tsunka taught us to braid the garlic we'd grown into long traipsing bundles and bring these to town for trade at the co-op.

There were trucks of organic peas, beans and squashes; trucks of poles and firewood going down the road and building materials, tools and other supplies coming back up the road. And the carrots. The carrots. Beaucoup de French variety sweet crisp carrots. In a very un-mechanized scene we were digging carrots, carting carrots, scrubbing carrots, rinsing carrots, bagging carrots and lugging them carrots onto the truck. It was a lot of work even for dedicated back-to-the-landers.

The deep valley-bottom soil could sure enough produce more carrots than we could manage to care for. And we either had to have a refrigerator truck ready to come pick them up or be ready to truck them to town markets because we didn't have refrigerated storage on site.

I don't think it was exactly the thought of endlessly hauling hay for mulch. And I don't think it was the sheer work of the carrots either. But the idea of an endless ongoing existence of these things, these farm routines for a lifetime ahead steered Karen's thinking to places beyond the farm. She re-enrolled in college, at the U of O in Eugene. The move out to the farm from the city environment years before and the experiments with communal lifestyle had appealed to her. Her stabilizing, thoughtful influence on that scene was enormous. Her influence shaped and helped define the balance between femininity and masculinity in that emerging Pacific Northwest communitarian culture. And I think the adventure of the Gathering appealed to her. She did much to communicate the original invitation. Still, the idea, after all that, of just living endlessly on the farm harvesting vegetables and apples and sacks of carrots didn't seem to be the whole of the life she wanted. More and more she spent her evenings and then her days at classes. I could see us veering apart. I was staying where I was and she was moving on.

There was wood to be gathered and split. All of the houses were heating *and* cooking with wood. Split and stacked. Kindled, stoked and 'banked down' for the night during the winter. Providing one's own energy takes energy too. That was a huge job. Trucks, chainsaws, hauling, loading, driving, then stacking in sheds whose sole purpose often was simply to keep these fuel sticks dry.

Sarah practiced midwifery and there were born a number of children.

We measured out a tipi design and began making tipis. All told we sewed about a dozen of them on a treadle sewing machine. We used the big floorspace of the A-frame to lay things out. There are a lot of very particular canvas parts in a good tipi. Tipis are a seriously sophisticated construction even though they appear simple. There are parts that provide strength and stability, parts that channel water, parts that channel smoke, parts that provide draft, and warmth, and a door that fits so it sheds water and so on.

The hillside above was dense with tipi pole size trees and we were able to thin *countless* sets of poles that when "skinned" were smooth and strong and light—just right for tipi lodges.

We chipped in and purchased a 40-foot-long steel-framed semi-portable saw mill and set it on a landing at the bottom of the big hill. It had its own engine and a huge blade. Honest John, the second hand store owner from town, showed us how to use it. We made a well-planned harvest of crowded trees and maneuvered 30-foot logs downhill to the mill. On the hillside crews were thinning the trees, trimming the branches, measuring the lengths, bucking the logs to the right length and then below crews were positioning logs on the mill, running the sawmill, moving the guides and running the saw again, removing and stacking the boards. But it was an old mill. And it had a hard time staying exactly straight. Some of the boards were a tad thicker at one end than the other. And 'a tad thicker' is no good for fine carpentry; rough uses yes, but fine work, no. We had a lot to learn.

Baking filled the houses with activity. Of course we had the wheat to begin with and we had the fruit from the orchard. So we began to keep bees. An old beekeeper taught us how to tend the hives in exchange for keeping a truck of his hives there as well. It was a wonderful deal. He was almost 80 years old (that was in 1978) and he had lost one of his legs in WWI. "Came home and started keeping bees. Been doin' it ever since." He was able and capable on his own. He just wanted to teach beekeeping to as many young people as he could.

So we had honey and pies and breads and cookies and muffins and cakes all sweetened with home grown honey. It was beginning to seem that it was possible to provide a good life from the efforts of a bunch of city kids who wanted to live close to the land. But it seemed like a torrent of endless effort. Work that was highly physical, often difficult and occasionally dangerous.

We began somehow, without planning it, to have regular full moon parties. One of the things these did was to help bring the cycle of work to conclusions and rational stopping places. People would try to finish jobs, get in harvests, finish plowing or planting, or bring construction projects to a halt so everyone could relax and have a good time at the full moon. Also over the years the community had spread a bit up and down the valley. New friends and acquaintances had moved in upriver and downriver. Full moon meant people could walk home in the moonlight, even in the middle of the night.

We began a custom of performances for the kids in the early evening of the celebrations. So the youngsters would have a full moon entertainment as well. Storytelling, puppets, clowning, songs and then off to bed.

Figure 71. Organic farming in Oregon's Coast Range. (Garrick Beck: 1979)

Each month we would concoct some different psychedelic elixir or tea or juice—for those who chose to imbibe. Psylocybin one month, maybe acid or mescaline the next. It was different every month. There was always a tasty non-psychoactive beverage as well. And one dedicated barkeeper who watched over the vats and served the beverages. We'd build an open fire on the hillside and play music and drums. Some folks would just come by for a taste of zuzu juice, chat for a few minutes and then wend their way home. Others would stay all night.

The rest of the month we were as busy as the proverbial Oregon beavers. Linda Lou baked pies and Eve Syapin split wood. Baker Paul baked loaves in racks that slid in and out of the woodstove's oven. Charlyn, fresh out of the Air Force, moved in with Cheyenne and began wearing all homemade buckskins. William and One-armed Bill Hasselback led the firewood brigades. Gene and Margie built a Mongolian wooden yurt. Gene ran the tractor and Margie

played guitar and serenaded us so beautifully in the evenings. Charlotte Levinson moved into the A-frame and I took up residence with her. Patrick Thompson scooted back and forth to Eugene, our nearest city, 50 miles away ferrying friends and visitors. Bluebird put his lodge up on the hillside and he and Jill birthed their baby there. Michael Eagle maintained the back trails and roads and built a wood-fired hot tub that was mounted on his trailer. He'd pull up during a full moon party and fire it up. Joy braided garlic, sewed and embroidered clothes, canned endless vegetables and sauces while William bucked and split endless firewood. Kunga Tyson and Kathleen inhabited Jake's old Place. Kunga and Fritz thinned the timber. Kathleen was one of those 'superpersons' who could do just about everything, which is just what she did. Terry Hubbard, aka Vision, and his partner Lynn moved into the dome. Vision lived to play guitar. They were the house band. Daphne set up a midwifery clinic next door. Old Carlos showed us how they used to grow pot in L.A. Menachem Kallus (on sabbatical from the Hebraic Hasids in Brooklyn) learned carpentry. Sharon Forestwoman planted and tended the herb garden. Sid Small moved into a debilitated breadtruck someone had parked and abandoned and began plans for building a community woodshed. Carla Newbre debarked from the Rajneeshee sect and moved her ingenious and practical self in with us. And the kids (the kids!) roamed up and down the valley helping and mischievous all at once. Mary and Rochelle and Mercy. Orissa and Eden and Jessica and Midge and Fontana and Crystal. Tom and Clarence and Billy Jr. and Stephan and Yuwipi. Robin and Melita and Ferralli and Gwen and Cassie. Jade and Chinima. Morning Glory and Sunrise Mist, Jerimiah and Ishna. Amelia Rose and Ophelia Rose. Ruby. Ebram, Josiah and Jedediah and Faye. Beniah, Shemiah and Thomas. Josh and Tameron, Darshan, Evam, Kriya and Missy. Andrew and Joseph and Rymin. All of them wild and free and wise and wonderful.

It was a rich, full time but did it have the "je ne sais quoi" to sustain itself? It's a long roster of people who came and lived there for a while. Learned or taught skills. Contributed and gained from the process. That life wasn't for everybody, but the visitors' help enabled the rest of us to hunker down for winter after winter. Half a decade went by. Always there was the struggle with the money for parts for machinery. Always the prices paid for agricultural products were dirt cheap. Always the battle with the weather. We were part of an old struggle—the struggle of the farmer to survive.

42. Q 7

Zack and Melody Record had driven the winding 14 miles into town and back for some list of errands and returned with—among other things—a copy of the daily paper. And they were eager to share the news highlighted in a small ad announcing an appearance and lecture by Dr. Timothy Leary.

Well indeed, we hill people were interested in listening to the philosophies and musings of the ranking psychedelic archon of the times, being in our own way acolytes of the sacraments ourselves.

"So who's bringing the good Doctor to town?" I asked.

"Dunno," said Zack, "all it says here is 'sponsored by Quantum Seven'."

"Right," chimes in Melody, "Here we are stationed outside Eugene for years. We know every group in town. Its probably Tim's latest circle or maybe its a code!"

"Yeah, the star people. Isn't that what he's been writing about lately?" I ask.

"Not star people. Seeds of life from the stars or comets. He's been writing, speculating about the origins of life," answers the well-read Melody. "Maybe he's on a book tour."

We all resolve to take the hour-long drive to town the following evening to check it out.

But come morning Zack and Melody are convincing us of a different plan.

"Listen, we want to go interview him," Zack is explaining.

"How're we gonna do that?" I ask.

"We'll call the airport. Find out his flight number and interview him right there at the airport."

"We've got press credentials," says Melody flashing a number of different colored cards, representing, I think, a smattering of extinct and nearly extinct California small presses.

I think: They're off on a wild guru chase. But I encourage them anyway, "Great idea. Give it a try."

A short while later Zack has the flight number, and he's talked to the airport administration about using the press room. "They don't," he reports, "have a 'press room,' but they could make available their 'V.I.P. room' for the occasion."

That settles it. We're off on the adventure. Another friend produces a sheet of four-way kisses, and with a quarter of a kiss on my tongue and then swallowed, I'm helping to load camera equipment, tape recorders, microphones and away we go to the Eugene, Oregon airport to interview the high saint of LSD.

Arriving at the small airport just outside Eugene, Zack and Melody are in the lead with their press cards and the rest of us are the grips, carrying the equipment while the airport office sends a young man to guide us to the trim bright room used mostly, he explains, for sheltering politicians or celebrities from public glare while they await their planes.

We begin setting up microphones on the table and fixing the tripods. The airport intercom announces that the Doctor's fight is arriving and Zack and Melody's baby wets its diaper just as they're about to go greet the flight. Melody looks at me questioningly, and without hesitation, I'm on my way, carrying her kid out to our parked car for changing.

Really it was their idea, and I was there to help in whatever way, so I'm out in the sunlight en route to the car when there appears coming into the dropoff lanes a splendid blue-green Mercury convertible with none other than Ken Kesey at the wheel. Ken Babbs is in the passenger seat. I'm waving at them, flagging them over.

They pull up and Kesey leans over and asks, "Are you with the Doctor's entourage?"

"Well, yes and no," I answer a bit goofily. "But he's arrived. We've got him inside. He's being interviewed in the" (Babbs is already out of the car) "V.I.P. Room. It's to your left past the ticket counters," I call after him 'cause he's already heading toward the doors.

Kesey prefers to wait in the vehicle absorbing the sunlight.

Then he pauses a moment, turns toward me, and with his broad welcoming grin extends his hand to shake. So I quickly transfer the baby to the crook of my left arm and extend my right arm shaking his big comfortable hand. Then he looks down as our hands part and he sees what I also see. Baby poop. Right on his palm, and my palm too. He just shakes his head. No, no, no, this can't be right. And in a moment I've got a hankie out and he's wiping it clean. I'm mortified, muttering something about changing the baby was why I'm out here, and I feel like I'm backing away stumbling toward our car. Kesey doesn't say a word. I look back and he's still just shaking his head.

Until Babbs got to the V.I.P. Room the questions had been mostly Zack and Melody's semi-scholarly efforts:

"And how do you feel the reaction to your new book, *Starseed* has been? Was the public's reaction what you expected?"

"Do you see any reason for hope that the laws concerning psychedelics will be changed in the near future?"

"What kind of message do you want to send the youth of today?"

Boring stuff like that.

And then enters Babbs. Hand waving excitedly like a kid at the back of a classroom who knows he's got the answer.

The Doctor nods to him.

"What do you think of Ascorbic Owsley?"

"What?" asks Leary in return.

"You know, Ascorbic Oswley. Fifty percent Acid, fifty percent Vitamin C. Gets you high and keeps you from getting sick all at once!"

And from there, he and the Doctor were off and running: changing and exchanging jokes and riffs and passing paisley patterned paragraphs covering most of human evolution, the development of pharmacology, the need for humans to communicate and to reach beyond Earth's atmosphere, the possibilities of internal time travel, the true meaning of the Beatles lyrics on Magical Mystery Tour and the repression of people's freedom of thought by the Cro Magnon militarists running the world's governments when Melody calls out, "That's it gentlemen. We're at the end of our tape."

So Babbs escorts the honored guest to the Convertible Chariot awaiting outside where the smiling Doctor Leary greets the esteemed Author Kesey at their first meeting—other than Ken's visit to Tim behind bars—since their famously-documented collision at the Millbrook estate years before.

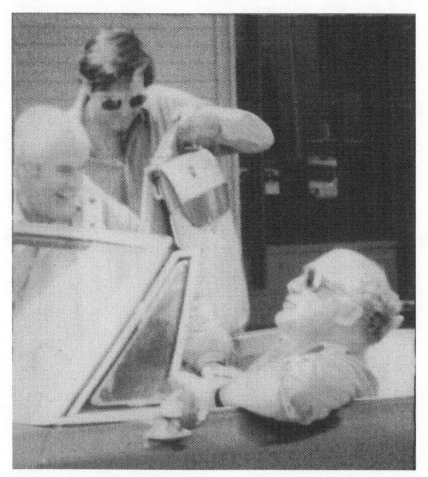

Figure 72. Dr. Timothy Leary and Merry Pranksters Ken Kesey and Ken Babbs greeting each other at the Eugene, Oregon airport, 1975. (Garrick Beck: 1975)

Standing and watching there in the sunlight it was clear to me that despite whatever the cynical press and media of the world may have reported about these fellas' differences all these years since their Millbrook run-in, about the rumored splits, the rifts in the psychedelic underground, these men were on the same wavelength, the same beam, the same vibrant vector of light and they were so glad, so very glad to be seeing each other again.

Babbs places the Doctor's valises into the back seat and with the convertible full of pranksters—and another jeep full to accompany them—off they all ride. No, Kesey's coming around the traffic circle again.

They're all waving. They don't know who on Earth we are, but we're there for them so they tool around one more time waving and then, then they ride off into the sun-filled day.

We stand there, with our small crew, mics and tripods already out on the sidewalk, waving as they exit the airport.

"So that's who 'Quantum Seven' in the newspaper ad really is," observes Melody, holding her index finger aloft and then pointing it at the distant cars. She smiles and we all smile.

We went that night to the high school (The High School!) where Leary addressed the crowds. His speech was one part a professor explaining mysterious unknown terrain to an attentive group of scholars, one part coach pep-talking to his team, and another part celestial comedian from some distant planetary nightclub satirizing and mimicking the primitives of 20th century Earth. Then he called on Kesey at half-time to do a commercial break. So Ken did a commercial for grass. I wish we had *that* on tape.

The party continued out back of the High School parking lot way after the hall had been emptied and the custodian shut the lights.

Both of them were surrounded by well-wishers. They were unafraid of the crowds, the questions, the acknowledgements, the questions, the praise, and the endless questions.

The rest of us meandered among our cars, laughing, talking,

getting to know one another. There must have been two or three cars full of pranksters plus a host of mud-tired pickups with the folks like us, from the hills outside of town, and sedans bearing teachers, VWs full of students, slick new rigs with the families of Eugene's more successful hippie entrepreneurs and someone (or maybe some*ones*) lit a fistful of bomber-sized joints and there we are all of us, like the renegades and rebels we truly are, all smokin' up out back of the High School, meeting, and greeting under the star-filled sky and then, at last, waving goodbye and goodnight.

43. The Hopi, The Hippies, The Missing Tablet and The Beautiful Blue Corn

Part 2

In The Rainbow Oracle, the booklet we printed just before the first Rainbow Gathering, we asked people to bring a stone from their own home turf and put these in a pile at the site of the July Fourth meditation, as a kind of representation of the Earth. And people actually did this. Skyblue carried our carved rock—the one we'd brought to the Hopi to Mina and David's houses—up Table Mountain and set it on the pile of stones that was heaped there. It sat there all day. But in the evening, with the cool Colorado wind beginning to blow she brought it back down the mountainside.

The carved rock continued along an odyssey. It was carried and cared for by many different people. It went to a petroglyph expert in Minneapolis who pronounced it "at least 100 years old." It was brought to a psychic reader in Northern Arizona who made taped readings about its connection to the great pyramids of mythic Lemuria. It was brought back to the Hopi lands and someone there saw a bear claw sign on it and remarked that was like marker stones left behind during the bear clan migrations long ago. Feather and Jaysun Hammond kept it for a while at their cabin in Lindrith, New Mexico. It traveled with the hard-drinking, spliff-smokin' warrior hippie named Kilo until Red David took it from him. Chuck received it and gave it to Youth Phil Hanson. Phil brought it back to New Mexico and used it for a pillow. It was wrapped and re-wrapped with each keeper adding perhaps another layer until after five years of travel a smiling bar-band guitarist named Pip got it from Phil and brought it in 1977 to the

New Mexico Rainbow Gathering alongside the Gila River.

That was a remarkable Gathering for many reasons. In Council we began to see that we could recognize the same returning faces from the past years. We were finally getting to know each other after five or six gatherings—for the first four days of July. So in Council that year it was brought up by Neriah Lothamer that four days wasn't enough to get to know each other properly or to build the kind of community we were striving for. So our Council consensed that from here on we would Gather from the First through the Seventh day of July. And it's been that way ever since.

Washboard Sid, a renowned (in the circle of buskers) street musician, rode into the Gathering in my and Charlotte's car with an amazing washboard that had more attachments, blowers, whistles, and honkers than you could shake a drumstick at.

Wavy Gravy, the Master of Ceremonies at the original Woodstock Festival, and one of the founders of the Hog Farm—the legendary 1960s commune from Northern New Mexico—showed up with his wife Jahanara and they set up camp in the midst of our Tipi Circle. Wavy, in his full regalia clown outfit, entertained the kids, yes, yes, kids of *all* ages, endlessly with his seamless rap and cosmic humor.

That year Grandfather David Monongye, who we had met at Old Oraibi, the ancient Hopi village, came to the Gathering. Pukalani Sweetwater picked him up at his home in Old Oraibi and drove him to the Gathering along the west fork of the Gila River in New Mexico. I remember him riding down the Gila Valley on a burro, pack baskets loaded on behind him. One day, while the Council was taking place, Jimmer took out the stone tablet and opened it on top of the blankets and cloths it had been wrapped in. Then Grandfather David came to speak in the Council.

He had someone draw out the symbols of the prophecy rock—the Hopi's prophecy rock—and slowly in the center of the tipi village under the midday sun, he retold the story of the Hopi people and the four worlds, full of detail and spoken slowly and

Figure 73. Hopi Grandfather David Monongye addressing the Rainbow Family Council, Gila National Forest, New Mexico, 1977. (Photographer unknown: Communities Magazine, 1979)

carefully as from long memory. Then he was done and he returned to his lodge and the council continued. Later that same day, after dinner and dark, the drums started up, the fire threw sparks into the desert sky, and, in one of those quiet places between the drummings, someone's voice said David would like to speak to the circle. So he came out from his lodge and by the evening firelight spoke to us again.

"It is not by accident that the words 'Hopi' and 'Hippie' sound alike. We are all people of Peace, we are all working for the same Great Spirit.

"You cannot rely on the banks, or the corporations or the government. They will never give you anything. They will never respect you unless you hold territory. You must take back the Earth, peacefully, one piece at a time. Plant seeds, and water them, and make the Earth beautiful again."

This time when he spoke he was not repeating the old stories of his people, he was speaking directly to us, with a passion and a purpose: "You must take back the Earth, peacefully, one piece at a time. Plant seeds, and water them, and make the Earth beautiful again...."

Figure 74. Hopi Grandfather David Monongye addressing the Rainbow Family Council, Gila National Forest, New Mexico, July, 1977. (Pukalani Sweetwater: 1977)

From there the tablet was brought back to The Farm in Oregon. We kept it under wraps except for full moon celebrations or when someone came who expressed a desire to see it.

In 1978 at the Oregon Gathering, on the sixth of July, Harold and Jeannie suggested we bring it out and re-share the story.

As each blanket and cloth was unfolded, revealing its own hidden shells or feathers or beadwork, people began to gather 'round, straining to get a view of the rock. At the outside of the crowd people were trying to tell people what was going on and to relay the parts of the story being told. It was almost too much because everyone wanted a chance to see this thing with their own eyes—make sense or no sense of it themselves—and this meant there was jostling and a little bit of pushing forward at the outside of the circle so people were stumbling forward pressing in closer at the circle's center. Don Freedom, with his inimitable twinkle in his eye said, "Y'all finish this story up fast before anyone gets hurt." So finish it up we did, and the stone was re-wrapped in all its stuff, and that was the last time I saw it.

It went from the Oregon Gathering up and down the West Coast, and then to Mexico where it was brought to Palenque, under the full moon to the top of the Jaguar Pyramid and then to the Huichol lands. It passed through the hands of many Carriers of The Tablet as we pass things among ourselves with love and delight and it went with Birdie Guzman on her way to a bluegrass festival outside of Lincoln, Nebraska. On their route it was so hot, Birdie and the people she was traveling with stopped to go down to a river for a swim, but the pickup truck and people she had a ride with left unannounced without even knowing anything about the wrapped bundle in the back of their truck bed.

That was in 1979. But this was no rock in a bag. This was an elaborate bundle, inside her backpack, containing something carved and beautiful and mysterious. I do not believe that it has been 'thrown away.' I believe that it is somewhere waiting to be re-found.

Is there a Tablet that is somehow Our Tablet? Or, are we just trying to mimic other tribes who have a tablet, or several tablets, or a lost tablet? And does this tablet have some meaning more than its mysterious carvings?

I can tell you what we do have. We have a social program that cares for our young, our weak, our sick, our old, and as best as we can for ourselves and each other. We have an evolving culture that cares about the Earth and all its inhabitants. We have a growing community that respects the land, the water, the sky. And I know that when we live in conscious awareness of doing good for each

Figure 75. Ears of the Hopi blue corn. (Garrick Beck: 1997)

other and the Earth, that the signs are everywhere along the way; that omens spring up at each turn; that there are natural wonders and mythical symbols that appear as markers, as if to guide us, every day of our lives...but usually our eyes are closed to such things, and our minds occupied with just getting by.

Is the Lost Tablet of the Hippies ever going to be found? Does whoever has it know what it is? Perhaps hearing this story someone will come upon it and recognize it for what it is. Could it be brought back to the Gathering? And....What would we ever do with it then?

And remember the Hopi corn whose planting led us to find the carved rock in the first place? This is the all-time great drought-resistant corn. It can produce even in the driest and harshest of climates. If we are really facing climactic climate changes that will dry up aquifers and irrigation waters sources, then maybe, just maybe, this Hopi corn will be one of the things that can save us and tide us through times of a great drought. Corn from the seed of that very same seed is alive and still being grown today. It can be super productive even in parched environments. Each single kernel yields 200 kernels—or more—every season. It may be that it's not the tablet that's at the heart of the story—it's the corn.

44. Solar Epiphany

In the spring of 1979 our lower field had been planted in organic vegetables. There was also a cover crop of buckwheat put in over areas we'd planted in previous years. The buckwheat was providing rich nectar for the bees and becoming a source of future green nutrient for the soil. It was a good cool weather crop, so it could thrive in the damp, chilly Oregon spring nights.

Charlotte and I were living in the A-Frame by the river. Our son, Robin, was born there. Sarah midwifed. The house was finally getting insulated to keep out the cold. Rugs, blankets and tapestries lined the floors and hung from the walls—or ceilings, in an A-Frame it's hard to tell.

By now the Gatherings had begun to expand into several regional events—in addition to the annual first-week-of-July gathering. There was still a *Howdy Folks* information mailing that was going out from the farm through a P. O. Box in Eugene. We collated addresses on 3x5 cards.

A regional Gathering was being planned for West Virginia, below Old Rag Mountain and the folks from that area also secured a slot to participate in ACT '79 on the Washington D. C. Mall. ACT '79 was one of the first 'Energy Fairs,' an event designed to showcase alternatives to the fossil-fuel-based world. The gas shortage of 1974 was still a clear memory and there had been a lot of steps toward 'greening up' the environment during the mid-seventies. Those were the Carter years and events like ACT '79 got funding.

From my perch in Oregon I couldn't quite see how we fit into this, but our job would be to represent the 'Wilderness.' The Old Rag Gathering was the week before the D. C. event and we could have time to plan for it there.

So I took off with Melody and Zack and Rainbow Hawk and Hanna in Hawk's old station wagon gallivanting East on another adventure.

Old Rag was a grand rolling mountain with dense underbrush and just enough open space to let the sun shine down on us. We drove in in the early morning sunlight.

Two years earlier at the New Mexico Gathering in 1977 there'd been so many newcomers entering the Gathering and we wanted to convey so many of the things we'd learned during our five years of gathering so far. The terrain that year in New Mexico had an entry trail that ran through a narrow pass at about the halfway point of the hike in. So we put a small camp there and as hikers came through they'd stop for tea and Washboard Sid and a crew of folks would entertain them with music while someone gave them the info rap. It was just basic stuff about meals and doing this all 'for free' and Councils, and 'C.A.L.M./Mash' (for medical), and sanitation and recycling, and the Magic Hat for donations, and simple basics of health and community.

Now, two years later at the entryway to the Old Rag Gathering here's this newly-christened 'Rap 107' all colorfully written out on giant cardboards. I've got my pad out and I'm copying it word for word. Some of its phrases we all know and use; some is just the excellent easy way to say things and get the ideas across clearly. A few of the phrases are even my own turns of the tongue. It's the distilled simple way to say all these things, collected over two years and already repeated orally, like an oral tradition poem at a few years' worth of gatherings, and now…written out the first time.

Big Susan Bernstein greets us and—ever the provident earth-mother—serves us hard-boiled eggs. I meet Challe Erb a performing clown and Robbie Gordon, an inestimable mandolineer. He was one of the mainstays of the New Buffalo community in New Mexico and now this wise philosopher of the new world culture has transplanted to West Virginia where he strums on his strings and dispenses wisdom and stories like a modern day Heraclitus.

A week later we are prepared to head to D. C. In the dusk we unload a natural canvas tipi and its poles at one end of the Washington Mall near the Lincoln Memorial. Half an hour later the lodge is set up, taut and noble-looking, alongside a couple of graceful shade trees. In the early morning we set tables in a row for displays and someone rolls logs off a truck which we roll into a circle for seats around an unlit neatly arranged faux 'woodfire.' The Wilderness was ready and I went off to look at the rest of the fair.

ACT '79 was set up to stretch from the Washington Monument the length of the reflecting pool with representations of different parts of society. At the densest center near the obelisk were urban models. Walk-through displays were made to look like a bank (which had exhibits about credit unions) or schoolhouses (which had

Figures 76 (i–viii). ACT '79, America's first Energy Fair, held on the Washington D.C. Mall, showed off early examples of solar panels, wind generators, hydrogen cars and much, much more. (Garrick Beck: 1979)

exhibits about new ideas like environmental education) or a town hall (which served as an information center) or 'shopping plaza' (which showcased energy-saving and recycling-oriented home products).

As you walked away from the urban center of ACT '79 you came to areas that represented suburbia, industrial zones and then farms. Each of these had private companies, public agencies, individual inventors and do-gooder community groups of all kinds hosting booths, displaying their stuff. It was quite a marvelous array. Especially because here was the gamut from individual

people right through corporations—all out on the lawns proposing and promoting ideas and products for a greener world together.

In 'suburbia' for example there were bicycle groups describing the advantages of public bike paths.

In an 'Inventors' section a woman from Chicago had set up a window-duct exhibit showing attachments which could be fitted slanting down below windows that—by convection and a couple of ventgates—would bring warm air in during wintertime and cool air in during hot summer nights. "You want to save energy?" she was asking the crowd, "Put one of these on *every* apartment window in the country. That'll save us energy. Uses the sun's temperature and a natural venting system to let the air move where *it* wants to go naturally."

In the industrial sector GM was making quite a hubbub with its prototype hydrogen-powered car. There were engineers and press all crowded around it. Some people were complaining that here were the giant corporations once again trying to control society.

Farmers were promoting ethanol made from corn. And an exhibit about the vanishing American family farm was heart-rending in its depiction of the disappearance of one of the best pieces of the American landscape.

And there beyond the farmers was a 25-foot by 4 1/2-foot silver-blue mosaic gleaming in the morning light. Behind it rose a bubbling fountain of water. It was an array of solar panels. I felt like a primitive gently touching them, running my fingers over their smooth plexi-covers. Beneath the covering, delicate solar crystals transmit energy from the photons of the sun into a network of wires that powers the fountains. "Why aren't you in the downtown of this ACT '79?" I ask one of the fellows at the solar panel exhibit. "Why aren't you powering all the buildings?" "I guess," he says, "they see us an irrigation device. So we're down here with the farms." I continue to look with amazement. Silent smooth flow of energy. Water spurting upward into the air. No exhaust. Almost no moving parts. I saw the emancipation of our species from fossil fuels in an instant. I saw that it was possible, probable, actually inevitable that we would be using this bi-level silicon crystal to extract energy from sunlight to power our world, safely, securely, and soon. How wrong I was about 'soon.'

I asked all the questions I could think of and got lots of good information. After he published his renowned Relativity Theory, Albert Einstein put his mind to this energy source which had been observed (and even measured) for decades but which no one understood. Einstein explained "The Photovoltaic Effect" describing (in sub-atomic detail) how two slightly different crystals alongside each other can 'pull' electrical energy from sunlight. "That's who explained it to the rest of us originally," concluded my guide at the exhibit.

At the furthest end of all these exhibits, past the urban, suburban, industrial and farm displays stood the Wilderness of the Rainbows and the Puerto Rican Worm Farm. Actually these folks were from the South Bronx. They had developed an urban composting model and were collecting huge amounts of compost from restaurants, individuals and the leftovers from the Hunts Point Market, the great produce distribution point for the City of New York. So back in the Bronx they had *hills* of compost and they'd built these rotary compost tumblers that worms just loved.

They brought a couple of these rotating tubes and set them up here on the Mall, filled them with compost and the earthworms were happily chewing their way through the stuff churning out rich droppings, simply the best soil additive imaginable.

They explained that projects like this could recycle all the compostables from every major city, employ people, reduce landfill and deliver a precious, useful product.

We enjoyed being next to these people.

At our own exhibit Big Susan, Jenny 'Starlight' and Hanna set up a display of medicinal healing herbs and flavoring spices from the mid-Atlantic region—actually from the Old Rag mountain region, where we'd been the week before.

There was a scheduled herb walk and tree identification class. People could enter the tipi and sit inside.

I planned a workshop on wilderness survival for 'unexpected circumstances.' At least we could be entertaining by talking about wild foods, keeping warm, purifying drinking water, and signaling for help.

But then came something we hadn't counted on: *school groups*. One after another groups of schoolchildren began to arrive. They had been bussed to ACT '79 on school trips. All morning long in the hot Washington sun they'd been marched through the walkways of the exhibition and they were tired. The green grass and

Figures 77 (i–iv). The Rainbow Family's 'Wilderness Camp' on the D.C. Mall. (Garrick Beck: 1979)

logs in a circle offered just the right place to sit.

So Medicine Story, a Wampanoag Indian, and master storyteller, rose to the occasion. He strode to the circle's center (by the unlit firewood) and began weaving tales about the early days of these Potomac River's shores. He told stories of the animals and birds who used to live here, bringing them to life in character.

The D. C. area children were spellbound. Of course, they were good and tired by the time they got to us, so it was a prime audience for listening quietly. But school group after school group passed through the 'Wilderness' over the next days. I told stories, Barry told stories, others told stories. Medicine Story was a virtual encyclopedia of legends, myths and history. He held forth and brought me in, as well as other taleweavers to spell him.

The students could wander over to the tipi and go inside if they wanted. They asked questions about the herbs and spices. Robbie played mandolin. Jugglers juggled.

And if that wasn't enough, the children could go visit the Worm Farm right next door!

When an older group of high school students arrived I led the imaginative discussion about wilderness skills. The folks from the Geshundheit Institute, a people's medical clinic, came to participate and Dr. J. J. an M. D. from Geshundheit held a fascinating workshop on wilderness medicine and rescue techniques.

It was eye-opening to see the resources that were all really within our grasp.

I left ACT '79 with impetus to set up a solar array back on the farm in Oregon. It was time to start putting the new technologies to use, in league with the old close-to-the-earth lifestyle.

Before going home we visited the South Bronx compost and worm farm. It really was amazing. Right on the edge of the Bronx bay, heaps of sweet smelling decay. There were backhoes and loaders to turn the stuff. And a system of pipes and ducts to blow air under the heaps. Then there were the beautiful, slowly

Figure 78. The main house cabin at the farm with its new solar panels. (Garrick Beck: 1981)

revolving worm-breeding bins. This set-up was light years ahead of what so-called civilization was ready for.

Back in Oregon by the end of the summer of '79 we had managed to install two solar panels which were charging a 12-volt system pumping pure sun juice into a series of marine batteries, providing light and radio and music.

Thirty-five years later these same panels would still be in tip-top operation.

45. Journey to Mexico

I first met Uncle Billy on a cross-country caravan to the West Virginia Rainbow Gathering in 1980. I was traveling in a VW van piloted by Yarrow Aka Logan who picked me up along with my Gathering gear from The Farm's front porch. We rendezvoused outside Seattle with Uncle Billy and his family in their fire-engine red station wagon and Serious from the Love Family commune. Serious came equipped with a huge blue converted schoolbus full of travelers. Off we all went heading to the very first East Coast Annual Rainbow Gathering.

Back at The Farm in Oregon, Charlotte and I had been having a rugged time. It certainly wasn't working for either of us. Eventually she moved in with other friends at another organic farming community 80 miles north and nearer the coast. Now she was planting her gardens in a different valley and banding together with different neighbors to save the lives of a different forest's old growth. I think I was taking on too much. Too many projects, both there at the farm, *as well as* in Eugene, *plus* these larger ventures toward Gathering the Tribes *and* the constant, endless peace actions, plus the No Nukes demonstrations left not enough time, not nearly enough time for the vital parts of being a family together. We separated, got back together and then ultimately separated again. She was always the devoted eco activist, devoted to the earth, and devoted to *how* people work together with the earth. Separating from me wasn't going to change any of that.

Going east with Uncle Billy seemed like a refreshing step. I'd heard mention of him for years. He used what he called 'Native Overdrive' on the downhills putting his big red station wagon into neutral and turning off the engine. "Saves gas. Everybody should do it," he said.

Billy and his sons were members of the Bird Dancer Tribe, the Kumeyaay Sycuans, from just outside what's now Los Angeles. They'd kept alive many of the traditional dances from long ago and brought some of these to the back-to-the-land tribes in the Pacific Northwest. The Hippies of the Northern California-Oregon- (I'm tracing a path here) Washington-Idaho-Montana 'fertile crescent' of back-to-the-land and spiritual communes couldn't get enough of Uncle Billy and his small crew. Billy was a pretty serious guy. He took his mission of passing the wisdom of Native practices to Hippiedom very seriously. He made us chuckle all the time, but his overall approach was deeply serious. At the sweatlodges which he showed us how to build, he talked on and on about reverence for our own ancestors and their ways, their traditions. He wasn't trying to make us Indians, he was trying to convey wisdom that was tribal in nature to show us how these traditions and ceremonies help all people maintain their culture and their reverence for life.

Many months later, after the Gathering, we got a message from Uncle Billy—sent by a young courier—asking us, from the Rainbow to go meet this man named Kuiz. Billy had never really asked *us* to do anything…it was always us asking him. The message is just that Kuiz is going to be at the Paiute-Shoshone Lands for their Sun Dance and we should try to meet him there.

It's a long ride from anywhere to the Paiute Shoshone Reservation along the northern border of Nevada by the far eastern end of Oregon. There is very little out there but sagebrush and rocky land and nearby, well, nothing is nearby.

We arrive late at night and are ushered to Tibor Bruer's tipi. He is a cheerful Hungarian, skilled in the outdoors and he explains the respectful traditions of the encampment. We are among very few Whites in the village. Our friend Rome is among those tending to the Native American Church meeting there and we find that Kuiz is dancing in the Sun Dance. He starts tomorrow morning, and since the ritual of fasting and dancing will go on for four days, we won't be able to have a word with him until at least four days from now.

A young messenger arrives from one of the chief's lodges. He tells Tibor that his new visitors should head out to the front gate to help with the nighttime parking and traffic. A message goes back asking if this is right, these are newcomers, they don't know a thing about their way around here. And the young courier returns saying, right, they know that. And they know these guests have festival and outdoor parking experience, so that's a way we could contribute.

In minutes we are off to the front gate and for the next days we direct traffic, park cars and vans and trucks and busses and help with the 101 things that happen up at front gates of fiestas and festivals. We are good at this and it does let us be helpful. On the final day we get told to come into the arbor area and be spectators to the dance.

I will leave the particulars of the Sun Dance unsaid because these things are better experienced than told about. And that's always part of the mystery of ceremonies: that there are surprises and meaningful moments that take one's breath away and these must be observed or experienced to be understood.

After the dance we went to Kuiz' lodge and waited outside while he rested, drank water and broke his fast. Then he came outside and we told him Uncle Billy had asked us to come meet him here.

Kuiz spoke quietly and very briefly. He said that next year in the spring of 1982, there would be a very rare alignment of the visible planets. He explained this was noted by a raised dot on the great Aztec calendar stone and that he, an Aztec, was inviting the tribes from the Bering Strait to Tierra del Feugo to come to Mexico for an 'Alignment of the Planets' ceremony and since we would probably be the closest to a 'spiritual tribe' from the mixed-culture people of the United States, we should come and be part of this. Then he took some of our addresses and went back inside his lodge. That was it.

At the end of the following winter I attended the New England Storytellers' Conference, which was held at the Another Place community in New Hampshire, a beautiful colonial era farmhouse now used as a conference center and futon factory. Medicine Story and Emmy Rainwalker were among the founders of that community. Mareba Jos lived there. She and I had met the previous summer at the West Virginia Gathering and traveled together to the Black Hills Survival Gathering—on the Lakota Lands in July of 1980. John Trudell gave the Keynote address at that Gathering: a brilliant assessment of the history of imperial encroachment over indigenous peoples. One of the best political speeches I ever heard. Frank Fools Crow made an Invocation. There were energy and water and peace exhibitions. Jackson Browne and Bonnie Raitt played together, headlining the performances on stage. Mareba and I romanced in that season and now, a year later, we have a newborn son, Tameron.

Another Place, where Mareba's been living, first began as an offshoot of Project Place, Boston's legendary youth and community drop out/drop inn 'self-help' center of the late-1960s. They re-opened this overgrown farmhouse and used it as a retreat. Then it was turned over to the community, which inhabits it to this day, a group of social and environmental activists who have used it to serve numerous community needs of rural New England—including this conference of storytellers. Medicine Story has helped arrange this meeting where New England, New Age, and Native keepers of the folklore are gathering to share yarns, epics, mythologies and also some round-the-hearth discussions of the venerable history of the Spoken Word.

After the Storytellers' Conference I drove back West with Mareba, Tameron and Jodey Bateman who is an amazing multi-lingual folksinger. You name the language, he sings you the song—in dialect!—with translations!—and anecdotes!—annotations!—side stories!—and—and then!—another song! All the way to Arizona. That's where our small band was assembling for the Journey to Mexico to meet up with Kuiz.

At the farm in Oregon the previous fall we had received a packet containing an invitation from the anthropological cultural foundation Kuiz was working with. There was more explanation about the Alignment of the Planets and its relation to both modern times and the ancient peoples of this continent. It was clear many tribal peoples were coming together for this. They were going to use one of Mexico's famous pyramid sites for the celebration.

But *after* I'd left The Farm for the Storytellers' Conference in New Hampshire another packet arrives there. Sid opens it. It contains a Paho, a ceremonial message from Hopi Grandfather David Monongye. In the letter David explains that he has commitments with his own people on their own lands at that time, so he cannot come to the ceremony in Mexico. The paho is a ceremonial message—a feather about 3 inches long wrapped in colored threads. David wrote that he has put his prayers into this paho and asked that it be placed on the east side of the pyramid on the ceremonial day.

Sid decides to carry this to the Mexico ceremony.

After Sid departs for Mexico still *another* letter arrives. This one contains an apology from Kuiz indicating that the whole event is called off.

North of the border we rendezvous with Jaysun and Feather and their son Shawn; Barry and Sunny and their children Shaneca and Megan; Eve and Suzanna; Feather also has the no-show letter from Kuiz, which she reads to us. That's the first I'm hearing anything about the ceremony being called off. There's no explanation just a one line cancellation. Feather has also been to see Grandfather David who has given her a message to take to Kuiz's Alignment of the Planets

Feather says, "We're going to that ceremony." And we are. Sid is already ahead of us. Smiling Sun, the golden-haired mechanic and pilot will drive us to the train station at Nogales. In Mexico City we have a contact with the Arts and Ecology Institute simply named Gea whose members kindly host us in their little enclave—a small eco-paradise nestled in the crowded capital. From them we hear the rumors that the reason Kuiz quit was because Mexican authorities in the form of the police, the Ministry of Culture and the Ministry of Justice and someone from the Mexican Army visited him and told him, "Forget you ever had such an idea." Seems like the last thing the current Mexican government wants is a resurgence of the Aztec.

From there we travel on southward by bus to the monastery at Yautepec where we link up with our friends in the international arts group, The Illuminated Elephantes. For years they've been coming to the Gatherings, this band of artists from a dozen countries. For a decade and a half they have been wandering the globe performing in remote villages across Turkey, the Mideast, half of Asia, all of Scandinavia and now Mexico. They are skilled masters of puppets, mime, musicals, children's theatre, comedy, tragedy and now they are looking here in Mexico for a place to establish a more permanent base. Temporarily they've moved into this abandoned monastery, well actually we find out it's a crematoria. All the little houselets we're going to be sleeping in were once the burn chambers for the decent disposal of the dead.

Earlier that morning was when the Spring Equinox had occurred—signaling the beginning of the four-day planetary alignment. Sid had arrived there several days ahead of the rest of us and he and Los Elephantes had considered the situation. They could see there wasn't going to be a major coming-together of the tribes "from North to South America," but there *is* ancient demarcation of this event on the stone calendar. Los Elephantes are maestros in the art of Pageantry (they have been awarded a commission from the Mexican government to help small villages develop pageants and feast day ceremonies based on each village's own unique history, heroes and legends). They decide to go to a remote, un-excavated very ancient Olmec pyramid and give their offerings to the cosmos and the earth there. So they do. Sid brings the Paho sent to the farm.

Arriving there in time for the equinox they walk around the base of the pyramid. It was about 200 feet long on each side and had a flat top about 30 feet across with a tree in each corner.

Toward evening the local mayor along with police arrived and wanted to know what was going on. They thought this was some kind of witchcraft. There was an anthropology professor among the Elephantes troupe who was known to the locals and he explained honestly what was happening, so the officers left. There were petroglyphs there with mysterious markings which were examined and contemplated and in the morning, at dawn those still awake went back to the top of the pyramid for meditation and prayer and Sid tied the paho to the Eastern tree. And so the deed was done.

The following night we get to party with Los Elephantes. Svante, a Swedish photographer takes Spirit Changing photographs where he projects a slide onto the darkly lit person's form and voila! the spirit of the slide is emblazoned onto the person's body. Snap that shot and there's another whole photograph ready to view or project later. We play flutes and drums and out behind the funeral chapel people dance under the stars.

We plan several days of adventures. A trip to Cuernavaca, the colorful town where Timothy Leary and Richard Alpert had met the *curandera* who had suffered them to ingest the mushroom tea. We shop in the market and feel the whole town reverberate to the gonging of its churchbells.

A visit to land at Oldoldcoyote, where the group plans to settle and establish an arts colony. Alberto Ruiz, one of the group's founders says, "We traveled by oxcart for weeks across Eastern Turkey and not a single photograph. We were too busy living in The Present to think about recording it for the future. Now? Now we don't go to 'the store on the corner' without our cameras." There is a trickle of water from the heights of the land that they intend to catch and collect in a cistern. There are house sites. We sit on the ground in a circle at a spot where they envision a central studio. Everyone in turn offers a dedication or an invocation.

We visit the Museo Antropología where we view the stone calendar and 'the dot' that Kuiz supposes represents the Alineación de los Planetas.

And a visit to the great sun pyramids surrounded by vendors and hawkers offering soft drinks and souvenirs. Still the immense stone bleachers and colossal scale of the whole Avenue of Pyramids does cause a pause for awe. At the top of the sun pyramid Sid says, "Let's make a pyramid. You know, like we did in gym class, or the cheerleaders do." And in a minute several of us are on all fours with the next tier rising on top of us and the next on top of them with our lightest one on top. There's a moment, a quiet moment, when we're just in the breeze, a living pyramid on top of a stone pyramid. Other tourists snap pictures. We are laughing, tumbling apart and hiking down leaving after a beautiful

Figure 79. The pyramid on top of the pyramid. (Photographer unknown: Collection of the author, 1982)

day in the ruins, leaving behind in the shadows the eerie memories of the blood-ceremonies that the masses attended here in the era of that empire.

But even with all these daily adventures we two groups of cultural evolutionists have begun planning a performance to do together. We can't do anything commercial—we don't have any working papers. Jorge explains that in Chapultapec Park—the main urban park of Mexico City—there is a place where families come to celebrate children's birthdays. And performers, clowns and jugglers offer their entertainments for the families (for a donation) and this is a longstanding traditional performance area.

So we began to create a children's play, based on children's games from around the world. The play opens with an eagle alighting at (!) Chapultapec Park and offering to take a birthday child on a flying tour around the world to visit children in other lands. The child climbs on the eagle's back and they and everybody 'flies' around the world stopping on each continent to play a children's game from that part of the globe. Jaysun and Jodey and Deva are writing music and a song that everyone can learn. Tove and Andreas are producing masks, Mareba and Mercedes are making costumes, Suzanna and Eve are painting rattles, Liora and Tonya are teaching us the songs in Spanish, Alberto is arranging staging, Barry is strumming his two-stringed Plunker, Jaysun is going over the chords on the guitar, Don Arceneaux is demonstrating the eagle's flight, everyone is busy as can be preparing this collective creation. We are going to do "In and Out My Window" (where hand-holding children weave in and out of 'windows' made from other participants' arched arms); a version of 'Duck, Duck, Goose' (Feather is just hysterical waddling about in the duck mask), a Central American favorite about melons and sandias (which are watermelons); and several more. At last, after flying 'round the circle already many times, the eagle and the entourage of arm-flapping children 'land' back home again in Chapultapec park where everyone returns to their birthday celebrations. We called the play, *"Obras de Paz."*

The day of the performance is all sunshine and blue skies. Children's families dot the gentle curve of parkland with their blankets and picnic baskets. Their birthday parties are already underway. Alberto, Mercedes and Tonya present themselves and the proposal for the troupe's entertainment to a few of the birthday families. They talk a bit about wanting to pay us—it's the tradition—but Tonya explains that some of us are from other countries and not supposed to work for money here, and Alberto adds that we are a 'funded arts group.'

We form a big circle on the green grass and the production begins. Soon all the children are following the eagle, swooping from land to land, riding on the turtle's back, flying in and out of the windows with the bluebirds, closing their eyes and counting to ten in many different languages, and singing the "*Obras des Paz*" song together at the end. It was just wonderful.

We sit together in the shade afterwards and enjoy our own picnic lunch. Then we decide—especially considering all the effort we put into the creating the play—we decide we should do it again for some of the families who hadn't watched and for the Birthday-ing families who are just getting there. So those fluent in Spanish go to talk to newly arrived birthday children's families. The rest of us begin to assemble on the open grassy area when suddenly there's Kuiz and an entourage arriving ready to join us and initiate at last The Alignment of the Planets Ceremony.

Some of us wanted to go on with the children's play. But Kuiz explained this was the only possible place where we could do this freely. It was open and yet it was protected.

Besides, accompanying Kuiz's small clan there were more of our friends from the Pacific Northwest, some of the crew that we had camped with at the Paiute-Shoshone lands. They had traveled south also for the *Alineación* here too, And before we know it we are beginning the Ceremonia.

It starts with a procession in which we form a spiral representing Time. When we come to a stop we have reached the

Figure 80. Feather Hammond as "The Duck" in Obras de Paz, in Chapultapec Park, Mexico City. Jaysun Hammond on guitar, Jorge and Barry Adams on drums. (J. Svante Vanbart: 1982)

present. Kuiz spends some time arranging us and re-arranging us. I think he's putting us in places representing the planets in the sky and the sun and moon. But there's no chance to raise a hand and ask questions.

There are embroidered cloths unrolled on the grass and participants are encouraged to put something there as some kind of symbol. People are coming forward and placing flowers, shells, rocks, rattles, other ceremonial-type objects.

Some of the birthday children and their friends are looking on curiously. Some of their parents and families are watching attentively. Sid takes the children like a pied piper around the outside of the circle and they pick up all the litter, bringing it to the center, to the same altar where other participants are placing their contributions.

Then a musical part of the Ceremony begins. There are ancient songs. There is a 600-year-old wooden drum. There is an old eagle bone whistle. Kuiz and friends already know that the paho was placed days ago at the Eastern edge of the ancient pyramid.

But! Look, Feather's got the other message given to her by Grandfather David. So she comes forward and slowly the message is unwound, sort of like a spiritual piñata, revealing the four colors of corn wound together symbolizing, say the readers, the coming together of the differently colored peoples. Children are continuing to bring bits of trash to the altar. It's a perfect symbol: the future generation cleaning up the earth.

Whatever do ceremonies like these mean? Do they actually do anything? Can they? Are they just the continuation of a long gone culture, a straw in the wind? With no meaning but to amuse and entertain some watching families out for a day in the park? Is there some Great Awareness that hears or sees these prayers and offerings and is likewise pleased or amused? Isn't every moment a raised point on the universe's calendar? Can we sanctify a few moments, or a few days out of the endless stream of days to give praise and thanksgiving to the Power that spins the planets and the stars?

As the Ceremony continues I recognize some of the songs from other Native American rituals and Elaine from Los Elephantes leads us in "Circle Around" a chant-song that has English and Spanish verses so those of us who only speak one or the other can chant together. It is very beautiful, and goes on and on. I sit, just trying feel the mass of the good Earth under me. At least the ceremony was able to occur.

In the end there are hugs and goodbyes. The clans part ways. Our journey to Mesoamerica is all but done. Of course we all make 'intentions' to keep in touch—though how quickly the years pass and how long the miles between.

46. Short Takes

Swami Mommy

The Gatherings had been recycling their trash since the very beginning. Andy C gathered a crew and began sorting out the trash up at Strawberry Lake in 1972. Speaking of waste, he said, "Never leave brown out of the Rainbow." He explained that how we treat our 'waste' or our 'trash' was going to determine what happens to us as a species.

And so the trash got sorted and then trucked to specialty places that would take glass or aluminum. In the early 1970s these were mostly small-scale processors. They were few and far between and often long drives away from the Gatherings' sites. The infrastructure for recycling was basically non-existent. Just about everything back then was placed in municipal 'dumps.'

For us, wood and cardboard were burned. Compost was composted. But sorting all these messed up boxes and bags of garbage was a huge and messy job. And in the early days of the Gatherings an awful lot of it got by us unmixed and went to the dumps.

And then a yoga teacher came to the Gatherings and saw this. She had the inspiration to separate the garbage at the source, so she made signs to label the different kinds of trash—easily readable black and white signs. And people hardly paid them any attention, but then….then!...She had the vision that the types of garbage matched up with the chakras of Yogic practice, and each category matched the color of the rainbow associated with each chakra! She began promoting what she called Rainbow Garbage Yoga. She made *colored* signs for each of the kinds of recyclables and she began promoting this with songs, with parades, with clowning (inspired by the inimitable Patch Adams), with serious talks about the state of our world and with a relentless visionary passion. And she taught people to separate our garbage at the start—*before* it winds up in mixed bags!

This may not seem like such a big deal today, but at the time this was unheard of. Nobody did that. She became known as Swami Mommy, the Guru of Garbage. She made and distributed colorful labels that matched the colors of the Chakras of the inner body with the seven main categories of 'trash' and she set up centers—along the woodland trails—where lashed logs held bags and boxes where we could put our trash. 'Recycling Centers' was what she called them.

Suddenly the seemingly-impossible job of processing our trash became possible. It was still a lot of work. It will always be a lot of work. But it's what we have to do if we want to live on a clean, healthy planet.

Swami Mommy taught recycling classes. She made up—and taught—songs about source separation of garbage. She designed a series of yoga poses around the process. She created a chart of

Figure 81. Source separation of Garbage at one of Swami Mommy's 'recycling centers' in the woods. (Photographer unknown: collection of the author, 1978)

Figure 82. Swami Mommy. (Gabe Kirsheimer: 1992)

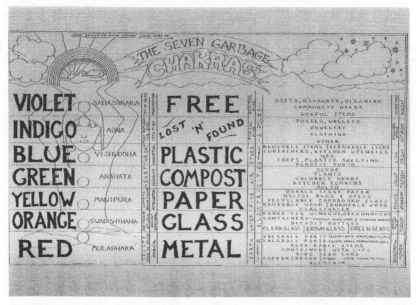

Figure 83. Swami Mommy's 'Seven Garbage Chakras' recycling chart (Swami Mommy: 1978)

recycling categories matched to the chakras—which she had me draw out to her specifications.

I can't prove it, but it might be true that the Rainbow Gatherings are the first large-scale community on earth to source separate and recycle its garbage. We don't need credit for this. We just need everyone to recycle their trash.

The W.O.W. Hall

In the winter of 1973 the American Indian Movement occupied the site of the 1890 Wounded Knee massacre in South Dakota as a protest against civil rights abuses toward Native Americans. That occupation became national and even world news. It was a watershed moment in realizing that civil rights were not just an issue for black people—and just as Cesar Chavez and his farm workers made it clear that civil rights issues extended to the Latino community, so did the Wounded Knee occupation make clear that civil rights for Native Americans were also part of the human equation for justice.

The Rainbow folks in the Eugene, Oregon area talked together about wanting to be supportive toward this occupation. We decided to hold an event like a fundraiser, but more of a food-and-supply-raiser to send material goods to the occupation. So we started to look for a place to hold that event.

We found the almost-abandoned Woodmen of the World hall. It was built and operated by the Woodmen of the World, an old-timey union of loggers. They built it with a great wooden dance floor and held events there for decades. But in current times, the loggers 'union' hadn't built itself up the way other workers' unions had and its membership declined and operating the hall had become a burden.

They were glad to rent it to us for our event for 35 dollars. So we put up posters and used word-of-mouth as promotion. The

Figure 84. The W.O.W. Hall, Eugene, Oregon. (Garrick Beck: 2014)

price of admission was to bring something to donate to Wounded Knee. And so we sent a truckload of goods (canned foods, warm clothes and sleeping bags, lamps and kerosene, batteries, tools, and—of course—the truck itself) to South Dakota to the occupation at Wounded Knee. This would be the first of many, many projects of mutual support between Rainbow clans and the American Indian Movement.

But it was also the first time that the W.O.W. Hall was used for a counterculture event. After this it was rented again and again by community groups for benefits and for entertainment. In 1975, when the Woodmen of the World was going to sell the building, community groups banded together and produced a 'Wowathon'—a 24-hour-a-day ongoing cavalcade of entertainers, along with an arts auction, to raise the down payment and buy the building. Which we did.

Today it stands as a wonderful example of community support for the arts, as a center for emerging artists, as a place where benefits can be held for today's causes and as a beautiful art deco building that has been rescued, renovated and maintained by community process. Wow.

Trojan

The Trojan Nuclear Power Plant was located along the Columbia River just thirty-five miles from the city of Portland, Oregon. There had been chatter by environmentalists about the possible calamities from this water-pressurized reactor from the very start of its construction. But those concerns were muted by the nation's love affair with the so-called 'safe' and 'clean' energy supplied by the nuclear industry.

Small independent groups of activists had made protests at the plant but got little attention and even less support from the mainstream. One group even entered the plant area at night and wheat-pasted anti-nuclear posters all over the buildings. They finally had to wake up the plant's night watchmen in order to get arrested!

My friends and I were among the environmentalists who were opposed to nuclear energy but we were also convinced that conventional demonstrations were not going to bring about change. We held meetings and, with the incredible insight of Lloyd Marbet (a Portland area activist), Robert McCullough, an old friend from anti-war protests at Reed College (who later went on to blow the lid off the Enron energy company's scandalous operations in California and Texas), with Nina Bell and Norman Solomon (two completely brilliant strategists)—we formed the Trojan Decommissioning Alliance.

The idea was that we needed a comprehensive plan that both the public and officialdom could relate to—and not just marches and protests. Lloyd moved ahead toward promoting ballot measures and voter initiatives. Robert uncovered illegal kickback deals

Figure 85. Protesters marching on the Trojan Nuclear Power Plant. (Photographer unknown: 1977)

that violated state laws, and Nina and Norman rallied the public both with informative meetings and with highly publicized sit-ins and marches.

Overall our plans called for not just shutting down the plant but also for taking the whole thing apart and finding ways to pay for that.

The history of the successful decommissioning of the Trojan Nuclear plant deserves a whole book to itself. My friends and I were on the minor scale of the actions, but we did help rally lots of folks—from bell-bottomed hippies to civic-minded mainstreamers—to participate in the demonstrations. We sat in after passing through the gates of the plant. I was arrested and eventually sentenced to three days of public service. To fulfill our sentence Michael Bear and I were assigned to firewood duties. So for three days we felled and bucked, split and stacked cords of firewood for a group of four old-timers living deep in the hills of the county where the power plant was located.

The Trojan plant itself helped the movement by having one of its steam pipes rupture and scaring the living daylights out of

Figure 86. Protesters entering the Trojan Nuclear Power Plant. (Photographer unknown: 1977)

everyone in Portland. Eventually the plant was decommissioned, taken apart and the pieces sent to the Hanford repository in Washington State where they can cool off for the next 100,000 years.

The key thing I learned here is that merely protesting isn't enough; there has to be a plan. There has to be a way to show the larger public what the problems are. There has to be a plausible, possible, practical solution, and there has to be a coordinated community effort to make it happen.

Ram Dass

Ram Dass, the Harvard professor turned psychedelic sadhu, was a guiding force in the evolution of new world culture ever since he and his cohort, Dr. Leary, burst into the spotlight of notoriety surrounding the use of mind-expanding elixirs.

His trip took him to India where he fed LSD to the gurus and came away with an insight into the unified nature of spiritual experiences. He wrote the book *Be Here Now* and advocated for meditation as a psychedelic activity. It was only natural that his path would lead down the trail to the Rainbow Gatherings.

The first time I saw him at the Rainbow in 1979 he was with his friend Medicine Story. Each one was standing on either side of the trail leading up to the Fourth of July meditation meadow. The slow pilgrimage of Gatherers was wending its way up the trail from the encampment below to the higher meadow. Everyone was already in silence—mostly—and there beside the trail just before the huge meadow opened out up ahead, each one stood with an index finger held against their lips, almost statue-like, signaling silence.

Later I watched him holding 'classes' in the Arizona pine forest. Hippies, hobos, hotshots and hipsters crowded round him to ask advice, or challenge him on some point of his writings. People thought they were going to see the Guru. But he was more like Ann Landers—a charming advice columnist—giving the most sensible and wise replies.

And that's (generally) how the modern Western world adapted to the yogic wisdom of the East. Despite the Western media's mockery

Figure 87. Ram Dass and Medicine Story stood beside the trail. (Photographer unknown: Courtesy Medicine Story, 1979)

Figure 88. Ram Dass holding 'class' at the Arizona Rainbow Gathering, 1979. (Photographer unknown: Courtesy Medicine Story, 1979)

of the yogis and teachers and gurus who came to America to ply their trade, and despite some westerners' urge to become followers, and despite some gurus' relish for devotees to adhere to their every word, for the most part those introduced to the meditative practices, the yogic postures, and the spiritual teachings of the Hindu, Tibetan and Nepalese traditions, for the most part people followed these traditions *not* by mindlessly following the dictums of gurus, but by learning the meditations and breathing exercises and calming techniques, and then adapting these lessons as part of life.

Patch Adams

Patch was a medical doctor in the long tradition of M.D.'s who came to the gatherings, the country faires, the renaissance faires, the barter faires, the no nukes rallies, etc.—and offered their services to the people: Dr. Ken Osgood, Dr. Rusty Nichols,

Dr. Watts, Painless (the dentist), Dr. Jim 'Jimbo' Berg, among many, many others. Patch was also a comedian. He believed in the old adage that "Laughter is the best medicine."

He was working, in 1979, to establish a permanent healing center where free services could be given to the patients. A true medical revolutionary.

Rainbows had been scouting the hills of Virgina and West Virginia helping him find a locale for his soon-to-be-named Gesundheit! Institute.

Through that connection, Patch came to the Gathering and noted that we suffered perennially from the 'rainbow runs.' We all pretty much thought the diarrhea was due either to changes in people's diets, or the largely stew-like dinner meals plus the largely porridgy breakfasts. Or that it just spread through the camp because of the mix of so many children from so many

Figure 89. Dr. Patch Adams speaking to the Council, Arizona Rainbow Gathering, 1979. (Garrick Beck: 1979)

different places, that one of them must have brought in this 'bug' and it just spread.

But Patch said, "No. That's not it." He began to explain the 'fly connection' and how it leads from the slit latrines to our stomachs. So he went to council one afternoon and in a riveting speech explained exactly how flies land on the excrement at the latrines (even if we try to coat the waste with lime or ash) and *then* land on unwashed dishes where they deposit their own droppings, and from there pass to people's hands, mouths and stomachs where those germs multiply and make us sick. It was a marvelously clear talk. And he finished up by explaining that we needed three-part dishwashing (hot soapy water, hot rinse, and cold santize) and hand washing for *everyone* preparing or serving food.

I thought it was one of the most intelligent information-sharings I'd ever heard in our councils. Afterwards, I went over to thank him for the clear, concise message. I shook his hand, "Patch," I said, "that was terrific. You really taught the lesson."

"Nope," he said, shaking his head. "They didn't get it."

"Whaddya mean they didn't get it?" I asked, puzzled. "Everyone was listening completely. Really," I said trying to reassure him.

"No," he went on, "*they* got it, but not enough to go back to their camps and tell everyone else. I've got to do this better. Come back tomorrow afternoon and I'll give it a better try."

The next day Patch again addressed the council. This time he had prepared a play with characters and costumes. Out came Joe and Jane Sunshine, two gatherers, with a big spoon and big bowl. There they were on their way to dinner. Yumm. They were eating. As Patch narrated they finished their dinner and went back to their camp (by the edge of the council circle) and then they went to visit the slit latrine (by a little rise at the edge of the woods). They dropped their drawers and out rolled (wrapped in burlap) other actors who lay there in a pile. Now Joe and Jane went to their 'tent' (a tarp held up and folded over by Patch's 'stagehands'). They carefully put their dirty bowl and giant spoon down outside the 'tent' and went inside giggling to make love! You can hear the crowd howling and cheering. Now, from over the hill came the buzzing flies. Patch has everyone make the buzzing sound. The flies buzz around the whole circle and land—you guessed it!—on the burlap-covered actors. The flies are having a field day frolicking among the turds. Now the flies buzz away looking for another meal. And there are the unwashed bowl and spoon of our young couple. The flies descend on the utensils. Patch has everyone boo. You know the rest of the story. The couple comes out in the morning, uses the bowl and spoon for breakfast and they get sick, sick, sick.

It was a great scene. Afterwards I met up with Patch and nodded at him. "Yeah," he said, "I think we got it that time."

Of course *everyone* who was there told *everyone* back at their own camps what they had just seen. In fact, it's forty years since that happened and people are still telling people about it.

Three-part dishwashing got instituted at every kitchen, hand washing became a standard for food preparers and servers, and the Gatherings got healthy.

Mana

Immanuel 'Mana' Trujillo enlisted as an underage recruit during World War II with the British Merchant Marine. After sustaining a severe blast injury (and transferring to the U.S. forces), at the end of the war he went to New York to show his paintings in the gallery scene that was soaring and filled with new talent. He soon learned the hard way that his Native American background limited the interest in his artwork.

As he explained to me, after we met in 1979, "I went to gallery after gallery and everyone told me the same thing: 'You're an Indian, and no one's interested in Indians' paintings. Why don't you make some baskets or some pottery or some blankets?' It didn't take me long to see the writing on the wall, so I started doing my art on pottery."

Figure 90. Painting by Mana, (Immanuel Trujillo: 1979, Collection of the author)

As a longtime motorbiker, he joined the Ching-a-Lings biker club in the South Bronx and moved in there with the club.

He told me he was adopted but didn't know he was half Apache until, at age eighteen, he had received a portion of an inheritance from his Apache father. His father's will had been witnessed by two men who were to become his spiritual mentors: Native American Church road chief "Apache" Bill Russell and aging Spanish American War veteran Eugene Yoakem. These men introduced him to the Native American Church and he experienced the spectacular visions of peyote and became a lifelong devotee of the sacred cactus' 'buttons.'

Mana, as he was called, joined the Native American Church, a legally recognized peyote religion, but he was bothered when he learned that the Church had a requirement of blood quantum (25 percent) for membership. Being only '50 percent' Apache himself, he reasoned that his blond grandchildren, the issue of the children of his non-Indian unions, would be prevented from practicing his chosen religion.

So he petitioned the Native American Church to allow for changes in its membership rules. When his petition was rejected, he formed a chapter of the Church made up specifically of veterans of WW II and the Korean War. And (uh-oh!) he made changes to the blood quantum requirement for his chapter of the Church.

He called his chartered chapter the Native American Church All Race Group. A year later, the Native American Church revoked the license of the chapter and ordered it disbanded.

What was he to do? Mana cast about trying to find a way to establish an all-race peyote religion, independent of the NAC.

When Timothy Leary and Ram Das were fired from Harvard University for their LSD experiments—amid great fanfare and national attention—they set up an institute at Millbrook, New York on an estate owned by William Mellon Hitchcock, an heir to the Gulf Oil fortune. There they continued their psychedelic experiments, research and partying. When (by no small coincidence) they met Mana, they were curious how peyote, the psychedelic sacrament was managed within the Native American Church. Mana was more than happy to share what he had learned.

Some of the upper crusty Bostonians were not at all impressed by the salty-talking Native American seaman who arrived at their estate, and he was mutually not impressed by them. Their psychedelic scene was much more oriented toward the intellectual elites, the Hollywood celebrities and collegiate scientists. Still, they gave Mana the gatehouse at the front end of the grounds to use as his pottery studio.

Mana lived there and made, painted and glazed his beautiful pottery and watched in wonder as the massive police scene arrived at Millbrook to bust the psychedelic pioneers. The police cars, all flashing their lights, were headed by former F.B.I. agent G. Gordon Liddy (Liddy would later be disgraced as the chief bungler of the infamous Watergate burglary). They drove up the driveway, arrested Leary and all his cohorts and drove back down the long drive, never paying a moment's notice to the crazy Indian who stayed busy working his clay.

After that debacle, Billy Hitchcock and Mana hightailed it out west to find and purchase property in the Southwest for the League of Spiritual Discovery (Ram Das and Leary's organization). Mana ultimately purchased three properties for the League through Hitchcock.

In 1966, during a time in this country when psychedelic use was hotly condemned by the authorities, Mana's pottery studio in Denver was raided. The police saw the peyote button hanging on a string around his neck—which Mana promptly ate, right in front of them. He was arrested and the trial was a public spectacle.

Mana raised issues relating to the 1st, 5th, 11th and 14th amendments to the U.S. Constitution but the key in the trial came when Mana asked the Judge how he could be a member of a bona fide religion to which his children or grandchildren might not be able to belong. The result of this trial was the creation, in the Colorado statutes, of the first ceremonial use exemption for peyote regardless of ancestry. This ruling paved the way for Mana (along with two non-Indian co-founders) to establish the Peyote Way Church of God, an all race religion, with Peyote as a lawful sacrament. Let there be wonder! Let there be astonishment!

When his elderly adoptive Uncle Bill became ill in Northern New Jersey, he moved back to the South Bronx—where the Ching-a-Lings still had him on their roster. He'd ride his bike from the clubhouse over to Jersey to give his Uncle Bill the extra care he needed. And he was forming, firing and glazing his pottery in a garage at the Ching-a-Lings. He began a free, after-school pottery program for neighborhood children, and he'd ride his bike (with full biker escort) to deliver his wares to the Smithsonian Institute, which was now purchasing and displaying his pottery in their permanent collection.

By then, the Ching-a-Lings were inhabiting a whole neighborhood. They had houses, garages, and a neighborhood watch for safety and security, because the New York cops simply stayed out of those 'free' areas. They had a pool hall, a gallery and of course, their amazing bikes. But most important, for all the Ching-a-Ling's reputation as tough a gang as ever was, they were (unlike many other clubs) distinctly and completely non-racist. They were open to anybody regardless of skin color. And now they had Mana holed up with them as well.

During that time, in the early 1980s, the East Village scene in Lower Manhattan was its own hotbed of cross-fertilizing cultural adventure: the burned out buildings were being inhabited by adventurous artists; the Shuttle Club opened a late-night jazz sanctuary in a truly underground, unlicensed basement; performances spaces like Gargoyle Mechanique, 8BC, ABC No Rio, and The Fort became focus points of a poetic revival where old Beatnik wordsmiths Herbert Hunke, Jack Michelin and Taylor Meade came to share the small stages with a whole new generation of weirdo artists like Winchester Chimes, Latch, Matthew Courtney, and comedians like Zero Boy and the Mike and Steve Buscemi brothers. Tiny art galleries sprang up showing Luka Pentrovski's piano assemblages and Keith Haring's visionary, chalky outlines. Jeanne Liotta's meditative and splashy art films splayed themselves across gallery walls. The hole-in-the-wall club, CBGB's was already attracting national attention and garage rock 'palaces' like Gorgio's, Meow Mix, and the Pyramid hosted Dino and Wendy Wild's Mad Violets, Dave Herrera's Handouts, They Might Be Giants, The Fuzztones, the Cramps, the Optic Nerve and more. The Gas Station—a totally burned out old filling station on the corner of Avenue B and Second Street—became *the* place for post-midnight theatrical escapades, where groups like Shock Troupe Theater performed poet David Boyle's version of William Yeat's *The Wisdom of the King*. Just down the block, the Newyorican Poets Café thrived with packed houses for their poetry slams and up the street, Save The Robots opened at 4 a.m.—a truly after hours club for those who just could not get enough. The midnight denizens of Alphabet City (where the streets were named Avenue's A, B, C, and D) now had an *entire* community to call their own. C and D had long stood for coke and dope, but cocaine and heroin were rapidly being replaced by MDMA (Ecstacy) and a huge renewed interest in 'magic' mushrooms.

It was during that time that I had the opportunity, through my fortunate acquaintance with Mana, to introduce the wild, incredible East Village garage band scene to the wild, incredible

South Bronx biker scene. The two groups actually had a lot in common: certainly, a disdain for oppressive authority and a genuine liking for getting mind-blowingly high.

Figures 91, 92 & 93. Mana Pottery. (Immanuel Trujillo: 2007, Collection of the author)

47. Saskatchewan A.I.M.

The 1982 Idaho Rainbow Gathering was the rainiest ever. Unbelievable. Six days into a continuous downpour you could hear voices chime out from under tarpaulins and inside cramped tents, "They've seeded the clouds!" and "When're we gonna start building our Ark!!?" The mud was ankle deep everywhere. At night it was shivering cold. Families huddled together and in the short breaks in the torrent everyone went out collecting wet firewood. My tipi had twenty plus people lodging in it.

The terrain provided a narrow loop road that came up one side of the mountain and curved around to the gathering entrance, winding its way back down the other side. So we planned to use a one-way route to avoid traffic facing itself on the mountainous road. Well, one stretch of road got so soggy it just washed out and slid off down the mountainside leaving a gaping, impassable hole.

The remaining half of the loop would have to serve for both up and down traffic. It was a muddy mess. Cars, trucks, even buses got stuck. The word from the front gate crew was passed through the camp and about 50 people, myself included, went off to help with traffic and movement of people up and down the mountain. We brought gear and tents to maintain way stations along the road. John Buffalo figured it out: he organized a baton system so whole caravans could leave town, all the vehicles traveling along more or less together, helping each other if one got stuck, until the last vehicle made it to the top then the baton was passed and the next caravan would begin its journey down the hill. It was an incredible lesson in group effort and coordination.

At one of our waystations along the mountainous route I overheard an Idaho State Police Captain say to a Forest Ranger, "I never saw anything like this outside of the military."

Finally the weather started drying up and after that we had a chance to dry out. I remember watching some youngsters wringing out sleeping bags like huge wet washcloths, twisting as the water just spewed out of them.

In the days that followed the gathering flourished. There was a fabulous bakery/shower system that heated the water from the same flames that fueled the ovens by running copper water pipe through the ovens' rock walls. Wavy Gravy from the Hog Farm community led the Fourth of July Children's Parade. We had a peacefully, mutually-agreed-to Operating Plan worked out with the Forest Rangers. Council went on each day in the middle of the tipi circle. An all-night full moon celebration brought all the drums and drummers to the rocky-topped mesa above the encampment. A couple from Mexico announced in council that we had been given an invitation to a Gathering of all the nations on the continent. They said the Native Nations were holding a Powwow of dancers from all the tribes of North America and we were being invited to bring a troupe of our own dancers and drummers to participate.

Meanwhile the sun was baking the wet clay ground dryer and harder. After all our tromping in the mud and then dancing while it was drying out, several of the open areas got pretty compacted. The land would take some aerating and breaking up with tools to allow root growth. Even summer seeding might be advisable. So I volunteered to stay on with the cleanup crew. The land naturalization was tough work, but we made a good scene of it, so it was kind of fun too. There were some abandoned vehicles stuck up to their gunnels in the now-dried mud. Those needed to be winched out by larger equipment. We were learning that there's less trash brought in if the hike in is uphill and it's easier to get the trash out if the hike out is downhill. And that's how it was there. So the naturalization of the land and the recycling was done about as efficiently as could have been.

Done in fact, before the bus leaving for the Saskatchewan

Gathering of Nations had left Missoula. And that was not far from where I was sitting in Idaho.

It took a half-day's travel in the last car leaving the Idaho Gathering site for me to catch up with dreadlocked Feliche's black roadster and Black Lewis's and Yolanda's industrial green bus with the rainbows painted over the wheels. Almost twenty of us were aboard the two vehicles including my sister Isha, 14 years old, visiting for the summer. She is petite, dark-eyed, with an expressive face and an opinion about everything. She had been living with the Living Theatre all her life, traveling the performance circuits of Europe, North Africa and South America. This caravanning toward the 'show' was nothing new to her.

Our first stop was just outside Kalispell, Montana in the idyllic Flathead valley near where Barry and Sunny had a small cabin. We stayed down the road at Alberto Ecco's small farm. I went horseback riding in the evening with Kim Estes. It was beautiful.

Then the long, long, jouncy bus journey begins. Some of us help consume some LSD pills someone has found so we can cross the border *completely clean*. There's a small highway that wends its way from the small towns of eastern Montana up to the small towns of Alberta, Canada. We choose that road as our route. Mareba Jos gathers all our passports, visas, money and the all-important invitation letter from the Council of Nations.

At the little customs house she presents all of our papers and the rest of us just lounge onboard. A Canadian official sticks his head inside for a moment then clears us all for entry into his country. Cool, all of us entering Canada without even having so much as to talk to the border patrol.

But then the bus wouldn't start. There's no choice but to give it a push. "Everyone off the bus! Let's do this as fast and easily as we can."

So off we go, in a stream of dreadlocks, embroidered hippie garb, colored Guatemalan shirts, hair glitter. The customs officials are not sure why we're disembarking. Then all together we stand to the rear of the bus and heave to. T-ॐ (yes, that's his name) calls out, "Hold it! Hold it!" We all stop. "This calls for a picture!" he continues while he fumbles in his woven sidebag for his camera. He's got it out, we all begin heaving to again, the bus begins to move, T-ॐ snaps the shutter, the engine r-r-r-u-m-mbles into action and we are all filing back onto the bus waving and smiling to the officers. They are waving slowly back.

It's a long, beautiful ride. Sarra Sunshine, Sunny Adams, Feather Hammond, Dorothy, Howard, Feliche, Garrick, Tameron, Mareba, T-ॐ, Lewis, Yolanda, their son, many others, and one young lady originally from southern midwestern Canada who's just astonished that the little road we're taking out in the middle of these plains leads right through the tiny one-silo town she grew up in. She's narrating the stories of the farmers, the

Figure 94. Pushing the bus across the border. (T-ॐ: 1982)

schoolhouse, the preacher, the town and its people bringing the passing landscape into perfect clarity.

Outside of the northern city of Saskatoon, Saskatchewan on the Canadian Great Plains, the Assembly of Nations was spreading out its blankets and its village. As we drove the last 50 miles a terrific thunderstorm shot lightning burst after burst along the vast panoramic horizon of the modern world's wheat basket. The thunder just kept going and going. It was the first time I'd really heard 'rolling thunder.'

In the morning light at the Powwow we parked amid the vast array of motorhomes and tipis. There were more lodges than I'd ever seen.

A little inquiry into where we should set up our camp brought us this story: a couple of our dancers had arrived a few days before us. The night before last they'd had a bit of a marital dispute, in the middle of the night, in the quiet of the encampment,

Figure 95. At the Saskatchewan Gathering of Nations—more lodges than I'd ever seen. (Garrick Beck: 1982)

Figure 96. Our Rainbow bus and tipis set up next to the A.I.M. encampment. (Garrick Beck: 1982)

they'd had a huge screaming match. They used the f-word, the mf-word, all the &*%$#@!* words. As one of the Native guides explained it, "I think everyone here's seen about all the dancing from your group that they want to see—or hear—already." We were pointed to a place on the far end of the encampment and told to set up there. And that we should, please, stay, but that we had already done all the performing anybody wanted.

We drove to the nice open place we were shown, parked the vehicles and began setting up our tipi and tents. Right next to us was the American Indian Movement camp, the A.I.M. camp. These were Native Americans from many different tribes who were activists in the causes of Native Peoples' civil rights. Just as there was an African American civil rights movement in the Sixties, so had there been a smaller but equally motivated civil rights movement among Native Americans. These were the people who had kept with that movement into the 1980s. The racism against Indian peoples is worse than legendary. It's a true genocidal story whose residues are racism, poverty, loss of lands, culture, and traditions. In many parts of Canada (where there are very few black people) racism manifested itself toward the Indian peoples. These A.I.M. advocates were coming from causes they had been campaigning for from all over North America: school benefits, voting rights, housing rights, job opportunities. They were coming from many different tribes, states and provinces. They were not happy about us camping next to them.

They were not happy that they themselves had been put so far from the center of things either. Nor were they being treated as a recognized tribe. They were a social/political movement it was true, but they were disappointed in the Council of Nation's determination to view them as different from the tribes. And then to have us—the mostly white kids of the rainbow—placed next to them. That just seemed to be one more push in the wrong direction. We didn't know what to do, so we just set to work making a good camp. We built a small kitchen and wash area; we set up lean-tos for shade; we stacked firewood and hauled water.

The A.I.M. folks just stolidly ignored us. But the kids, yes the kids, theirs and ours, began to play together. And that broke the ice. Slowly the Moms communicated and by the following day we had heard their side of the story.

This whole huge thing, this whole festival of dancers of all these tribes was a ruse, a front, to bring tribal governors together to meet with executives of big oil and gas and coal corporations to get them to sign over huge contracts for the extraction of minerals and petroleum. This dancing stuff and the drumming and the singing powwow—that everybody got paid to come to— was like a bone thrown to the elders and spiritkeepers of the Nations while their 'officials' signed over countless land, water and (especially) energy rights at meetings in the air-conditioned hotels in Saskatoon.

The A.I.M people were outraged by this. They called it the largest takeaway of Native peoples' heritage in a generation. The hotel meetings were closed to ordinary tribespeople. And out here on the plains everyone was just havin' a good old time at the party paid for by the giant energy corps. What a hoax! What a weaselly hoax! The A.I.M. people wanted to address the crowds at the festivities at the main dance area but they weren't given a performance slot.

The next day—while there was dancing going on at the arena—there was also a meeting and speechmaking by elders of many tribes. They had huge tipi made of several tipis all laced together. It was spread out over a wide area with the sides open. We took seats at the outer edge and sat listening for hours. These were not the 'officials of the tribal governments,' these were the traditional wisdomkeeper elders. Some told their tribes' creation stories; others told a particular tale to illustrate some lesson; each speaking in turn. It was quiet. In the Saskatchewan summer heat it was easier just to stay still and be absorbed by the talking and the tales. The A.I.M. folks waited patiently near the back of the great lodge. Close to the end of the meeting they were recognized to speak by the old ones at the front.

Several of the A.I.M. clan stood up. One mapped out the 'truth' about the nature of the powwow we were all drawn into: sweetheart mineral rights deals being 'negotiated' in town where the Tribal Officers are being wined and dined by the Executives. And about the environmental degradation that is going to happen to our Mother Earth if we let these unrestrained deals go through. One asked the elders to make a statement to the public through the press condemning the 'hotel agreements' as fraud.

The elders responded with weary looks. They had seen so many protests before. They talked about how we had to see the brighter side of things; how it was good for all the tribes to come together like this; that this hasn't happened for a very long time; how these deals being made would at least bring some jobs and income to impoverished people.

The A.I.M. people talked among themselves for a few moments and then one of them turned to the assembly and made a proposal.

He said that as the A.I.M. movement wasn't going to be doing a formal dance, the dance they would do would be a 50-mile walk from the powwow site to the Provincial Jail, where there was a large percentage of Native American prisoners—all without access to sweatlodge, pipe ceremony or any other vestiges of traditional religion; without access to medicine people of their tribe; and frankly even without basic health care. They were going to walk this walk as their part of the powwow dance in hope of drawing attention to the plight of these poorly-treated prisoners. Christians, Protestants, Catholics, Jews, all had access to clergy and to religious services in the Provincial Jails. But Native Peoples? Not allowed! And the Natives were the majority population in this joint. He suggested that whoever wishes would join their walk and that they could use the power of this event to shed light on the situation and bring some spiritual relief to their people. I thought it was a brilliant idea, completely appropriate and full of potential to work.

We had a day to prepare. We made sandwiches and cookies to snack on along the way. We rounded up broad-brimmed hats for each of us.

In the light of dawn we loaded up daypacks, filled our water bottles and laced up our best walking boots. We went over to the A.I.M. camp ready as could be. They were in gear too. Looking us over, they said they'd like us to walk behind them. That this was essentially a Native American demonstration and that was the way it had to be. A couple of the Rainbows weren't so happy about this and were objecting. But I—and others—spoke up about the basic cause we were supporting and however the 'look' of the march would be—Native Peoples in front, peoples of other races, tribes, religions marching behind in support—however that would look best, we all were together in the cause.

We waited for other tribal groups to show up. It was getting clear that not a lot of other people were going to walk this walk along with us. A few folks from different tribes arrived at the

A.I.M. camp one or two at a time. It was time to get going. We set off at a fast clip onto the blacktop highway. About fifty of us all together, the A.I.M. people and native tribespeople leading the way, and we a little ways behind.

It didn't take long for the sun to rise above that flat open horizon and start to fry, then bake and finally broil us as it rose slowly above the wheat, drying it on their stalks in the fields all around us for as far as we could see.

Moms and dads had kids in backpack carriers and cradleboards. There were some banners and flags being carried at the front. We were setting a blistering clip to get to the prison destination by early evening hopefully to meet with news teams there. A press release and leaflet had been printed and were ready to distribute.

But first we had to get there. Feliche's car served as one of several support vehicles hauling extra water, or letting some of the older marchers or children ride for part of the trip. Sarra (where does she get the energy?) is dancing up and down along the line of marchers. Someone is playing a wooden flute and the haunting sounds whisper by us as we trudge along the roadside. Slowly, one at a time A.I.M. folk drop back to chat with one or another of us as we walk along. One of the Blackfeet A.I.M. people knows Sunny from Montana. Another was to a couple of Rainbow Gatherings years before. Even if A.I.M. is not going to be recognized as a Tribe, and A.I.M. is surely not going to recognize us as a Tribe, at least we were another clan not dancing to the corporations' tune. And we were finding some common ground with these dedicated activists.

As we moved into the afternoon the grueling nature of the walk felt painful like the heat of the sweat lodge or a fasting day's foodless effects. There is kinship of compassion that bonds one with those who are oppressed when the ritual act has some reminder of the suffering of others. This heat, this glistening black asphalt, this is a small ordeal compared to what people denied medical help or religious freedom go through. So on we trudged.

The support cars that had gone back to the encampment found people waiting for rides to catch up with the march. So they brought them and other vehicles followed. The march was growing in numbers. As we approached the prison there were two or three hundred of us. We Rainbows—black, white and Hispanic—just about vanished in the crowd.

The press was really there too, with cameras and microphones. This was a story behind the story. Something going on about real issues, really being brought forward because of the opportunity presented by this Council of Nations. And while the protest did not address the land, mineral and water takeaways; it did address the very real issue of Native American's prison conditions: their neglect, particularly while other prisoners of other races are receiving medical, educational, recreational and religious benefits.

The press did their job. They started investigating independently, confirming the accusations brought to light. The prison system responded merely that they would look into these 'allegations.' The press played on the alternative type of 'Dance' this march represented.

The result was real changes in people's lives. Prisoners—regardless of race—receiving the minimal benefits that the taxpayers were already paying for. I'm not saying that suddenly the prisons became nice places. But Native People in Saskatchewan's detention system were newly allowed religious clergy visits, observance of ceremonial days, basic reading and math skills courses and access to some health care. What a good use of public focus. What a small but meaningful victory! What an example of an effective demonstration.

The object of a demonstration is *to demonstrate* something to a wider public; to take an action that is connected to—or symbolic of—a situation. By making that action we educate a wider public to the problem and—hopefully—to the solution. It's not always a matter of huge numbers of people. It's a matter of how clearly the idea is *demonstrated*.

It's so easy to be disappointed by progressives' or radicals' ideas of what a demonstration should do. Demos to 'close down the xyz' or to 'stop the abc' are almost always disappointments because they don't immediately shut down or stop cold the problem. No. A successful demonstration is one that opens a larger public's eyes, so the larger public can take the actions to make change.

We shuttled back slowly to the Village of Nations. It was a good end to a remarkable journey. On the way back home my sister Isha and I visited Karen's mother, Gerry McPherson, who was then a professor at the University in Saskatoon. She was teaching sociology and knew all about the problems of Native American rights in the Provinces. I asked her about solutions. "Education," she pondered aloud, "education, starting right in childhood, that's the best solution I know."

PART TEN

In the Canyons of the City
(1983–1984)

The lessons of this generation blossom forth in actions that return to our roots in the city. The Theatre returns from its decades-long tour in foreign lands leaving a changed world in its wake, and we receive clues about the unfolding of the future from a utopian architect.

48. Gardenopolis

After twelve years of back-to-the-land life in the hills of Oregon we still had not solved the economic puzzle. Granted that early-on much of that time had been spent struggling with community dynamics, and our own personal foibles or 'issues' as they later came to be called; granted that we had strayed into territory both social and agricultural that we had no real training for; granted that we were young, full of belief and enthusiasm but without experience, without knowledge and without tradition; granted that we were stoned on organics as well as inorganics; *granted all these* it's a wonder that we survived as long and as well as we did.

We did become much more mellow just as aging country casks should get. And we did learn how to produce the produce, to coax the bountiful harvest right out of the earth. But marketing was another matter. And preserving freshness en route to market still another. And storage was another. And transportation, weighing, packaging, bagging, boxing, lifting, loading. All of these are steps in the economic reality of farming, especially for the new foundling 'Organic Farming,' where the steady routes from field to consumer market weren't yet established.

Even after all the plowing and tilling and planting and growing (and the season's worth of maneuvers with equipment and irrigation) many more steps remained before there was any economic return.

Also, we were subject to the conundrum of 'Competitive Good Ideas.' Multiple good ideas could be put forward by several very enthusiastic participants. And in our collaborative style we tried to accommodate everyone. We were good at making room for everybody's plans, but we were not at all skilled in the taking-*and*-giving art of compromise. So instead of one marketable crop being planted on the 'gentle slope below the road' we'd end up with four smaller crops—harder to water, harder to care for and much harder to find a market for. The Farmer's Market in Eugene, 50 miles away, wouldn't even be open for another five years. And in town? Our sweet backwoods logging town? No local farmers' market there even by the turn of the millennium.

Plus, when a part burst on the water pump or the tractor's carburetor, there went hundreds of dollars, looking to me like bushels of organic Italian Romano green beans turning themselves into finely tooled small metal parts. And the mechanical work that went along with it consumed more time than I'd ever imagined. It was constant wrangling with the equipment: hitches, motors, valves, rotors, *huge* tires to change. To run a farm you have to be able to run a full machine shop too.

The fall field crops were harvested, seeds and garlic were drying. My cousin was getting married in Denver, so I took a thirty-day bus ticket to go to the wedding in Denver and then visit my daughter Eden, now in middle school on the East Coast.

Eden was thriving in the Connecticut public schools and her mother, Karen, was wrapping up her own graduate studies at Yale. I stopped in New York on the return trip where I still had a key and access to my grandparents' old apartment.

It was my parents' now, and they were still away on the endless pilgrimage tour—Scandinavia for the third time, residencies in Italy and France, touring a dozen cities in Spain, travelling up and down Eastern Europe where among other public venues they played a seriously clandestine performance in a darkened basement in Czechoslovakia during the hardest-line days of Soviet control, and in Sicily they produced Judith's translation of Brecht's version of Sophocles' *Antigone* in the grand, ancient amphitheatre *where the play had first opened* (!) two millennia ago while Sophocles was still alive.

There was no reason not to hole up in the apartment for a few days and see old friends in the city.

Even a cheap bus ticket can cost more than it seems: there are endless stops and (for a vegetarian) endless grilled cheese sandwiches. But there wasn't any new money coming in, and in the time it takes to get from 'here to there' a lot of days go by, so by the time you're 'there' there's less money in your pocket than you ever planned. Just ask anyone who's done long distance bus travel.

I called up a few old pals, walked downtown, all 110 blocks to save the subway fare and bought a few oranges instead.

Joanee Freedom was living in a run-down duplex loft in the then-very-wild East Village. Joanee was heating the place with a woodstove. We scavenged wood from old broken pallets and anything wooden in the trash on the streets. The landlords of her building had also quit making any repairs. Because the neighborhood was so dilapidated, drug-ridden and crime-prone, the rents were so low that they didn't cover repairs and greedy slime-bucket building owners wouldn't dip into their century's worth of profits to fix the places so there could be (at minimum) hot and cold water, heat, light, and safe stairs. But in her building the tenants had taken on the jobs themselves. Celtic Bard and constructionist David Boyle lived there and engineered the community aspect of building renovation. They patched roofs; they fixed staircases; they repaired the electric. And they stopped paying rent. They even put solar panels on the roof.

Inside her loft Joanee was silk-screening banners, posters and tee shirts for the first ever Whole Life Expo. It was being held the following week at some gigantic uptown hotel. Her friends have a food booth there and could use some help flipping veggie burgers. It's a dawn-to-night job but it pays ... a hundred dollars a day. And it's a four-day affair. I can hardly turn it down.

By the end of the Expo there are thirty restaurants and independent health food stores signed up to receive our burgers. Now all of a sudden we've really got work to do. There's bakery space being rented to produce the burgers and I've got a job. It seemed like it happened in the blink of eye.

I return to Oregon still inside my thirty-day's ride, tie up a few loose ends and pack my bags for the return to the Big Apple.

In a couple more months I have an apartment shared with a young artist, Alex Rotner, on the top floor of a six-floor walk-up just around the corner from Joanee's.

Joanee has the big idea to bring the Rainbow Gatherings somehow into the city. We meet with Mike, a philosophical wizard—and wiseguy—who is trying to make working examples that can help some of the homeless young people who are out on the streets. He runs both a crafts business and a construction business. He's been rescuing 'displaced' (aka homeless) young people and teaching them how to make simple craft items for resale and also how to do basic carpentry. They build loft spaces in the city's tiny apartments and renovate run down studios to make them more livable. Artist Brant Kingman and his dancer girlfriend Wingbow are meeting with us too, and all together we conceive of holding a Rainbow-style picnic in Central Park. Wingbow draws up a flyer with a big apple and rainbow logo and we choose the third Sunday of May as our target date.

Word is spread through the Rainbow grapevine and that is the beginning of the many potluck Rainbow picnics that have occurred ever since in New York's Central Park… and in many other cities' public parks as well. In a few years time, the New York picnics grow huge with giant circles of people holding hands in a Circle of Grace before the picnic feast.

I was beginning to see how the ideas inherent in the Rainbow experience could translate into an urban setting.

Directly kitty-corner from Joanee's loftspace loomed a colossal even-more-run-down skeleton of a building. There was a flophouse on one end of it, a dice hall in the corridor on the eastern side, a bordello wagon that parked every evening on the north and a crackhouse on the far other end. Why, in an old huge rathouse like that there was room for everybody. The owners had long ago stopped making repairs; the tenants had long ago stopped paying rent. The building had slowly been stripped of all its valuable fixtures: copper wire, railings, flooring, plumbing all torn out by

Figure 97: A thousand or more people holding hands in a Circle for Peace before the meal at the Rainbow Picnic in Central Park, New York City. (Garrick Beck: 1986)

hands willing to sell it for scrap. The owners defaulted on the taxes and now the City owned this dissolute harbor.

The following winter during an ice storm, tiles and bricks slide off the roof. They land Ka-blam! on the streets and sidewalks below. The city has no choice but to rope off the corner and begin plans for demolition. In the end they leave a rubble-heaped open lot.

Behind one of the hills of brick bats and iron parts—almost entirely hidden from the street—Joanee dumps some soil and plants some tomatoes. By mid-summer her plants are knee high and look!—there's another patch of green behind another rubble mound. There's someone else gardening! It's Melinda Futrell, the black community activist who lives one block south. From Joanee and Melinda's alliance sprang a vital and vigorous community movement. Sure, there were community gardens in the neighborhood before this. But most of them were 'fiefdoms'—small city

lots held by one group of friends or relatives, gardened and protected but not really open to the community or the city. Yes, there were others, even nearby, whose members formed not-for-profits or community trusts.

But out of this particular alliance there grew a network of community gardeners, *and* a neighborhood harvest fair, *and* a series of arts events and poetry readings and a community stage got erected where performances—open and free to the public—became regular events, *and* a program for the elderly in the home nearby and so on. The community garden founded on that spot became a nexus for the neighborhood and *all* its people.

By then, my son Tameron was living with me and going to pre-school at Children's Liberation, a school which had been formed from the union of two 1960s-founded daycares. They asked all the parents to come up with some activities the classes could do. I had a connection in the children's theatre world that could let me invite a couple of the classes to their puppet shows.

I got the 60 tickets for two classes from Marc, a puppeteer who lived just downstairs from Joanee, and Tameron's school arranged for all the grownup chaperones needed to move the youngsters through the subway system.

It was a sweltering day. The air conditioning was off in the subways. The trains were hot and densely packed. Midtown was steaming. Cars and people rushing everywhere. By the time we got to the midtown theatre the children were ready for a nice romp in a cool green park. Instead they got moved through stairways and halls and told to sit quietly in their seats. They were bouncing off the walls. There were two other school contingents: one a religious school all in matching uniforms, and the other another private school, all the well-dressed children stepping off air-conditioned busses that had brought them into the city. They were *very* well behaved. Our kids wanted to jump and climb and play. It was a very trying experience.

True, the folks back at Kids Lib gave me credit for trying. But it was months before I gained the courage to propose another outing. This time I suggested bringing a class to our nearby community garden.

And this was a different experience entirely. In the cool green-shaded morning with all those amazing plants, flowers, bushes and trees, there were interesting sculptures, and rocked walkways between the garden plots that the children could follow like a maze. As we toured along the pathway I found myself telling little stories about the plants, their leaves, the roots and stems. I watched myself as the children watched, fascinated.

"Does anyone know how plants breathe? Do plants breathe? Yes, they do. Well, where do they breathe from? Okay, make your two hands like a leaf: put your two palms *together* and turn them flat, so the back of one hand is down, and the back of the other is up, facing the sun. That's right. Just like that. Doesn't the part of your hand facing the sun feel warm? Sure it does. Well that's where the plant gets its energy, the strength to grow. And the

Figure 98. Before and After (i): The 6th Street and Avenue B Community Garden. (Joanee Freedom: 1982)

Figure 99. Before and After (ii): The 6th Street and Avenue B Community Garden. (Garrick Beck: 2003)

part of your hands facing down... the 'bottom' of the leaf: what happens there? No one knows? Well, that part of the leaf has tiny, tiny holes and that's where the plant breathes from! Yes, that's right, it's true for all the leaves on *every* plant. Do you think you can remember that?" All their heads nod vigorously.

The children spent some time scampering about the garden and we returned easily to the school. I saw that the experience in the garden wasn't just recreational, it had the essence of education built into it.

Over the next few years this turned into a program involving thousands of schoolchildren transforming dozens of vacant lots into oases of green in the canyons of our city.

First we brought the Purple Room and the Blue Room students from Children's Lib to the garden on a regular basis. The garden had common areas used by all the members and the public, but there were also individual plots (mostly 4 by 8 feet) that each member maintained. Through the garden meetings we got each class its own individual garden plot. Initially there was some controversy about encouraging children in the garden. "It's not a playground." "They'll pull up flowers and plants and they don't know the difference between a garden bed and a place to play." "The shrubs and plants in the city parks are much hardier than what we grow. We have a lot of delicate plants here."

But the responses (of which I was a part): "The children are the real future of the garden. We have to teach them so 10 years from now they'll be teenagers who are respecting and protecting this place." "How are they going to learn to love and care for nature if we don't show them?" The responses carried the day. I agreed to draw up a poster directed towards parents about how to supervise their children in the garden areas. Eventually a small children's playspace and sandbox got built. But at the start we got the Purple and Blue Room classes each a 4-by-8 foot area to plant and tend.

Over the next seasons I learned that I could meet classes once every week and gear an activity to the cycle of growth for that time

Figures 100 & 101. The 6th Street & Avenue B Garden, open to the public, with the handprints of all the gardeners embedded in its border and gate design. (Garrick Beck: 2013)

of year. There were some natural progressions. First we'd plant marigold and radish seeds and learn to use the watering can. The marigolds had the most distinctive seeds: sort of arrow-y feathery things. The radishes would come up first (usually by the next week) in bright green easy-to-see rows. Then the marigolds would poke their first little leaves up. We did the digging with hand trowels. Later we would bring plant starts (little plants in tiny pots grown at a plant nursery) and the children would learn the difference between 'planting' and '*trans*-planting' as they carefully took the little plants out of their containers and placed them into the small hole their partner had dug. Then they'd cover the little roots gently with soil and pat it down just like they were tucking a baby into bed.

We used marigold transplants so there could be bright yellow and orange flowers already blossoming while whatever we were planting from seeds got started. Before the end of the spring the flowers we planted from seed were just starting to bloom … and the *trans*-planted marigolds' first flowers were now wilted, turning brown and drying up. I take one of the dried flower heads in my hands. I stoop low so all the children can see and I open up the base of the dried flower. What do they see packed inside? Tiny seeds. Looking exactly like the flower seeds they planted, the little pointy things with the feathery tail! Dry and ready to plant again. Eye-opening lessons like this stay with us the rest of our lives.

Christine Datz, another great East Village activist, brings classes from another school. Between her two classes and my two classes—and the children of the members and the neighbors—the garden is becoming known as a place that's good for children.

We get photographed and photographed again. People stop all the time to watch the classes in the garden. One day a group steps from a van, tours through the garden, watches us for a while and then, before they leave one of the group hands me a note and asks me to get in touch. So a few days later I'm downtown at the offices of The Trust for Public Land. They have helped the garden by sponsoring training weekends in the past where ordinary people can learn about committees, agendas, note taking, how Robert's Rules of Order can help manage a community garden's meetings, and similar skills to help the community, *our* community, run its garden.

Now it's being suggested that an educational program like the one they saw there last week could be incorporated into public schools. I tell them, "I'm your guy. Let's make this happen." I know how to direct the classes and how there can be a program based on once-a-week class sessions. "These can run from just before spring break until school closes for the summer." The Trust for Public Land people explain they are planning to work on contacting and hopefully making arrangements with The City's school system.

By the next spring we have opened a pilot program with two public elementary schools. One will use garden beds in an already-existing community garden and the other will use a vacant, rubble-strewn area of its own schoolyard.

Jackie Betz, who I know from years at the Rainbow Gatherings, is an award-winning public school science teacher. She comes up from Florida visiting me and other friends in New York. She watches me with a couple of classes and she explains that what I'm teaching is really the life cycle of the plants.' "Each of these weekly classes you're teaching is a lesson," she tells me. "You need to write down these lessons. That's what a curriculum is. Make a curriculum guide so the teachers in the classes can work along with you, so they can prepare the students with additional activities, so they have a vocabulary list afterward." Jackie is encouraging me to work with whichever teachers seem most interested to develop this guide.

One enthusiastic second grade science teacher, Julie Kirkpatrick, leads me through the arcane language of 'science learning objectives' at the State level, at the Federal level, and here in New York, even at the City level. I pore through the big volumes that enumerate 'learning.' Jackie sends me examples of science lesson plans for the second to fourth grades. Another eager teacher,

Mary Nissen, schools *me* in the unique dynamics of the City's schools' processes. There are things you can't say, custodians to be worked with, parents with concerns, principals, vice-principals and permissions for taking the children outside the school building. Mary guides me through all of these and more. She works with me to encourage in-class lessons that back up the hands-on outside lessons, and to create drawn or written workbook pages for the students to fill in.

I contact my friend Jay Kurley, another friend from the Rainbow Gatherings. He's a grade school teacher from California whose classes have been used to evaluate numerous proposed science programs. He helped develop a 'Lifelab' curriculum where there is indoor equipment set up to study agriculture and biology. He sends me examples of whole sets of lessons—curriculum guides for children's science programs. I am beginning to see how these in-the-field lessons I am giving can be translated into lesson plans and activity guides that can be used by teachers who can teach the program themselves.

I began writing the outline for each week's lessons according to templates of lesson guides already in use. A parochial school contacted us and we began classes with their students at a fourth garden location. Another progressive kindergarten asked us to find a garden we can bring their kids to.

After two years of tracking the progression of the four public school classes, it became clear that the gardening program helped improve the students' science test results. The city was encouraging the Trust for Public Land to continue sponsoring the program. Andy Stone, who became the Program Director for this at TPL, was a convincing advocate with the city, the community boards, the gardens, and the Department of Education. I was caught between the best of both worlds: on one side schools wanted the gardens and on the other, gardens wanted the schools.

Over the next years the Childrens Gardening Program flourished. It spread to South Jamaica, Queens; the South Bronx;

Figure 102 (i–iv). In the pilot program we began with a city-owned vacant lot adjacent to a public elementary school. (Garrick Beck: 1984)

Harlem; the edge of Chinatown—anywhere there were vacant lots. I pitched the advantages of this program to the city schools science program advisors, to the community boards, to parent groups, to gardeners' alliances.

I never had been part of anything so good that had so little opposition.

A young energetic and innovative teacher, Paula Watson, originally from Children's Lib, joined the program full-time. She supplied the hand-inked illustrations that made clear many of the activities described in the curriculum guide. The book, *Plant and Grow!* by Paula and me was finished and printed. We began a formal program to teach teachers the program. Paula designed a hands-on build-a-garden-bed activity with pre-drilled 2x6 and 2x10 lumber. We introduced a mentor program so program 'graduates' now in middle school or high school could assist in teaching the classes. We grew 'wheatfields' two feet by two feet square and explained that most wheatfields were "as big as New York

Figure 103 (i & ii). The same vacant lot after working with parents, students, teacher, school custodians and the community to create a growing and learning environment. (Garrick Beck: 1984)

City!" We drew the buds week-by-week as they developed on trees. Students learned multiplication because they saw three rows of tomatoes with four tomato plants in each row. We added a special component to learn about worms. Worms!? The children *loved* it. We used a scaled down version of the worm beds the South Bronx composters had shown us years ago. We asked the children what they'd like to grow most. Over and over again one of the answers I heard was, "Grass to sit on." So we began to include an ordinary grassy area as part of the garden's design. It seemed that everywhere I turned the program was sprouting and proliferating just like plants gone wild under ideal conditions.

Everything I'd learned in Oregon on the farm had suddenly become useful in these narrow greenlandia at the feet of the tall cliff-like buildings. Here in the dry canyons of the city, I could see the greenery returning.

I learned to work with the school custodians. They are a force to be reckoned with. Without their help nothing moves. But my years in Oregon also showed me how to be plainspoken and direct. We held up our end of the agreements with the custodians and they held up theirs.

In the more devastated inner city neighborhoods the available vacant lots were horrific messes to start with. It was too much to ask parent or neighborhood groups to come for an evening to clean it up. Some of these lots had been dumps for years. So TPL arranged for prisoners from Rikers Island to come under armed guard escort as part of a day-release program where they donned thick gloves and used rakes to clear and level the lots. Once that was done the creative part of gardening could begin.

The students moved soil with wheelbarrows. They planted shade and fruit trees. We hand-built rock walkways with rubble. They planted rose bushes and we built trellises for them out of bamboo. They grew snap peas and slender baby carrots and ate them in the lunchroom. Some classes harvested the wheat, 'threshed' it back at the classroom, ground it up and baked their own cookies.

Figure 104 (i & ii). The children loved it, the community enjoyed it, and students' science test scores improved dramatically. (Garrick Beck: 1984)

The program was covered by network newscasts. *Green Card*, a goofy romantic Hollywood film about community gardens, used children from our program for its cast. Some people said The Trust for Public Land was using the program as a fundraising

Figure 105 (i–iv). The children learn tool use and teamwork as well as gardening techniques. New York City. (Garrick Beck: 1985)

showcase. I said "So what? I'm using TPL to further my own aims; TPL is using me to advance its efforts; the city is using its neglected property; the children are using their hands and brains, the schools are using once-vacant lots as if they were quarter-of-a-million-dollar science classrooms; the neighborhoods are using the gardens as little paradises of green in the jumble of their city. It looks like a win-win-win-win-win-win situation to me."

Figure 106. From vacant lots to community gardens in the cement canyons of New York City. (Garrick Beck: 1985)

49. The Return of the Theatre

When The Living Theatre returned from its 'extended tour' in the winter of 1983 the art scene in New York was a different place. The great playful art of the beatnik era had multiplied. And moved in different directions.

Instead of a few bold galleries hosting unusual painting, there were galleries from Harlem to Brooklyn, galleries on *every block* of the East Village. Action painting, collage, construction, abstract, pop art, neo-this and post-neo-that. There were now *thousands* of struggling painters. And the original Beat painters were being 'inducted' into the lofty art history heights as The New York School, aka The Abstract Expressionists.

Instead of a few daring clubs with an open mic for spoken word, there were more venues than nights of the week to visit them. ABC No Rio, The Knitting Factory, The Fort, Gargoyle Mechanique, 8BC, Café Bustelo. Folkies playing folk, poets reciting, and performance artists carrying on *by the hundreds*. All adept, all heartfelt, all creative, some even bound for celebrity and fame.

Instead of a few underground late night jazz masters, jazz was everywhere. Uptown, downtown, out-of-town, everywhere. Some of the greats, like Don Cherry, trumpeter, came to visit the seriously underground East Village Shuttle Club bringing his classic sound into the amalgam of the new jazz frontier. Jazz was everywhere—as well it should be—integrated into the mainstream sound.

The world of advertising had opened its doors to a new generation of graphics and video artists who easily adapted the optical art, pop art, surrealism, dada, collage and paint-splattering styles. They made the innovations of the Beat era painters commonly available and put them to use in eye-popping TV commercials and slick-paged magazine ads. But the audience-involving live action of The Living Theatre was light years away from the new remote controls that so easily changed the channels on the TVs in people's living rooms. To most of these young graphic/sound/design/video artists the Beat era and its associated plays, poetries and performances were honored but bygone history.

It was a dance company that made the decision to bring The Living Theatre back across the Atlantic and produce 'Le Living' (as they were called in Europe) at their own Joyce Theater. These were the people in the family circle of the Feld Ballet Company. They had converted an old 'midnight movie' house on Eighth Avenue, turning it into a beautiful jewel box of a theater. They remembered The Living from the strongest days of the Off-Broadway theatre experiments. Julian and Judith thought the time was right for a return to the city of their beginnings. They had played 44 countries in over 20 languages, and brought modern theatrical productions to South America, Africa, Scandinavia and Eastern Europe. They had played for free in churchyards, hospitals, school auditoriums and in the small theaters of countless towns of Europe. They had played the major theater districts of Paris, Rome and London. Often they would translate key passages into the language of the country they were playing. Or do as the playwright Brecht did: add a series of 'bridge' lines that briefly described the action—like the sidenotes in Coleridge's *Rime of the Ancient Mariner*—which could be spoken in the language of the people in the audience. No other American theatre company, no other theatre company period, did anything like that.

The last time the company had been in the United States was a decade earlier when they had come for a season and created the play, *The Money Tower*. That outdoor epic was built around a five-story construction that was meant to be put up and played outdoors near factory environments. The top story had a giant revolving green neon dollar sign and that was the place of the 'super rich.' Each story below was broader so the whole thing was like a slender pyramid. The next floor down was held by the military and the police. Below them were the white collar workers. On the floor below that were the blue collar workers and on the very bottom, the poor and the unemployed. Paper money is dispensed from the top, fluttering to the grasping hands below. The play enacts many realistic scenes: the spiral of inflation, the pain of the underclass, and the fear employees have of losing their jobs.

The structure gets built in plain sight of the industrial zone where the performance is to take place. The production is played in less than an hour during the change of shifts. So the factory folks have seen these bohemian actors and actresses building the steel construction all day long; then the shift changes and the

Figure 107. The Living Theatre's spectacular production, *The Money Tower*. (Photographer unknown: Courtesy of The Living Theatre Archives: 1975)

play begins. In the middle of the construction is an elevator, really a small dumbwaiter that brings props and people up and down the money tower. At the heart of the play the elevator gets stuck, breaks and 'kills' a performer. Then there is a long argument on the money tower about what to do. The classic arguments:

"Forget about it. Just be more careful than he was when you're near the elevator."

"We should petition the management to put in a safer elevator."

"They'll never do that."

"We should strike if they won't give us a safer workplace."

"Do that and *you* won't have *any* workplace."

"There was someone killed last year too. In the same elevator. We gotta get some changes. Next time it could be me."

"Strike!"

"No way. No strike for me. I got a family I'm supporting. I'm not going to get fired, lose *my* wages."

And then one of the performers turns to the audience and says, "What do I know? I'm an actor not a factory worker. You, you tell me what we should do!" Throwing the discussion open to the workers changing shifts. Real theatre.

Because of their 'leftist' social leanings and willingness to criticize the United States, The Living Theatre got invited by the Italian Communist Student Arts League to do a tour in Soviet bloc Eastern Europe. They played in Poland and performed near the shipyards at Gdansk. Standing in that audience that day were the core of the early Solidarity Movement. Strike? What do *you* think? What did they think! Months later they went on strike at those shipyards and the whole entire complex of the Soviet dominated domino states tumbled down. Don't ever let it be said that art does not walk hand-in-hand with history.

Coming back to the United States, Julian and Judith and the 23-person company brought four plays. The classic, *Antigone*, the anti-war masterpiece that simply won't go out of style. As long as we make wars it just needs to be played. A revival of *Mysteries and Smaller Pieces*, the trance-like production from the 1960s. A new production, *The Yellow Methuselah*, combining the text of George Bernard Shaw with the design and style of Vassily Kandinsky. The theme was the quest for immortality. Julian painted the largest-ever (at the time) canvas painting that ran as a slowly moving backdrop—from two gigantic rollers—across the back of the stage. An homage to Kandinsky's painting styles, it moved ever so slowly inch by inch behind the actors as they performed Shaw's play about the quest for extended life.

The fourth play, *The Archaeology of Sleep*, was something *entirely* different.

Julian wanted to do something more than tell another story in a beautiful style (or a poetic style) (or a political style) (or an audience involving style) (or any regular tried and true dramatic style). The modern motion picture industry had become so adept at storytelling with all the available techniques and technologies. Theatre, live theatre, is of course different. It has the power to affect us deeply. But how does live theatre do more than tell a story? How does a creator of theatre-type spectacle reach beyond the old-fashioned world of stage-play storytelling?

To do this Julian needed a theme that could be well presented by the multi-layered possibilities: sounds, lights, songs, actions, acrobatics of actors and the extension of that energy beyond the stage.... So he chose sleep, whose dreams are themselves very like the kind of production Julian was envisioning. *The Archaeology of Sleep*, an exploration of the depths as Julian put it, "of the largest unexplored realm on Earth...the sleeping mind."

The play's 'plot' consisted of the dreams of the real cast members, mixed into the personalities of cats in an old-style sleep laboratory. The scenography of the play follows the true sleep cycle of the human being: alpha, beta, delta, gamma, the 'REM' cycle, the stages of entering sleep, breathing cycles, twitching, dreams.... And the cats and the cast enact dramas of great beauty and great terror, eros and wonder, in a multi-imaged experience more like a trance than a play-in-three-acts. Many of the dreams were so beautiful like those tiny 'Christmas' souvenirs that you hold in your hand and shake and a scene of a city or cathedral is shimmering with tiny snowflakes, all in your palm, and chimes are softly gongalaling in the distance. But does it tell a story in the traditional sense? Well, there's a maniacal doctor (obviously the evil authority figure) and certainly some animal rights themes, but a story? Only the stories of each of the cast members' dreams.

Just as Julian's collage paintings of the mid-1950s heralded a new multi-layered form of seeing into the canvas' depths, here Julian was making an overlay of images, one melting into the next to be presented to the spectator, live and coming from all sides, tantalizing, touching, inviting the spectators to join in. In several sequences, how the spectators choose or choose *not* to participate affected the course of the play's action.

The press in New York was abuzz. Every media ran stories about the Theatre's history, its adventures, the foreign acclaim, the prizes, the various causes the group had supported around the world. All good press. I gushed about this to Judith. She raised a warning eyebrow and explained how the press loves to put someone on a pedestal and then Whack! knock them off. "It's the reviews that really matter," she said knowingly.

We got the whole company housed in New York. The giant downtown arts collectives Charas and Quando opened up rehearsal space and set-building space for us and we hustled to get the four plays ready to open in rapid succession. My own experience on the farm gave me tool handiness. Joanee Freedom worked with Julian on the costumes. Languages were everywhere as the company spoke to each other in a potpourri of tongues.

The Joyce management was gracious and supportive. We loaded in the sets and began the run.

Opening night was packed. The lights went down, hush enveloped the room and the descent into the realm of sleep had begun.

Oh, how the press loved to hate us. First, they berated everyone's accents: Scandinavian, Eastern European, European,... this to a company that had brought Americanized English plays into countless foreign dialects. But more important, *much* more important: they didn't get the imagistic, multi-layered live theatre experience. Where is the theater that used to discuss political ideas? Or, where is the plot to this? What is all this supposed to be about? Who are they to be *touching* audience members? Asking *us* questions? The same old incomprehensible Off-Broadway stuff that we didn't like twenty years ago either!

A few of the small press and politically far left magazines had nice things to say—especially about the time-honored *Antigone* production—Judith's translation of Brecht's adaption of Sophocles' anti-war masterpiece. But the valuable New York 'quotable' press that inspired box office revenue was simply not on our side.

The old friends of the theater all came to see the plays, of course. So there were endless reunions in the green room and lobby after the shows. Many of the old Beats were more staid in appearance; the academic look having overtaken the firebrand. Many still spoke affectionately of the dreams of a more poetic society and were clearly astounded that the Great Changes hadn't already descended on all of us! Pretty much everybody was involved in neighborhood environmental or educational causes. And all were still relentlessly productive: music, writing, teaching, filming, sculpting, painting, etcetera.

Practically all of the city's young performance artists, the experimental visual and political artists came to see the performances. But that is not a large group, even in New York. Beyond that? Into the masses of, say, college students, or nightlife partiers, or well-off theater-goers or tourists who might get tickets to an Off-Broadway feature? Hardly. And that hurt. Because to sustain a run in The City you have to tap into those groups' economic power to survive.

The Empire of the West was going to be a harder nut to crack than the Soviet Union.

50. Percival's Story

Shortly after my arrival back in New York City, as the winter chill was beginning to set in, I called on many of my old friends for visits. Steve Ben Israel was one of the Living Theatre greats, having been central to the tremendous productions of *The Brig, Frankenstein, Antigone* and *Paradise Now*. I stopped over at his place and he cooked up a marvelous kasha dish while we spoke about so many people from our past.

I wondered aloud what I would be doing for winter holidays and Steve reminded me about the Eve after Christmas Eve party at the home of Naomi and Percival Goodman. This intellectual couple brought together their many friends, and their friends' children, for an end-of-year soiree and philosophical re-capping.

During my childhood we went just about every year, my parents and I, to the Goodman's home, just across the street from the old castle-like entranceway of the Museum of Natural History. The grownups pondered the same old ageless questions while we kids ran about—Joel, Percival's oldest leading the way, making moiré patterns out of television static with a set of revolving discs (some kind of scientific Christmas gift) and painting designs on the furniture legs with the new holiday gift paint set.

Percival was an architect. His outstanding chapel graced the hills above Colorado Springs' Air Force Academy and his work encompassed a host of inspired dwellings and public places as well as a professorship at Columbia University.

His younger brother, Paul, was by trade a psychologist, but was truly a challenging philosopher whose conversational intrigues and dialogues had already made him one of the fountainheads of the entire Beat Generation. He influenced everybody, raised each ordinary conversation to the level where cause, motive, will and the ethics of each action were debated and pondered so the thoughts of people advanced through their own self inquiry.

He stood like a Socratic character; here assembled about him are a band of young thinkers, painters, dancers, writers, poets and political activists and he tests them all with criticism and wit—why wait for some appointment or seminar—just get on with figuring it out right now—and he sends forth his ideas of ethical action through the art of his contemporaries. Everyone in that whole New York arts and intellectual scene respected him. Paul's pipe-smoking, academic scholarly approach met the wild free Beatnik fun-loving artistic spontaneity and he knotted together a socially aware creative force that felt the tides of evolution in its veins, and engaged the minds of a creative culture to put forth a message—a beatific message—as Kerouac said it—to an as yet unheralded generation.

Paul wrote a slew of books and essays. Powerful stuff. *Growing Up Absurd*, his classic treatise on mis-education in America; *People or Personnel,* his writings about how people are treated and mistreated in the modern industrial state; and a majestic novel—*The Empire City*—about the metaphoric rise and fall of rich and poor in New York. He also penned a decisive philosophical work called *Drawing the Line* about how each of us interprets ethical choices and then "draws a line"—according to our own conscious dictates—between what we call right and what we call wrong.

Years before, in 1948, the brothers Paul and Percival wrote a book *together*. It was called *Communitas* and it merged Paul's social theory with Percy's architectural insights. *Communitas* was abundantly illustrated and described and advocated a new style of human environment. One that combined the best of modern urban culture with the best of greenspaces, waterways, fertile farms, educational and healthcare structures, recreational areas and industrial zones—all mapped out in a harmonic order that even today—over half a century later seems more like some utopian dream than a wonderful or genuine goal that we have moved even a couple of inches toward. What a piece of work is this book—the forerunner of so many of the concepts laid out years later by Stewart Brand who was inspired in part by their work to mint his Whole Earth Catalogs. *Communitas* is the first advocate for incorporating solar and wind power on a massive scale into the grids of urban electricity, and of urban greenbelts, and of the European model "Urban Ring" cityscapes, and on and on....

Paul had been close with The Living Theatre. He wrote one of the first plays they ever produced, *Childish Jokes*, and the third of the major plays they put up at the 14th Street theatre, *The Cave at Machpelah*. It told the story of the reunion of Isaac and Ishmael at the death of Father Abraham, a family feud issue that is still today—obviously—unresolved. James Earl Jones splendidly played Black Ishmael, the magnificent outcast.

Paul wrote a short comedy that was part of a Monday Night series of one act plays, so as a child actor I had the opportunity to perform in his tale of an underdog boy who outfoxes his bullies.

The Goodmans and their crowd also held an annual softball game at a field on Roosevelt Island, which stretches its slender self north-south in the East River between the boroughs of Queens and Manhattan. We'd walk over the arching footbridge and out onto one of the playing fields below. Matthew, Paul's son, grew in those years to become the power hitter on whichever team chose him, but the rest of us kids were mostly too little at 8-9-10-11 years old, so we ambled and played about, encouraged every year to do some batting to slow pitches for fun and practice after the game. Still, there they were: Beatniks at Play, and under the shady sycamore trees, ourselves playing in their shadows.

Now, decades later, later I found myself back in New York again. Paul, I know, had passed some years ago to the world ahead of us, but Steve Ben tells me that Percival survives along with Naomi, and that at 79 years he's still teaching one day a week at Columbia University. So on a cold solstice day I look up their number and call. Naomi answers the phone unsure about who I am, but I identify myself through my parents and she exclaims, "Well of course you'll come over for the holiday party. How many years has it been?—Please, please, don't hesitate to come by. I'll be sure to tell Percy you're coming."

The next evening I stroll by the site of the Women's House of Detention—another regular stop on my childhood Christmases in New York. It really *has* become a public garden now. Although closed at this hour, a welcoming sign posts its open times. There are walkways, flowerbeds, benches for sitting in the sun, a fountain. It seems that we have advanced in some small ways at least.

Three evenings later I'm ringing the doorbell at the Goodman's apartment. The glow of many bright lights and the hubbub of many guests greet me. I am ushered in, put my small house-visiting gifts under the tree and am welcomed by Percival.

He sizes me up, one hand on the outside of each shoulder—he is a small man himself. "Well," he says, his head nodding as he looks me up and down, "well, you seem to be doing quite OK for yourself. He smiles, and his unobtrusive question prompts me to answer, "Thankfully, yes, I'm in good health."

But without further small talk he turns us both around toward the mix of people in the larger rooms before us. "I don't know just who here you are acquainted with, it's been such a while."

I owned up, "Off the top of my memory, I don't recognize anybody."

"Well then," continued my adept white-haired host, "Let me introduce you to this cluster of fine companions." And he leads me towards a standing circle of drink-holding folks a few years older than myself. "Go on, just all of you introduce yourselves. This is Garry," he remarked (referring to me by the name I was called as a child) as he led me into their perimeter. "He's been out West a few years...." He begins to turn away and back to his other hostly duties, then turns his head again, "I'm sure you'll find yourself in most excellent company." He twinkles his eyes and slowly turns back to his many guests.

His lead-in lends itself to my new companions—whose lives are old friends to each other's already. It leads them to ask after my 'Western sojourn' which gives me grace for easy, summary answers about leaving New York for Reed in 1967, living on an organic farm in collective counter-culture experimental fashion, working with alternative energy, "and other projects" to leave as much unsaid as said.

The next while was spent in what must be one of our species' attainable goals: insightful conversation. Mutually or collectively undertaken, or by turns led by a particular participant, alternatively questioned or challenged by others, with each other's comments, building idea by idea, and based—in the very best cases—on our experiences and expertise. Thus does good conversation proceed, resulting in what has—since the development of language—been called 'contemporary thought'—the current thinking of our current time. This is how our human culture evolves ideas—by talking about them!

Not that we five or so figures, standing together that eve had any aspirations to earth-shaking insights, still we touched on small-press publishing, the media agglomerates, brain chemistry, the question of whether there is any neurological truth to the conventional 'new age' wisdom that our 'right brain' and our 'left brain' have certain divisions of power relating to artistry and creativity on the one side, and organization and analysis on the other. We rallied to another small circle of guests to buttonhole a professional neurological researcher for his considered opinion. And so the evening flowed along.

None of the Goodman children were in attendance that year and I missed seeing them, though some of the guests did remember me from long ago and told only moderately embarrassing stories about we zany youngsters.

On the way out at evening's end, Percival asks, "Are you free next week sometime? We're having a *small* dinner (he names a January date) and we'd love to have you over as well." I'm completely pleased he'd even consider extending such an invitation.

My evenings are all open. "Yes. Sure I could make it."

"Good. Then please come. It's so hard to talk at length at these big get-togethers."

The following dinner at the Goodman's was with three other Goodman friends—we made a full table and Percival and Naomi took gracious turns asking each guest about their latest projects, families and prospects. They inquired of me about the travels and sagas of the Living Theatre, and the lives of other particular friends of the theatre who were friends of theirs. Some I knew and some not.

As to myself, they asked and I told briefly the highlights of my progression from Reed through Drain, Oregon and back through to New York. They followed with some interest in the whole-systems, close-to-the-earth approach of the Drain farm and the application of the ideas gained to my just-beginning children's gardening program here in the city. Then I described the Gatherings. As best I could in a few short images: the people; the non-organized process for sustaining 20,000 people; the gentle relation with the ecology of the territory, and the meditation.

One guest says she's heard of these things, and another says he thinks he knows someone whose kid has gone.

Percival leans forward, "So where is all this going?" he asks.

I'm not sure how broad to take the scope of his question. Does he mean to ask: What am I doing next; or: where is this effort with all this Gathering going?

I answer toward the latter and evoke some of the original dreams, some of the stuff we mapped out in *The Rainbow Oracle*, "The possibility," I say, "of a longer-term community village, year round, on land that could accommodate such an experiment, with interlaced systems stretching from barefoot-friendly forest paths to mag-lev monorails."

He's listening, nodding slowly,

I go on, "There are ancient whole systems like heirloom seed strains, tried and true methods like wind power, and the now-available-for-the-first-time: solar voltaics, and perhaps, soon, undiscovered sources for our energy."

I'm talking crisply, to the point, about the village-to-be, the skills for which are being learned through the Gatherings. Where community processes are modeled on circles of cooperative participation, which is the way neighborhoods and the Gathering village self-govern. And about how—as this is the dawn of the computer chip age—all these energies: solar, tidal forces, electromagnetics, biomass—are going to be unified as a harmonic whole systems energy source. And how all these technologies can finally make the job of matching human needs with available supplies within our potential to accomplish. I have waxed a little bit poetic.

"My boy, my boy," says Percival grinning, "people have always had the technology," he places a palm against the edge of the tabletop, and presses back, raising himself up slightly, then continues, "We have always had the technology, the tools to live—all of us—in prosperity, in peace and abundance. We already have, we've always had, since the earliest days of civilization all the tools we need. All the providence is already here for we humans to survive in happiness. It's *not* new technology that we need." He shakes his head and continues, "What we need is a change, improvement, in the human character."

He looks wistfully around at his guests. Truly enough we all understand what he is saying and for the next while we pile up agreements noting that we've always had enough good water, food sources, enough places for shelter, and sources for fuel, but our own managing and mis-managing has been to blame for the inequities and inequalities of goods and freedoms.

Perhaps, yes, these Gatherings, the gardens, these inquiries into the workings of our brains, the cooperation and experiences of "Communitas," promote the shared ideal that we people can—or should—make of ourselves a commonwealth that is in harmony with the natural powers and provident toward our weakest, most needy members. But this remains to be seen, remains yet un-accomplished in the history of our times, and yet—as ever—within our reach.

Perhaps these efforts, these gardens, these Gatherings, lead toward an experience that encourages people—especially young people—to reach toward what could be do-able, what could be possible, if only there were enough trust, love, compassion, wisdom and courage in the human character.

Percy is so right.

These other actions, these Gatherings, these gardens, these cooperative arts and social efforts are meaningful to a degree as far as we learn skills for living in sync with each other, but they're more meaningful as they bring together people to confirm through experience that a neighborhood garden, a cooperative forestland encampment, a small-scale farm are possible in reality, and not just fictions.

Does this help advance the human character? Maybe only time and nature do that, as though some new evolutionary step ahead is coming to salvage us from our own destructive tendencies by molting us into some more advanced human form. Maybe it's our own process to use our skills and our dreams to try to move us ahead.

The conversation continues around the table with savvy comments, more comparisons, laughter, examples, statistics, opinions and finally dessert.

Eventually, at half past tea and coffee, we say our goodbyes. We leave promises to keep in touch, and I depart, down their old elegant hallway and out into the crisp air gusting westward out of the park.

Somehow what Percival said that night has struck clear with me ever since. I think because as a utopian planner and writer in his youth he saw the potential, as well as the technology. And because he was familiar with the history of Utopian efforts and certainly of some of the back-to-nature movements of the late 1960s and 1970s, Percy was keenly aware of what's holding all this back from blossoming, flowering, and spreading through the mainstreams of the world's cultures. Well, says the maestro, it's not our lack of technical ability, nor lack of communications or coordination, no, it's something deeper, closer to who we are, something "in the human character," that needs to evolve further.

Epilogue

Where are they now?

Dorothy Day is being considered for sainthood by the Catholic Church. Pope Francis invoked her "Social activism, her passion for justice and for the cause of the oppressed" in his 2015 speech to the United States Congress.

Nina Gitana lived out her days peacefully and gracefully on a Sikh farm in Vermont.

The Carlebach Shul is still conducting services and teaching peace in its tiny synagogue.

The Living Theatre continues to present new theatrical work. It is now the longest continually producing theatre company in the country. Julian and Judith lived until 1985 and 2015 respectively. A blend of Living Theatre old-timers and young talent now manage the company.

The compulsory conscription of young men into the U. S. military—the Selective Service System (the military 'draft')—was abandoned by the government in 1975.

The evolution of organic agriculture and the consumption of organic foods has blossomed into a immense part of the food chain.

The Oregon Country Faire is entering its fifth decade. And a multitude of similar folk faires thrive, bringing art and commerce into rural settings.

The Rainbow Gatherings have spread worldwide. Even in some of the most oppressed and conflicted areas of the world people from the different cultures, religions, races, social backgrounds, and even 'warring' sides find their way into nature's sanctuary to gather in peace.

Community Kitchens from the Gatherings have taken on positions in disaster relief at the Katrina and Sandy superstorms, in

Figure 108. European Rainbow. Fasgar, Spain, 1988. (Garrick Beck: 1988)

Haiti after the earthquake, and in other emergency situations.

Solar energy and wind power have taken a piece of their place in the energy formulae of the modern world.

The farm in Oregon is a productive organic farm and a productive organic forest. Groups like Oregon Tilth and the Forest Stewardship Council, which certify organic and stewardship standards are creating a groundwork (literally) for sound, sensible, and sustainable agriculture and forestry.

Marijuana criminality and the fear/policing/imprisonment that grew from that is becoming a thing of the past.

The psychedelic movement is still largely underground. There is so much potential here for awakening human wisdom.

The destruction of Black Mesa for the coal and uranium within it has been delayed—for now. This is an ongoing environmental struggle emblematic of the issues, the results and the ecological challenges the world faces.

Community gardens are a regular part of urban existence in all major cities, introducing neighbors to each other and young people to the wonder and goodness of nature.

Numerous human rights and earth rights movements not specifically chronicled in this volume have advanced causes and set in motion real changes. The events and people portrayed in this book did not somehow create a new world culture on their own. No, they were a part of a huge series of interlinked cultural changes that are continuing today and are connecting with each other in recognition that each share enormous underlying common principles.

The colossal effects of the Civil Rights, Gay Rights and Women's Liberation movements are still shaking the earth.

Rachel Carson with her watershed book, *Silent Spring* almost singlehandedly set in motion worldwide environmental education. Recycling in some degree is happening almost everywhere. Many of

Figure 109. Author speaking in council at the European Rainbow Gathering, 1988. (Joanee Freedom: 1988)

the most poisonous pesticides and herbicides have been banned. For 20 years no new nuclear power plants opened in the United States.

Rights of the handicapped and disabled have become public policy.

All of these are part of the mosaic of movements that make up a new and evolving world culture.

And every one of these causes has remarkable people and amazing stories.

I have tried here to tell some of the tales of events I personally witnessed and in some cases, helped nurture.

There is a long road and a lot more difficult territory ahead of us.

But there is a global movement with an amazing number of different parts that sees the long-term goals in the same visionary landscape. And that landscape includes people cooperating with each other, helping, sharing and caring for each other, advancing our common interests and protecting the earth, the children, the old, our climate, and all the diverse species including our own. And that is the terrain we are moving toward.

✻ ✻ ✻

Photo Credits

Front Cover. Garrick Beck. *1979. Rainbow Hot Air Balloon over Tipi Village, Arizona Rainbow Gathering.* Collection of the author.

Figure 1. Photographer unknown. 1957. *Christmas Eve, 1957. Author, center, between Judith Malina, Julian Beck. Dorothy Day at far right.* Courtesy the Estate of Judith Malina.

Figure 2. Ruth Kuzub. 1960. *Nina Gitana.* Courtesy the Living Theatre Archives.

Figures 3 & 4. Ruth Kuzub. 1960. *In rehearsal for Spenser Holst's play, The Devil's Mother. From the left: Spencer Holst; my mother, Judith Malina; author; Nina Gitana; actor Jerome Raphael.* Courtesy the Living Theatre Archives.

Figures 5 & 6. Don Loomis. 1959. *Jack Kerouac, Allen Ginsberg, Gregory Corso, Eileen Fulton (at far left bottom) at the opening night party at our apartment following the debut of W. C. Williams' Many Loves, New York City, January 13, 1959.* Collection of the author.

Figure 7. Don Loomis. 1959. *Judith Malina looks on while Eileen Fulton reads the NY Times' review of Many Loves.* Collection of the author.

Figures 8 & 9. Don Loomis. 1959. *Poet Allen Ginsberg (with Gregory Corso and Jack Kerouac) shows me how to blow over the champagne bottle's top to make a rhythm sound while I pop paper bags as percussion.* Collection of the author.

Figure 10. Don Loomis. 1959. *Kerouac lying down by the door, cigarette still in his hand, waited for his friends.* Collection of the author.

Figure 11. Charles Rotmil. 1961. *Julian Beck and Judith Malina incredibly happy after the opening of their new theatre.* Courtesy the Estate of Judith Malina.

Figure 12. Photographer unknown. 1963. *On the set of Kenneth H. Brown's play, The Brig.* Courtesy The Living Theatre Archives.

Figures 13 & 14. Photographers unknown. 1964. *My parents, Julian Beck and Judith Malina, in the office at the 14th Street Theatre.* Courtesy the Estate of Judith Malina.

Figure 15. Photographer unknown. 1963. *Padlocked for Non-Payment of Back Taxes, the Living Theatre Defies the Law....* New York World-Telegram & Sun.

Figure 16. Photographer unknown. 1965. *Velletri, Italy, June 1965. Living Theatre members including Steve Ben Israel (with guitar), Jimmy Tiroff, Petra Vogt, Judith Malina.* Courtesy the Estate of Judith Malina.

Figure 17. Photographer unknown. 1965. *The Chord from The Living Theatre's Mysteries and Smaller Pieces.* Courtesy the Living Theatre Archives.

Figure 18. Photographer unknown. October 19, 1967. *"Reed College Students protested the draft by blocking the entrance to Selective Service headquarters in Portland, Ore., by chaining themselves to the main door. The students, shouting "Hell No, We Won't Go," were hauled away in a police wagon after officers removed the chain with cutting tools."* (Bettmann: Getty Images, 1967)

Figure 19. Marty Topp. 1969. *The Living Theatre cast and audience enact ritual ceremonia onstage.* Courtesy the Living Theatre Archives.

Figure 20. Photographer unknown. 1969. *Morocco, 1969. The author at the Living Theatre's collective creation discussions, high on majoun, in the big whitewashed rehearsal room.* Collection of the author.

Figure 21. Kenn Kushner. 1969. *Mandala.* Pen and ink on paper. Collection of the author.

Figure 22. Lee Meier. 1970. *Building the Vortex Stage, McIver Park, Oregon (i).* Courtesy Lee Meier, MonoGraphicsStudio.com

Figure 23. Lee Meier. 1970. *Building the Vortex Stage, McIver Park, Oregon (ii).* Courtesy Lee Meier, MonoGraphicsStudio.com.

Figure 24. Glenn Davis. 1970. *Building the Vortex Stage, McIver Park, Oregon (iii).* Courtesy Matt Love, "The Far Out Story of Vortex 1," Nestucca Spit Press, Astoria, Oregon.

Figure 25. Glenn Davis. 1970. *Building the Vortex Stage, McIver Park, Oregon (iv).* Courtesy Matt Love, "The Far Out Story of Vortex 1," Nestucca Spit Press, Astoria, Oregon.

Figure 26. Clackamas County Sheriff's Office. 1970. *Building the Vortex Stage (v), McIver Park, Oregon.* Courtesy Matt Love, "The Far Out Story of Vortex 1," Nestucca Spit Press, Astoria, Oregon.

Figure 27. Glenn Davis. 1970. *Joseph set up a battleship's array of steam kettles,*

Vortex 1, September, 1970. Courtesy Matt Love, "The Far Out Story of Vortex 1," Nestucca Spit Press, Astoria, Oregon.

Figure 28. Clackamas County Sheriff's Office. 1970. *Vortexers chopping vegetables in front of Joseph's deisel-powered boiler, Vortex 1, September 1970.* Courtesy Matt Love, "The Far Out Story of Vortex 1," Nestucca Spit Press, Astoria, Oregon.

Figure 29. Gerry Lewin. 1970. *Shoveling rice from Joseph's amazing 'kettle drum' cookers to feed tens of thousands of people. Vortex 1, September 1970.* Courtesy Gerry Lewin.

Figure 30. Oregon State Parks. 1970. *Vortex 1: The line of cars stretched for miles.* Courtesy Matt Love, "The Far Out Story of Vortex 1," Nestucca Spit Press, Astoria, Oregon.

Figure 31. Kerry Haas. 1970. *Bathers and sunbathers at the Clackamas River.* Courtesy Matt Love, "The Far Out Story of Vortex 1," Nestucca Spit Press, Astoria, Oregon.

Figure 32. Gerry Lewin. 1970. *Looking out from the stage, Vortex 1, September 1970.* Courtesy Gerry Lewin.

Figure 33. Gerry Lewin. 1970. *Chuck 'Windsong' Mills (center) playing drums at the tipi circle, Vortex 1.* Courtesy Gerry Lewin.

Figure 34. Gerry Lewin. 1970. *Shanti Sena tipi and volunteer peacekeepers, Vortex 1.* Courtesy Gerry Lewin.

Figure 35. Gerry Lewin. 1970. *One of the Rainbow tipis at Vortex 1.* Courtesy Gerry Lewin.

Figure 36. Photographer unknown. 1971. *The Hippies have landed! Top row, from the left: Heath, Bear, Teri, Dana, Terri, Maggie, Laika, Rob Roy. Front row, from the left: Garrick, Karen, Major & John.* Collection of the author.

Figure 37. Photographer unknown. 1971. *It was a joyous occasion.* Collection of the author.

Figure 38. Garrick Beck. 1974. *In the lower field we fenced two acres and grew all manner of vegetables and greens.* Collection of the author.

Figure 39. Garrick Beck. 1974. *The Main house cabin at the Rainbow Farm with new porch, cedar shake roofing and greenhouse made of recycled windows.* Collection of the author.

Figure 40. Photographer unknown. 1971. *Barry 'Plunker' Adams 'flying' at the Spring Equinox Celebration, Rainbow Farm, Drain, Oregon.* Collection of the author.

Figure 41. Garrick Beck. 1971. *Building the dome: Leonce (who came with the Medical Opera from San Francisco and helped midwife for Karen and my daughter, Eden), with David and Marco cinching the bolts that hold the framework of the dome together.* Collection of the author.

Figure 42. Garrick Beck. 1981. *The dome at Rainbow Farm.* Collection of the author.

Figure 43. Photographer unknown. 1972. *Sihu, Kaushal and Peyto Yellin.* Courtesy Sihu Yellin.

Figure 44. David Roberts. 1972. *Author, Karen McPherson and our daughter, Eden Star at the farm in Oregon.* Courtesy David Roberts.

Figure 45. Michael Green. 1972. *Artist Michael Green's cover for The Rainbow Oracle printed at Visionworks Press, Eugene, Oregon, May/June, 1972.* Courtesy Michael Green.

Figure 46. John Papp. 1972. *Hiking up to Strawberry Lake, Arapahoe National Forest, June, 1972.* Courtesy Nathan Koenig and the Woodstock Museum, © White Buffalo Multimedia, Inc. WoodstockMuseum.org.

Figure 47. John Papp. 1972. *The trail was terrifically steep, switchback after switchback at 11,000 feet elevation.* Courtesy Nathan Koenig and the Woodstock Museum, © White Buffalo Multimedia, Inc. WoodstockMuseum.org.

Figure 48. Photographer unknown. 1972. *Starting to dig our first latrines, Colorado Rainbow Gathering, June 1972. Notice the banjo player helping keep spirits high.* Collection of the author.

Figure 49. John Papp. 1972. *Paul Geisendorfer addressing the massive assembly on his land at Granby, Colorado.* Courtesy Nathan Koenig and the Woodstock Museum, © White Buffalo Multimedia, Inc. WoodstockMuseum.org.

Figure 50. John Papp. 1972. *The assembly on Paul's land right before the march to the Gathering at Strawberry Lake. June 1972.* Courtesy Nathan Koenig and the Woodstock Museum, © White Buffalo Multimedia, Inc. WoodstockMuseum.org.

Figure 51. Photographer unknown. 1972. *Barry 'Plunker' Adams says he's going to shoulder his backpack and hike to the lake.* Collection of the author.

Figure 52. John Papp. 1972. *Gathering at Strawberry Lake, Colorado, July 1972.* Courtesy Nathan Koenig and the Woodstock Museum, © White Buffalo Multimedia, Inc. WoodstockMuseum.org.
Figure 53. Alan Carey. 1972. *Playing the cymbals at Harmony Kitchen.* © Alan Carey.
Figure 54. Alan Carey. 1972. *Strawberry Lake.* © Alan Carey.
Figure 55. Nathan Koenig. 1972. *Author speaking in Council, Strawberry Lake, Colorado, July 1972.* Courtesy Nathan Koenig and the Woodstock Museum, © White Buffalo Multimedia, Inc. WoodstockMuseum.org.
Figure 56. Alan Carey. 1972. *Omming at the first Gathering.* © Alan Carey.
Figure 57. Alan Carey. 1972. *Council at Strawberry Lake, July 2, 1972.* © Alan Carey.
Figure 58. John Papp. 1972. *Dawn, Fourth of July, 1972, from the top of Table Mountain.* Courtesy Nathan Koenig and the Woodstock Museum, © White Buffalo Multimedia, Inc. WoodstockMuseum.org.
Figure 59. Alan Carey. 1972. *July 4th, 1972, Silent Circle for World Peace, first Rainbow Gathering.* © Alan Carey.
Figure 60. Garrick Beck. 1974. *How it was left.* Collection of the author.
Figure 61. Garrick Beck. 1974. *Karen pitching hay into the main house garden.* Collection of the author.
Figure 62. Garrick Beck. 1975. *Tera with cauliflower.* Collection of the author.
Figure 63. Garrick Beck. 1975. *Ron tilling the field with Bo.* Collection of the author.
Figure 64. Garrick Beck. 1976. *Diversity is the key to a healthy forest...providing habitat for zillions of creatures and forest products for people's uses.* Collection of the author.
Figures 65 & 66. Garrick Beck. 1977 & 1997. *Perpetual yield forestry is not only productive... it's beautiful, turning forests of thin poles into stout timber while increasing birds, bees, brush and wildlife.* Collection of the author.
Figure 67. Garrick Beck. 1981. *William horse-logging with neighbor Jim Ward's team.* Collection of the author.
Figure 68. Garrick Beck. 1978. *Bo, the horse, pulling the carousel seeder.* Collection of the author.
Figure 69. Garrick Beck. 1980. *The seeder attached to the tractor with Kunga Tyson driving and Baker Paul following behind.* Collection of the author.
Figure 70. Photographer unknown. 1974. *Author in the carrot patch.* Collection of the author.
Figure 71. Garrick Beck. 1979. *Organic farming in Oregon's Coast Range.* Collection of the author.
Figure 72. Garrick Beck. 1975. *Dr. Timothy Leary and Merry Pranksters Ken Kesey and Ken Babbs greeting each other at the Eugene, Oregon airport. 1975.* Collection of the author.
Figure 73. Photographer unknown. 1977. *Hopi Grandfather David Monongye addressing the Rainbow Family Council, Gila National Forest, New Mexico, 1977.* Courtesy Communities Magazine.
Figure 74. Pukalani Sweetwater. 1977. *Hopi Grandfather David Monongye addressing the Rainbow Family Council, Gila National Forest, New Mexico, July 1977.* Courtesy Pukalani Sweetwater.
Figure 75. Garrick Beck. 1997. *Ears of the Hopi blue corn.* Collection of the author.
Figures 76 (i–viii). Garrick Beck. 1979. *ACT '79, America's first Energy Fair, held on the Washington D.C. Mall, showed off early examples of solar panels, wind generators, hydrogen cars and much, much more.* Collection of the author.
Figures 77 (i–iv). Garrick Beck. 1979. *The Rainbow Family's 'Wilderness Camp' on the D.C. Mall.* Collection of the author.
Figure 78. Garrick Beck. 1981. *The main house cabin at the farm with its new solar panels.* Collection of the author.
Figure 79. Photographer unknown. 1982. *The pyramid on top of the pyramid.* Collection of the author.
Figure 80. J. Svante Vanbart. 1982. *Feather Hammond as "The Duck" in Obras de Paz, in Chapultapec Park, Mexico City. Jaysun Hammond on guitar, Jorge and Barry Adams on drums.* Courtesy J. Svante Vanbart.
Figure 81. Photographer unknown. 1978. *Source separation of garbage at one of Swami Mommy's 'recycling centers' in the woods.* Collection of the author.

Figure 82. Gabe Kirsheimer. 1992. *Swami Mommy*. Courtesy Gabe Kirsheimer.
Figure 83. Swami Mommy. 1978. *Swami Mommy's 'Seven Garbage Chakras' recycling chart*. Courtesy Swami Mommy.
Figure 84. Garrick Beck. 2014. *The W.O.W. Hall, Eugene, Oregon*. Collection of the author.
Figure 85. Photographer unknown. 1977. *Protesters marching on the Trojan Nuclear Power Plant*. Collection of the author.
Figure 86. Photographer unknown. 1977. *Protesters entering the Trojan Nuclear Power Plant*. Collection of the author.
Figure 87. Photographer unknown. 1979. *Ram Das and Medicine Story stood beside the trail*. Courtesy Medicine Story.
Figure 88. Photographer unknown. 1979. *Ram Das holding 'class' at the Arizona Rainbow Gathering, 1979*. Courtesy Medicine Story.
Figure 89. Garrick Beck. 1979. *Dr. Patch Adams speaking to the Council, Arizona Rainbow Gathering, 1979*. Collection of the author.
Figure 90. Immanuel Trujillo. 1979. *Painting by Mana*. Collection of the author.
Figures 91, 92 & 93. Immanuel Trujillo. 2007. *Mana Pottery*. Collection of the author.
Figure 94. T-ॐ. 1982. *Pushing the bus across the border*. Courtesy of T-ॐ.
Figure 95. Garrick Beck. 1982. *At the Saskatchewan Gathering of Nations – more lodges than I'd ever seen*. Collection of the author.
Figure 96. Garrick Beck. 1982. *Our Rainbow bus and tipis set up next to the A.I.M. encampment*. Collection of the author.
Figure 97. Garrick Beck. 1986. *A thousand or more people holding hands in a Circle for Peace before the meal at the Rainbow Picnic in Central Park, New York City*. Collection of the author.
Figure 98. Joanee Freedom. 1982. *Before and After (i): The 6th Street & Avenue B Community Garden*. Courtesy Joanee Freedom.
Figure 99. Garrick Beck. 2003. *Before and After (ii): The 6th Street & Avenue B Community Garden*. Collection of the author.
Figures 100 & 101. Garrick Beck. 2013. *The 6th Street & Avenue B Garden, open to the public, with the handprints of all the gardeners embedded in its border and gate design*. Collection of the author.
Figures 102 (i–iv). Garrick Beck. 1984. *In the pilot program we began with a city-owned vacant lot adjacent to a public elementary school*. Collection of the author.
Figures 103 (i & ii). Garrick Beck. 1984. *The same vacant lot after working with parents, students, teachers, school custodians and the community to create a growing and learning environment*. Collection of the author.
Figures 104 (i & ii). Garrick Beck. 1984. *The children loved it, the community enjoyed it, and students' science test scores improved dramatically*. Collection of the author.
Figures 105 (i–iv). Garrick Beck. 1985. *The children learn tool use and teamwork as well as gardening techniques*. Collection of the author.
Figure 106. Garrick Beck. 1985. *From vacant lots to community gardens in the cement canyons of New York City*. Collection of the author.
Figure 107. Photographer unknown. 1975. *The Living Theatre's spectacular production, The Money Tower*. Courtesy the Living Theatre Archives.
Figure 108. Garrick Beck. 1988. *European Rainbow. Fasgar, Spain, 1988*. Collection of the author.
Figure 109. Joanee Freedom. 1988. *Author speaking in council at the European Rainbow Gathering, 1988*. Courtesy Joanee Freedom.
Back Cover. Nancy Kraskin. 2015. *Author photograph*. Courtesy Nancy Kraskin.

Index

5 Beekman 48, 50-1, 54
6th Street and Avenue B Community
    Garden 429
14th Street Theatre 35
Abbie Hoffman 106, 150
Acid 36, 257, 360
ACT '79 370, 372-4, 376-7
A.I.M. 409, 411, 413-19
Alan Watts 280
Alberto Ecco 411
Alberto Ruiz 385
Allen Ginsberg vii, 26-7
Alpert 102, 385
American Legion 197-8, 213
An Evening of Bohemian Theatre 8
Andy C 391
Andy Stone vi, 434
Ansche Chesed 13
Antigone 122, 423, 443, 446-7
Anuha 322
Arti 120-1
Arupa 328
Asparagus 81, 83
Auggie 225, 239-40, 245, 254
AWOLS 152
Babbs 254, 359-62
Baker Paul 339, 350, 355
Bana Devi vi
Banana Boats 60
Baron de Lima 133
Barry 174-80, 187, 201, 212, 241-4, 264-6,
    270, 275, 279, 283-5, 304, 306, 317,
    322, 377
Barry Adams 174, 201, 304, 389
Be-In 149-50
Beanbat 104, 149, 168
Bear 148, 221, 223, 227, 240, 243, 264,
    273, 275, 327, 397
Beatnik vii, 1, 11-12, 407, 448
Beatniks 11, 25, 449
Beaver Hall 77, 97, 106, 197
Bellingham Arts Fair 173, 181-2, 189, 223
Ben Wright 196, 208
Beniah 356
Bill and Cindy Wooten 155, 331
Bill Hassleback 332
Bill Shari 43
Billy Jr. 356
Birdie Guzman 368
Black Hills Survival Gathering 382
Black Panthers 162
Bluebird 267, 356
Bobbie Wehe 196, 200
Brant Kingman 425

Brotherhood of Eternal Love 325
Bruce 285, 340
Buffalo Party vi, 36, 190-2, 194
Café Wha? 64
Carl Einhorn 136
Carl Oglesby 55
Carla Newbre 356
Carlebach Shul 15, 456
Carol Kushner vi
Cassie 356
Castle Tioram 129
Catwoman 75
Centenary Wilber Community 162
Challe Erb 371
Charley 149
Charlie Martin 340
Charlotte 356, 365, 370, 379
Charlotte Levinson 356
Charlyn 355
Che Guevara 12
Cheyenne 355
Chicago Democratic Convention 163
Children's Gardening Program ii, vi
Chinima 356
Christine Datz vi, 432
Chuck 118-19, 122-3, 174, 177, 179, 181,
    185-7, 201, 214, 253-4, 322, 364
Chuck Mills 174, 177, 185-6, 201
Chuck Yellin 118
Clarence 356
Colorado Rainbow Gathering 304
Council 242-4, 311, 314, 365-7, 401, 410-11,
    415, 419, 457
CRO 240, 245
Crystal 77, 97, 356
Dadaji 98
Dan Galusha 196
Dana Gottlieb 125, 148
Daphne 356
Darshan 356
Dave Herrera 407
Dave McReynolds 53
David Boyle 407, 424
David Lescht 201
David Monongye 265, 365-7, 383
David Sweet 84
David Zeltzer 270, 324
Dean Dudman 113
Denny 282
Deva 387
Dick Coffin 84
Dino and Wendy Wild 407
DMT 105
Dominic 254

Don Arceneaux 387
Dorothy 2-7, 20, 412, 456
Dorothy Day 3-5, 456
Doug 149, 347
Dr. Bronner 277
Dr. Jim 'Jimbo' Berg 401
Dr. J.J. 377
Dr. Ken Osgood 400
Dr. P. H. Martin's Magical Medicine
    Show 173
Dr. Timothy Leary 107, 358, 361
Dr. Watts 401
Drain, Oregon 241, 324, 452
Duke 186-7
Ebram 356
Eden i, 250, 272-3, 315, 319-20, 322, 324,
    330, 338, 356, 423
ee cummings 37
Eileen Fulton 26-7
Elaine 390
Elizabeth 270-1, 273, 275, 277-81
Ellen Light vi
Emmy Rainwalker 382
Essaouira 135
Esupé 328
Evam 356
Eve 4-5, 7, 253-4, 355, 383, 387, 447
Familiar Musing 146-7, 149-51, 153, 175
Family of the Mystic Arts 183
Fantuzzi 278
Feather 270, 301, 322, 364, 383, 387, 389-
    90, 412
Feather Hammond 301, 389, 412
Feliche 411-12, 418
Ferralli 356
Findhorn 72, 312
Fontana 356
Frank Fools Crow 382
Frankenstein 42, 92, 122, 447
Fred Nemo vi, 332, 335
Free Store 175, 190, 195
Gabe Kirsheimer 393
Gai 125
Gail Varsi 279
Garrick ii, 114, 129, 221, 226, 229, 250-1,
    320, 333, 337-9, 341, 350, 412-14,
    435-6, 438-9
Garrick Beck ii, 226, 229, 250-1, 337-9,
    341, 346, 350, 354, 361, 369, 372,
    413-14, 435-6, 438-9
Gary Ewing 173
Gary Snyder 148, 181
Gatchell 236-7
Gea 383
Gene Gordon 136
General Strike for Peace 21, 48

Gerry McPherson 420
Glen 186, 193, 196, 200, 215
Glen Swift 196, 215
Goose Hollow vii, 77, 97, 149, 161-2, 173
Granby 293, 298, 305, 315
Granby, Colorado 305
Gregory Corso 25-7
Grinell, Gene 349
Gulf of Tonkin 88, 160
Gunga-dar 149
Gwen 356
Haight-Ashbury vii, 77-8, 175, 225
Hanna 370, 375
Hanon Reznikov 121
Harold 179-80, 188, 200-1, 212, 217, 327-
    8, 367
Heath 221
Hendrix 66-7
Henry Howard 136
Hippie 12, 202, 243, 246, 270, 366
Hippies 98-9, 221, 242, 248, 262-3, 265,
    267, 269, 364-5, 367, 369, 380, 399
Hog Farm 192, 365, 410
Holly Hart 161
Honest John 353
Hopi 262-5, 267-9, 286, 364-7, 369, 383
Howard 136, 412
Howdy Folks 279, 291, 370
Howdy Johnson 254
Hubert Humphrey 97
Ian G. Ensign vi
Illuminated Elephants 384
IRS 33-4, 36-8
Isha 70, 142, 411, 420
Ishna 356
Jack Armstrong 229, 254, 326
Jack Kerouac vii, 25-8
Jackie Betz vi, 433
Jackson Mac Low 3, 45
Jade 356
Jahanara 365
Jake 271, 336, 339, 356
Janis Olson 76
Jay Kurley vi, 434
Jaysun 322, 364, 383, 387, 389
Jaysun Hammond 364, 389
Jeanne Liotta 407
Jeannie 367
Jenny Felmley vi
Jenny Hecht 36, 136
Jeremy Lawrence 75
Jerimiah 356
Jerome Raphael 18
Jerry Rubin 150
Jessica 356
Jesus Christ 6, 180

Jesus Freaks 256, 258, 260
Jim Ward 346-7
Jimmer 365
Jimmy Anderson 136
Jimmy Diamond 63, 65
Jimmy Tiroff 41
Joanee vi, 193, 424-6, 428-9, 445, 458
Joanee Freedom vi, 193, 424, 429, 445, 458
Jodey Bateman 382
John Cage 17, 106
John Harriman 22
John McIver 293
John Trudell 382
Jorge 387, 389
Joseph 206-8, 356
Josh 356
Josiah 356
Joy Tsunka 351
Judith i, vii, 3-5, 8, 11, 14, 17-18, 20-1, 26-7, 29, 35-7, 41, 70, 334, 445-6
Judith Malina i, vii, 3, 5, 8, 18, 26, 29, 35, 41
Judy Sachter 270, 324
Julian i, vii, 4-5, 8, 11, 14, 17, 20-1, 29, 35-7, 45, 139-40, 142, 334-5, 443-5
Julian Beck i, vii, 4-5, 8, 29, 35
Julie Kirkpatrick vi, 433
Karen 76-7, 102, 104, 118, 123-5, 128-9, 131-3, 138, 140-1, 143-5, 220-3, 272-5, 282-3, 319-20, 329-32
Karen McPherson vi, 76, 273
Kathleen 356
Katie Jackrabbit 285
Kaushal 123-4, 129-31, 149, 161, 164, 168-9, 171, 174, 190, 198-200, 217-18, 224, 264-5, 273-5, 322
Ken Babbs 254, 359, 361
Ken Kesey vii, 181, 253, 359, 361
Kenn Kushner vi, 146-7
Kenneth Anger 94
Kenneth H. Brown 34
Kenny 99-100, 155, 157, 159-60
Kesey vii, 181, 253, 255, 257, 259-60, 359-62
Kim Estes 411
King Crimson 128
Kinswoman 332
Kitty 270-1, 273, 275, 277-81
Koinonia House 97, 196-7
Kriya 356
Kuiz 380-4, 386, 388-90
Kunga Tyson 350, 356
Laika 187, 201, 221, 223, 227, 254, 272, 321-2, 327
Latch 407

Laurie 149
Le Living 135, 140, 441
Leda 322
Lettvin 93
Lewis 149, 162, 411-12
Lila 185, 187, 201
Linda 53, 55, 174, 355
Linda Lou 355
Liora 387
Living Theatre i, vi-vii, 3, 5, 8-9, 18, 20, 22-3, 33-4, 39-41, 44, 91-3, 121-2, 440-3, 456
Lloyd Marbet 396
Love Family 311, 379
LSD 99, 128, 131, 140, 202, 215, 242, 248, 257, 280, 325, 359, 398, 405, 411
Lynn 356
Ma Beebe 233-5
Mabel Beck 40
Maggie 221
Major 162, 221, 254, 326
Majoun 136-8, 356
Mana 403-8
Mandala City 136, 176, 279-80
Many Loves 23, 26
Marblemount 177, 182, 184, 187, 200, 223
Mareba Jos 382, 411
Margie 355
Mark Amitin 121
Mary vi, 6, 42, 140, 264, 283, 322, 356, 434
Mary Mary 140
Matthew Courtney 407
MDMA 407
Medicine Story 332, 377, 382, 399-400
Megan 383
Meher Baba 196, 277
Melinda Futrell 426
Melita 356
Melody Record 358
Menachem Kallus 356
Merce Cunningham 20
Mercedes 387-8
Merry Pranksters 361
Mescaline 210
Michael Crater vi
Michael Eagle 356
Michael Green 286-7
Midge 356
Mike 94-5, 224, 227, 282, 407, 425
Mike and Steve Buscemi 407
Millie 351
Mimi Leland vi, 77, 84
Mina Lansa 267
Mitch Mitchell 201, 291
Morning Glory 356
Morning glory seeds 277, 326

Morocco 134-5, 137-40, 142
Mousa 136, 138
Murray Paskin 23
Mushrooms 120, 224, 407
Mysteries and Smaller Pieces 42, 44, 444
Naomi and Percival Goodman 447
Naphtali Carlebach 15
Nathan Koenig 296-7, 305, 307, 311, 316, 319
New Buffalo 171, 249, 371
New World Culture viii-ix, xi, 1, 69, 127, 167, 219, 261, 289
Nina Gitana 9, 18, 456
Nina Graboi 280
Nissen, Mary 434
Nona Howard 136
Norman Solomon 396
Obras de Paz 387, 389
Oregon Country Faire 154, 158, 456
Orissa 273, 356
Orpheus 8
Paradise Now 92-3, 122, 184, 241, 447
Patch Adams 391, 400-1
Paterson Brown 291
Patrick Thompson 294, 356
Paul Breslin 123, 224
Paul Geisendorfer 294, 305
Paul Goodman 8, 106
Paul Hultburg 22
Paul Prensky 22
Paul Rosenberg 76
Paula Watson vi, 435
Peggie Morrison vi
People's Army Jamboree 195-6, 200
Pepe 249
Petra Vogt 41
Peyto 265, 273
Phedre 3, 8
Phil Hanson 364
Plunker 241, 264, 306, 387
Portland Zoo 77, 181
Pride Family 249
Prince of Wales 128
Psylocybin 355
Pukalani Sweetwater 365, 367
Radical Theater Repertory 121
Rain 186, 200-1
Rainbow 171-2, 199, 215, 217-18, 240-1, 261-2, 268-70, 286-7, 317-19, 364-7, 379-80, 394-5, 399-401, 425-6, 456-8
Rainbow Family 218, 276, 324, 366-7, 376
Rainbow Family Council 366-7
Rainbow Family of Living Light 218, 276, 324

Rainbow Farm 229, 240-1, 244, 248, 251, 330
Rainbow Gathering 36, 304, 318, 332, 364-5, 379, 400-1, 409, 458
Rainbow Hawk 370
Rainbow Oracle ii, 269, 286-7, 290-1, 293, 313, 364, 452
Rainbow Picnic 426
Ralph Di Gia 53
Ram Das 405
Raquel Shapira vi
Ray Johnson 35
R.D. Laing 120
Reed 75-6, 80, 83, 85, 87-90, 102, 108, 113, 115-16, 121-2, 124, 148, 160-1, 224-5, 451-2
Reed College 75-6, 85, 87, 90, 108, 148, 396
Renaissance Faire 154-5, 157-8, 174, 182, 241, 244
Richard 97, 106, 165, 196-7, 385
Richard Nixon 97
Rob Roy Rowley 174, 254
Robbie Gordon 371
Robert McCullough 396
Robin i, 155, 356, 370
Robin and Ron Ulrich 155
Rock 'n Roll Circus 132
Roland Hanselman 339
Rolling Stones 128
Rome vii, 40, 42, 265-6, 327, 329, 380, 441
Ron 84, 155, 273, 328, 339, 349
Ron and Tera Rutecki 339
Ron Anderson 84
Rose 14, 98, 149, 162, 197, 356
Rufus Collins 136
Rusty Nichols 400
Sahara 139, 142
Samuel and Leah Sleeper 57
Sara Sunshine 332
Sarah 340, 352, 370
Saul Gottleib 121
Sean O'Reilly 285
Selmah 208, 224
Seranol 101
Serious 379
Sernyl 101-2
Seth Booky 196, 200
Shaneca 383
Shanti Sena 214-15
Sharon Forestwoman 356
Shawn 383
Shemiah 356
Sherwood Forest 128
Sid vi, 356, 365, 371, 383-6, 389
Sihu 264-5, 273-4

Sky River 200, 213
Skyblue 264, 283, 285, 291, 302, 322, 338, 364
Spenser Holst 18
Spiro Agnew 97
Stephan 356
Stephen Gaskin 158
Steve Ben Israel 41, 136, 447
Steve Berman 274, 290
Steve Lebow 331
STP 241, 243
Strawberry Lake 36, 295-8, 301, 303-7, 310-11, 314-15, 318-19, 324, 391
Street Songs 45
Student Peace Union 51, 55
Students for a Democratic Society 54
Summer of Love 71, 77-8
Sunny 320, 322, 383, 411-12, 418
Sunny Adams 412
Susan Bernstein 371
Svante 385, 389
Swami Mommy 391-3
Swami Satchitananda 98
Symond's Yat 128

T- ॐ 412
Table Mountain 282, 286, 290, 293-5, 298, 306, 314-17, 324, 364
Tall Paul 340
Tameron i, 356, 382, 412, 427-8
Temple Tribe 184, 195
Tennessee Williams 37
Tera vi, 339
Teri 221, 224, 227
Terri vi, 194, 221, 225, 239, 250-1, 254, 321-2
Terri Faires vi, 194, 225
Terry Hubbard 356
THC 99
The Age of Anxiety 8
The Archaeology of Sleep 444
The Brig 32-9, 293, 447
The Catholic Worker 2
The Cauldron 330
The Chord 44, 157
The Devil's Mother 18
The Idiot King 8
The Money Tower 441-2
The Paragon 330
The Spook Sonata 8
The Wayfarer 106, 196, 208

The Yellow Methuselah 444
The Young Disciple 8
Tibor Bruer 380
Tim 63-8, 245, 280, 327, 333, 358, 361
Tim Hardin 63-6
Tintern Abbey 128
Tisa Jewell 332
Titanic Co-op 273, 290-1, 293, 298, 302
Toad Hall 167-8, 170, 172-82, 184, 186, 188, 190, 192, 194, 196, 198, 200, 202, 204, 206
Tom vi, 64, 121-2, 187, 200-1, 209, 218, 242, 347, 356
Tom Walker vi, 121
Tonight We Improvise 8
Tonya 387-8
Tracey 301
Uncle Billy 379-81
Universal Life Church 282, 291
Vietnam 21-2, 36, 46-7, 53-4, 94, 97, 115, 196, 198
Visionworks Press 282-3, 285, 287
Vortex vii, 167, 190, 195-200, 203-7, 209, 211-15, 220, 223, 293
Wamsutta 57
War Resisters League 48, 53
Wavy Gravy 365, 410
Wayne 89, 160-1, 328-9
Whole Life Expo 424
Willamette Bridge 154
William 22, 346, 355-6, 405, 407
William Carlos Williams 23
Winchester Chimes 407
Wingbow 425
Women's House of Detention 4, 450
Woodstock 190-2, 278-81, 283, 290, 296-7, 302, 305, 307-8, 311, 316, 319, 365
Woodstock Museum 296-7, 305, 307, 311, 316, 319
World Family Gathering 178, 188, 270, 275, 289-90, 292, 294, 296, 298, 300, 302, 304, 306, 308, 318
Wounded Knee 394-5
Yippie 106, 274, 313
Yogi Bajan 98
Yolanda 411-12
Yuwipi 356
Zack 358-60, 370
Zero Boy 407

About the Author

Garrick Beck grew up in a pioneering Off-Broadway theatrical family. He attended Reed College and lived for a dozen years on an organic community farm in the Coast Range of Western Oregon. He was instrumental in the founding of the Rainbow Gatherings and the creation of a children's gardening program in New York City. He co-authored Plant and Grow! a teachers' curriculum guide for that program. He has been in the forefront of the sustainble forestry movement and has worked with numerous children's outdoor education activities. Beck owns a gem and mineral business, has three children and lives with his wife, Jenny, in Santa Fe, New Mexico.

Printed in the United States
By Bookmasters